Examkrackers MCAT®

BIOLOGY 1: MOLECULES

9th Edition

Jonathan Orsay

Major Contributors:
Joshua Albrecht, M.D., Ph.D.
Jennifer Birk-Goldschmidt, M.S.
Stephanie Blatch, M.A.
Lauren Nadler
Mark Pedersen, M.D.
Colleen Moran Shannon

Contributors:
Max Blodgett
David Collins
Ashley Feldman, Esq.
Darby Festa
Amanda Horowitz
Jay Li
Mohan Natrajan
Laura Neubauer
Steven Tersigni, M.D., M.P.H.

Advisors:
North de Pencier
Ahmed Sandhu
Morgan Sellers, M.D.
Sara Thorp, D.O.
Charles Yoo

Art Director:
Erin Daniel

Designers:
Dana Kelley
Charles Yuen

Layout & composition:
Nick Williams

Illustrators:
Stephen Halker
Kellie Holoski

Published in the United States of America by Osote Publishing, New Jersey.

ISBN 10: 1-893858-72-3 (Volume 1)
ISBN 13: 978-1-893858-70-1 (6 Volume Set)
9th Edition

To purchase additional copies of this book or the rest of the 6 volume set, call 1-888-572-2536 or fax orders to 1-859-255-0109.

Examkrackers.com
Osote.com

Printed and bound in the United States of America.

PHOTOCOPYING & DISTRIBUTION POLICY

Acknowledgements

The hard work and expertise of many individuals contributed to this book. The idea of writing in two voices, a science voice and an MCAT® voice, was the creative brainchild of my imaginative friend Jordan Zaretsky. I would like to thank Scott Calvin for lending his exceptional science talent and pedagogic skills to this project. I also must thank seventeen years worth of Examkrackers students for doggedly questioning every explanation, every sentence, every diagram, and every punctuation mark in the book, and for providing the creative inspiration that helped me find new ways to approach and teach biology. Finally, I wish to thank my wife, Silvia, for her support during the difficult times in the past and those that lie ahead.

Read this Section First!

Introduction to the Examkrackers Manuals

The Examkrackers books are designed to give you exactly the information you need to do well on the MCAT® while limiting extraneous information that will not be tested. This manual organizes all of the information on molecular biology tested on the MCAT® conceptually. Concepts make the content both simple and portable for optimal application to MCAT® questions. Mastery of the biological and biomolecular material covered in this manual will increase your confidence and allow you to succeed with seemingly difficult passages that are designed to intimidate. The MCAT® rewards your ability to read complex passages and questions through the lens of basic science concepts.

An in-depth introduction to the MCAT® is located in the Reasoning Skills manual. Read this introduction first to start thinking like the MCAT® and to learn critical mathematical skills. The second lecture of the Reasoning Skills manual addresses the research methods needed for success on 50% of questions on the science sections of the MCAT®. Once you have read those lectures, return to this manual to begin your study of the biology you will need to excel on the MCAT®.

How to Use This Manual

Examkrackers MCAT® preparation experience has shown that you will get the most out of these manuals when you structure your studying as follows. Read each lecture three times: twice before the class lecture, and once immediately following the lecture. During the first reading, you should not write in the book. Instead, read purely for enjoyment. During the second reading, highlight and take notes in the margins. The third reading should be slow and thorough. Complete the twenty-four questions in each lecture during the second reading before coming to class. The in-class exams in the back of the manual are intended to be completed in class. Do not look at them before class.

Warning: Just attending the class will not raise your score. You must do the work. Not attending class will obstruct dramatic score increases.

If you are studying independently, read the lecture twice before taking the in-class exam and complete the in-lecture questions during the second reading. Then read the lecture once more after the in-class exam.

The thirty minute exams are designed to educate. They are similar to an MCAT® section, but are shortened and have most of the easy questions removed. We believe that you can answer most of the easy questions without too much help from us, so the best way to raise your score is to focus on the more difficult questions. This method is one of the reasons for the rapid and celebrated success of the Examkrackers prep course and products.

A scaled score conversion chart for the in-class exams is provided on the answer page, but it is not meant to be an accurate representation of your score. Do not be discouraged by poor performance on these exams; they are not meant to predict your performance on the real MCAT®. **The questions that you get wrong or even guess correctly are most important. They represent your potential score increase. When you get a question wrong or have to guess, determine why and target these areas to improve your score.**

In order to study most efficiently, it is essential to know what topics are and are not tested directly in MCAT® questions. This manual uses the following conventions to make the distinction. Any topic listed in the AAMC's guide to the MCAT® is printed in **red, bold type**. You must thoroughly understand all topics printed in **red, bold type**. Any formula that must be memorized is also printed in **red, bold type**.

If a topic is not printed in **bold and red**, it may still be important. Understanding these topics may be helpful for putting other terms in context. Topics and equations that are not explicitly tested but are still useful to know are printed in *italics*. Knowledge of content printed in *italics* will enhance your ability to answer passage-based MCAT® questions, as MCAT® passages may cover topics beyond the AAMC's list of tested topics on the MCAT®.

Features of the Examkrackers Manuals

The Examkrackers books include several features to help you retain and integrate information for the MCAT®. Take advantage of these features to get the most out of your study time.

- **The 3 Keys** – The keys unlock the material and the MCAT®. Each lecture begins with 3 keys that organize by highlighting the most important things to remember from each chapter. Examine the 3 Keys before and after reading each lecture to make sure you have absorbed the most important messages. As you read, continue to develop your own key concepts that will guide your studying and performance.
- **Signposts** – The new MCAT® is fully integrated, asking you to apply the biological, physical, and social sciences simultaneously. The signposts alongside the text in this manual will help you build mental connections between topics and disciplines. This mental map will lead you to a high score on the MCAT®. The post of each sign "brackets" the paragraph to which it refers. When you see a signpost next to a topic, stop and consider how the topics are related. Soon you will begin making your own connections between concepts and topics within and between disciplines. This is an MCAT® skill that will improve your score. When answering questions, these connections give you multiple routes to find your way to the answer.

Thermodynamics
CHEMISTRY

- **MCAT® Think** sidebars invite deeper consideration of certain topics. They provide helpful context for topics that are tested and will challenge you just like tough MCAT® passages. While MCAT® Think topics and their level of detail may not be explicitly tested on the MCAT®, read and consider each MCAT® Think to sharpen your MCAT® skills. These sidebars provide essential practice in managing seemingly complex and unfamiliar content, as you will need to do for passages on MCAT® day.

Text written in purple is me, Salty the Kracker. I will remind you what is and is not an absolute must for the MCAT®. I will help you develop your MCAT® intuition. I will offer mnemonics, simple methods of viewing a complex concept, and occasionally some comic relief. Don't ignore me, even if you think I am not funny, because my comedy is designed to help you understand and remember. If you think I am funny, tell the boss. I could use a raise.

Additional Resources

If you find yourself struggling with the science or just needing more practice, take advantage of the additional Examkrackers resources that are available. Examkrackers offers a 9-week Comprehensive MCAT® Course to help you achieve a high score on the MCAT®, including 66 hours with expert instructors, unique course format, and regular full-length MCAT® exams. Each class includes lecture, a practice exam, and review, designed to help you develop essential MCAT® skills. For locations and registration please visit Examkrackers.com or call 1-888-KRACKEM.

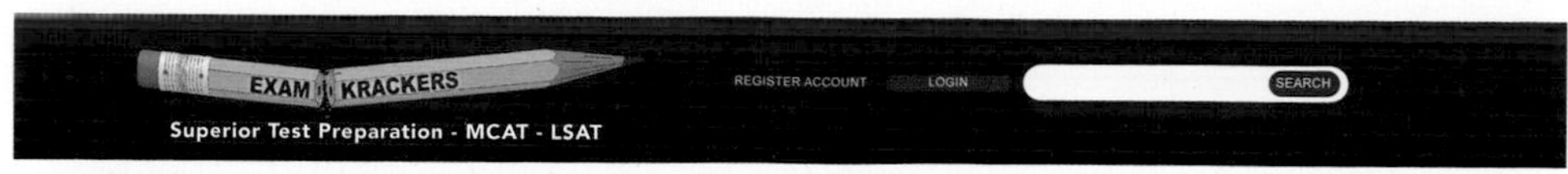

Study with Examkrackers MCAT Books
If you have questions about the problems in the Examkrackers books, ask them here. Our MCAT experts will answer your questions shortly. To Post a question, simply choose the subject of which you have a question about.

ON

Examkrackers MCAT Biology 2: Systems
Under this topic, Dr. Jerry Johnson will answer any questions that you have concerning the Examkrackers MCAT Biology manual. To post a question for this topic, simply choose the lecture of which you have a question about and then select "new topic" on the following page. When posting your question, please include the page number and question number.

Lecture 1 · Lecture 3 · Lecture 5
Lecture 2 · Lecture 4 · Lecture 6

2 2

Examkrackers MCAT Chemistry
Under this topic, Sam Crayton will answer any questions that you have concerning the Examkrackers MCAT Chemistry manual. To post a question for this topic, simply choose the lecture of which you have a question about and then select "new topic" on the following page. When posting your question, please include the page number and question number.

Lecture 1 · Lecture 4 · Lecture 6
Lecture 2 · Lecture 5 · Lecture 7
Lecture 3

2 2

Examkrackers MCAT Physics
Under this topic, Sam Crayton will answer any questions that you have concerning the Examkrackers MCAT Physics manual. To post a question for this topic, simply choose the lecture of which you have a question about and then select "new topic" on the following page. When posting your question, please include the page number and question number.

Lecture 1 · Lecture 3 · Lecture 5
Lecture 2 · Lecture 4

Your purchase of this book new will also give you access to the **Examkrackers Forums** at www.examkrackers.com/mcat/forum. These bulletin boards allows you to discuss any question in the book with an MCAT® expert at Examkrackers. All discussions are kept on file so you can refer back to previous discussions on any question in this book. Once you have purchased the books you can take advantage of this resource by calling 1-888-KRACKEM to register for the forums.

Although we make every effort to ensure the accuracy of our books, the occasional error does occur. Corrections are posted on the Examkrackers Books Errata Forum, also at www.examkrackers.com/mcat/forum. If you believe that you have found a mistake, please post an inquiry on the Study with Examkrackers MCAT Books Forum, which is likewise found at www.examkrackers.com/mcat/forum. As the leaders in MCAT® preparation, we are committed to providing you with the most up-to-date, accurate information possible.

Study diligently, trust this book to guide you, and you will reach your MCAT® goals.

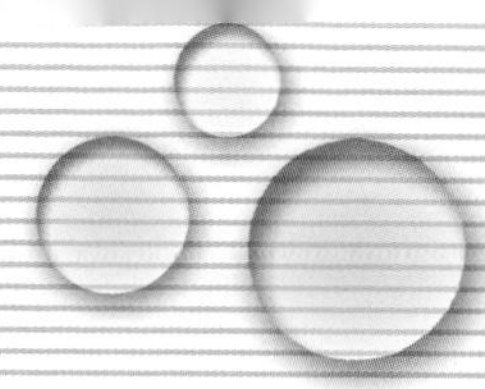

Table of Contents

30-Minute In-Class Exams 119

Answers & Explanations to In-Class Exams 145

Answers & Explanations to Questions in the Lectures 159

Photo Credits 175

BIOLOGICAL SCIENCES

DIRECTIONS. Most questions in the Biological Sciences test are organized into groups, each preceded by a descriptive passage. After studying the passage, select the one best answer to each question in the group. Some questions are not based on a descriptive passage and are also independent of each other. You must also select the one best answer to these questions. If you are not certain of an answer, eliminate the alternatives that you know to be incorrect and then select an answer from the remaining alternatives. A periodic table is provided for your use. You may consult it whenever you wish.

PERIODIC TABLE OF THE ELEMENTS

1 **H** 1.0																	2 **He** 4.0
3 **Li** 6.9	4 **Be** 9.0											5 **B** 10.8	6 **C** 12.0	7 **N** 14.0	8 **O** 16.0	9 **F** 19.0	10 **Ne** 20.2
11 **Na** 23.0	12 **Mg** 24.3											13 **Al** 27.0	14 **Si** 28.1	15 **P** 31.0	16 **S** 32.1	17 **Cl** 35.5	18 **Ar** 39.9
19 **K** 39.1	20 **Ca** 40.1	21 **Sc** 45.0	22 **Ti** 47.9	23 **V** 50.9	24 **Cr** 52.0	25 **Mn** 54.9	26 **Fe** 55.8	27 **Co** 58.9	28 **Ni** 58.7	29 **Cu** 63.5	30 **Zn** 65.4	31 **Ga** 69.7	32 **Ge** 72.6	33 **As** 74.9	34 **Se** 79.0	35 **Br** 79.9	36 **Kr** 83.8
37 **Rb** 85.5	38 **Sr** 87.6	39 **Y** 88.9	40 **Zr** 91.2	41 **Nb** 92.9	42 **Mo** 95.9	43 **Tc** (98)	44 **Ru** 101.1	45 **Rh** 102.9	46 **Pd** 106.4	47 **Ag** 107.9	48 **Cd** 112.4	49 **In** 114.8	50 **Sn** 118.7	51 **Sb** 121.8	52 **Te** 127.6	53 **I** 126.9	54 **Xe** 131.3
55 **Cs** 132.9	56 **Ba** 137.3	57 **La*** 138.9	72 **Hf** 178.5	73 **Ta** 180.9	74 **W** 183.9	75 **Re** 186.2	76 **Os** 190.2	77 **Ir** 192.2	78 **Pt** 195.1	79 **Au** 197.0	80 **Hg** 200.6	81 **Tl** 204.4	82 **Pb** 207.2	83 **Bi** 209.0	84 **Po** (209)	85 **At** (210)	86 **Rn** (222)
87 **Fr** (223)	88 **Ra** 226.0	89 **Ac=** 227.0	104 **Unq** (261)	105 **Unp** (262)	106 **Unh** (263)	107 **Uns** (262)	108 **Uno** (265)	109 **Une** (267)									

*	58 **Ce** 140.1	59 **Pr** 140.9	60 **Nd** 144.2	61 **Pm** (145)	62 **Sm** 150.4	63 **Eu** 152.0	64 **Gd** 157.3	65 **Tb** 158.9	66 **Dy** 162.5	67 **Ho** 164.9	68 **Er** 167.3	69 **Tm** 168.9	70 **Yb** 173.0	71 **Lu** 175.0
=	90 **Th** 232.0	91 **Pa** (231)	92 **U** 238.0	93 **Np** (237)	94 **Pu** (244)	95 **Am** (243)	96 **Cm** (247)	97 **Bk** (247)	98 **Cf** (251)	99 **Es** (252)	100 **Fm** (257)	101 **Md** (258)	102 **No** (259)	103 **Lr** (260)

For your convenience, a periodic table is also inserted in the back of the book.

Biological Molecules and Enzymes

1.1 Introduction

This lecture discusses the structure and basic functions of the major chemical components of living cells and their surroundings. Most biological molecules can be classified as lipids, proteins, carbohydrates, or nucleotide derivatives. Each of these types of molecules possesses a carbon skeleton. Together with water and minerals, they form living cells and their environments. The functions of these biological molecules can be understood by considering the match between the ways they are employed and each of their unique features. Knowledge of these biological molecules and their roles in the cellular environment provides a strong base from which to understand the biology and biochemistry required for the MCAT®.

THE 3 KEYS

1. Each category of biological molecule has a "personality" - think structure and polarity - that matches its practical uses in living organisms.
2. Enzyme-substrate fit correlates with enzyme effectiveness and a lower K_m.
3. Competitive inhibitors block the active site; noncompetitive inhibitors bind to a separate site, changing the shape of the active site; uncompetitve inhibitors bind the enzyme-substrate complex, decreasing the concentration of substrate that can react.

Lipid: phospholipid

Protein: collagen

Carbohydrate: amylose

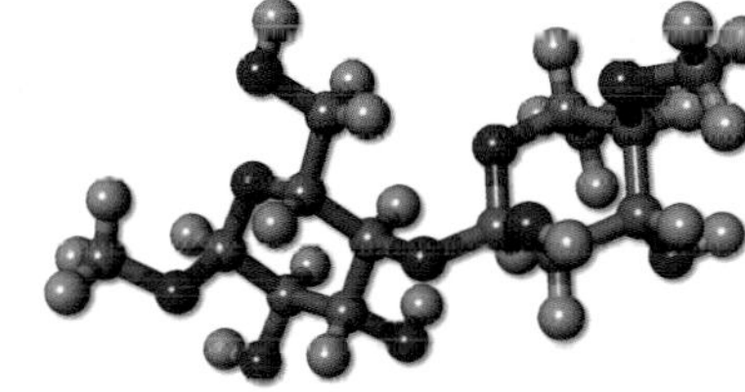

Nucleotide: ATP

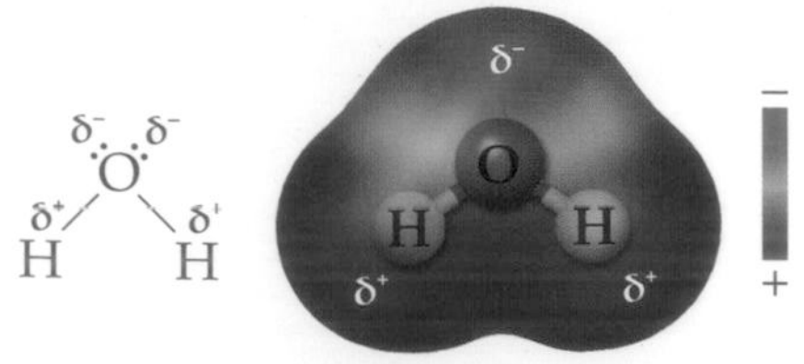

When you think about water, think polarity. The polarity of water is what makes it a perfect solvent for chemical reactions in the body. As you read this lecture, consider how the polar and nonpolar regions of biological molecules affect their interactions with water. Due to polarity and hydrogen bonding, water molecules pull apart polar molecules or ions and form ordered networks around them. On the other hand, water molecules force nonpolar molecules to congregate together. These interactions play an important role in biological reactions.

1.2 Water

Water is the solvent in which the chemical reactions of living cells take place. 70 to 80 percent of a cell's mass is made up of water. Water is a small polar molecule that can participate in **hydrogen bonding**. Most compounds as light as water would exist as a gas at typical cell temperatures. The ability of water molecules to form hydrogen bonds with each other elevates the boiling point; as a result, water remains in a liquid state in the cellular environment. Hydrogen bonding also provides strong cohesive forces between water molecules, thus "squeezing" **hydrophobic** (Greek: hydros → water, phobos → fear) molecules away from water and causing them to aggregate. By contrast, **hydrophilic** (Greek: philos → love) molecules or ionic compounds dissolve easily in water because their negatively charged ends are attracted to the partial positive charge of water's hydrogens while their positively charged ends are attracted to the partial negative charge of the oxygen (Figure 1.2). Thus, water molecules surround (solvate) a hydrophilic molecule or ion.

Besides acting as a solvent, water often acts as a reactant or product. Most macromolecules of living cells are broken apart via **hydrolysis** (Greek: lysis → separation) and are formed via dehydration. In a hydrolysis reaction, a macromolecule is broken into two smaller molecules through the addition of water. The hydrolysis of ATP molecules provides the body's major source of energy. Digestion is primarily the hydrolysis of macromolecules, breaking a bond by adding the H and OH of water to either end. **Dehydration** is the reverse reaction of hydrolysis, where two molecules are combined to form a larger molecule and water is formed as a byproduct. As will be described later in this lecture, a dehydration reaction allows the formation of the bonds that make up biological molecules, such as the peptide bonds that make up proteins and the ester bonds that are essential to triglycerides.

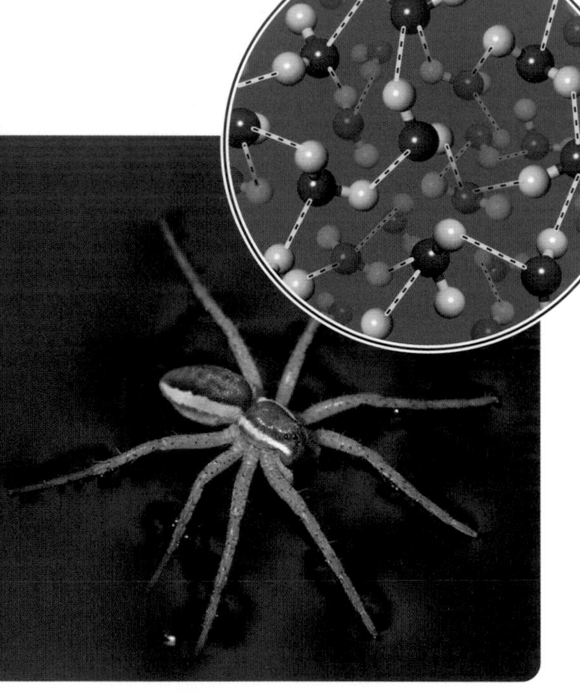

FIGURE 1.1 Hydrogen Bonds

Hydrogen bonding between individual water molecules creates cohesive forces that are strong enough to support this raft spider.

FIGURE 1.2 Water as a Solvent

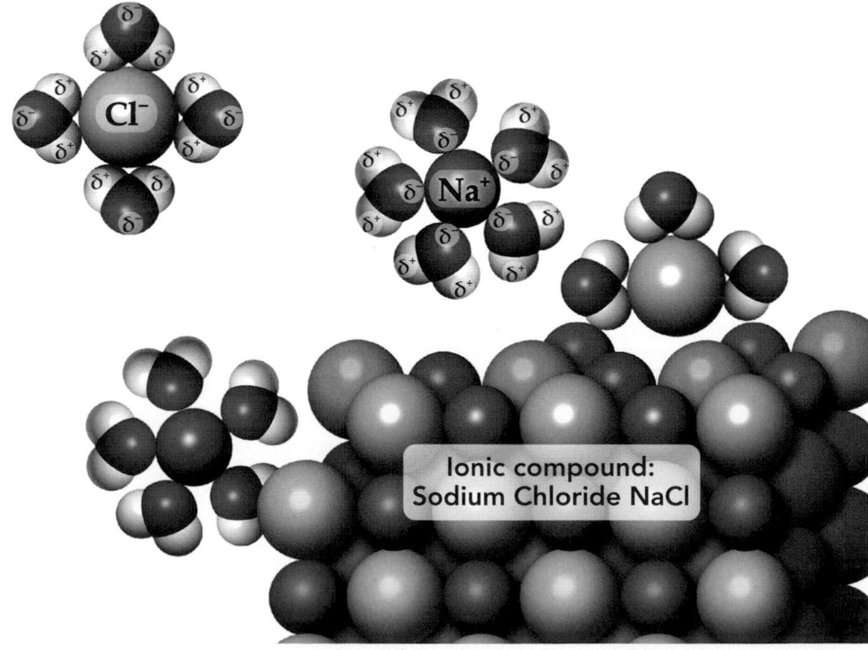

Polar molecules or ionic compounds are readily solvated by water; nonpolar molecules are not. This is an example of how "like dissolves like."

1.3 Lipids

Omega-3 fatty acids are lipids. They are found in fish and other seafood including algae and krill, some plants, and nut oils.

Lipids are essential to life and perform a variety of functions in the body. While the types of lipids are characterized by a variety of structures and functional groups, they all share the same defining characteristics: low solubility in water and high solubility in nonpolar organic solvents. In other words, lipids are nonpolar and thus hydrophobic. This property determines the behavior of lipids in the watery environment of the cell.

The roles played by lipids in an organism can be placed into three categories: 1. energy storage; 2. cellular organization and structure, particularly in the membrane; and 3. provision of precursor molecules for vitamins and hormones. The structural features of different lipids make them ideally suited for these cellular functions.

The major groups of lipids include fatty acids, triacylglycerols, phospholipids, glycolipids, steroids, terpenes, and waxes.

FIGURE 1.3 Types of Lipids

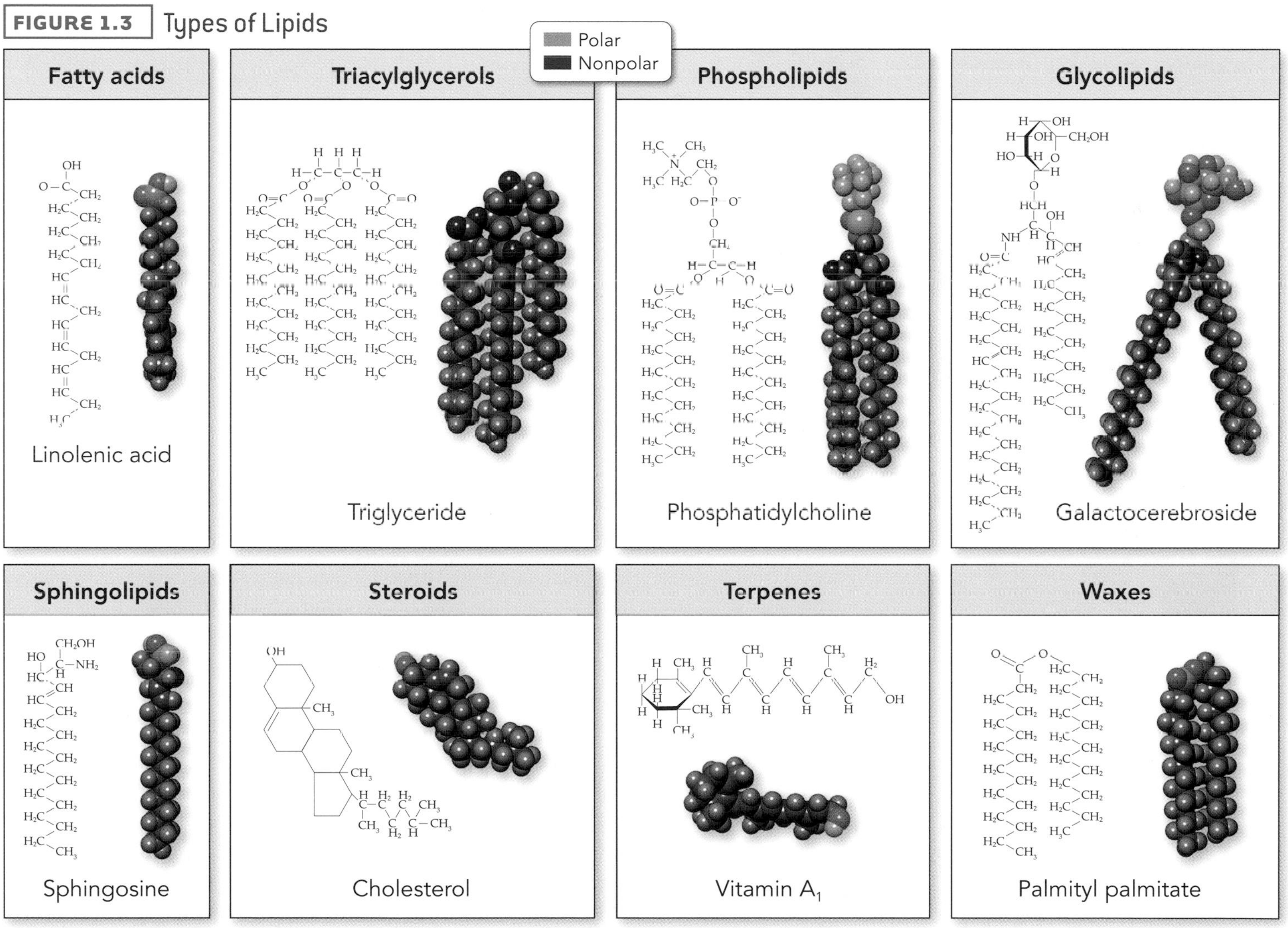

Polar
Nonpolar

Fatty acids — Linolenic acid

Triacylglycerols — Triglyceride

Phospholipids — Phosphatidylcholine

Glycolipids — Galactocerebroside

Sphingolipids — Sphingosine

Steroids — Cholesterol

Terpenes — Vitamin A_1

Waxes — Palmityl palmitate

As you read about the following types of fats, relate each of them back to the three major functions of lipids. Remember that long carbon chains allow energy storage; that fats assemble into barriers separating aqueous environments because they are hydrophobic; and that lipids are useful as precursors for signaling molecules because they can pass through cellular membranes.

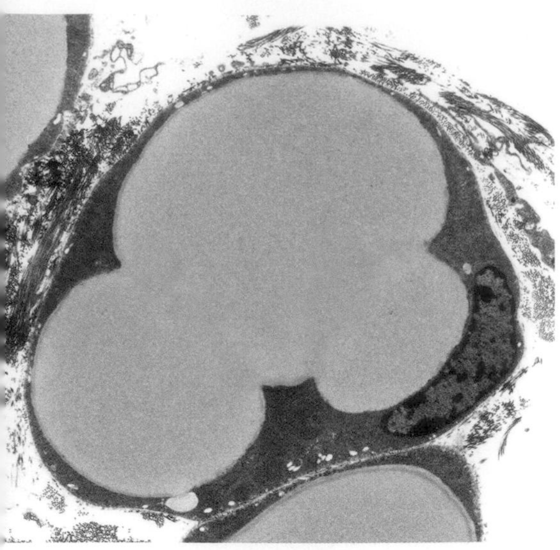

Each fat cell or adipocyte consists of a large central lipid droplet (yellow) surrounded by a thin layer of cytoplasm (red) containing the nucleus (blue). Fat cells store energy as an insulating layer of fat under the skin.

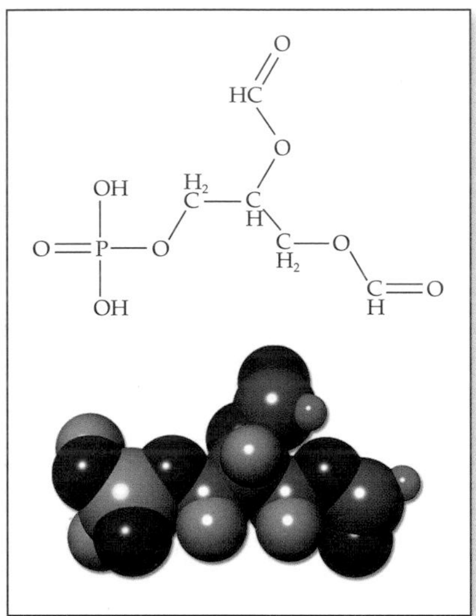

The simplest phosphoglyceride is phosphatidic acid. All other phosphoglycerides except one type, *plasmalogens*, have a phosphatidic acid backbone, which is just another way of describing the glycerol backbone with a phosphate group attached. They can thus be referred to as **phosphatids**.

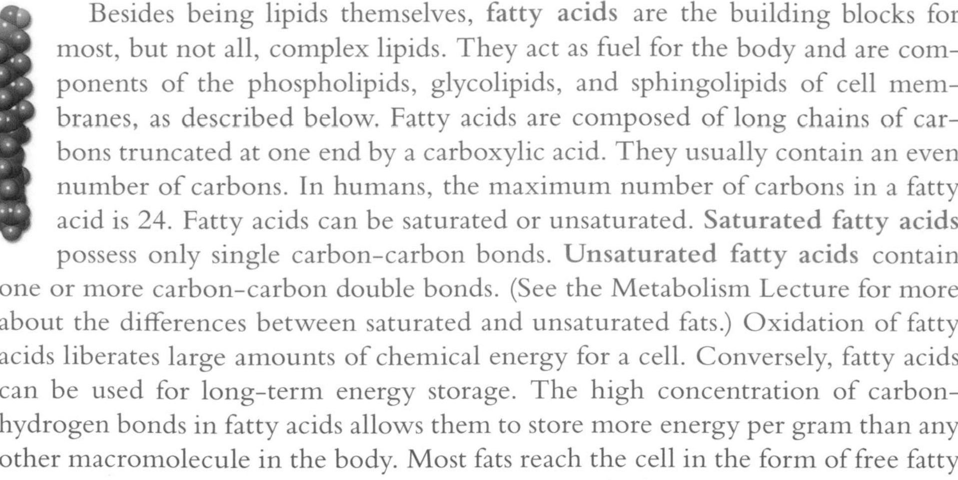

Besides being lipids themselves, **fatty acids** are the building blocks for most, but not all, complex lipids. They act as fuel for the body and are components of the phospholipids, glycolipids, and sphingolipids of cell membranes, as described below. Fatty acids are composed of long chains of carbons truncated at one end by a carboxylic acid. They usually contain an even number of carbons. In humans, the maximum number of carbons in a fatty acid is 24. Fatty acids can be saturated or unsaturated. **Saturated fatty acids** possess only single carbon-carbon bonds. **Unsaturated fatty acids** contain one or more carbon-carbon double bonds. (See the Metabolism Lecture for more about the differences between saturated and unsaturated fats.) Oxidation of fatty acids liberates large amounts of chemical energy for a cell. Conversely, fatty acids can be used for long-term energy storage. The high concentration of carbon-hydrogen bonds in fatty acids allows them to store more energy per gram than any other macromolecule in the body. Most fats reach the cell in the form of free fatty acids, meaning fatty acid chains not attached to a backbone, rather than as triacylglycerols.

Triacylglycerols, phospholipids, and glycolipids are sometimes referred to as fatty acids. **Triacylglycerols** (Latin: tri → three), commonly called **triglycerides** or simply **fats** and *oils*, are constructed from a three carbon backbone called **glycerol**, which is attached to three fatty acid chains (as shown in Figure 1.3). Their function in a cell is to store energy. They can also provide thermal insulation and padding to an organism. **Adipocytes** (Latin: adips → fat, Greek: kytos → cell), also called fat cells, are specialized cells whose cytoplasm contains almost nothing but triglycerides.

Phospholipids are lipids with a phosphate group attached. For the purposes of the MCAT®, the most important phospholipids are phosphoglycerides. Like triglycerides, phosphoglycerides are built from a glycerol backbone, but a polar phosphate group replaces one of the fatty acids. The phosphate group lies on the opposite side of the glycerol from the fatty acids, making the phospholipid polar at the phosphate end and nonpolar at the fatty acid end. Molecules that have a polar and nonpolar end are referred to as **amphipathic** (Latin: ambo → both), and this quality makes phospholipids especially well suited as the major component of biological membranes. When forming bilayer membranes, the polar heads of phospholipids are able to face toward the watery environment within and outside the cell, while the tails create a nonpolar inner layer within the membrane, creating a barrier to polar molecules that allows the regulation of their passage in and out of the cell.

Glycolipids (Greek: glucus → sweet) are similar to phosphoglycerides, except that glycolipids have one or more carbohydrates attached to the three-carbon glycerol backbone instead of the phosphate group. Glycolipids are also amphipathic. They are found in abundance in the membranes of myelinated cells in the human nervous system.

Sphingolipids are also similar to phosphoglycerides, in that they have a long chain fatty acid and a polar head group. However, rather than glycerol, the backbone molecule is an amino alcohol called a sphingosine. (One type of sphingolipid, *sphingomyelin,* has a phosphate group attached to the sphingosine backbone and is thus a phospholipid, although it is not a phosphoglyceride.) Like phospholipids, glycolipids, and steroids, sphingolipids make up part of the cell membrane.

Steroids are four ringed structures. They include some hormones, *vitamin D*, and cholesterol, an important membrane component. See the Endocrine System Lecture in *Biology 2: Systems* to learn about the steroid class of hormones, and see the Cell Lecture in the same manual for how steroids affect the characteristics of the cellular membrane.

Terpenes are a sixth class of lipids that are often part of pigments in the body. They include *vitamin A*, which is important for vision.

Waxes are another type of lipid that are formed by an ester linkage between a long-chain alcohol and a long-chain fatty acid. They have a variety of functions in different types of organisms, determined by their characteristic water-repellent texture. Ear wax is an example of a wax in the human body.

Another class of lipids (not shown in Figure 1.3 but often listed as a fatty acid) are the 20 carbon *eicosanoids* (Greek: eikosi → twenty). Eicosanoids include **prostaglandins**, thromboxanes, and leukotrienes. Eicosanoids are released from cell membranes as local hormones that regulate, among other things, blood pressure, body temperature, and smooth muscle contraction. Aspirin is a commonly used inhibitor of the synthesis of prostaglandins.

Because lipids are insoluble in aqueous solution, they are transported in the blood via *lipoproteins*. A lipoprotein contains a lipid core surrounded by phospholipids and *apoproteins*. Thus the lipoprotein is able to dissolve lipids in its hydrophobic core, and then move freely through the aqueous solution due to its hydrophilic shell. Lipoproteins are classified by their density. The greater the ratio of lipid to protein, the lower the density. The major classes of lipoproteins in humans are chylomicrons, *very low density lipoproteins (VLDL), low density lipoproteins (LDL),* and *high density lipoproteins (HDL)*. (For more on lipoproteins, see the Digestive and Excretory Systems Lecture in *Biology 2: Systems*.)

Vitamins are a particular type of organic molecule that are essential, meaning they cannot be produced by the body. Vitamin A and Vitamin D are examples of **fat-soluble vitamins**. Fat-soluble vitamins are transported in the body along with fats obtained from the diet, and also assist in the absorption of these fats.

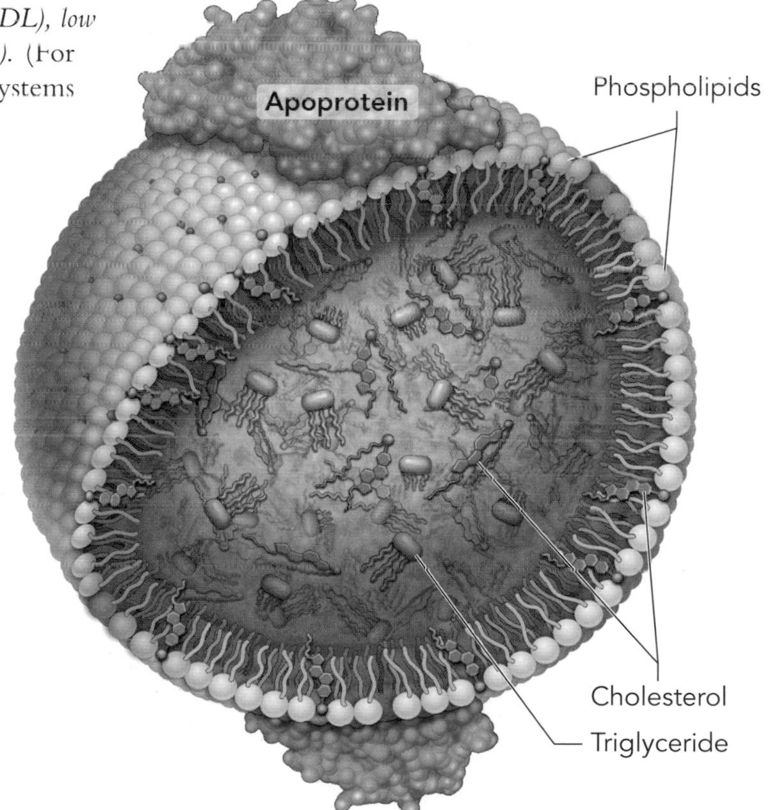

When the ratio of protein to lipid is larger, the density of a lipoprotein is greater. Think about a solidly built athlete and remember that the proteins comprising muscles weigh more than an equivalent volume of fat. Because proteins are more dense than lipids, the greater the ratio of protein to fat in a lipoprotein, the denser the lipoprotein will be.

Know these major functions of lipids:

1. phospholipids serve as a structural component of membranes;
2. triacylglycerols store metabolic energy and provide thermal insulation and padding;
3. steroids regulate metabolic activities; and
4. some fatty acids (eicosanoids) even serve as local hormones.

1.4 Carbohydrates

The primary biological importance of **carbohydrates** lies with their usefulness in energy storage and providing easily accessible energy to the body. As with fats, the high concentration of C-H bonds in carbohydrates allows for the storage of a large amount of energy. However, carbohydrates do not store as much energy per gram as lipids simply because they do not have as high a concentration of C-H bonds; alcohols are also present along the carbon chain. The consistent structure of carbohydrates allows them to be easily stacked together in the cell, which contributes to their usefulness for energy storage. The structure of carbohydrates also makes it possible for them to join together through a dehydration reaction, forming long chains, **polysaccharides**, for energy storage. The reverse hydrolysis reaction allows the release of single sugar molecules, **monosaccharides,** that the tissues can use for energy.

Carbohydrates can be thought of as carbon and water in a fixed one-to-one ratio. For each carbon atom there exists one oxygen atom and two hydrogen atoms. The formula for any carbohydrate is:

$$C_n(H_2O)_n$$

The carbohydrates most likely to appear on the MCAT® are fructose and glucose. Both are six carbon carbohydrates called **hexoses. Glucose** (Greek: glucus → sweet) is the most commonly occurring six carbon carbohydrate. The Fischer projections of fructose and glucose are shown in Figure 1.4. Glucose normally accounts for 80% of the carbohydrates absorbed by humans. Almost all digested carbohydrates reaching body cells have been converted to glucose by the liver or enterocytes (intestinal cells).

The cell can oxidize glucose to transfer its chemical energy to a more readily usable form, ATP. If the cell already has sufficient ATP, glucose is polymerized to the polysaccharide form, glycogen, or converted to fat. As shown in Figure 1.5, **glycogen** is a branched glucose polymer with alpha linkages. Glycogen is found in all animal cells, but especially large amounts are found in muscle and liver cells. The liver regulates the blood glucose level, so liver cells are one of the few cell types capable of reforming glucose from glycogen and releasing it back into the bloodstream when needed. Only certain epithelial cells in the digestive tract and the proximal tubule of the kidney are capable of absorbing glucose against a concentration gradient. This is done via a secondary active transport mechanism down the concentration gradient of sodium. All other cells absorb glucose via facilitated diffusion. Insulin increases the rate of facilitated diffusion for glucose and other monosaccharides. In the absence of insulin, only neural and hepatic cells are capable of absorbing sufficient amounts of glucose via the facilitated transport system.

Just like animals, plants join glucose molecules to form polysaccharides. Plants use **starch** for long-term storage instead of glycogen. Starch comes in two forms: *amylose* and *amylopectin*. Amylose may be branched or unbranched and has the same alpha linkages as glycogen. Amylopectin resembles glycogen but has a different branching structure.

Plants also use glucose molecules to form **cellulose.** Cellulose is used as a structural material rather than for energy storage, and in contrast to starch and glycogen, it is composed of beta linkages. Like most animals, humans have enzymes to digest the alpha linkages of starch and glycogen but do not have enzymes that can digest the beta linkages of cellulose. Some animals such as cows have bacteria in their digestive systems that release an enzyme to digest the beta linkages in cellulose. Recent research suggests that certain insects do produce an enzyme to digest the beta linkages of cellulose.

See the Oxygen Containing Reactions Lecture in the *Chemistry Manual* for more on carbohydrates, including the chemistry behind the formation of polysaccharides.

FIGURE 1.4 Glucose and Fructose

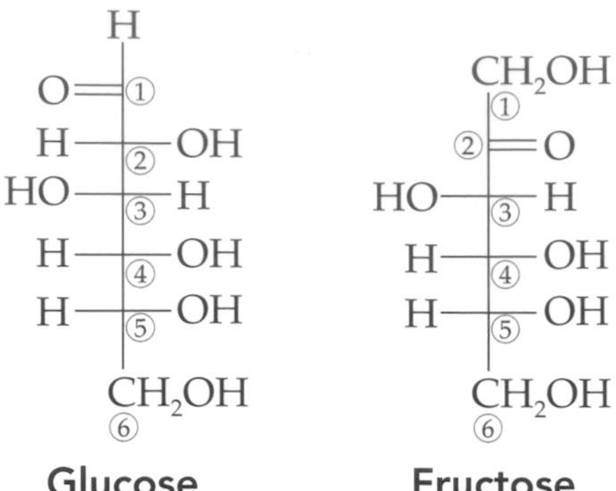

In the absence of insulin, only the brain and the liver continue to absorb glucose.

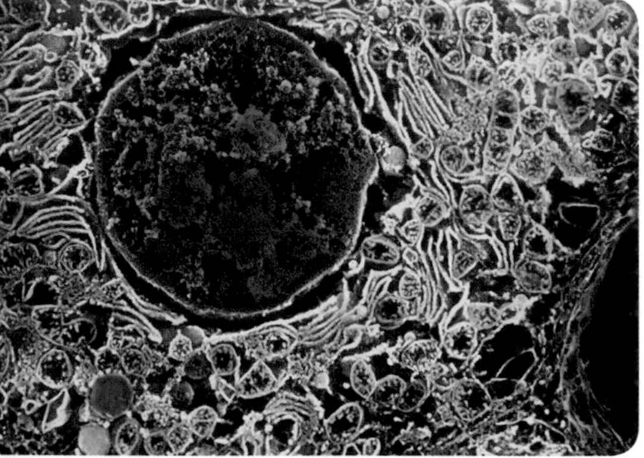

Liver cells contain large amounts of glycogen. This helps the liver regulate blood glucose levels.

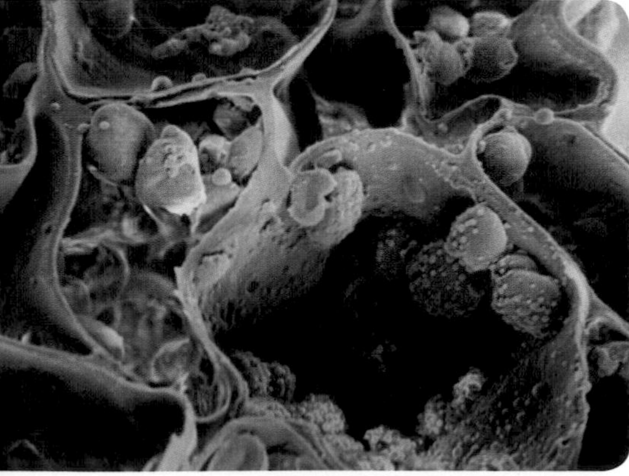

Large chloroplasts (found in plants) contain starch granules made by photosynthesis.

FIGURE 1.5 Glucose and Glucose Polymers

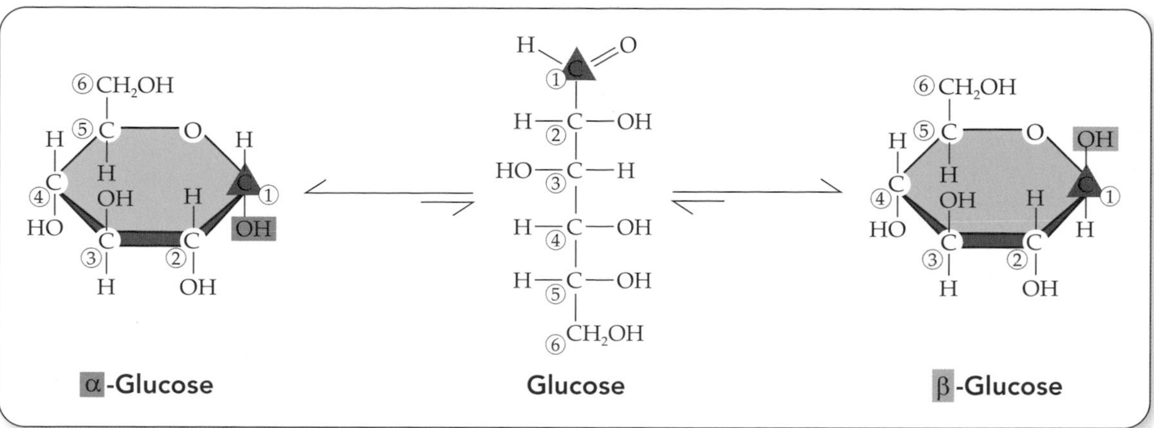

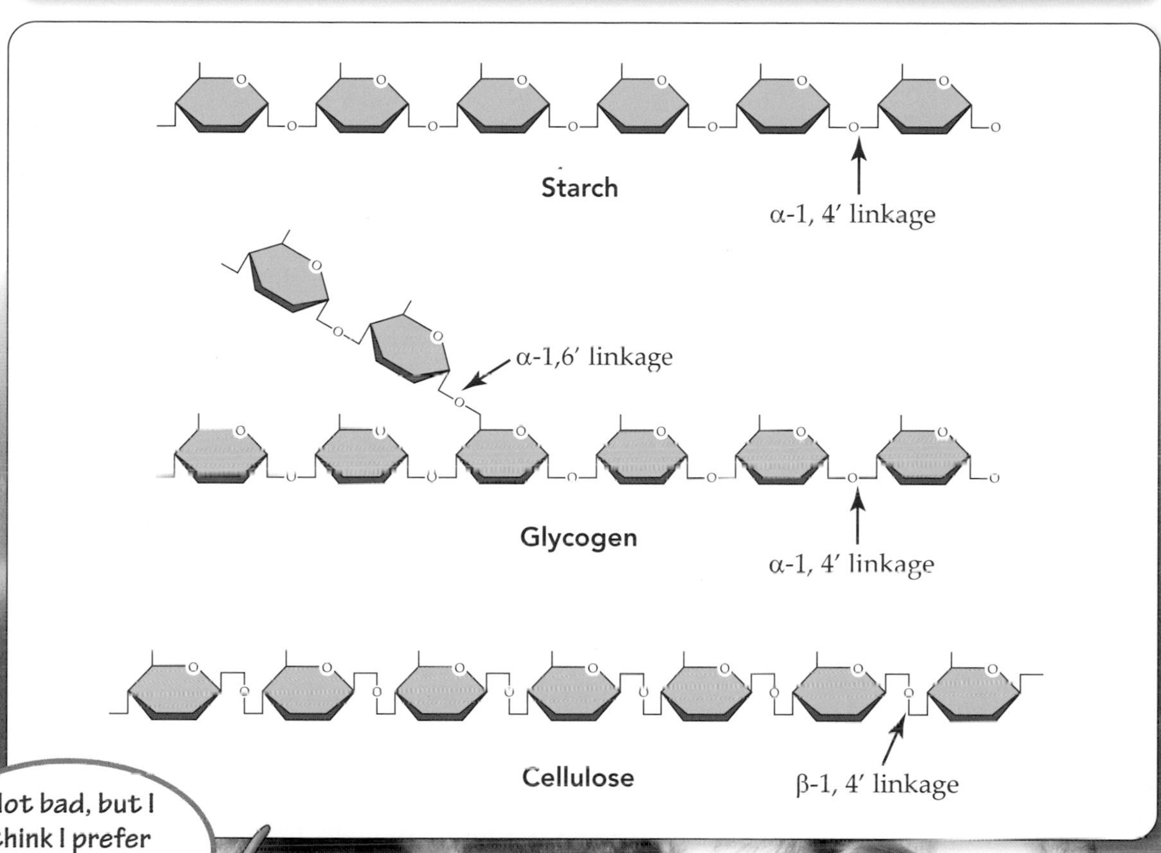

For glucose polymers, remember that animals eat the alpha linkages, but only bacteria break the beta linkages. The stability of the beta linkages of cellulose makes it a tough, stable molecule that can be used to build plant cell walls.

Watson and Crick discovered the double helix structure of DNA.

1.5 Nucleotides

Nucleotides are an important class of molecules that are involved in the cell's use of energy as well as comprising the building blocks of every organism's genetic material. They are made up of three components:

1. a five carbon (pentose) sugar;
2. a nitrogenous base; and
3. a phosphate group.

The three components of nucleotides allow them to form the characteristic structure of DNA, as described below. The highly stable sugars, along with the phosphate groups, are able to link together to form a stable and organized backbone. Both are polar and thus can face outward into the watery solvent of the cell. Meanwhile, the nitrogenous bases can form weak hydrogen bonds with each other that stabilize the double-stranded structure of DNA but can also be separated to allow the replication of genetic material.

A **nucleoside** consists of a pentose sugar attached to a nitrogenous base. Nucleotides are formed by the addition of one or more phosphate groups to a nucleoside. Nucleotides form polymers to create the **nucleic acids**, DNA and RNA, which allow for the expression of genetic traits by specifying the production of proteins (see the Genetics Lecture).

In nucleic acids, nucleotides are joined together into long strands by **phosphodiester bonds** between the phosphate group of one nucleotide and the third carbon of the pentose sugar of the other nucleotide, forming a **sugar-phosphate backbone**. By convention, a strand of nucleotides in a nucleic acid is written as a list of its nitrogenous bases. A nucleotide attached to the number 3 carbon (3') of its neighbor follows that neighbor in the list. In other words, nucleotides are written in the 5' to 3' direction (5'→ 3'). By convention, DNA is written so that the top strand runs 5'→ 3' and the bottom runs 3'→ 5'.

Four nitrogenous bases exist in **DNA (deoxyribonucleic acid): adenine** (A), **guanine** (G), **cytosine** (C), and **thymine** (T). Adenine and guanine are two ring structures called **purines**, while cytosine and thymine are single ring structures called **pyrimidines.** DNA usually exists in a particular form described by the **Watson-Crick model,** named for the scientists who are credited with first theorizing the structure of DNA. In this typical structure, also known as the *B form*, the two strands lie side by side in opposite 3′ → 5′ directions (**antiparallel**) bound together by hydrogen bonds between nitrogenous bases, forming a **double stranded** structure. This hydrogen bonding is commonly referred to as **base-pairing**. The length of a DNA strand is measured in **base-pairs (bp)**. Under normal circumstances, the hydrogen bonds form only between specific purine-pyrimidine pairs; adenine forms 2 hydrogen bonds with thymine, and guanine forms 3 hydrogen bonds with cytosine. Therefore, in order for two strands to bind together, their bases must match up in the correct order. Two strands that match in such a fashion are called **complementary strands**. When complementary strands bind together, they curl into a **double helix** (Figure 1.7). The double helix contains two distinct grooves called the major groove and the minor groove. Each groove spirals once around the double helix for every ten base-pairs. This structure of DNA is stable in the cellular environment and allows for replication of genetic material.

FIGURE 1.6 NADH

NADH is an example of a dinucleotide. Notice that here a phosphomonoester linkages join the two nucleotides.

FIGURE 1.7 DNA Double Helix

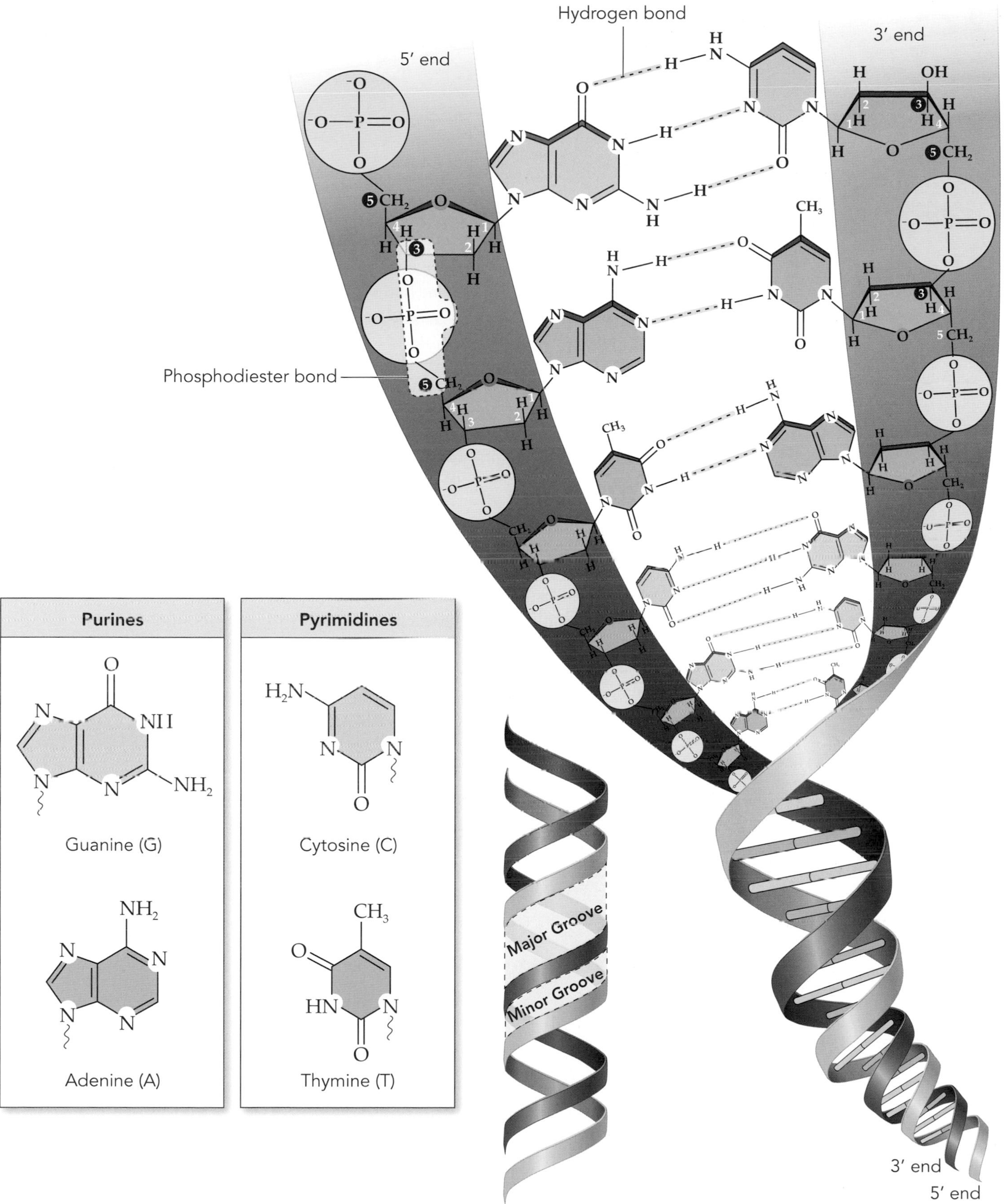

Remember that DNA is a polymer of nucleotides, and each nucleotide is made up of three parts: the phosphate group, the 5-carbon sugar, and the nitrogenous base. Know the names of the purines (adenine and guanine) and the pyrimidines (cytosine and thymine). A good way to remember this is: "pyrimidine" contains a "y," and so do "cytosine" and "thymine." Uracil, a nitrogenous base in RNA, is also a pyrimidine. This is easy to remember since it replaces the pyrimidine thymine. Know the pairings (AT, GC) and the number of H-bonds between each pair. Two hydrogen bonds hold together AT, while three hold together GC. This means that more energy is required to separate GC bonds.

Uracil (U)

RNA (**ribonucleic acid**) is identical to DNA in structure except that:

1. carbon number 2 on the pentose is not "deoxygenated" (it has a hydroxyl group attached);
2. RNA is almost always **single stranded**; and
3. RNA contains the pyrimidine **uracil (U)** instead of thymine.

Unlike DNA, RNA can move through the nuclear pores and is not confined to the nucleus. Three important types of RNA, which will be described further in the Genetics Lecture, are mRNA (messenger RNA), rRNA (ribosomal RNA), and tRNA (transfer RNA). Also, notice the similarity in structure between uracil and thymine. This is a common cause of mutations in DNA.

In addition to forming genetic material, nucleotides also serve other purposes in the cell. Important nucleotides include **ATP (adenosine triphosphate**: Figure 1.8), the main source of readily available energy for the cell; cyclic AMP (cAMP), an important component in many second messenger systems; and NADH and $FADH_2$, the coenzymes involved in the Krebs cycle.

FIGURE 1.8 ATP

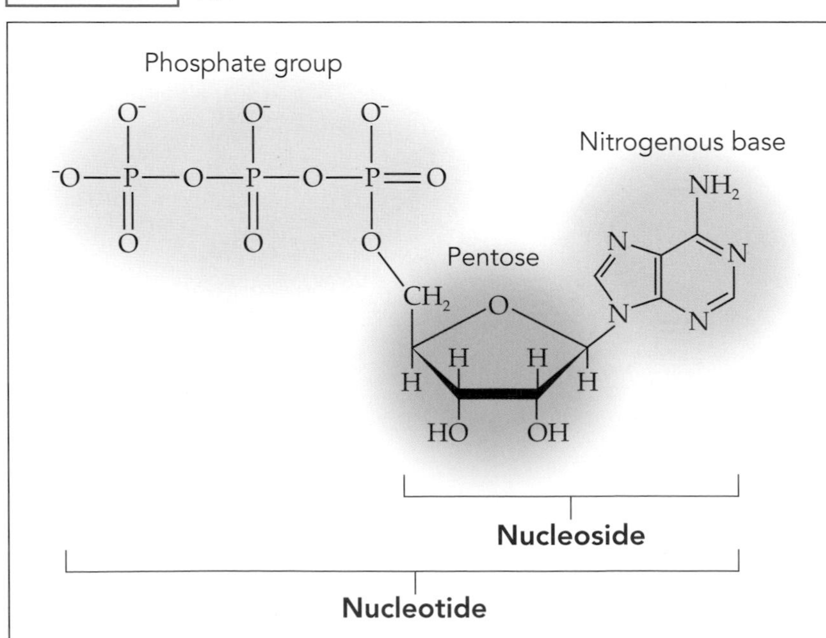

You will learn much more about the role of ATP as an energy source in Metabolism and Muscle, Bone, and Skin; about second messenger systems in Endocrine; and about NADH and $FADH_2$ in Metabolism.

These questions are NOT related to a passage.

Item 1

The most common catabolic reaction in the human body is:

- O A) dehydration.
- O B) hydrolysis.
- O C) condensation.
- O D) elimination.

Item 2

A molecule of DNA contains all of the following EXCEPT:

- O A) deoxyribose sugars.
- O B) polypeptide bonds.
- O C) phosphodiester bonds.
- O D) nitrogenous bases.

Item 3

Which of the following is a carbohydrate polymer that is stored in plants and digestible by animals?

- O A) Starch
- O B) Glycogen
- O C) Cellulose
- O D) Glucose

Item 4

Metabolism of carbohydrate and fat spares protein tissue. All of the following are true of fats EXCEPT:

- O A) Fats may be used in cell structure.
- O B) Fats may be used as hormones.
- O C) Fats are a more efficient form of energy storage than proteins.
- O D) Fats are a less efficient form of energy storage than carbohydrates.

Item 5

Which of the following is found in the RNA but not the DNA of a living cell?

- O A) Thymine
- O B) A double helix
- O C) An additional hydroxyl group
- O D) Hydrogen bonds

Item 6

Like cellulose, chitin is a polysaccharide that cannot be digested by animals. Chitin differs from cellulose in that it possesses an acetyl-amino group at the second carbon. What molecule is a reactant in the breaking of the β-1,4 glycoside linkages of cellulose and chitin?

- O A) Water
- O B) Oxygen
- O C) α-1,4-glucosidase
- O D) β-1,4-glucosidase

Item 7

Which of the following is always true concerning the base composition of DNA?

- O A) In each single strand, the number of adenine residues equals the number of thymine residues.
- O B) In each single strand, the number of adenine residues equals the number of guanine residues.
- O C) In a molecule of double stranded DNA, the ratio of adenine residues to thymine residues equals the ratio of cytosine residues to guanine residues.
- O D) In a molecule of double stranded DNA, the number of adenine residues plus thymine residues equals the number of cytosine residues plus guanine residues.

Item 8

All of the following types of lipids can be found in cell membranes EXCEPT:

- O A) glycolipids.
- O B) steroids.
- O C) prostaglandins.
- O D) sphingolipids.

Peanuts are a source of protein.

1.6 Amino Acids and Proteins

Amino acids are the building blocks of proteins. As described below, amino acids contain differing side groups with varying physical and chemical properties. The large number of possible combinations of amino acids with different properties allows different types of proteins to have a wide variety of structures, contributing to the multitude of functions that proteins carry out in the body. A single protein is built from a chain of amino acids linked together by peptide bonds; thus proteins are sometimes referred to as **polypeptides** (Greek: polys → many).

It is important to be able to recognize the general structure of an amino acid and a polypeptide. A peptide bond creates the functional group known as an **amide**, an amine connected to a carbonyl carbon. It is formed via a dehydration reaction of two amino acids. The reverse reaction is the hydrolysis of a peptide bond.

FIGURE 1.9 Hydrolysis of a Peptide Bond

$$HO{-}C({=}O){-}C(H)(R){-}N(H){-}C({=}O){-}C(H)(R){-}N{-}H + H_2O \rightleftharpoons HO{-}C({=}O){-}C(H)(R){-}N(H){-}H + HO{-}C({=}O){-}C(H)(R){-}N(H){-}H$$

Amide

Peptide bond

Dipeptide

Amino acids

Since nitrogen is most stable with four bonds and oxygen attracts electron density, resulting in a partial negative charge, electrons delocalize to give the peptide bond a partial double bond character. This double bond character prevents the bond from rotating freely and affects the secondary and, to some extent, the tertiary structure of the polypeptide (these types of protein structure are described later in this section).

Nearly all proteins in all species are built from the same 20 α-amino acids. They are called alpha amino acids because the amine is attached to the carbon in the alpha position to the carbonyl. In humans, nine of the amino acids are essential, meaning that they cannot be manufactured by the body and thus must be ingested directly. Digested proteins reach the cells of the human body as single amino acids.

Notice the R group on each amino acid. The R group is called the **side chain** of the amino acid. Each amino acid differs only in its R group. Like the amino group, the side chain is attached to the α-carbon. The R groups have different chemical properties, which can be divided into four categories: 1. acidic; 2. basic; 3. polar; and 4. nonpolar. All acidic and basic R groups are also polar. Generally, if the side chain contains carboxylic acids, then it is acidic; if it contains amines, then it is basic. These properties of the side chains affect the overall structure of the protein.

FIGURE 1.10 The 20 Common Amino Acids

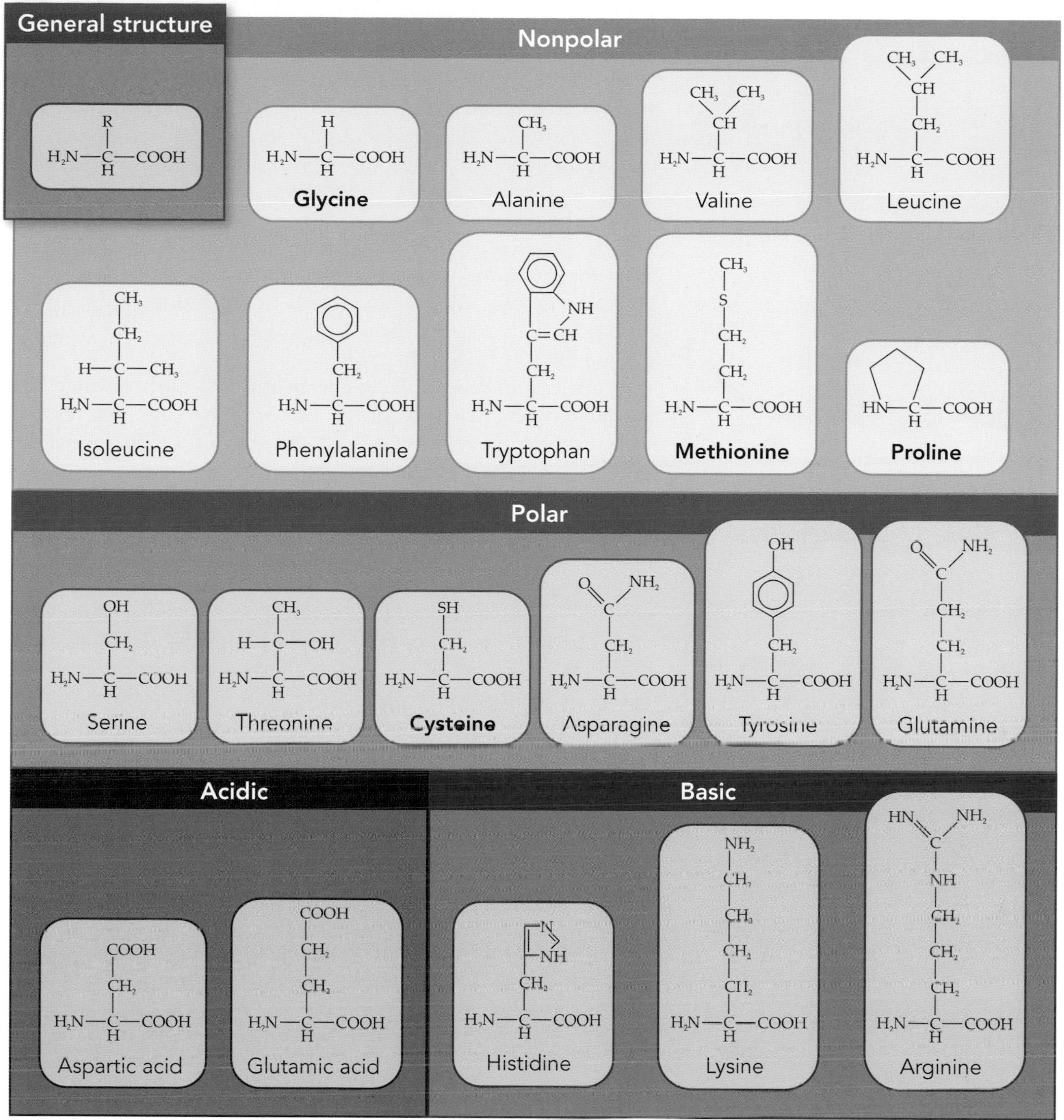

The structure of a protein is described according to several levels of organization. The number and sequence of amino acids in a polypeptide is called the **primary structure**. Once the primary structure is formed, the single chain can form into distinct shapes known as the **secondary structure** of the protein. The polypeptide can twist into an **α-helix**, or lie alongside itself and form a **β-pleated sheet**. With β-pleated sheets, the connecting segments of the two strands can lie in the same direction or in opposite directions. Both α-helices and β-pleated sheets are reinforced by hydrogen bonds between the carbonyl oxygen of one amino acid and the hydrogen on the amino group of another. A single protein usually contains both structures at various locations along its chain. These areas of secondary structure contribute to the **conformation**, or overall shape, of the protein.

The amino acid structures shown in this figure are artificial representations. Amino acids in solution, such as in the biological environment, will always carry one or more charges. The position and nature of the charges will depend upon the pH of the solution.

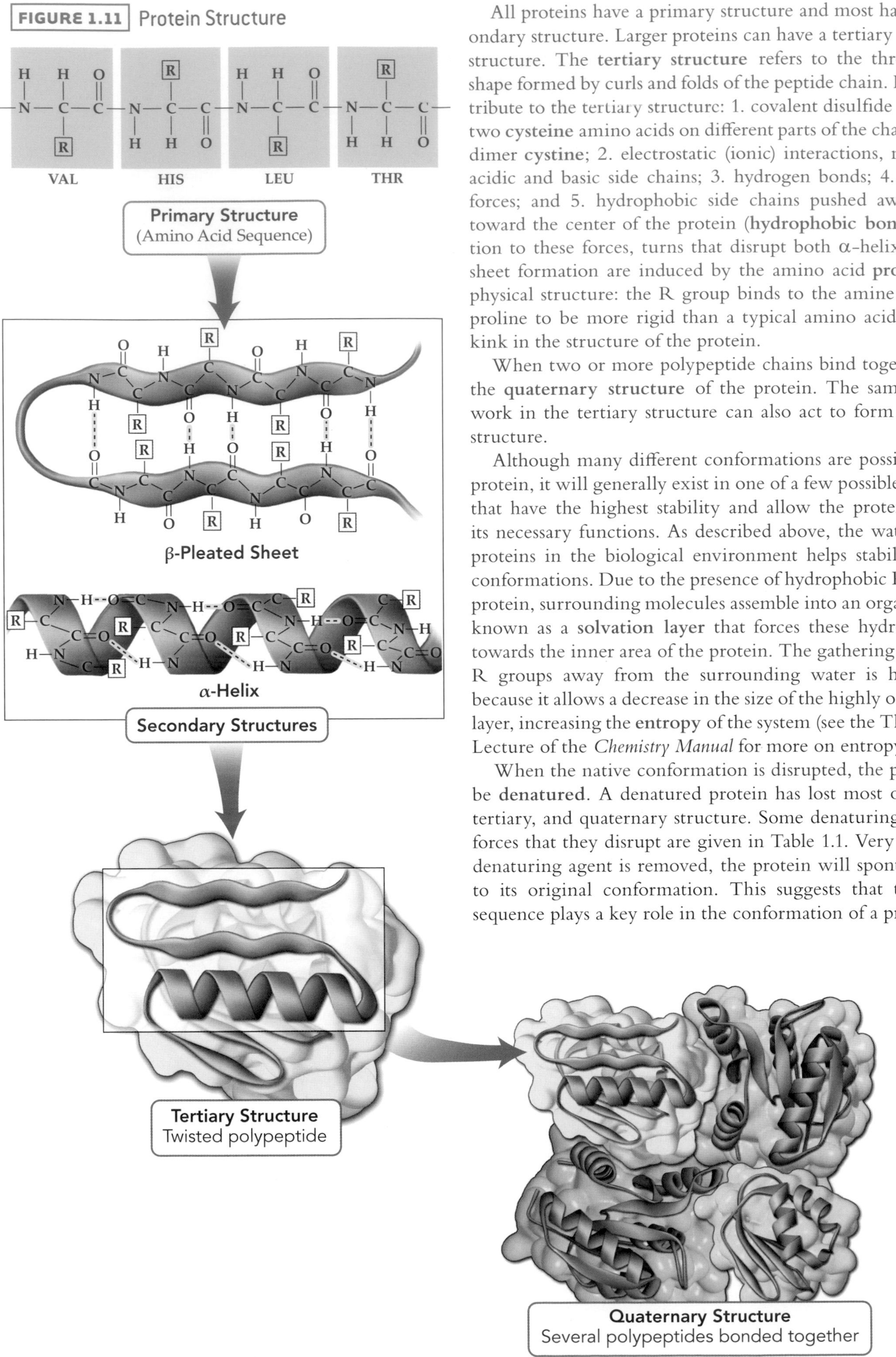

All proteins have a primary structure and most have areas of secondary structure. Larger proteins can have a tertiary and quaternary structure. The **tertiary structure** refers to the three dimensional shape formed by curls and folds of the peptide chain. Five forces contribute to the tertiary structure: 1. covalent disulfide bonds between two **cysteine** amino acids on different parts of the chain, creating the dimer **cystine**; 2. electrostatic (ionic) interactions, mostly between acidic and basic side chains; 3. hydrogen bonds; 4. van der Waals forces; and 5. hydrophobic side chains pushed away from water toward the center of the protein (**hydrophobic bonding**). In addition to these forces, turns that disrupt both α-helix and β-pleated sheet formation are induced by the amino acid **proline** due to its physical structure: the R group binds to the amine group, causing proline to be more rigid than a typical amino acid and creating a kink in the structure of the protein.

When two or more polypeptide chains bind together, they form the **quaternary structure** of the protein. The same five forces at work in the tertiary structure can also act to form the quaternary structure.

Although many different conformations are possible for any one protein, it will generally exist in one of a few possible conformations that have the highest stability and allow the protein to carry out its necessary functions. As described above, the water surrounding proteins in the biological environment helps stabilize these *native* conformations. Due to the presence of hydrophobic R groups on the protein, surrounding molecules assemble into an organized structure known as a **solvation layer** that forces these hydrophobic groups towards the inner area of the protein. The gathering of hydrophobic R groups away from the surrounding water is highly favorable because it allows a decrease in the size of the highly ordered solvation layer, increasing the **entropy** of the system (see the Thermodynamics Lecture of the *Chemistry Manual* for more on entropy).

When the native conformation is disrupted, the protein is said to be **denatured**. A denatured protein has lost most of its secondary, tertiary, and quaternary structure. Some denaturing agents and the forces that they disrupt are given in Table 1.1. Very often, once the denaturing agent is removed, the protein will spontaneously refold to its original conformation. This suggests that the amino acid sequence plays a key role in the conformation of a protein.

Later in this lecture, proteins' function as enzymes will be discussed extensively, but proteins have MANY additional roles in the body that will be covered throughout *Biology 1: Molecules and Biology 2: Systems.* Remember that the large array of possible functions is made possible by the numerous possible combinations of amino acids that have different physical properties. See the immune section of Lecture 4 in *Biology 2: Systems* for proteins that are involved in the immune system; the Muscle, Bone and Skin Lecture in the same manual for motor proteins that enable the movement of muscles; and the Genetics Lecture for DNA binding proteins.

Protein is found in nearly all unprocessed foods.

There are two types of proteins: *globular* and *structural*. There are more types of globular proteins than there are types of structural proteins. Globular proteins function as enzymes (e.g. pepsin), hormones (e.g. insulin), membrane pumps and channels (e.g. Na^+/K^+ pump and voltage gated sodium channels), membrane receptors (e.g. nicotinic receptors on a post-synaptic neuron), intercellular and intracellular transport and storage (e.g. hemoglobin and myoglobin), osmotic regulators (e.g. albumin), in the immune response (e.g. antibodies), and more.

FIGURE 1.12 Six Factors that Contribute to Tertiary Structure

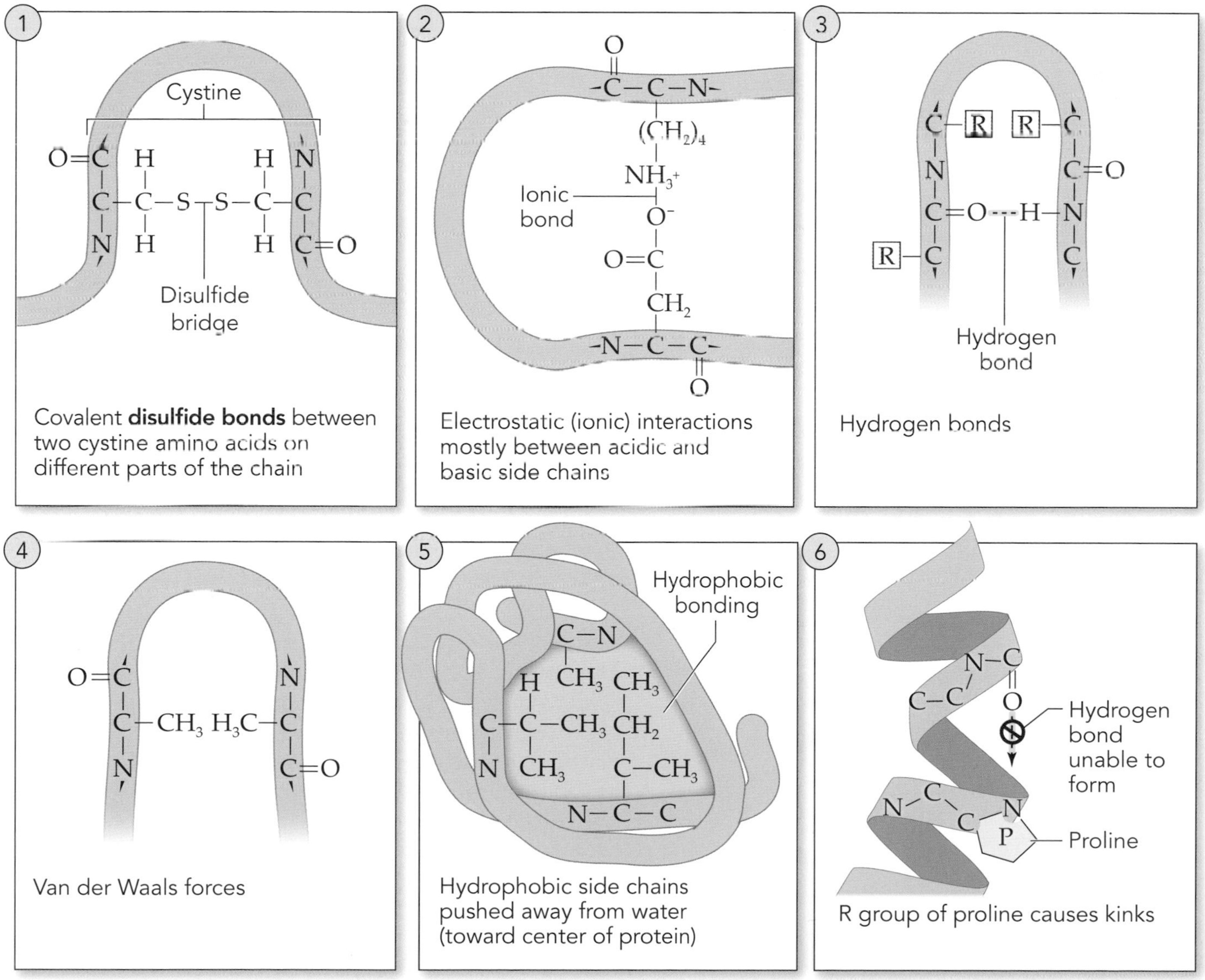

1. Cystine; Disulfide bridge — Covalent **disulfide bonds** between two cystine amino acids on different parts of the chain
2. Ionic bond — Electrostatic (ionic) interactions mostly between acidic and basic side chains
3. Hydrogen bond — Hydrogen bonds
4. Van der Waals forces
5. Hydrophobic bonding — Hydrophobic side chains pushed away from water (toward center of protein)
6. Hydrogen bond unable to form; Proline — R group of proline causes kinks

Properly folded protein

Denatured

Denatured protein

TABLE 1.1 > Denaturing Agents

Denaturing Agents	Forces Disrupted
Urea	Hydrogen bonds
Salt or change in pH	Electrostatic bonds
Mercaptoethanol	Disulfide bonds
Organic solvents	Hydrophobic forces
Heat	All forces

Heat, salt, and changes in pH can cause a protein to lose its higher-level conformation. Notice, for example, that the denatured form of the protein does not contain any of the α-helices that the properly folded protein has. Denaturing agents rarely affect the primary structure of a protein, which contains the essential information for conformation. Thus, mildly denatured proteins can often spontaneously return to their original conformation.

Remember to think "sugar" when you see "glyco-." Just as glycolipids are lipids with sugars attached, glycoproteins are proteins with sugars attached.

Structural proteins are made from long polymers. They maintain and add strength to cellular and matrix structure. *Collagen*, a structural protein made from a unique type of helix, is the most abundant protein in the body. Collagen fibers add great strength to skin, tendons, ligaments, and bone, among other structures. Microtubules, which make up eukaryotic flagella and cilia, are made from globular tubulin, which polymerizes under the right conditions to become a structural protein.

Glycoproteins are proteins with carbohydrate groups attached. These are a component of cellular plasma membranes. *Proteoglycans* are also a mixture of proteins and carbohydrates, but they generally consist of more than 50% carbohydrates. Proteoglycans are the major component of the extracellular matrix.

Cytochromes (Greek: kytos → cell, chroma → color or pigment) are proteins which require a *prosthetic* (nonproteinaceous) *heme* (Greek: haima → blood) group in order to function. Cytochromes get their name from the color that they add to the cell. Examples of cytochromes are hemoglobin and the cytochromes of the electron transport chain in the inner membrane of mitochondria. Proteins containing nonproteinaceous components are called *conjugated proteins*.

Cytochrome proteins carry out electron transport via oxidation and reduction of the heme group.

Proteins are important. Understand the different levels of structures, 1°, 2°, 3°, and 4°, and the bonding involved. You need to know the forces that contribute to the stability of protein conformations and what denaturation means. You don't have to memorize the structure of each amino acid, but recognize the basic structure of a generic amino acid. Although nucleic acids, some lipids, and even some carbohydrates contain nitrogen, when you see nitrogen on the MCAT®, think protein.

1.7 Minerals

Minerals are the dissolved inorganic ions inside and outside the cell. By creating electrochemical gradients across membranes, they assist in the transport of substances entering and exiting the cell. They can combine and solidify to give strength to a matrix, such as *hydroxyapatite* in bone. Minerals also act as cofactors (discussed later in this lecture) assisting enzyme or protein function. For instance, iron is a mineral found in *heme*, the prosthetic group of *cytochromes*.

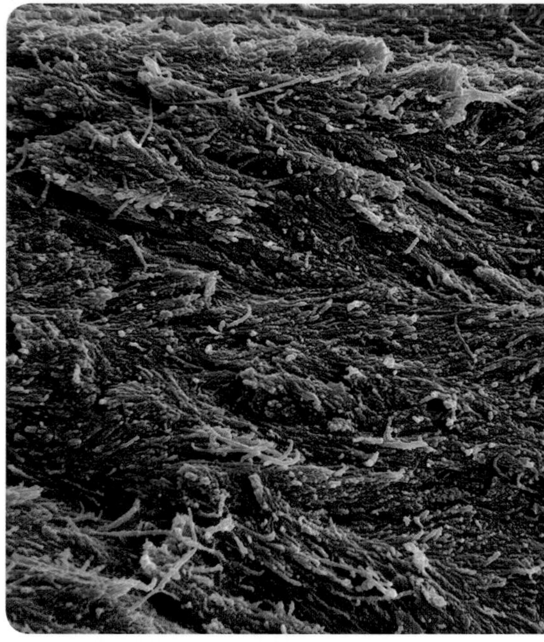

This fractured surface of a bone consists of an organic matrix of collagen fibers and mineral-based molecules such as hydroxyapatite and chondroitin sulfate.

This completes an overview of the major chemicals acting in the body. Your emphasis should be on understanding functions, not memorizing details. That doesn't mean that breezing right through this section. A large portion of your success on biology and biochemistry questions on the MCAT® depends on reading comprehension. Since it is impossible to know the exact topic of the passages ahead of time, you can't do well just by memorizing facts. Instead, it is helpful to become familiar with the terms and dialect in which the passages are written. Try to see the big picture and how each little piece fits into the big picture. Be certain that you thoroughly understand all the terms that are bolded and red! Your goal by the time you finish *Biology 1: Molecules* and *Biology 2: Systems* is to attain a general overview of how the body functions on each level of organization (i.e. molecular, cellular, tissue, organ, system, organism), and to know the specific contribution of any bold and red term or concept.

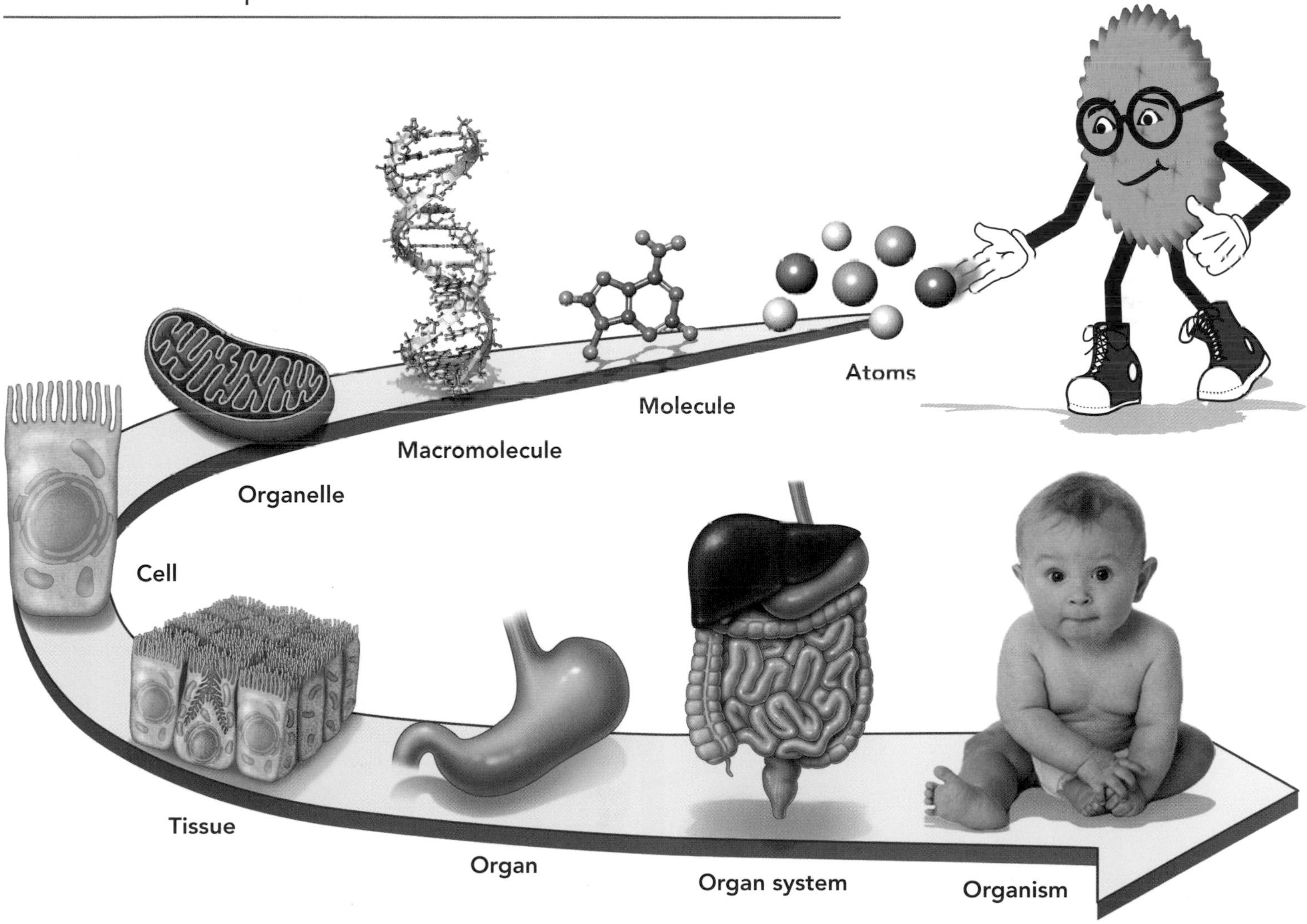

Atoms
Molecule
Macromolecule
Organelle
Cell
Tissue
Organ
Organ system
Organism

1.8 Features of Enzymes

Virtually all biological reactions are regulated and made possible by **enzymes**. Enzymes are typically globular proteins, although there are a few nucleic acids that act as enzymes. Just as the variability in structure of proteins makes them well-suited for many different biological functions, this variability also facilitates their action as enzymes. The differing characteristics of enzymatic R groups accounts for the specificity of enzymes for certain substrates, as will be described below.

The function of any enzyme is to act as a **catalyst**, lowering the energy of activation for a biological reaction and thus increasing the rate of that reaction. Enzymes increase reaction rates by magnitudes of as much as thousands of trillions. This is a much greater increase than typical lab catalysts. Such extreme control over reaction rates gives enzymes the ability to pick and choose which reactions will or will not occur inside a cell. Without the catalytic effect of enzymes, the energy of activation of essential biological reactions would be impossibly high. Thus, enzymes have a regulatory ability, making the body's chemical reactions possible, but ensuring that they occur only when needed. Enzymes, like any catalysts, are neither consumed nor permanently altered by the reactions which they catalyze. Only a small amount of catalyst is required for any reaction. Also like other catalysts, enzymes do not alter the equilibrium of a reaction; in other words, they do not alter the relative amount of reactants and products at equilibrium.

The reactant or reactants upon which an enzyme works are called the **substrates**. Substrates are generally smaller than the enzyme. The substrate binds to the enzyme at a particular location called the **active site**, usually with numerous noncovalent bonds. The enzyme and substrate bind together to form the **enzyme-substrate complex**.

Normally, enzymes are designed to work only on a specific substrate or group of closely related substrates. This is called **enzyme specificity**. The **lock and key model** is an example of enzyme specificity. In this theory, the active site of the enzyme has a specific shape like a lock that only fits a specific substrate, the key. The lock and key model explains some but not all enzymes. A second theory called the **induced fit model** says that the shapes of both the enzyme and the substrate are altered upon binding. Besides increasing specificity, the alteration actually helps the reaction to proceed by destabilizing the substrate. In reactions with more than one substrate, the enzyme may also orient the substrates relative to each other, creating optimal conditions for a reaction to take place.

Hexokinase lowers the activation energy for the phosphorylation of glucose.

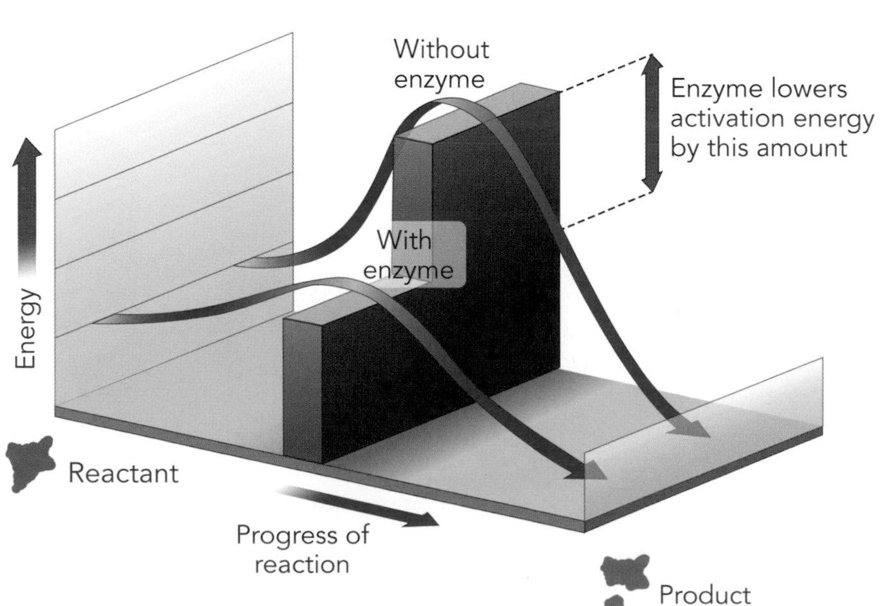

FIGURE 1.13 Enzyme-Catalyzed Reaction

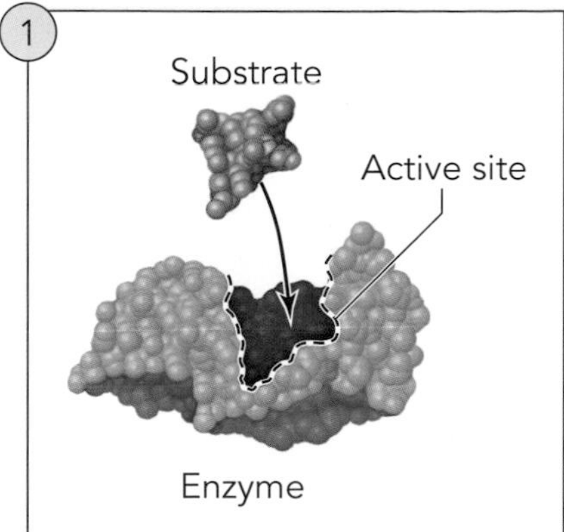

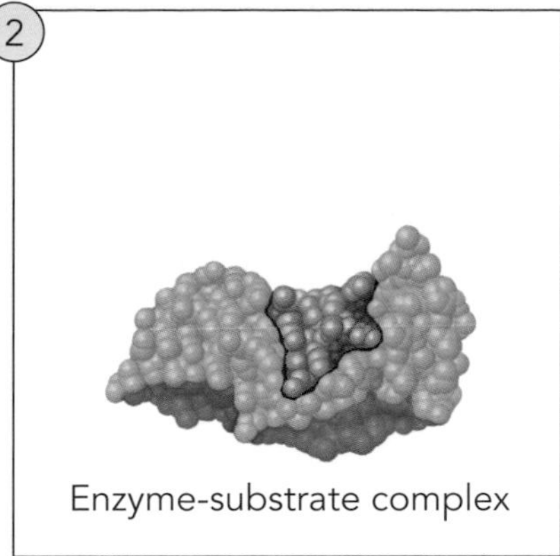

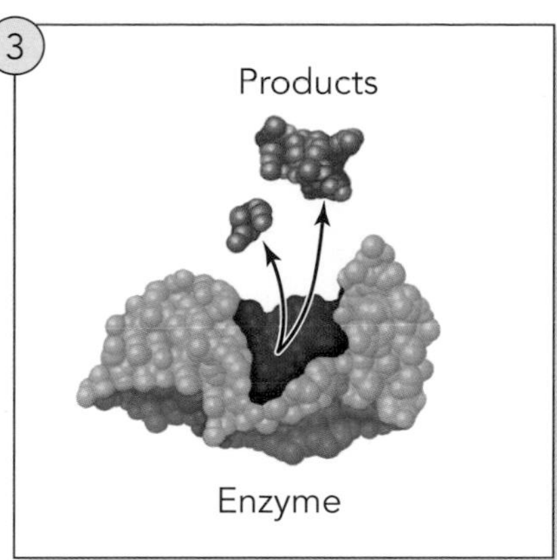

Enzymes exhibit **saturation kinetics**; as the relative concentration of substrate increases, the rate of the reaction also increases, but to a lesser and lesser degree until a maximum rate, the V_{max}, has been achieved. This occurs because as more substrate is added, individual substrates must begin to wait in line for an unoccupied enzyme. Thus, V_{max} is proportional to enzyme concentration. *Turnover number* is the number of substrate molecules one active site can convert to product in a given unit of time when an enzyme solution is saturated with substrate.

Related to V_{max} is the **Michaelis constant**, also known as the K_m. The K_m is the substrate concentration at which the reaction rate is equal to $\frac{1}{2}V_{max}$. The value of the Michaelis constant indicates how highly concentrated the substrate must be to speed up the reaction. If a higher concentration of substrate is needed, the enzyme must have a lower affinity for the substrate. Thus K_m is inversely proportional to enzyme-substrate affinity. Unlike V_{max}, K_m does not vary when the enzyme concentration is changed; in other words, it is a characteristic of the intrinsic fit between the enzyme and substrate, rather than reflecting the amount of substrate present. However, the value of K_m can be altered by certain types of enzyme inhibition.

Michaelis-Menten curves plot reaction velocity as a function of substrate concentration and show an enzyme's V_{max} and K_m (Figure 1.14). They are valuable tools for recalling and understanding the types of enzyme inhibition, as will be discussed further in this lecture.

Temperature and pH also affect the rates of enzymatic reactions. At first, as the temperature increases, the reaction rate goes up. However, since enzymes are generally proteins, at some point the enzyme denatures and the rate of the reaction drops off precipitously. For enzymes in the human body, the optimal temperature is most often around 37° C. Enzymes also function within specific pH ranges. The optimal pH varies depending upon the enzyme. For instance, pepsin, which is active in the stomach, prefers a pH below 2, while trypsin, which is active in the small intestine, works best at a pH between 6 and 7.

In order to reach their optimal activity, many enzymes require a non-protein component called a **cofactor** (Latin: co- → with or together). Cofactors can be coenzymes or metal ions.

Coenzymes are cofactors that are organic molecules. Many types of **water-soluble vitamins** serve as coenzymes or their precursors. Coenzymes are divided into two types: *cosubstrates* and *prosthetic groups*.

Cosubstrates reversibly bind to a specific enzyme, and transfer some chemical group to another substrate. The cosubstrate then reverts to its original form via another enzymatic reaction. This reversion to original form is what distinguishes a cosubstrate from normal substrates. ATP is an example of the cosubstrate type of coenzyme.

FIGURE 1.14 Michaelis-Menten Curves at Different Enzyme Concentrations

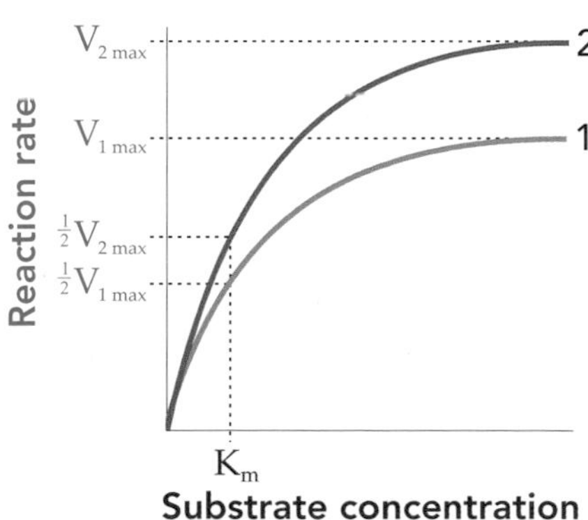

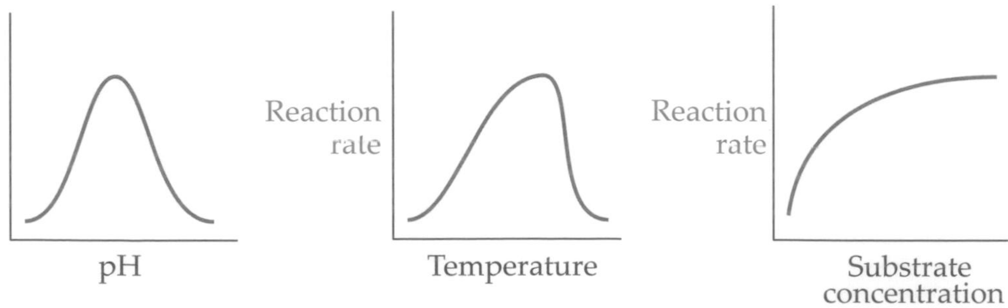

The important relationships between enzymes and their environment are represented by these three graphs. Memorize the basic shapes of the graphs and understand how to use them to predict relative rates of enzymatic reactions under different environmental conditions.

Prosthetic groups remain covalently bound to the enzyme throughout the reaction, and, like the enzyme, emerge from the reaction unchanged. As mentioned previously, *heme* is a prosthetic group. Heme binds with *catalase* in peroxisomes to degrade hydrogen peroxide.

Metal ions are the second type of cofactor. They can act alone or with a prosthetic group. Typical metal ions that function as cofactors in the human body are iron, copper, manganese, magnesium, calcium, and zinc.

An enzyme without its cofactor is called an *apoenzyme* (Greek: apo- → away from) and is completely nonfunctional. An enzyme with its cofactor is called a *holoenzyme* (Greek: holos → whole, entire, complete).

Just know that some enzymes need cofactors to function, and that cofactors are either minerals or coenzymes. Also remember that many coenzymes are vitamins or their derivatives.

These questions are NOT related to a passage.

Item 9

Excessive amounts of nitrogen are found in the urine of an individual who has experienced a period of extended fasting. This is most likely due to:

- O A) glycogenolysis in the liver.
- O B) the breakdown of body proteins.
- O C) lipolysis in adipose tissue.
- O D) a tumor on the posterior pituitary causing excessive ADH secretion.

Item 10

Proline is not technically an α-amino acid. Due to the ring structure of proline, it cannot conform to the geometry of the α-helix and creates a bend in the polypeptide chain. This phenomenon assists in the creation of what level of protein structure?

- O A) Primary
- O B) Secondary
- O C) Tertiary
- O D) Quaternary

Item 11

Enzymes are required by all living things because enzymes:

- O A) raise the free energy of chemical reactions.
- O B) properly orient reactants and lower activation energy.
- O C) increase the temperature of reacting molecules.
- O D) increase the number of reacting molecules.

Item 12

All of the following must change the rate of an enzyme catalyzed reaction EXCEPT:

- O A) changing the pH.
- O B) lowering the temperature.
- O C) decreasing the concentration of substrate.
- O D) adding a noncompetitive inhibitor.

Item 13

Since an increase in temperature increases the reaction rate, why isn't the elevation of temperature a method normally used to accelerate enzyme-catalyzed reactions?

- O A) Raising the temperature causes the reaction to occur too quickly.
- O B) Raising the temperature does not sufficiently surmount the activation energy barrier.
- O C) Heat changes the configuration of proteins.
- O D) Heat does not increase the probability of molecular collision.

Item 14

The partial double bond character of a peptide bond has its greatest effect in which level of structure of an enzyme?

- O A) Primary
- O B) Secondary
- O C) Tertiary
- O D) Quaternary

Item 15

Which of the following nutrients has the greatest heat of combustion?

- O A) Carbohydrate
- O B) Protein
- O C) Saturated fat
- O D) Unsaturated fat

Item 16

All of the following are true of enzymes EXCEPT:

- O A) The active site of an enzyme can destabilize bonds in the substrate.
- O B) Enzymes increase the amount of product at equilibrium.
- O C) Some enzymes change shape after binding to the substrate.
- O D) Enzymes have a greater catalytic effect than lab catalysts.

1.9 Enzyme Regulation

Enzymes select which reactions take place within a cell, so the cell must regulate enzyme activity. Regulation of enzymes ensures that they are activated when needed by the cell, and that the amount of product created in the reactions that are catalyzed is at the level required for cellular functions. Enzymes are regulated by four primary means:

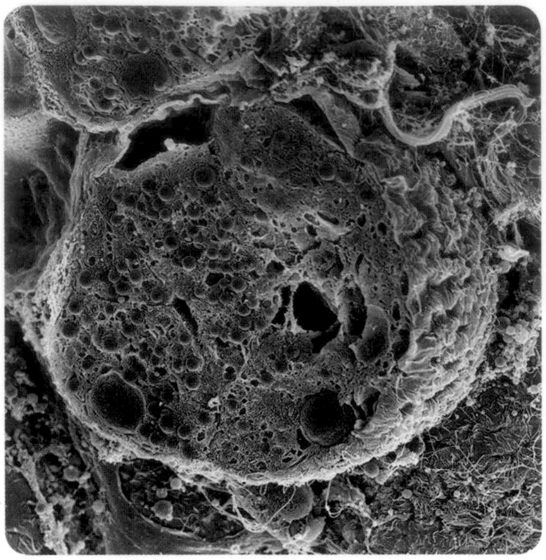

1. *Proteolytic cleavage (irreversible covalent modification)*—Many enzymes are released into their environment in an inactive form called a **zymogen** or *proenzyme* (Greek: pro → before). When specific peptide bonds on zymogens are cleaved, the zymogens become irreversibly activated. Activation of zymogens may be instigated by other enzymes, or by a change in environment. For instance, pepsinogen (notice the "–ogen" at the end indicating zymogen status) is the zymogen of pepsin and is activated by low pH.
2. *Reversible covalent modification*—Some enzymes are activated or deactivated by phosphorylation or the addition of some other modifier such as AMP (adenosine monophosphate). The removal of the modifier is almost always accomplished by hydrolysis. Phosphorylation typically occurs in the presence of a *protein kinase*, a type of catalytic enzyme.
3. *Control proteins*—Control proteins are protein subunits that associate with certain enzymes to activate or inhibit their activity. *Calmodulin* and *G-proteins* are typical examples of control proteins.
4. **Allosteric interactions**—Allosteric regulation is the modification of an enzyme's configuration through the binding of an activator or inhibitor at a specific binding site on the enzyme.

This acinar cell produces digestive enzymes in zymogen granules (purple). These enzymes are excreted into the pancreatic ducts and carried to the small intestine, where they are activated and aid in the breakdown of carbohydrates, fats, and proteins.

Think about why the body would release an enzyme in an inactive form. You will learn about the function of pepsin in Digestion, but for now it's enough to know that it digests proteins. The release of pepsin as a zymogen that is activated only by low pH ensures that pepsin only digests proteins where it is supposed to—in the stomach!

FIGURE 1.15 Enzymatic Regulation

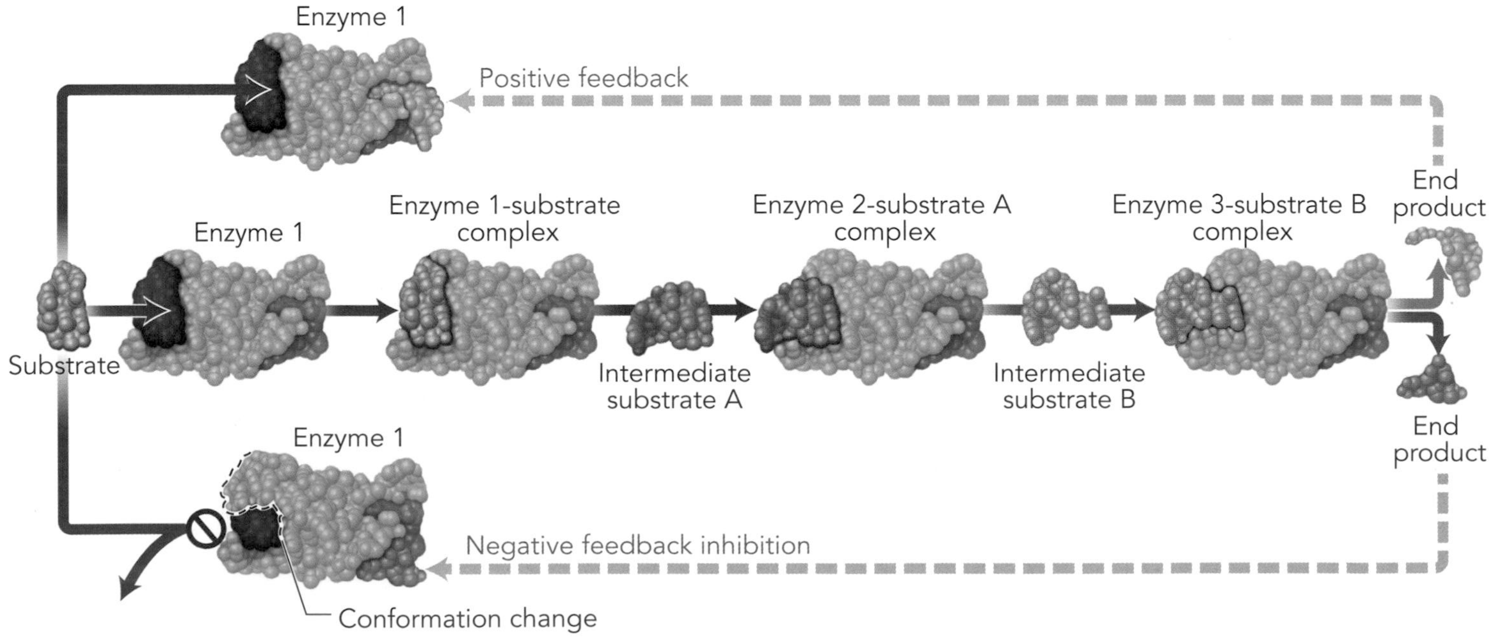

Normally, an enzyme governs just one reaction in a series of reactions. In a phenomenon called **negative feedback** or **feedback inhibition**, one of the products downstream in a reaction series comes back and inhibits the enzymatic activity of an earlier reaction. Negative feedback provides a shut down mechanism for a series of enzymatic reactions when that series has produced a sufficient amount of product. Most enzymes work within some type of negative feedback cycle. **Positive feedback** also occurs, where the product returns to an earlier step to activate the associated enzyme. Positive feedback occurs less often than negative feedback. Positive and negative feedback work in a complementary fashion to ensure that a reaction series leads to the right amount of product.

Negative feedback inhibition is typical in many amino acid synthesis pathways. It is wasteful and unnecessary to synthesize amino acids that are readily available in the environment. Therefore, upstream enzymes involved in a particular synthetic metabolic pathway typically have allosteric inhibitory sites that bind the final amino acid product. If the final product is present in the environment, it acts as an allosteric inhibitor in a negative feedback loop, preventing synthesis of additional product.

Products that exert negative feedback inhibition do not resemble the substrates of the enzymes that they inhibit and do not bind to the active site. Instead, they bind to the enzyme and cause a conformational change. This process is called **allosteric regulation** (Greek: allos → different or other, stereos → solid), which can be exerted by both **allosteric inhibitors** and **allosteric activators**. Not all allosteric inhibitors and activators are necessarily noncompetitive inhibitors (discussed in the next section), because many alter K_m without affecting V_{max}. Allosteric enzymes, meaning enzymes that have sites for allosteric regulation, do not exhibit typical kinetics because they normally have several binding sites for different inhibitors, activators, and even substrates. At low concentrations of substrate, small increases in concentration increase enzyme efficiency as well as reaction rate. The first substrate changes the shape of the enzyme, allowing other substrates to bind more easily. This phenomenon is called **positive cooperativity**. The opposite phenomenon, **negative cooperativity**, occurs as well. Cooperativity in the presence of the allosteric inhibitor is what gives the oxygen dissociation curve of hemoglobin its sigmoidal shape.

MCAT® THINK

Sometimes the effects of feedback inhibition can seem counter-intuitive. Glycolysis (described in the Metabolism Lecture) provides an example of negative inhibition. When there is a buildup of ATP, it exerts negative feedback on an enzyme earlier in the glycolytic pathway. This may seem strange because ATP is also a required reactant for the reaction to occur in the first place! However, as with all regulatory feedback, the point is to ensure that the amount of product created is the amount that the cell needs to function. If the cell has too little ATP it will not have enough energy; however, producing too much ATP would be a waste of cellular resources.

Hold on! Don't go overboard here. You will not be asked to distinguish allosteric inhibition from noncompetitive inhibition. Many good bio texts don't distinguish them, and the MCAT® certainly won't. However, it is crucial to understand negative feedback. Negative feedback will be tested on the MCAT®.

Negative Feedback

Hemoglobin's oxygen dissociation curve is similar to the Michaelis-Menten curves that you have seen throughout this lecture. The axes are analogous to those of a Michaelis-Menten curve: instead of reaction velocity there is oxygen saturation, and instead of substrate concentration there is partial pressure of oxygen. Just as reaction velocity levels off to a maximum as high concentrations of substrate are reached, the oxygen saturation of hemoglobin levels off at high partial pressures of oxygen. Expect that the MCAT® may ask you to apply your understanding of K_m and V_{max} to situations that are more complex than the typical Michaelis-Menten curve.

Enzyme Inhibition

Enzyme inhibitors provide an important mechanism for regulation of enzymatic activity in the body. Some inhibitors bind to the active site, thus blocking the substrate from binding. Others bind elsewhere on the enzyme and cause a change in its shape, thus disrupting its specific affinity for the substrate. These general mechanisms for altering enzymatic activity make regulation by positive and negative feedback possible.

In order to identify each of the four inhibitors, think first about where on the enzyme the inhibitor binds. If the inhibitor binds to the enzyme's active site when the substrate is not bound, it is a competitive inhibitor. If it binds to an allosteric site or to the E-S complex, it is one of the other three types. Next, ask whether it binds to the enzyme or to the enzyme-substrate complex. An inhibitor that binds only to the E-S complex is uncompetitive. If it can bind to either the enzyme alone or the E-S complex, it is a mixed inhibitor. A noncompetitive inhibitor is a special type of mixed inhibitor that binds with the same affinity whether to the enzyme alone or to the E-S complex.

Enzyme inhibitors can be broadly classified as either irreversible or reversible. Agents that bind irreversibly to enzymes and disrupt their function are **irreversible inhibitors**. Most inhibitors of this type bind to enzymes via covalent bonds, but a few bind noncovalently. Irreversible inhibitors tend to be highly toxic. Any of the following types of inhibitors can be irreversible if covalent modification occurs.

Competitive inhibitors compete with the substrate by binding reversibly with noncovalent bonds to the active site. They are the only type of reversible inhibitor that binds directly to the active site rather than binding to a different site on the enzyme. They typically bind directly to the active site for only a fraction of a second, blocking the substrate from binding during that time. Of course, the reverse is also true; if the substrate binds first, it blocks the inhibitor from binding. Thus, competitive inhibitors raise the apparent K_m but do not change V_{max}. In the presence of a competitive inhibitor, the rate of the reaction can be increased to the original, uninhibited V_{max} by increasing the concentration of the substrate. However, since an increased concentration of substrate is required to reach V_{max}, an increased concentration is also required to reach ½ V_{max}; thus the K_m is raised, reflecting the lowered affinity of the enzyme for the substrate. The ability to overcome inhibition by increasing substrate concentration is the classic indication of a competitive inhibitor.

FIGURE 1.16 Types of Enzyme Inhibition

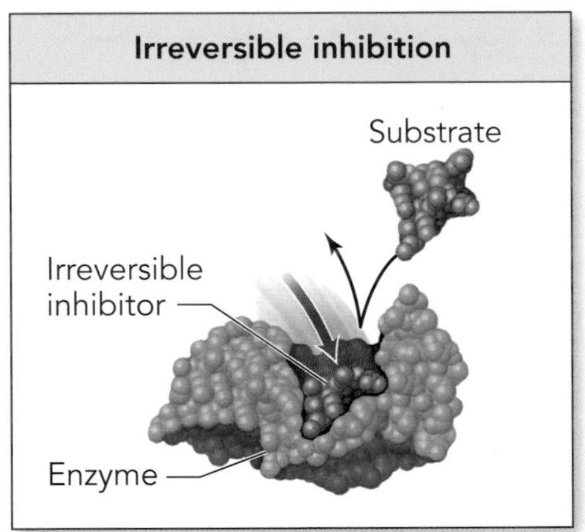

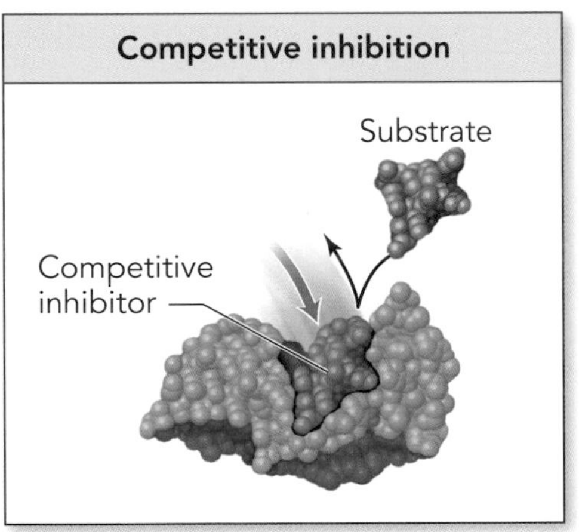

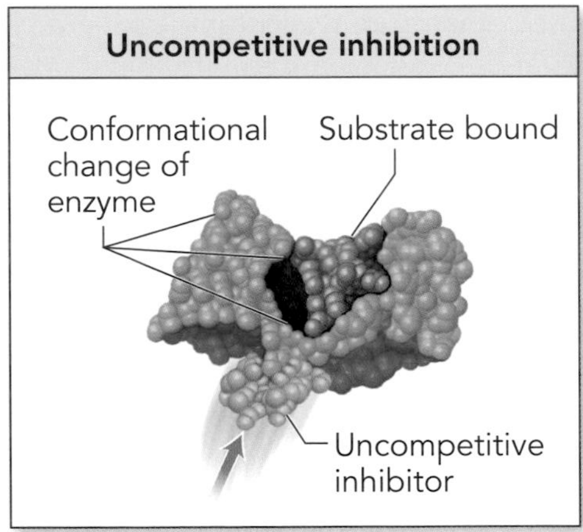

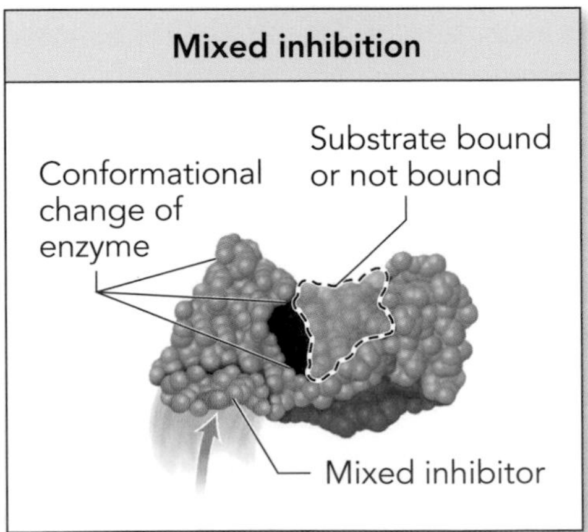

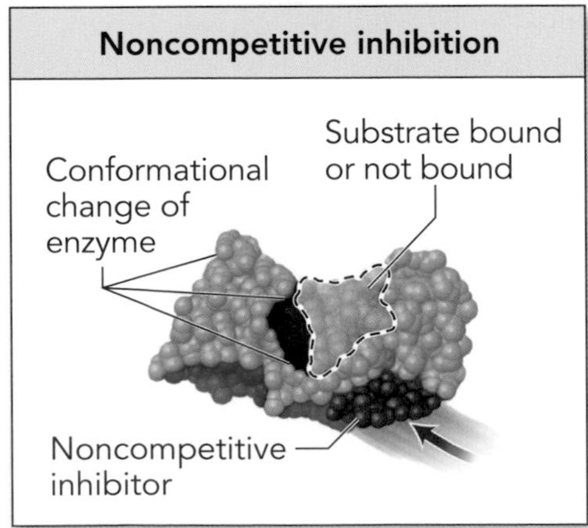

Irreversible and reversible inhibition are broad categories that include the four major types. For example, competitive inhibitor can be reversible or irreversible.

Competitive inhibitors often resemble the substrate. *Sulfanilamide* is an antibiotic which competitively inhibits a bacterial enzyme that manufactures folic acid, leading to the death of bacterial cells. Although humans require folic acid, sulfanilamide does not harm humans because we use a different enzymatic pathway to manufacture folic acid.

Unlike competitive inhibitors, **uncompetitive inhibitors** bind at a site other than the active site. Regulatory molecules can also bind to a site other than the active site and exert a positive feedback effect, rather than an inhibitory effect. Uncompetitive inhibitors do not bind to the enzyme until it has associated with the substrate to form the enzyme-substrate complex. Once the uncompetitive inhibitor has bound, the substrate remains associated with the enzyme. Thus the apparent affinity of the enzyme for the substrate increases, meaning that K_m decreases. Because the uncompetitive inhibitor only affects enzymes that have already bound substrate, adding more substrate does not overcome the affect of the inhibitor, and V_{max} is lowered.

Like uncompetitive inhibitors, **mixed inhibitors** bind at a site on the enzyme other than the active site and thus do not prevent the substrate from binding. However, their name comes from the fact that they can bind to either the enzyme alone or the enzyme-substrate complex. Most types of mixed inhibitors have a preference for one or the other, which dictates the effect on K_m and V_{max}. Mixed inhibitors that act like competitive inhibitors by binding primarily to the enzyme before the substrate is associated increase K_m, just as competitive inhibitors do. In contrast, mixed inhibitors that act more like uncompetitive inhibitors by preferring to bind to the enzyme-substrate complex lower K_m. All mixed inhibitors lower V_{max} to some extent.

Noncompetitive inhibitors are a special type of mixed inhibitors. They bind just as readily to enzymes with a substrate as to those without. Like other mixed inhibitors, noncompetitive inhibitors bind noncovalently to an enzyme at a spot other than the active site and change the conformation of the enzyme. Because noncompetitive inhibitors do not resemble the substrate, they commonly act on more than one type of enzyme. Unlike competitive inhibitors, they cannot be overcome by excess substrate, so they lower V_{max}. They do not, however, lower the enzyme's affinity for the substrate, so K_m remains the same.

Know the distinct characteristics of each of the inhibitor types shown in Table 1.2: where the inhibitor binds (active site or other site), to what the inhibitor binds (enzyme or E-S complex), whether and how it affects the fit of enzyme bound to substrate (fit is inverse to K_m), and how the kinetic features of the enzyme-catalyzed reaction are affected (V_{max}). Remember: NOncompetitive inhibitors have NO preference between the enzyme and enzyme-substrate complex. As enzyme-substrate fit decreases, K_m increases, and vice versa.

TABLE 1.2 > Characteristics of Enzyme Inhibitors

Type of inhibitor	Binding site	Inhibits binding of substrate?	Effect on K_m	Effect on V_{max}
Competitive	Enzyme (active site)	Yes	Increase	No change
Uncompetitive	E-S complex	No	Decrease	Decrease
Mixed	E-S complex or enzyme	No	Increase or decrease	Decrease
Noncompetitive	E-S complex or enzyme	No	No change	Decrease

FIGURE 1.17 Effect of Inhibition on V_{max} and K_m

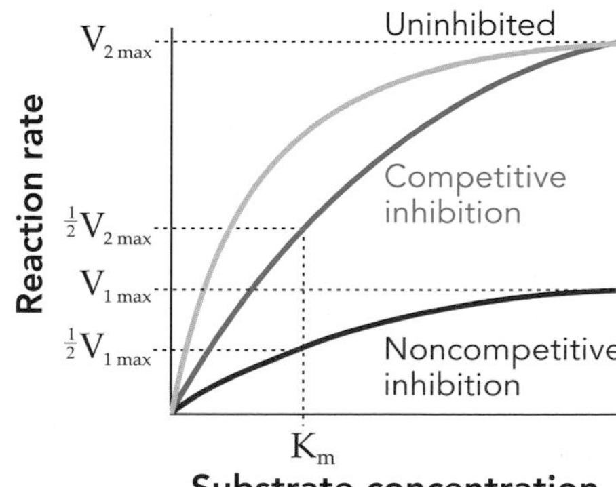

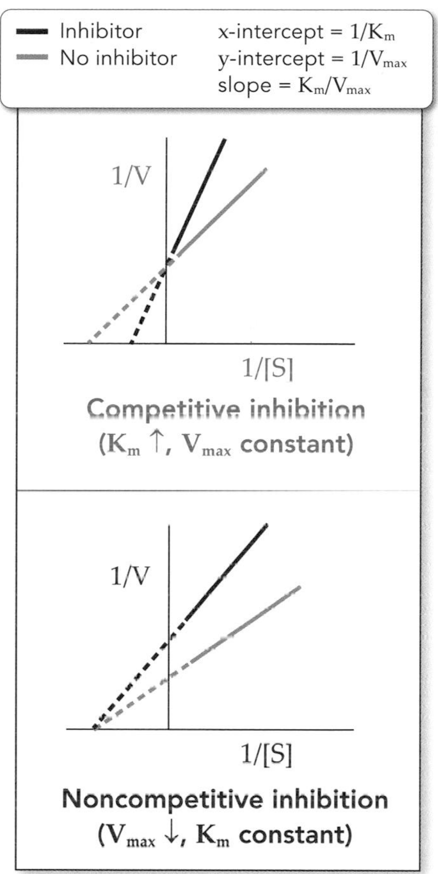

Recognize and reason through the graphs for each inhibitor type. Use the graphs to read the effects of inhibition on V_{max} and K_m. Remember, $1/K_m$ correlates with enzyme-substrate fit. V_{max} for any enzyme is its maximum rate of catalysis. If you see the linear graph, you may need to extend the lines to the axes. Think... the lines of competitors cross like swords.

1.10 Enzyme Classification

Look for the "-ase" ending. Often a seemingly complicated question about a complex chemical will depend upon the simple fact that the chemical is an enzyme, and the only clue is the "-ase" at the end of the name. Once you recognize that the chemical is an enzyme, you know that it contains nitrogen and that it is subject to denaturation. Similarly, many carbohydrates are easy to recognize by their "-ose" ending.

Enzymes are named according to the reactions that they catalyze. Very often, the suffix "-ase" is simply added to the end of the substrate upon which the enzyme acts. For instance, acetylcholinesterase acts upon the ester group in acetylcholine.

According to systematic naming conventions, enzymes are classified into six categories:

1. **Oxidoreductases** catalyze the transfer of electrons or hydrogen ions, i.e. oxidation-reduction reactions;
2. **Transferases** catalyze reactions in which groups are transferred from one location to another;
3. **Hydrolases** regulate hydrolysis reactions;
4. **Lyases** catalyze reactions in which functional groups are added to double bonds or, conversely, double bonds are formed via the removal of functional groups;
5. **Isomerases** catalyze the transfer of groups within a molecule, with the effect of producing isomers (discussed in the *Chemistry Manual*);
6. **Ligases** catalyze condensation reactions coupled with the hydrolysis of high energy molecules.

One major distinction between classifications is between lyases and ligases. The particular type of lyase that catalyzes the addition of one substrate to the double bond of a second substrate is sometimes called a *synthase*. ATP synthase is an example of a lyase. Ligase enzymes require energy input from ATP or some other nucleotide. Ligases are sometimes called *synthetases*.

As you learn more about the types of reactions described above in later lectures and other manuals, look back to refresh your memory on which reaction types are catalyzed by which enzymes.

Kinases and *phosphatases* may also come up on the MCAT®. A kinase is an enzyme that phosphorylates a molecule, while a phosphatase is an enzyme that dephosphorylates a molecule. Often a kinase phosphorylates another enzyme in order to activate or deactivate it. *Hexokinase* is the enzyme that phosphorylates glucose as soon as it enters a cell (see the Metabolism Lecture to learn how this phosphorylation assists metabolic processes).

The best way to remember the structures of different types of biological molecules is to think back from their functions. Carbohydrates need to be stable, uniform molecules so that they can be used for energy storage and release by all cells. Similarly, nucleotides have to be stable and highly organized molecules (including the carbohydrate component) in order to create a stable structure for genetic material. Carbohydrates and lipids are both used for energy storage, so they both must have a high density of C-H bonds. However, lipids are also used to construct membranes, so it makes sense for them to have a polar end and a nonpolar end. Finally, proteins are needed for many different functions in the cell, so they need to be able to have a wide array of possible structures. Thus the building blocks of proteins, in contrast to nucleic acids and polysaccharides, need to have a large variety of possible structures. Amino acids meet the needs of proteins through their R groups that vary in polarity and other structural features.

These questions are NOT related to a passage.

Item 17

Which of the following is (are) true concerning feedback inhibition?

I. It often acts by inhibiting enzyme activity.
II. It works to prevent a build up of excess nutrients.
III. It only acts through enzymes.

- A) I only
- B) II only
- C) I and II only
- D) I, II, and III

Item 18

One mechanism of enzyme inhibition is to inhibit an enzyme without blocking the active site, but by altering the shape of the enzyme molecule. This mechanism is called:

- A) competitive inhibition.
- B) noncompetitive inhibition.
- C) feedback inhibition.
- D) positive inhibition.

Item 19

The continued production of progesterone caused by the release of HCG from the growing embryo is an example of:

- A) positive feedback.
- B) negative feedback.
- C) feedback inhibition.
- D) feedback enhancement.

Item 20

Peptidases that function in the stomach most likely:

- A) *increase* their function in the small intestine due to *increased* hydrogen ion concentration.
- B) *decrease* their function in the small intestine due to *increased* hydrogen ion concentration.
- C) *increase* their function in the small intestine due to *decreased* hydrogen ion concentration.
- D) *decrease* their function in the small intestine due to *decreased* hydrogen ion concentration.

Item 21

The rate of a reaction slows when the reaction is exposed to a competitive inhibitor. Which of the following might overcome the effects of the inhibitor?

- A) Decreasing enzyme concentration
- B) Increasing temperature
- C) Increasing substrate concentration
- D) The effects of competitive inhibition cannot be overcome.

Item 22

Suppose that an enzyme inhibitor lowers V_{max} and has no effect on K_m. This inhibitor is likely to be:

- A) Uncompetitive
- B) Proteolytic
- C) Noncompetitive
- D) Mixed

Item 23

Which of the following is necessary for an enzyme to exhibit positive and/or negative cooperativity?

- A) The presence of a mixed inhibitor
- B) Multiple binding sites on the enzyme
- C) A high concentration of substrate
- D) Positive and/or negative feedback

Item 24

Why do uncompetitive inhibitors cause a decrease in K_m?

- A) The enzyme's apparent affinity for the substrate is decreased.
- B) The enzyme's apparent affinity for the substrate is increased.
- C) Uncompetitive inhibitors bind to the enzyme only before it binds substrate.
- D) Uncompetitive inhibitors do not actually cause a decrease in K_m.

TERMS YOU NEED TO KNOW

a-helix
b-pleated sheet
½ V_{max}
Active site
Adenine (A)
Adipocytes
Allosteric activators
Allosteric inhibitors
Allosteric interactions
Allosteric regulation
Amide
Amino acids
Amphipathic
Antiparallel
ATP (adenosine triphosphate)
Base-pairing
Base-pairs (bp)
Carbohydrates
Catalyst
Cellulose
Coenzymes
Cofactor
Competitive inhibitors
Complementary strands
Conformation
Cysteine
Cystine
Cytosine (C)
Dehydration
Denatured
DNA (deoxyribonucleic acid)
Double helix
Double stranded DNA
Entropy
Enzyme specificity
Enzyme-substrate complex
Enzymes
Fat-soluble vitamins
Fats
Fatty acids
Feedback inhibition
Glucose
Glycerol
Glycogen
Guanine (G)
Hexoses
Hydrogen bonding
Hydrolases
Hydrolysis
Hydrophilic
Hydrophobic
Hydrophobic bonding
Induced fit model
Irreversible inhibitors
Isomerases
K_m
Ligases
Lipids
Lock and key model
Lyases
Michaelis constant
Minerals
Mixed inhibitors
Monosaccharides
Negative cooperativity
Negative feedback
Noncompetitive inhibitors
Nucleic acids
Nucleoside
Nucleotides
Oxidoreductases
Phosphatids
Phosphodiester bonds
Phospholipids
Polypeptides
Polysaccharides
Positive cooperativity
Positive feedback
Primary structure
Proline
Prostaglandins
Purines
Pyrimidines
Quaternary structure
RNA (ribonucleic acid)
Saturated fatty acids
Saturation kinetics
Secondary structure
Side chain
Single stranded RNA
Solvation layer
Sphingolipids
Starch
Steroids
Substrates
Sugar-phosphate backbone
Tertiary structure
Thymine (T)
Transferases
Triacylglycerols
Triglycerides
Uncompetitive inhibitors
Unsaturated fatty acids
Uracil (U)
Vitamins
Water
Water-soluble vitamins
Watson-Crick model
Waxes
V_{max}
Zymogen

DON'T FORGET YOUR KEYS

1. Each category of biological molecule has a "personality" - think structure and polarity - that matches its practical uses in living organisms.

2. Enzyme-substrate fit correlates with enzyme effectiveness and a lower K_m.

3. Competitive inhibitors block the active site; noncompetitive inhibitors bind to a separate site, changing the shape of the active site; uncompetitve inhibitors bind the enzyme-substrate complex, decreasing the concentration of substrate that can react.

Genetics

LECTURE 2

THE 3 KEYS

1. DNA is potential; RNA is regulation; protein is action.
2. Location matters – nucleus or cytoplasm?
3. See mitosis, think replication; see meiosis, think reproduction.

2.1 Introduction

The study of genetics is central to understanding life forms: how they develop, how they function, how they reproduce, and how a species survives. Genes determine what proteins are created on a moment to moment basis for living organisms. The genome is, therefore, an essential contributor to both the regulation of processes within the body and to inheritance. This lecture will discuss the primary functions of genetic material, which include 1. coding for products necessary within the lifetime of an organism, 2. passing information between cells, and 3. passing information from one generation to the next. While the genome contains a vast wealth of information, the way a cell uses this information to make products is flexible, varying with the environment and needs of the cell. When considering the processes that lead to gene expression, location can be used as orienting tool. In eukaryotes, but not prokaryotes, the nuclear membrane separates the processes of transcription and translation in both space and time, which allows step-by-step regulation of gene expression.

This lecture will first introduce the basics of genetics, including the genome and the definition of a gene. It will then discuss the organization of genetic material and how that organization is involved in regulation. Next, the lecture will cover transcription and translation, the major processes involved in producing products based on the genome.

The passing of genetic information to new cells via cell division will be discussed, along with the errors that can occur. Finally, the lecture will address the passing of genetic information from one generation to the next. Throughout the lecture, environmental influences and regulation of genetic expression will be emphasized.

2.2 The Genome and Regulation

Genetic information is a mechanism of regulation; it provides the tools necessary for the moment to moment cellular processes that help cells survive in fluctuating environments. In addition, it allows these processes and adaptations to be passed on to future generations. Thus, genes are crucial for both the passing of hereditary traits and the cellular activities of an organism's lifetime.

The MCAT® will test your knowledge of genetics as a system of regulated gene expression. Keep in mind that gene expression is dynamic; it is constantly changing based on the environment and an organism's needs.

Genetic information exhibits a remarkable amount of similarity among living organisms. Variation of the nucleotide sequence among humans is small; human DNA differs between individuals at approximately 1 nucleotide out of every 1200, or about 0.08%. Humans share about 98% of their nucleotide sequence with chimpanzees, about 60% with a fruit fly, and about 50% with a banana! These similarities exist because the genetic language necessary to carry out the basic processes of life is universal. The amount of uniformity found in genomes of living organisms also demonstrates that small changes in the DNA sequence can make a significant difference. Additionally, differences between organisms are caused not just by variation in their nucleotide sequences, but also differences in the regulation of how those sequences are expressed. In other words, the sequence of nucleotides alone does not determine what an organism is like; how and when a sequence is read is also important. There is an enormous amount of variability in how the genetic code of an organism can be expressed in response to its environment. Even if certain genes are present, they may never be expressed during an organism's lifetime. Therefore, understanding the regulation of gene expression is critical to the study of genetics.

The versatility of the genetic code is best understood by first distinguishing between genetics and epigenetics. The raw material of genetics, the **genome**, is the complete sequence of nucleotides of the genetic material. The genome is usually DNA but can be RNA in some viruses. (See the Biological Molecules and Enzymes Lecture for a review of DNA and RNA structure.) These sequences of nucleotides comprise a huge repository of information. By reading the genome, the cellular machinery is able to make all of the proteins and products that sustain life. However, this process is not like reading a book cover to cover. The cell can create different products and different amounts of those products from the same single genetic code in response to the cellular environment. Changes in the kind or amount of gene products are not due to changes in the genome; instead, they depend on how the genome is read by the cellular machinery. The importance of being able to alter the expression of the genes in a genome is illustrated by considering how many different types of cells there are in a human body. Each cell contains the same complete genome, yet some cells become bone while others become muscle, liver, etc. Regulation affects which genes from the genome are expressed, and the products of that gene expression affect the cell's function and identity.

Epigenetic changes influence how the cellular machinery reads the genome. They can act like bookmarks saying "Read here!" or "Don't read here!" depending on the chemical signals present.

The concept of epigenetics explains how some of these changes in gene expression take place. *Epigenetics* (Greek: epi → around) is a term used to describe changes that are made around the genome that do not alter the actual nucleotide sequence. These changes instruct the cellular machinery how to read the genome, thereby altering gene expression. Epigenetic changes do not change the genome itself. Epigenetics include changes such as the attachment of chemical markers to the genome, histone protein modification, and use of non-coding RNAs to influence gene expression. These topics will be discussed in greater detail later within this lecture. The purpose of epigenetic control is to provide a system of regulation that allows gene expression to adapt to the needs of the organism. Epigenetic control of gene expression changes continually, allowing gene expression to adapt to changes in the organism's internal and external environment. In addition to changing gene expression throughout the lifetime of an individual, epigenetic chemical

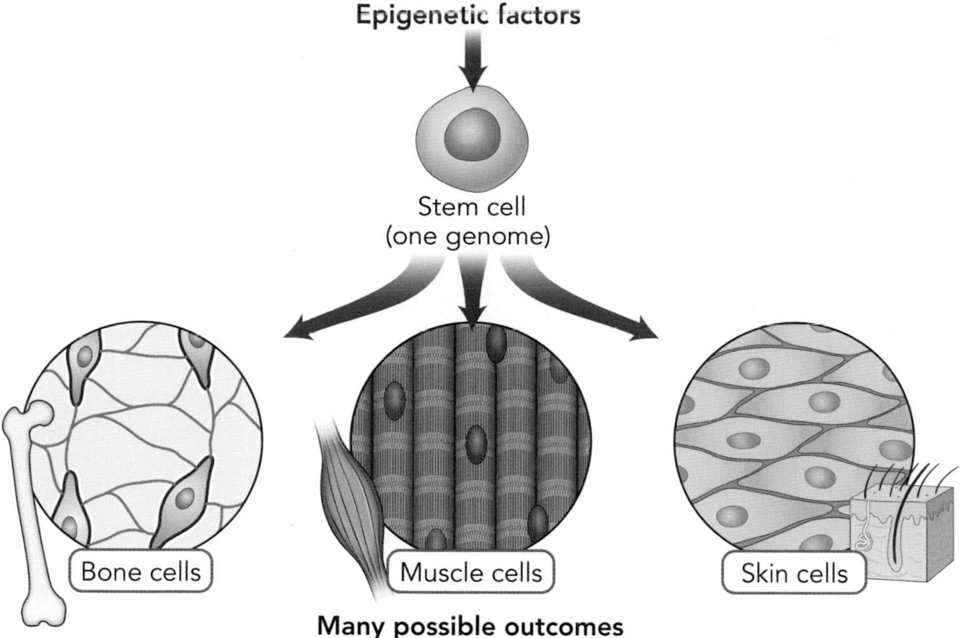

FIGURE 2.1 Epigenetic Regulation

You may encounter the term epigenome, which encompasses all of the epigenetic changes that affect gene expression. However, keep in mind that the epigenome is not a physical structure, but rather an ongoing process of regulation.

markers and histone modifications can be passed down from one generation to the next.

The genetic sequence is often thought of as a set of functional units called genes. For the MCAT® it is best to consider the definition of a gene in terms of its functions. A **gene** is a nucleotide sequence that can code for a certain product or set of products depending on factors such as alternative splicing and protein modification, which will be discussed later in this lecture. A gene is also a unit of heredity – a sequence of nucleotides that codes for a **trait**, meaning a genetically influenced characteristic.

Don't worry too much about the precise definition of a gene. For now, just remember that genes are sequences of nucleotides that code for protein products and that the way these sequences are read affects which products are created.

Within a cell's lifetime, the function of the genome is to code for the products, usually proteins, that are necessary for cellular processes. **The Central Dogma** of gene expression is that DNA is transcribed to RNA, which is translated to amino acids to form a protein. All living organisms use this method to express their genes. Retroviruses (which are not living organisms) store their information as RNA and must first convert their RNA to DNA in order to express their genes.

This lecture discusses how the genetic code performs its three major functions: 1. coding for necessary products during the lifetime of a cell, 2. copying genetic information for the creation of new cells within an organism, and 3. passing on genetic information to the next generation.

FIGURE 2.2 The Central Dogma

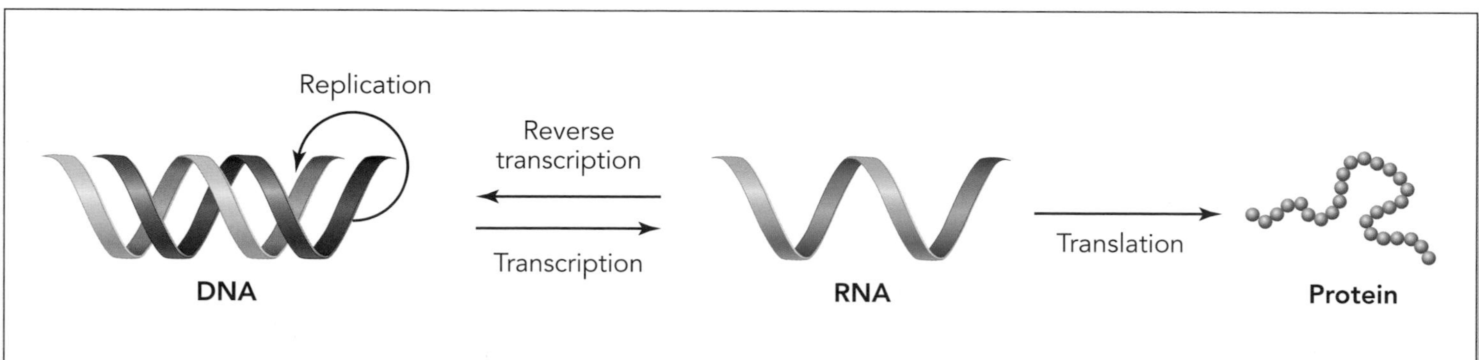

FIGURE 2.3 Chromatin

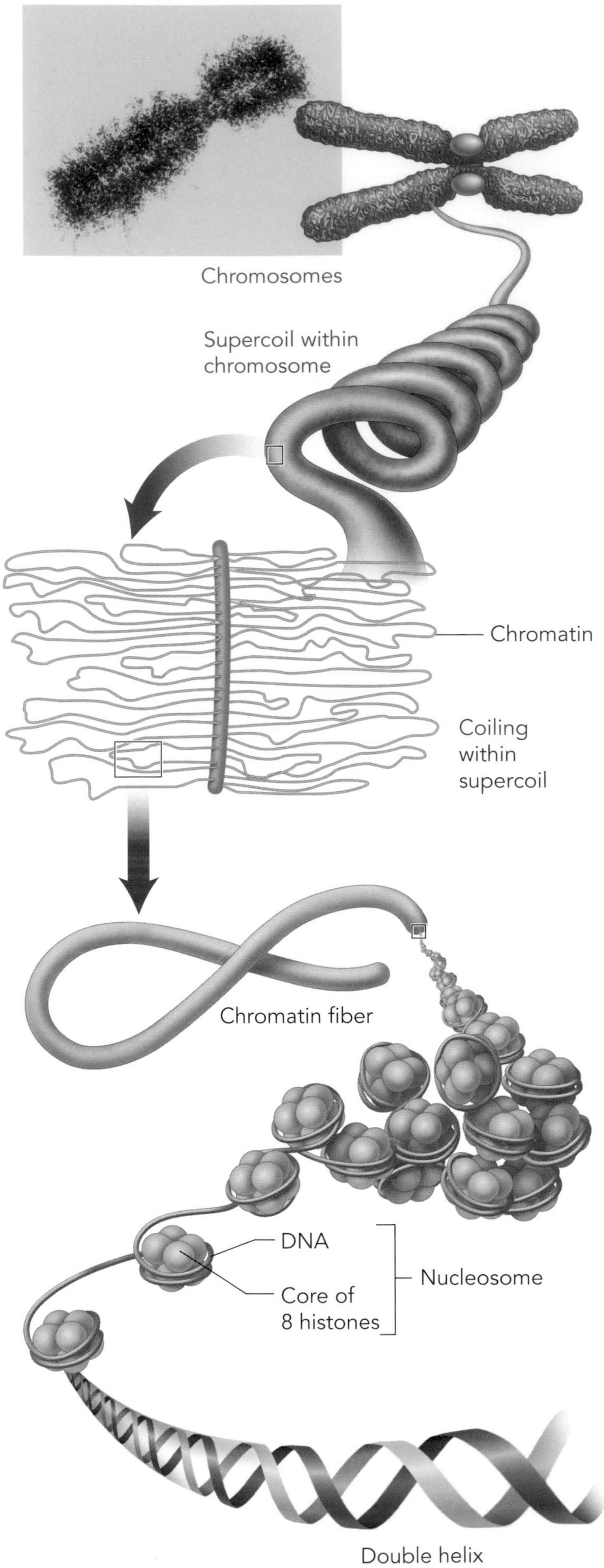

2.3 Organization of Genetic Material

Knowledge of the general structure and vocabulary of genetic material provides a base for the study of genetics. The Biological Molecules and Enzymes Lecture discusses the general structure of DNA and RNA nucleotides, how those nucleotides are joined together through phosphodiester bonds to form single-stranded nucleic acid sequences, and how complementary sequences of single-stranded DNA join in an antiparallel fashion to form double-stranded DNA. All living organisms have double-stranded DNA as their genetic material.

Chromosomes as a System of Organization

In eukaryotic cells, double-stranded DNA sequences are arranged into **chromosomes** (Greek: chroma → color, soma → body). This compact organization is necessary because of the large size of eukaryotic genomes. If a double strand of all the DNA in a single human cell were stretched out straight, it would measure around 5 feet in length. Of course, the nucleus of the cell is much smaller than this! Chromosomes allow the genome to be compressed and organized.

A chromosome consists of compactly wrapped DNA and protein in a hierarchy of organizational levels. The sections of DNA that are not in use are wrapped tightly around globular proteins called **histones**. Histones have basic functional groups that give these proteins a net positive charge at the normal pH of the cell (see the discussion of the isoelectric point in the Acids and Bases Lecture of the *Chemistry Manual*). The net positive charge attracts the negatively charged DNA strands and assists in the wrapping process. Eight histones wrapped in DNA form a **nucleosome**. Nucleosomes, in turn, wrap into coils called *solenoids*, which wrap into **supercoils**. The entire DNA/protein complex (including a very small amount of RNA) is called **chromatin** (Greek: chroma: color). By mass, chromatin is about one third DNA, two thirds protein, and a small amount of RNA. Chromatin received its name because the large amount of basic amino acid content in histones allows chromatin to absorb basic dyes.

Not all chromatin is equally compact. The cellular machinery that "reads" the genetic code can only act on chromatin that is uncoiled. Thus the structure of chromatin influences gene expression and is influenced by epigenetic regulation. Chromatin that is tightly condensed in the manner described above is called **heterochromatin** (Greek: heteros → other). Some chromatin, called *constitutive heterochromatin*, is permanently coiled. To manufacture the products encoded in a nucleotide sequence, the chromatin containing that section of the genome must be uncoiled. When chromatin is uncoiled and able to be transcribed (a process that will be further described later in this lecture), it is called **euchromatin** (Greek: eu → well or properly). Euchromatin is only coiled during nuclear division. Nucleotide sequences that code for protein products often contain **single copy DNA**, which are nucleotide sequences represented by only one copy of a nucleotide sequence, and are associated with regions of euchromatin that are being actively transcribed. In contrast, non-coding regions of DNA (found only in eukaryotes) often contain **repetitive DNA**, which has multiple consecutive copies of the same nucleotide sequence and remains tightly coiled in regions of heterochromatin.

In animals, DNA is found only in the nucleus and the mitochondria.

Regulation of Chromatin Structure

Because the structure of chromatin is important in determining which sequences of DNA are transcribed, the coiling and uncoiling of chromatin is highly regulated by epigenetic controls according to the needs of the cell.

Chemical changes to histone proteins help control which sections of DNA are tightly wound and which are accessible to cellular machinery. Chemical epigenetic changes can also control which coding sequences are unwound and transcribed. The most common example of epigenetic regulation through chemical change is **DNA methylation**, which involves the addition of an extra methyl group to particular cytosine nucleotides. Methylation causes DNA to be wound more tightly. Methylated sections are inaccessible to cellular machinery and cannot be transcribed, so the expression of genes in these sections is reduced. Sections of RNA that do not code for protein products, called **non-coding RNA (ncRNA)**, contribute to the regulation of the chemical changes that affect chromatin structure.

Patterns of DNA methylation can be inherited from previous generations. There is increasing evidence that the life experiences of your ancestors can affect gene expression in your lifetime. Inherited epigenetic changes can make people more prone to conditions such as asthma, obesity, and anxiety.

FIGURE 2.4 DNA Methylation

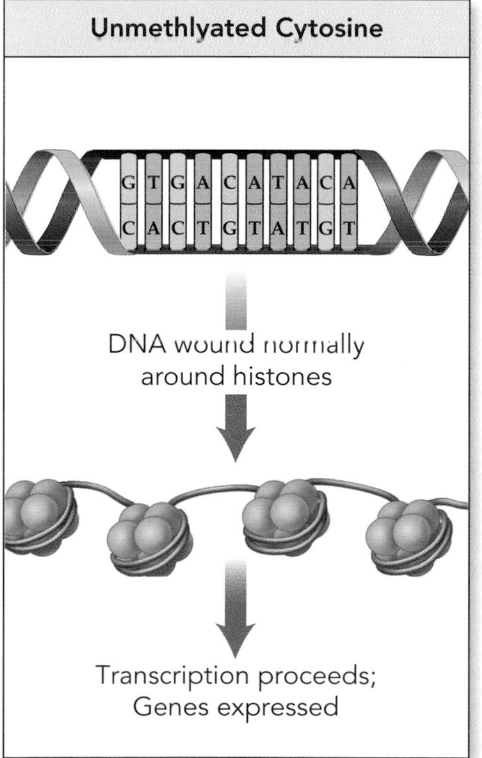

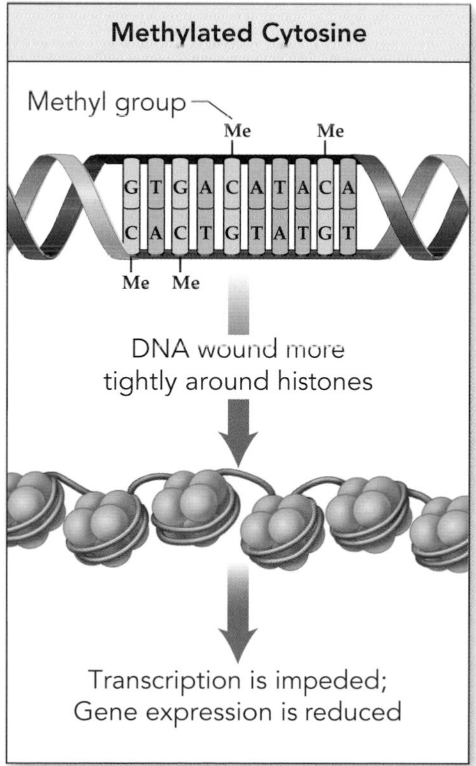

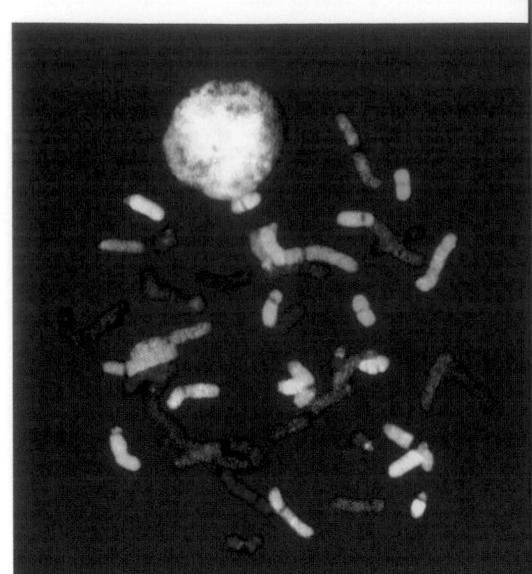

Chromosomes and nucleus stained to visualize individual chromosomes.

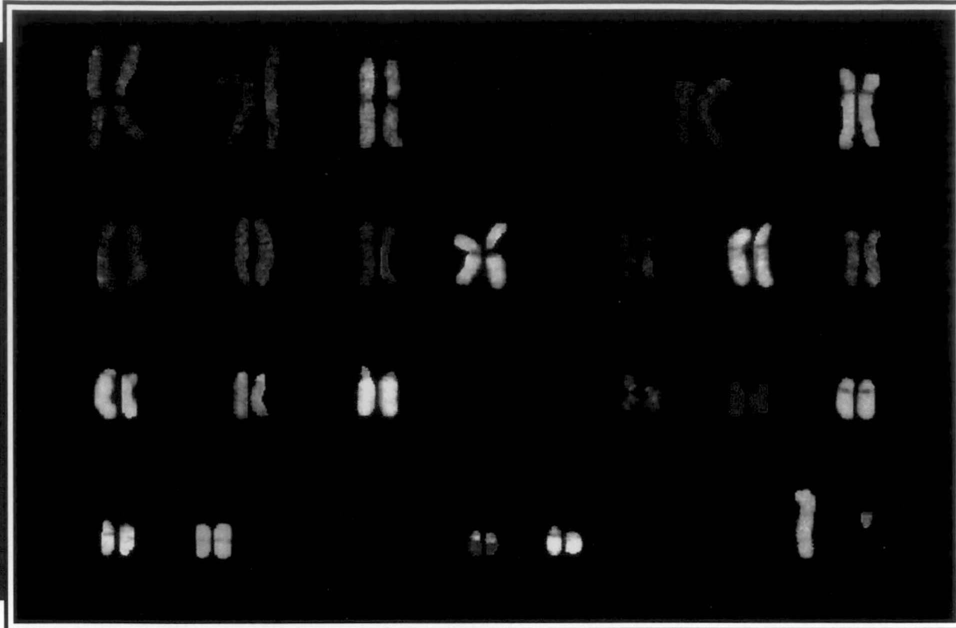

Chromosomal Vocabulary

Inside the nucleus of a human somatic cell, there are 46 double-stranded DNA molecules. The chromatin associated with each one is wound into a chromosome. In human cells, each chromosome possesses a partner that codes for the same traits as itself. Two such chromosomes are called **homologues** (Greek: homologein → to agree with, homo → same, logia → collection). Humans possess 23 homologous pairs of chromosomes. Although the traits are the same (e.g. eye color), the actual genes may code for different versions of the trait (e.g. blue vs. brown). Different forms of the same gene are called alleles, as will be discussed in greater detail later in this lecture. Any cell that contains homologous pairs of chromosomes is said to be **diploid** (Greek: di- → twice). Any cell that does not contain homologues is said to be **haploid** (Greek: haploos → single or simple).

Diploid means that the cell has homologous pairs. It's that simple. Diploid = homologues.

The tricky question about chromosomes is, "How many are there?" In the nucleus of a human cell, there are 46 chromosomes before replication, and 46 chromosomes after replication. The replicated and un-replicated versions of a chromosome are each considered to be a single chromosome. The duplicates can be referred to separately as sister chromatids.

FIGURE 2.5 Chromosomes

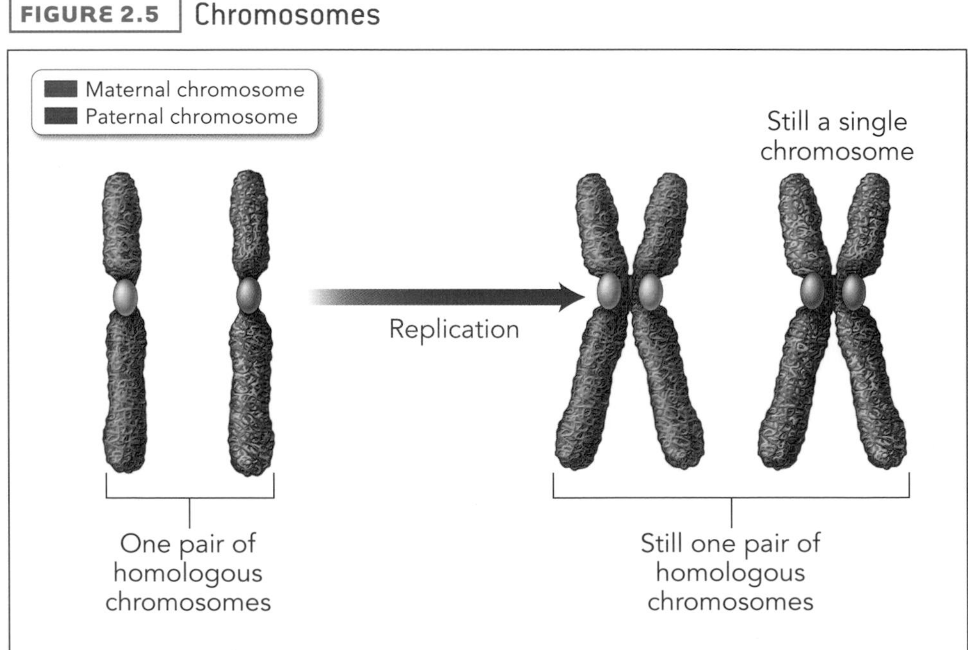

These questions are NOT related to a passage.

Item 25

Which of the following is NOT a major function of genetic information that is necessary for the survival of an individual organism?

- O A) Coding for necessary protein products
- O B) Coding for necessary non-protein products
- O C) Passing genes to future generations
- O D) Passing genetic information to new cells

Item 26

Which of the following best describes the relationship between genetic sequence and the environment?

- O A) Environmental factors affect gene expression only when they act at the level of translation.
- O B) Because genetic differences between living organisms are negligible, environmental effects play a large role in producing phenotypic differences.
- O C) Not all genes in the genome are expressed.
- O D) An organism can create different products or amounts of products in response to the environment.

Item 27

Which of the following statements about the genome is inaccurate?

- O A) The genome can be changed by environmental influence through epigenetic alterations.
- O B) The genome can be read in variable ways to produce different products.
- O C) The genome can be composed of DNA or RNA.
- O D) In multi-cellular organisms, different types of cells can read the genome differently.

Item 28

Epigenetic changes are one way the environment influences gene expression. Which of the following is NOT an example of an epigenetic change?

- O A) A methyl group is added to a cytosine residue in the DNA sequence.
- O B) A methyl group is added to a lysine within a histone protein.
- O C) ncRNAs influence chromatin structure.
- O D) Mutagens in the environment cause the creation of a new single nucleotide polymorphism.

Item 29

Scientists studying an autoimmune disease in mourning doves find that activation of a certain area of their genome (Section X) up-regulates the products of a gene (Gene Y) located downstream, and that the products of Gene Y caused increased symptoms of the disease examined. Increased DNA methylation of Section X would most likely result in which of the following?

- O A) Activation of Section X and decreased disease symptoms
- O B) Inactivation of Section X and decreased disease symptoms
- O C) Activation of Section X and increased disease symptoms
- O D) Inactivation of Section X and increased disease symptoms

Item 30

Which of the following correctly indicates increasing levels of complexity in the organization of genetic information around protein complexes?

- O A) Histones → Nucleosomes → Chromatin → Chromosomes
- O B) Nucleosomes → Histones → Chromatin → Chromosomes
- O C) Histones → Nucleosomes → Chromosomes → Chromatin
- O D) Nucleosomes → Histones → Chromosomes → Chromatin

Item 31

Which of the following is NOT true regarding nuclear DNA and its associated proteins?

- O A) Nucleosomes provide the structure for DNA to form into solenoids and supercoils.
- O B) Histones contain basic functional groups that result in a net positive charge.
- O C) Constitutive heterochromatin is transcribed by cellular machinery.
- O D) By mass, chromatin contains more protein than DNA.

Item 32

Which of the following is true regarding chromosomes?

- O A) The number of chromosomes in a human cell doubles during replication.
- O B) Diploid cells lack homologous chromosomes.
- O C) Homologous chromosomes can contain different alleles.
- O D) Chromosomes only form prior to transcription.

2.4 Transcribing DNA to RNA

A major function of the genome is to code for the products (usually proteins) that are necessary for cells to carry out the processes of life. Most cells spend the majority of their lives in the non-growing phase of G_0. Far from being a period of rest as the name implies, during G_0, cells are busy serving their various functions within the body and producing proteins for this purpose. Although cells manufacture protein products throughout the cell cycle, most production takes place during G_0 when the cell is not exerting energy in self-replication.

Genes undergo transcription and translation in order to make products. **Transcription** is the process by which RNA is manufactured from a DNA template. During transcription, an RNA transcript, which essentially copies the information in DNA, is created. Different genes can code for different types of RNA including ribosomal RNA (**rRNA**), transfer RNA (**tRNA**), small nuclear RNA (**snRNA**), and messenger RNA (**mRNA**). Some of these RNAs, such as rRNA, tRNA, and snRNA, are functional end products that serve important purposes in the cell. However, a large portion of the RNA transcribed is mRNA, which serves as the "message" that is translated for protein production.

FIGURE 2.6 The Cell Life Cycle

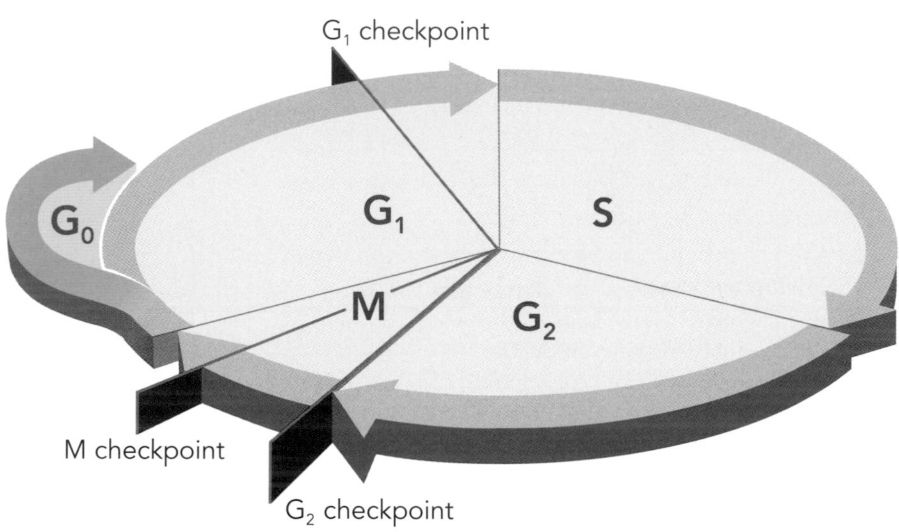

To produce proteins, transcribed mRNA must undergo the process of translation. **Translation** takes the nucleotide sequence of the RNA transcript and translates it into the language of amino acids, which are then strung together to form a functional protein. Recall from the Biological Molecules and Enzymes Lecture that proteins form the basis of many cell structures and regulate practically all cellular processes. Creating proteins through transcription and translation is essential to the processes of life.

Transcription

In eukaryotes, nuclear DNA cannot leave the nucleus and mitochondrial DNA cannot leave the mitochondrial matrix. Eukaryotic transcription takes place only in these two places.

The purpose of transcription is to create an RNA copy of a DNA template. Transcription is itself a form of regulation of gene expression. If transcription did not exist, and instead the whole genome was translated directly into proteins, every cell in an organism would be the same. Instead, only DNA which has first been transcribed into RNA has the opportunity to be translated into a protein.

Transcription includes three main stages: initiation, elongation, and termination. The beginning of transcription is called **initiation**. In initiation, a group of DNA **binding proteins** called **transcription factors** identifies a promoter on the DNA strand. A **promoter** is a sequence of DNA nucleotides that designates a beginning point for transcription. At the promoter, the transcription factors assemble into a *transcription initiation complex*, which includes the major enzyme of transcription, **RNA polymerase**. Promoter sequences help regulate where on the genome transcription can take place and how often certain sequences are transcribed. Promoter regions of DNA have some sequence variability, which serves a regulatory function. The most commonly found promoter nucleotide sequence recognized by a given species of RNA polymerase is called the *consensus sequence*. Variation from the consensus sequence causes RNA polymerase to bond less tightly and less often to a given promoter, which leads to the associated genes being transcribed less frequently.

After binding to the promoter, RNA polymerase unzips the DNA double helix, creating a *transcription bubble*. Next the complex switches to **elongation** mode. In elongation, RNA polymerase transcribes only one strand of the DNA nucleotide sequence into a complementary RNA nucleotide sequence. The transcribed strand is called the *template strand* or (–) *antisense strand*. The other strand, called the *coding strand* or (+) *sense strand*, protects its partner against degradation. RNA polymerase moves along the DNA strand in the 3′ → 5′ direction, building the new RNA strand in the 5′ → 3′ direction. There is no proof-reading mechanism that corrects for errors in the transcription process. (Errors in RNA are not called mutations, unlike errors in DNA.) Errors created in RNA are not transmitted to progeny. Most genes are transcribed many times in a cell's lifetime, so errors in individual instances of transcription are not generally harmful.

The end of transcription is called **termination**, which occurs when a specific sequence of nucleotides known as the *termination sequence* is reached. It can also involve special proteins, known as *Rho proteins*, that help to dissociate RNA polymerase from the DNA template.

FIGURE 2.7 Transcription

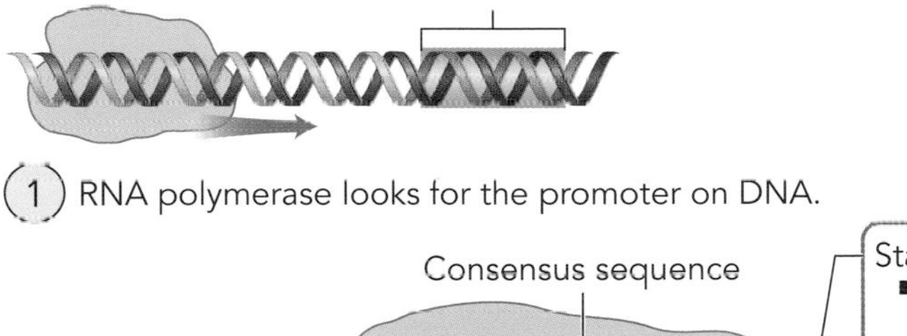

(1) RNA polymerase looks for the promoter on DNA.

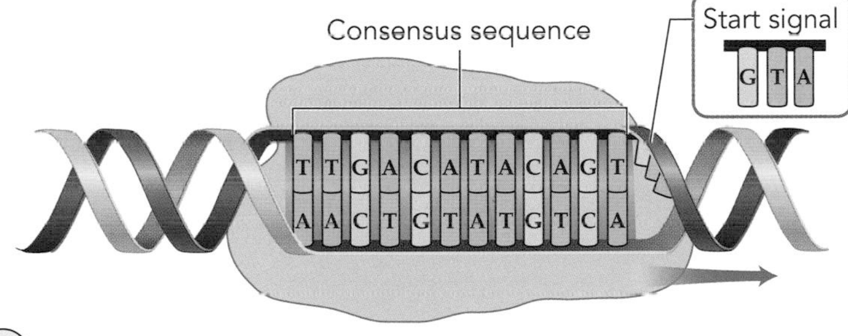

(2) RNA polymerase recognizes the promoter.

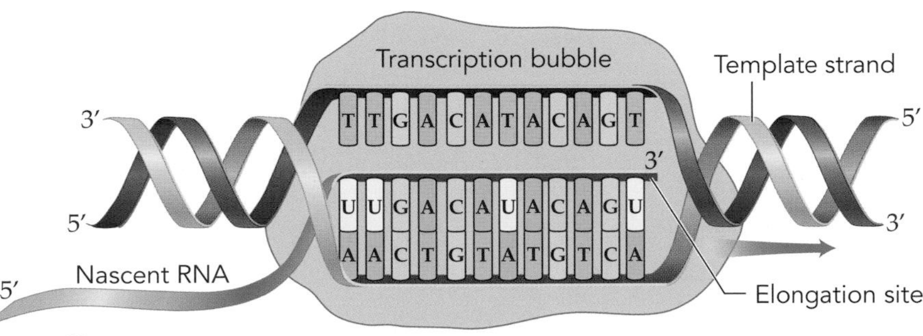

(3) A transcription bubble is formed and elongation begins.

Only the template strand of the DNA double helix is transcribed. The sequence of the coding strand resembles the sequence of the newly synthesized mRNA. Recall from the Biological Molecules and Enzymes Lecture that one of the major differences between DNA and RNA is that DNA is double-stranded while RNA is single-stranded. Make sure you understand that both the coding strand and the mRNA are complementary to the template strand. You could see a question about this on the MCAT®.

Use the simpler model of the prokaryotic genome to gain a basic understanding of the actions of activators and repressors. Know that eukaryotes also have activators and repressors along with many other forms of regulation for gene expression.

Transcription is the main level of activation or deactivation of genes. In both prokaryotic and eukaryotic cells, regulation of gene expression occurs at the level of transcription via proteins called activators and repressors. **Activators** and **repressors** bind to DNA close to the promoter and either activate or repress the activity of RNA polymerase. Activators and repressors are often allosterically regulated by small molecules such as cAMP. Gene regulation in eukaryotes adds complexity by involving the interaction of many genes and other proteins called enhancers. Because of this, more room is required than is available near the promoter. *Enhancers* are short, non-coding regions of DNA found in eukaryotes. They function similarly to activators but act at a much greater distance from the promoter.

Regulation of Transcription in Prokaryotes

Although regulation of gene expression occurs in both prokaryotes and eukaryotes, it serves different purposes. The primary function of gene regulation in prokaryotes is to respond to changes in the environment, such as changes in the concentration of specific nutrients in and around the cell. In contrast, the maintenance of *homeostasis,* or a stable and unchanging state of the intracellular and extracellular compartments, is the hallmark of multicellular organisms. The primary function of gene regulation in multicellular organisms is to control the intra- and extracellular environments of the cell.

Most genetic regulation occurs at the level of transcription. In other words, the amount of a given type of protein within a cell is likely to be related to how much of its mRNA is transcribed. One reason for this is that mRNA has a short half-life in the cytosol, so soon after transcription is completed, the mRNA is degraded and its protein is no longer translated. Also, many proteins can be transcribed from a single mRNA, creating an amplifying effect.

Prokaryotic mRNA typically includes several genes in a single transcript (*polycistronic*), whereas eukaryotic mRNA includes only one gene per transcript (*monocistronic*). In the **Jacob-Monod model** of prokaryotic genetic regulation, the genetic unit consisting of the operator, promoter, and genes that contribute to a single prokaryotic mRNA is called the **operon**. A well-studied and commonly used example of an operon is the **lac operon** in the species *E. coli*. *E. coli* generally prefer to use glucose as a fuel source when it is present in the environment. The lac operon codes for enzymes that allow *E. coli* to import and metabolize lactose when glucose is not present in sufficient quantities. The lac operon is activated only if both of two conditions are met: 1. glucose is scarce and 2. lactose is present. Low glucose levels lead to high cAMP levels. cAMP binds to and activates a *catabolite activator protein (CAP)*. The activated CAP protein binds to a CAP site located adjacent and upstream to the promoter on the lac operon. In an example of **positive control**, CAP activates the promotor, allowing the formation of an initiation complex and the subsequent transcription and translation of three proteins. A second regulatory site on the lac operon, called the *operator*, is located adjacent and downstream to the promoter. When lactose is not present in the cell, a lac repres-

FIGURE 2.8 Structure of Lac Operon

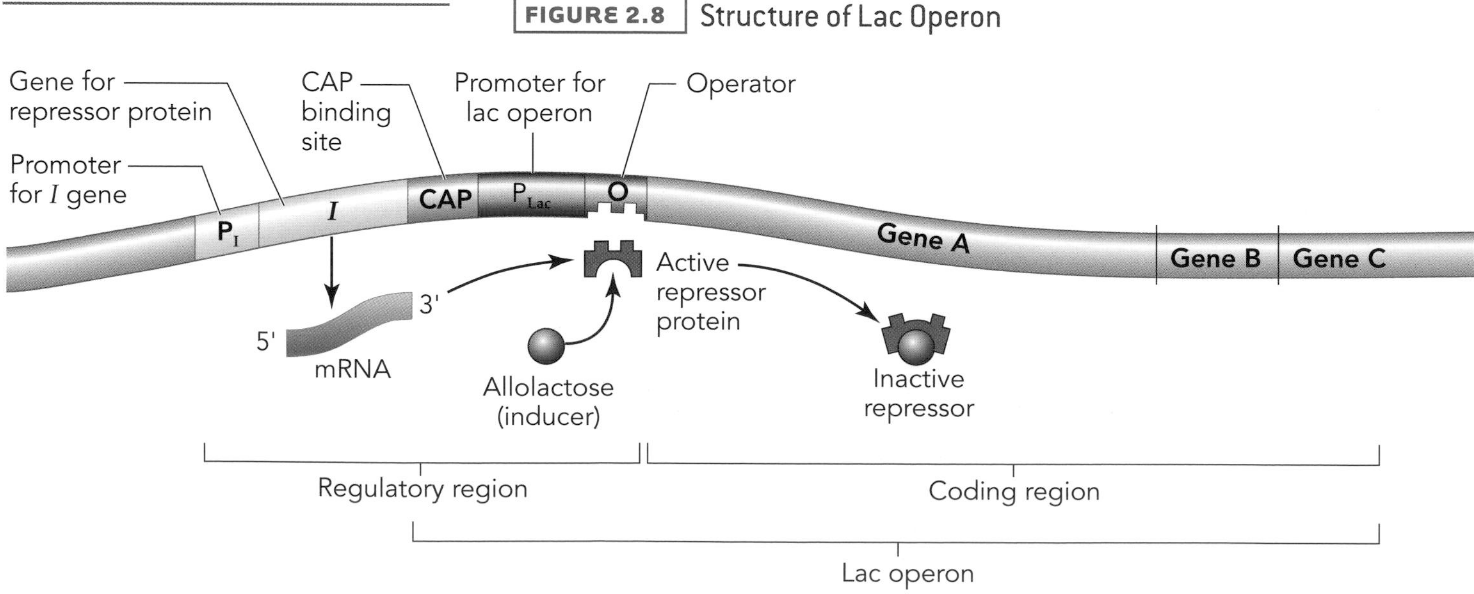

sor protein binds to the operator site and prevents transcription of the lac genes, thereby preventing gene expression. This process is called **gene repression**. When lactose is available, it will bind to the lac repressor protein, making that protein unable to bind to the operator site. Without inhibition from the repressor protein, transcription of the lac genes can proceed. The presence of lactose can therefore *induce* the transcription of the lac operon only when glucose is not present. The promoter and gene for the lac repressor are located adjacent and upstream to the CAP binding site.

An operon is a sequence of bacterial DNA containing an operator, a promoter, and related genes. The genes of an operon are transcribed on one mRNA. Genes outside the operon may code for activators and repressors.

2.5 Modification of RNA

When transcription is complete, the RNA products of transcription are modified by the cell. In addition to epigenetic modifications, the post-transcriptional modification of RNA is one of the major means through which gene expression is regulated. Post-transcriptional processing of RNA occurs in both eukaryotic and prokaryotic cells. In eukaryotes, each type of RNA undergoes post-transcriptional processing. Modifications to RNA transcripts, particularly to mRNA strands prior to translation, allow the cell to employ additional methods of gene regulation, which will be further described below. In prokaryotes, rRNA and tRNA go through post-transcriptional processing, but almost all mRNA is translated directly to protein.

Post-transcriptional modification of mRNA only occurs in the nucleus in eukaryotes. The bacterial genome does not contain introns.

Post-transcriptional Processing of mRNA in Eukaryotes

In eukaryotes, the initial mRNA nucleotide sequence arrived at through transcription is not ready to be translated into proteins until it has first been modified by the cell. The initial RNA nucleotide sequence arrived at through transcription is called the **primary transcript** (also called *pre-mRNA*, or *heterogeneous nuclear RNA [hnRNA]*). The modifications that change a primary transcript into a final, processed mRNA serve several purposes. These include: helping the molecules that initiate translation recognize the mRNA, protecting the mRNA from degradation, eliminating extraneous sequences of nucleotides from the transcript before translation, and providing a mechanism for variability in protein products produced from a single transcript.

Post-transcriptional processing includes modification of both ends of an mRNA sequence. Even before the eukaryotic mRNA is completely transcribed, its 5′ end is capped in a process using GTP. The **5′ cap** serves as an attachment site in protein synthesis during translation and as a protection against degradation by enzymes that cleave nucleotides, called *exonucleases*. The 3′ end of the transcript is similarly protected from exonucleases by the addition of a long series of adenine nucleotides. When this **poly A tail** has been added, the 3′ end is said to be *polyadenylated*.

The primary transcript is much longer than the mRNA that will be translated into a protein. Before leaving the nucleus, portions of the primary transcript are excised and discarded through the process of **splicing**. The portions of transcript that are removed are called **introns**, while the portions that become part of the mature mRNA and will code for proteins are called **exons**. Introns are generally much longer than exons. They do not code for proteins and are degraded within the nucleus. The process of splicing removes introns from the primary transcript and joins the ends of the exons together to form one, uninterrupted coding sequence of mRNA. The mechanism of splicing involves several small nuclear ribonucleoproteins (**snRNPs**, "snurps"). Each snRNP contains both an assortment of proteins and snRNA. During the splicing process, snRNA acts as a **ribozyme** – an RNA molecule capable of catalyzing specific chemical reactions. (Note that this is one of the few enzymes that is not a protein.) Splicing occurs when snRNPs recognize nucleotide sequences at the ends of the introns. The snRNPs pull the ends of the introns together, forming an intron loop or *lariat*.

FIGURE 2.9 Introns

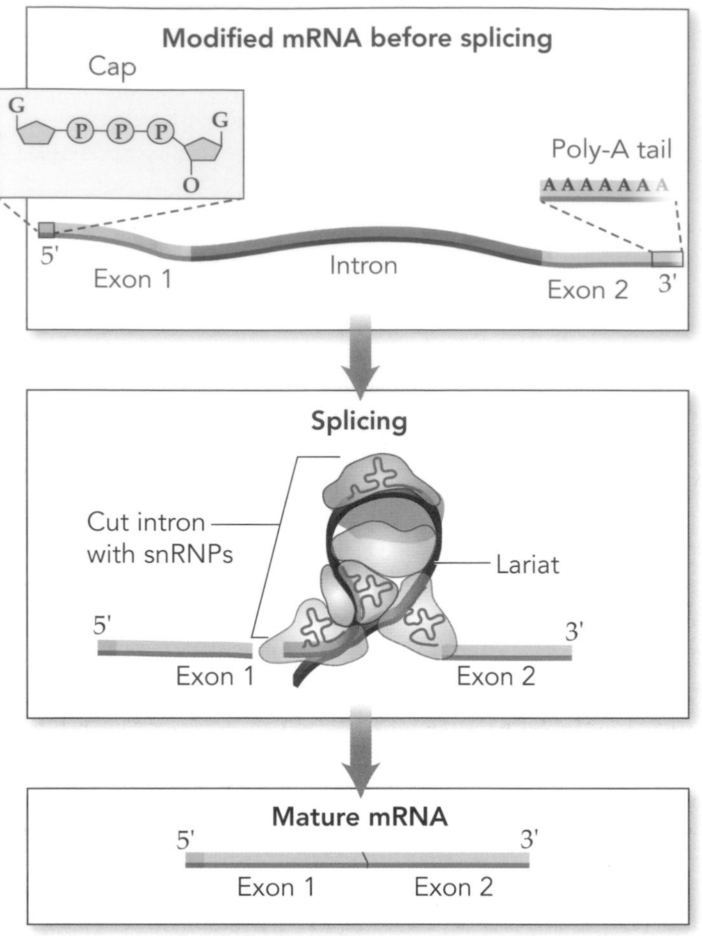

The complex formed from the association of the snRNPs and additional associate proteins is called a **spliceosome**. The spliceosome excises the introns and joins the ends of the exons together to form the single mRNA strand that ultimately codes for a polypeptide.

Remember that, in general, INtrons remain IN the nucleus, and EXons EXit the nucleus to be translated.

Eukaryotic cells exert control over gene expression and add to the variety of protein products possible through the process of alternative splicing, one of the major mechanisms in the regulation of eukaryotic gene expression. **Alternative splicing** allows the cell to incorporate different coding sequences into the mature mRNA. This highly regulated process can create a variety of mRNA molecules for translation from a single DNA coding sequence. The mechanisms for creating this variability include omitting certain exons, incorporating certain introns, and utilizing variable splicing sites. Increasing evidence indicates that introns play an important function in determining gene expression. The nucleotide sequences in both introns and exons determine the different ways a primary transcript may be spliced. Furthermore, sequences that contain introns are associated with amplified protein production compared to sequences that lack introns. Alternative splicing, together with other eukaryotic techniques such as the use of alternative promoter sites or terminating transcription at different sites, allows the cell to create a vast variety of proteins from a relatively limited number of protein-coding nucleotide sequences. Although the human genome is estimated to contain only 20,000-25,000 protein-coding gene regions, it can code for more than 100,000 proteins. Alternative splicing is an important contributor to this diversity of protein products.

Introns play a role in determining possible splicing patterns and promoting protein production. Because of their functional significance, many introns are highly conserved between species.

One reason there are more proteins than genes is that different splicing patterns of the same gene can create different polypeptides.

Transcription and post-transcriptional modifications take place in the nucleus of eukaryotes. The spatial separation between transcriptional and translational processes provided by the nuclear membrane is a form of regulation in eukaryotes. This separation allows the RNA transcript to be modified before it leaves the nucleus and before translation can begin. In contrast, prokaryotes have no nuclear membrane. The lack of spatial separation means that prokaryotes can carry out transcription and translation concurrently and that they do not modify RNA transcripts prior to the start of translation.

2.6 Translating RNA to Protein

Making Sense of the Genetic Code

When post-transcriptional processing is finished, a mature mRNA is ready for translation. Translation is the process through which a cell creates the protein products that are necessary to carry out the processes of life. As described earlier in the lecture, it involves the "translation" of the nucleotide sequence of mRNA into the amino acid sequence of the corresponding protein.

FIGURE 2.10 Alternative Splicing

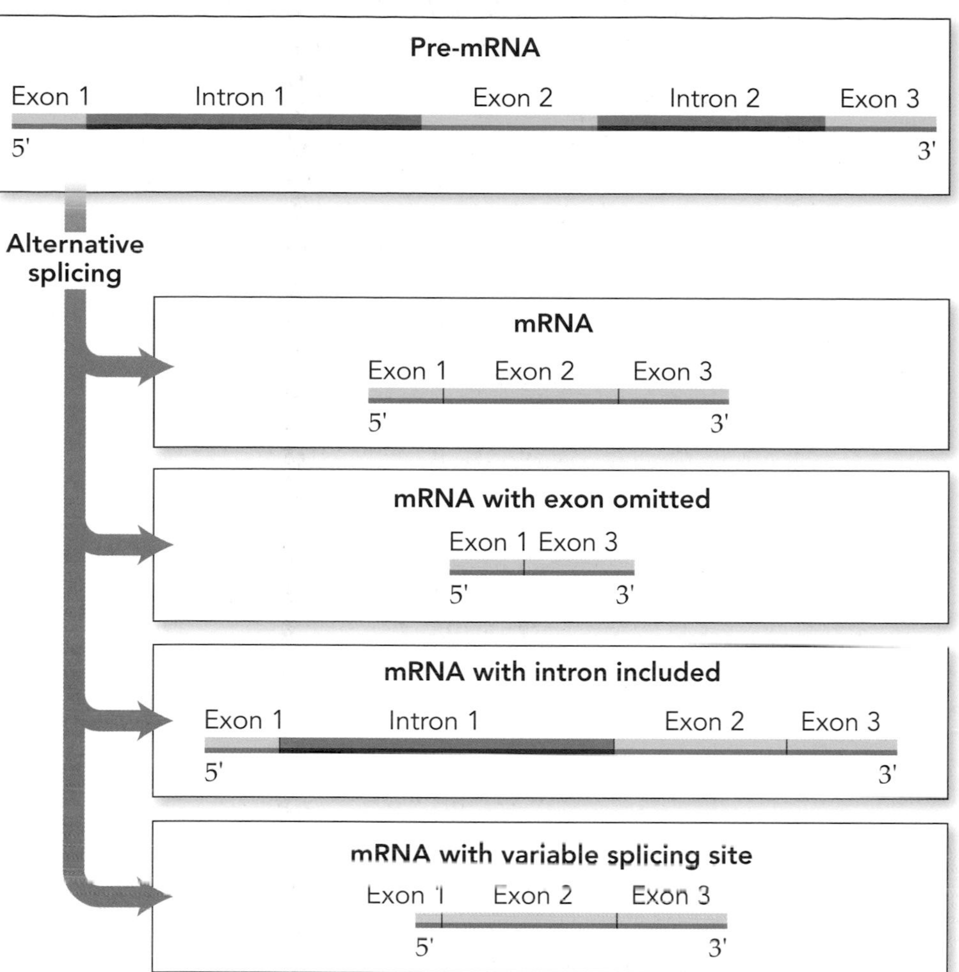

During the process of translation, the information contained in mRNA is used as a set of instructions to create a specific polypeptide chain. mRNA nucleotides are strung together to form a **genetic code** consisting of four different nucleotides, as described in the Biological Molecules and Enzymes Lecture. In nature, there are approximately 20 different amino acids that commonly make up functional proteins. The four RNA nucleotides (adenine, guanine, cytosine, and uracil) together must create a language that unambiguously codes for each of these common amino acids. The genetic code of mRNA accomplishes this task by using a series of three nucleotides to code for each amino acid – a system known as the **triplet code**. Some quick math reveals why sets of three nucleotides are needed. Because there are only four kinds of nucleotides, if each nucleotide coded for a different amino acid, only four amino acids would be possible. The number of possible combinations from a set of two nucleotides, where each nucleotide might contain any one of the four nitrogenous bases, is $4^2 = 16$, which is still not enough to code for the 20 amino acids (see Table 2.1). Therefore, the code must use a combination of three nucleotides for each amino acid. However, the number of possible combinations of any three nucleotides gives $4^3 = 64$, which is greater than the number of amino acids. The genetic code is therefore said to be **degenerative**, which means that more than one series of three nucleotides may code for the same amino acid. However, any single series of three nucleotides will code for one and only one amino acid. Therefore the code is also unambiguous. The use of three nucleotide series to code for a single amino acid works well and is highly conserved. The codes shown in Table 2.2 are almost universal; nearly every living organism uses these same codes to translate mRNA sequences into strings of amino acids.

TABLE 2.1 > Nucleotides in Pairs

	A	C	G	T
A	AA	CA	GA	TA
C	AC	CC	GC	TC
G	AG	CG	GG	TG
T	AT	CT	GT	TT

Memorize the start codon, AUG, and the stop codons UAA, UAG, and UGA. It is necessary to understand that a single codon (such as GUC) always codes for only one amino acid, in this case valine; but that there are other codons (GUU, GUA, GUG) that also code for valine. The first part of this means that the code is unambiguous, and the second part means that the code is degenerative. Finally, understand probabilities, such as figuring out how many possible codons exist. As discussed above, four possible nucleotides can be placed in each of 3 positions, giving $4^3 = 64$.

Try this: A polypeptide contains 100 amino acids. How many possible amino acid sequences are there for this polypeptide?

Answer: See page 63.

Three consecutive nucleotides on a strand of mRNA comprise a **codon**. All but three possible codons code for amino acids. The remaining codons, UAA, UGA, and UAG, are **stop codons** (also called **termination codons**). Stop codons signal an end to protein synthesis. The start codon (also called the **initiation codon**), AUG, indicates where translation will begin. The start codon codes for the amino acid methionine, which is always the first amino acid incorporated into a polypeptide during protein synthesis. By convention, a sequence of RNA nucleotides is written 5′→ 3′.

TABLE 2.2 > The Genetic Code

First position 5′ end ↓	Second position U	C	A	G	Third position 3′ end ↓
U	Phe	Ser	Tyr	Cys	U
U	Phe	Ser	Tyr	Cys	C
U	Leu	Ser	STOP	STOP	A
U	Leu	Ser	STOP	Trp	G
C	Leu	Pro	His	Arg	U
C	Leu	Pro	His	Arg	C
C	Leu	Pro	Gln	Arg	A
C	Leu	Pro	Gln	Arg	G
A	Ile	Thr	Asn	Ser	U
A	Ile	Thr	Asn	Ser	C
A	Ile	Thr	Lys	Arg	A
A	Met	Thr	Lys	Arg	G
G	Val	Ala	Asp	Gly	U
G	Val	Ala	Asp	Gly	C
G	Val	Ala	Glu	Gly	A
G	Val	Ala	Glu	Gly	G

The genetic code is given in Table 2.2. Be certain that you can interpret this table. For instance, the codons for lysine (Lys) are AAA and AAG. Understand that more than one codon can code for the same amino acid. It is not necessary to memorize which codons code for which amino acids.

Translation

Translation is the process by which the cellular machinery "reads" the mRNA transcript and translates it into a polypeptide. Each of the three major types of RNA plays a unique role in translation. mRNA is the template which carries the genetic code from the nucleus to the cytosol in the form of codons. tRNA plays a vital role in actually rendering the triplet code of the mRNA into a specific amino acid sequence. Each tRNA molecule has two distinct ends. One end contains a series of three nucleotides, called an **anticodon**, which will bind to the complementary codon sequence on mRNA. The other end of the tRNA carries the amino acid that corresponds to that codon, which can be added to a growing polypeptide chain as tRNAs bind to the codons along the mRNA strand (Figure 2.12). The first two base pairs in the codon and anticodon must be strictly complementary (A with U and C with G). However, there is some flexibility in bonding at the third base pair position. This flexibility is called **wobble pairing** and helps explain why multiple codons can code for the same amino acid.

All translation takes place using a specialized organelle called a **ribosome**. Ribosomes may be free-floating in the cytosol or attached to the outer surface of the endoplasmic reticulum to form rough ER, as described in the Cell Lecture in *Biology 2: Systems*. A ribosome is composed of a **small subunit** and a **large subunit** made from rRNA and many separate proteins. The ribosome and its subunits are measured in terms of *sedimentation coefficients* given in *Svedberg units (S)*. The sedimentation coefficient gives the speed of a particle in a centrifuge and is proportional to mass and related to shape and density. Prokaryotic ribosomes are smaller than eukaryotic ribosomes. Prokaryotic ribosomes are made from a 30S and a 50S subunit and have a combined sedimentary coefficient of 70S. Eukaryotic ribosomes are made of 40S and 60S subunits and have a combined sedimentary coefficient of 80S. The complex structure of ribosomes requires a special organelle called the **nucleolus** in which to manufacture them. (Prokaryotes do not possess a nucleolus, but synthesis of prokaryotic ribosomes is similar to that of eukaryotic ribosomes.) Although the ribosome is assembled in the nucleolus, the small and large subunits are exported separately to the cytosol.

Notice that the sedimentation coefficients don't add up: $40 + 60 \neq 80$.

FIGURE 2.11 tRNA and Ribosome Structure

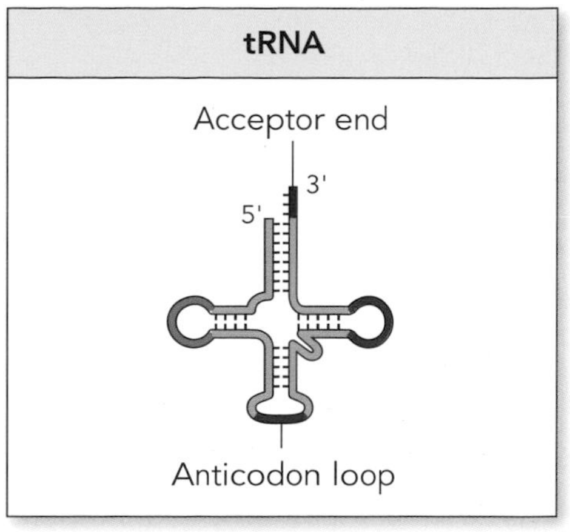

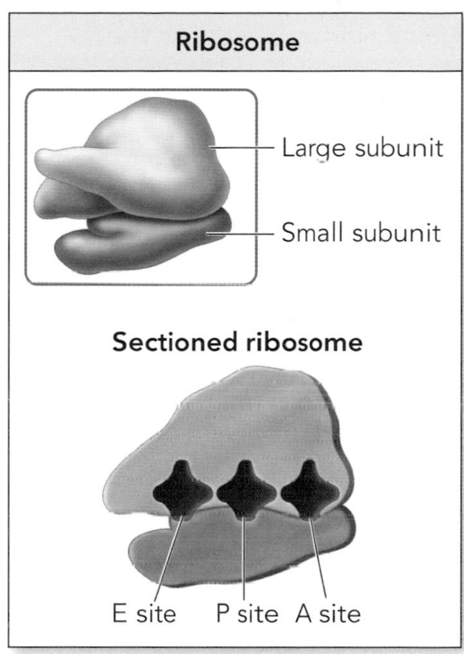

The process of translation is divided into the same three stages as transcription (initiation, elongation, and termination), but whereas transcription produces a strand of RNA, the product of translation is a chain of amino acids. After post-transcriptional processing in a eukaryote, mRNA leaves the nucleus through the nuclear pores and enters the cytosol. With the help of **initiation factors** (co-factor proteins), the 5′ end attaches to the small subunit of a ribosome. A tRNA containing the 5′-CAU-3′ anticodon sequesters the amino acid methionine and settles into the **P site** (peptidyl site). This is the signal for the large subunit to join and form the **initiation complex**. This process is termed **initiation**. Most of the regulation of translation occurs during the initiation stage through the recognition (or lack of recognition) between the ribosomal subunits and the secondary structure of the mRNA transcript.

Once the initiation complex is fully formed, **elongation** of the polypeptide begins. During elongation, the ribosome slides down the mRNA strand one codon at a time in the 5′→ 3′ direction while matching each codon to a complementary tRNA anticodon. The corresponding amino acids attached to these tRNAs are bound together into a growing polypeptide as the process proceeds. The mechanism of elongation requires the input of energy. Once a methionine-bearing tRNA has attached to the P site, a new tRNA, with its corresponding amino acid, attaches to the neighboring **A site** (aminoacyl site). The amino acid attached to the tRNA in the A site becomes the second amino acid in the polypeptide sequence. The C-terminus (carboxyl end) of methionine attaches to the *N-terminus* (amine end) of the amino acid at the A site in a dehydration reaction, forming a peptide bond. The bond formation takes place through peptidyl transferase activity, which is catalyzed by rRNA in the ribosome, another example of ribozyme function. After lengthening the polypeptide by a single amino acid, the ribosome shifts 3 nucleotides toward the 3' end of the mRNA. The tRNA that carried methionine moves to the **E site**, from which it can exit the ribosome. The tRNA carrying the newly formed dipeptide moves to the P site, leaving the A site open for the next tRNA. The elongation process is repeated until a stop codon reaches the P site.

It is helpful to consider location when thinking about the differences between prokaryotic and eukaryotic transcription and translation. In eukaryotes, mRNA is transcribed in the nucleus, where the DNA is kept. The mRNA must then leave the nucleus to be translated in the cytoplasm. Therefore, in eukaryotes, transcription and translation are separated both in both space and time. This separation is one mechanism to regulate which sequences are converted to products and which are not. Because prokaryotes have no separate, membrane-bound nucleus, transcription and translation can occur simultaneously.

Within each ribosome there are three sites where tRNA molecules can bind. At the A site the Anticodon matches up with the codon, ensuring that the correct Amino Acid is chosen. At the P site, a Peptide bond between amino acids is formed, lengthening the Polypeptide chain. Finally, at the E site, the tRNA, which now lacks an amino acid, is free to Exit the ribosome.

FIGURE 2.12 Translation

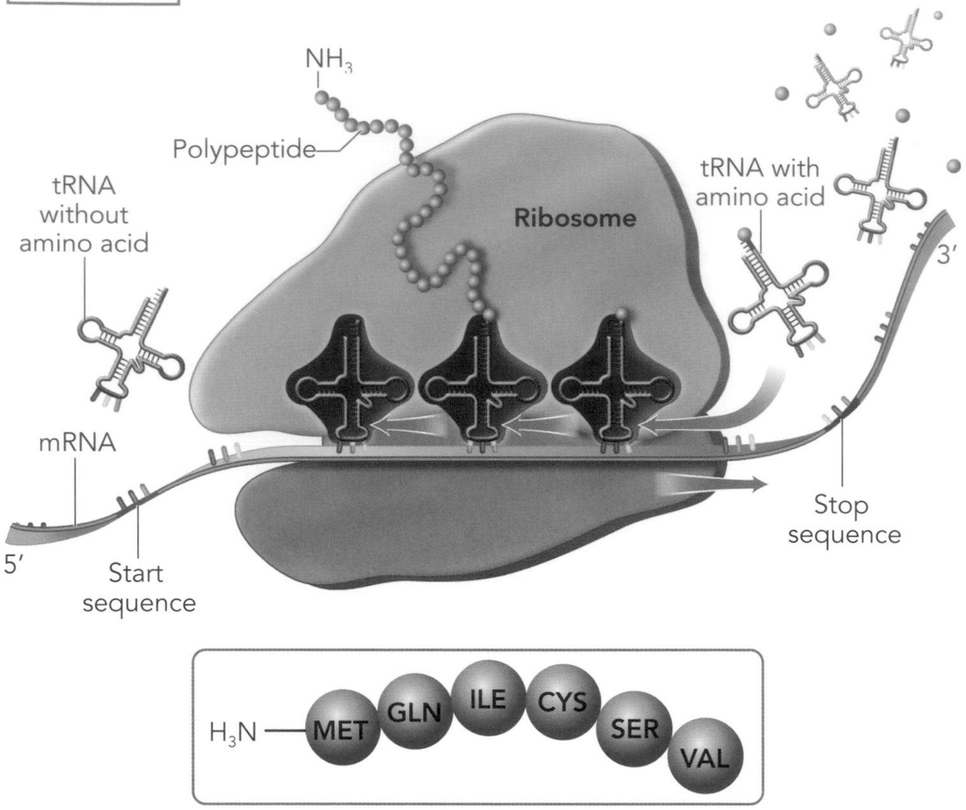

Newly formed polypeptide

Translation ends when the ribosome reaches a stop codon in a step called **termination**. When a stop codon (or **nonsense codon**) reaches the A site, proteins known as **release factors** (co-factor proteins) bind to the A site, allowing a water molecule to add to the end of the polypeptide chain. The polypeptide is freed from the tRNA and ribosome, and the ribosome breaks up into its subunits to be reused in later rounds of protein synthesis.

Even as the polypeptide is being translated, it begins folding. The amino acid sequence determines the folding conformation, and the folding process is assisted by proteins called *chaperones*. For further information on protein folding and structure, revisit the Biological Molecules and Enzymes Lecture.

After Translation: The Fates of Proteins

Know the steps of translation: initiation, elongation, and termination. Know the role of each type of RNA.

Once a protein is completely synthesized, it can still undergo **post-translational modifications**. These modifications are a mechanism for regulating gene expression by affecting which products of translation ultimately become functional proteins. Sugars, lipids, or phosphate groups may be added to amino acids to influence functionality. The polypeptide can be cleaved in one or more places. Separate polypeptides may join to form the quaternary structure of a protein.

The final destination of a protein is related to where it is translated. Proteins translated by free-floating ribosomes function in the cytosol, while proteins synthesized by ribosomes that attach to the rough ER during translation are injected into the ER lumen. Proteins injected into the ER lumen are destined to become membrane bound proteins of the nuclear envelope, ER, Golgi, lysosomes, or plasma membrane, or, often, to be secreted from the cell. Free floating ribosomes are identical in structure to ribosomes that attach to the ER. The growing polypeptide itself may or may not cause the ribosome to attach to the ER, depending upon the polypeptide. A 20 amino acid sequence called a **signal peptide** near the front of the polypeptide is recognized by a protein-RNA **signal-recognition particle**

(SRP) that carries the entire ribosome complex to a receptor protein on the ER. There the protein grows across the membrane, where it is either released into the lumen or remains partially attached to the ER. The signal peptide is usually removed by an enzyme. Signal peptides may also be attached to polypeptides to target them to mitochondria, the nucleus, or other organelles. In this way, proteins end up in locations appropriate to their structures and functions, and thus one of the main purposes of the genome, production and delivery of the products the cell needs, is achieved.

Translation begins on a free floating ribosome. A signal peptide at the beginning of the translated polypeptide may direct the ribosome to attach to the ER, in which case the polypeptide is injected into the ER lumen. Polypeptides injected into the lumen may be secreted from the cell via the Golgi body or may remain partially attached to the membrane.

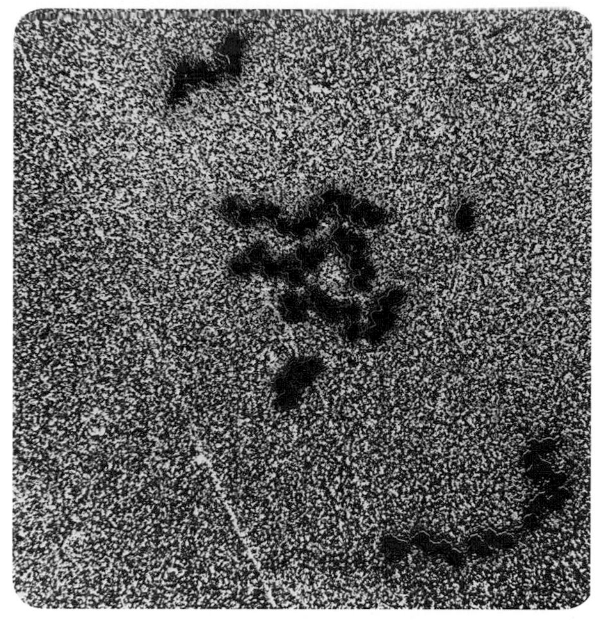

This false-color transmission electron micrograph (TEM) of a structural gene from the bacterium *Eschericia coli* shows the coupled transcription of DNA into mRNA and the simultaneous translation into protein molecules. The DNA fiber runs down the image (in yellow) from top left, with numerous ribosomes (in red) attached to each mRNA chain. The longest chains (called polysomes) are furthest from the point of gene origin.

FIGURE 2.13 Polypeptide Synthesis

CYTOSOL

ER LUMEN

ER membrane

Signal-recognition particle (SRP)

SRP receptor protein

Signal peptide

mRNA

Ribosome

Signal peptide removed

Protein

1. Polypeptide synthesis begins on a free-floating ribosome in the cytosol.
2. Signal peptide is recognized by the SRP.
3. The SRP carries the entire ribosome complex to a receptor protein on the ER.
4. The protein grows across the membrane where it is either released into the lumen or remains partially attached to the ER.
5. The signal peptide is usually removed by an enzyme.
6. The protein undergoes post-translational modifications.

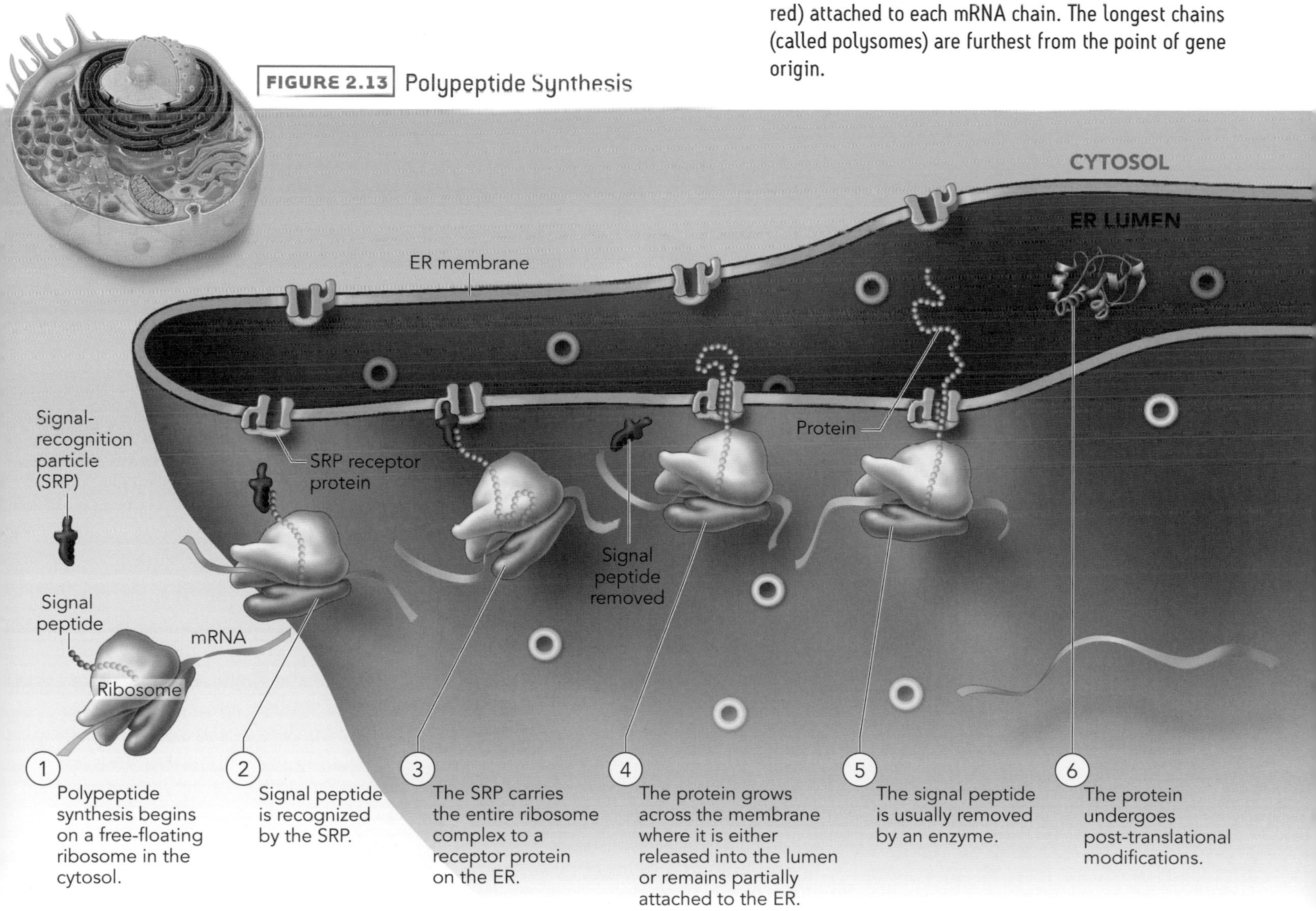

2.7 Genetic and Cellular Replication: Mitosis

Not all cell types in the body regularly undergo cell division. For example, fully differentiated neurons rarely divide to produce new cells. Instead, neurons primarily remain in the G_0 phase of the cell cycle and devote their time and energy toward carrying out the normal functions of a neuron (producing neurotransmitters, maintaining the resting potential, etc.) rather than toward producing new neurons. However, some cell types, such as skin and intestinal cells, have short lifespans or are lost to the environment and must regularly be replaced. To replace lost cells, some skin cell progenitors must routinely undergo cellular division to produce new cells. One of the major functions of the genome is its ability to direct the process of **DNA replication**, through which an exact copy of the genome is synthesized to be included in the newly created cell after division. As described in the Cell Lecture in *Biology 2: Systems*, cell division is a highly regulated series of phases. DNA replication takes place during the S phase of the interphase portion of the cell cycle. This allows two copies of the genome to be available during the M phase – one for each of the two resultant cells.

FIGURE 2.14 The Cell Life Cycle: S Phase

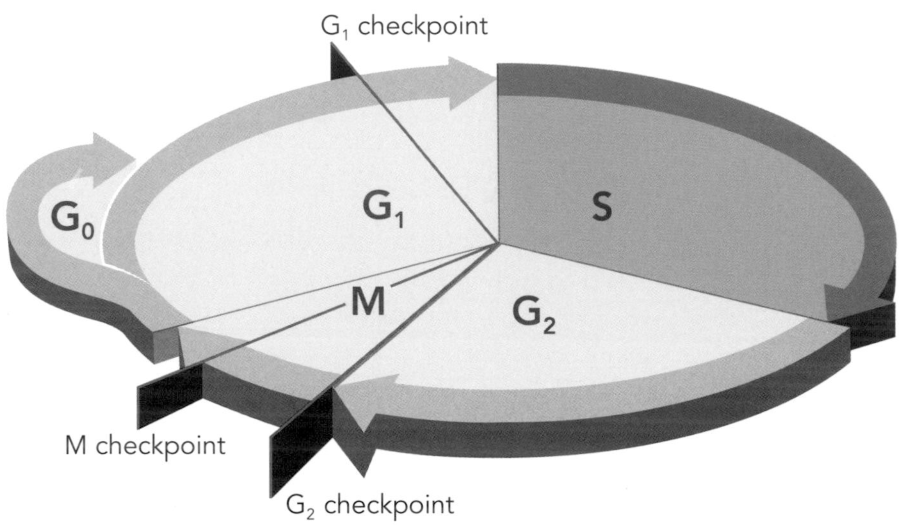

Replication of the Genome

The purpose of DNA replication is to produce two identical copies of the genome, each of which can be distributed to one of the cells created during division. This goal is accomplished by unwinding the DNA double helix and separating the two strands of DNA. Using the two single strands as templates, complementary nucleotides are matched along the lengths of each strand, resulting in two identical double-stranded copies of the same genome. Because each copy contains one strand from the original DNA, and one newly synthesized strand, the process of DNA replication is said to be **semiconservative**.

The mechanism of DNA replication is governed by a group of proteins called a *replisome* (Figure 2.15). Replication does not begin at the end of a chromosome, but toward the middle at a site called the **origin of replication**. Replication in prokaryotes usually takes place from a single origin on the circular chromosome. Eukaryotic chromosomes are much larger and therefore usually contain multiple origins of replication. Epigenetic markers designate the origins of replication and, therefore, help regulate how and where replication begins. At the origin of replication, two replisomes proceed in opposite directions along the chromosome, making replication a **bidirectional** process. The point where a replisome is attached to the chromosome is called the replication fork. Each chromosome of eukaryotic DNA is replicated in many discrete segments called *replication units* or *replicons*.

Included in the replisome are several enzymes necessary for DNA replication. The first of these enzymes, **DNA helicase**, unwinds the double helix, separating the two strands. **DNA polymerase** synthesizes the new DNA strands by pairing complementary free-floating deoxynucleotides with the sequence of nucleotides on the exposed strands of DNA. However, DNA polymerase cannot initiate a new strand of nucleotides; it can only add nucleotides to an existing strand. Therefore, **primase**, an RNA polymerase, creates an **RNA primer** approximately 10 ribonucleotides in length to initiate the strand. DNA polymerase adds deoxynucleotides to the primer and moves along each DNA strand, creating a new complementary strand. DNA polymerase reads the parental strand in the 3´ → 5´ direction, creating the new complementary strand in the 5´ → 3´ direction. By convention, the nucleotide sequence in DNA is written 5´ → 3´ as well. This direction is sometimes referred to as downstream and the 3´ → 5´ direction as upstream.

Transcription requires a promoter, whereas replication requires a primer. The words are similar, but don't get confused. A promoter is a spot on the DNA that tells RNA polymerase where to begin transcription. A primer is a short piece of RNA that jump starts replication.

Because DNA polymerase reads in only one direction, one strand of DNA is looped around the replisome, giving it the same orientation as the other strand. The single strand in the loop is prevented from folding back onto itself by *single strand binding* (SSB) *tetramer proteins* (also called *helix destabilizer proteins*). As is shown in Figure 2.15, at each replication fork, one of the separated strands is able to be read continuously in the 3´ → 5´ direction while RNA polymerase continuously synthesizes a complementary strand in the 5´ → 3´ direction. However, for the other original DNA strand, the polymerization of its new, complementary strand must be regularly interrupted and restarted with a new RNA primer so that the DNA may still be read 3´ → 5´ as the replication fork is unzipped. The continuous strand is called the leading strand, while the interrupted strand is called the **lagging strand**. The lagging strand is formed from a series of disconnected strands called **Okazaki fragments**. Okazaki fragments are approximately 100 to 200 nucleotides long in eukaryotes and about 1000 to 2000 nucleotides long in prokaryotes. Because the formation of one strand is continuous and the other

Replication proceeds in both directions from an origin. Each direction produces a leading and a lagging strand.

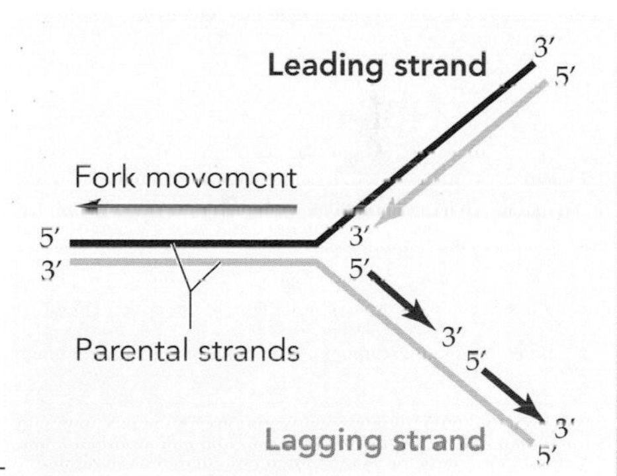

FIGURE 2.15 Prokaryotic Replisome

1 At the origin of replication, DNA helicase unwinds the double helix into a leading and lagging strand. Primase creates RNA primers to intiate the lagging strand. DNA polymerase synthesizes the new DNA strands by pairing the leading and lagging strands with complementary deoxynucleotides.

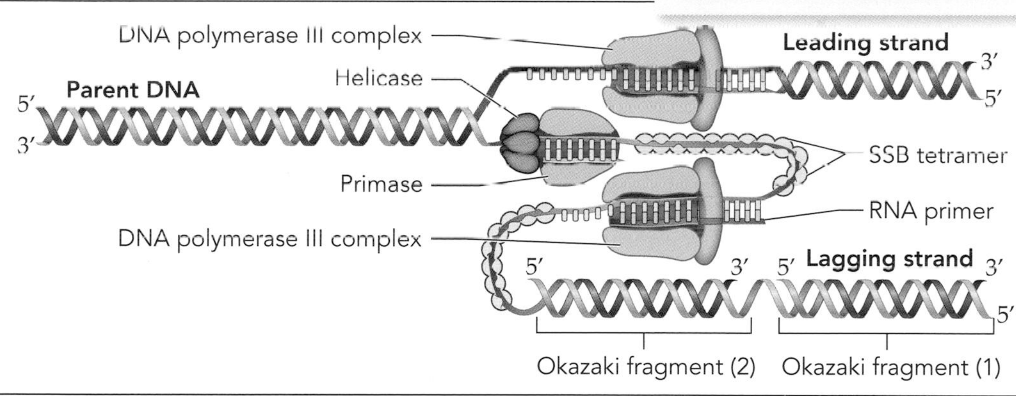

2 Because DNA polymerase reads in only one direction, the lagging strand is looped around the replisome, giving it the same orientation as the leading strand. DNA polymerase reads the parent DNA in the 3´ → 5´ direction, creating the new complementary strand in the 5´ → 3´ direction.

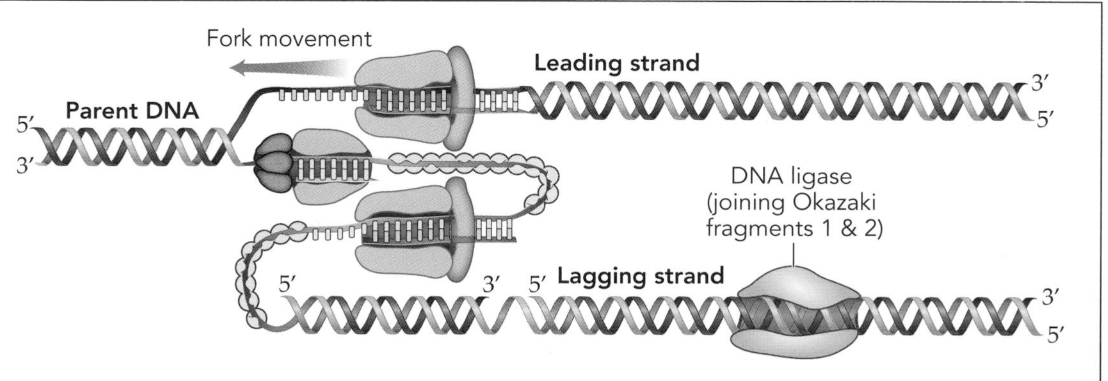

Know the five main steps of replication and which enzyme is involved in each step:

1. Helicase unzips the double helix;
2. RNA polymerase (primase) builds a primer;
3. DNA polymerase assembles the leading and lagging strands;
4. RNAse H removes the primers;
5. DNA ligase joins the Okazaki fragments together.

is fragmented, the process of replication is said to be **semidiscontinuous**. Once the new DNA strands are synthesized, the RNA primers are removed from the sequence by the enzyme RNAase H and the gaps created by the loss of the RNA primers are filled in with deoxynucleotides by DNA polymerase. In the final step of DNA replication, neighboring Okazaki fragments on the lagging strand are joined together by **DNA ligase** (Latin: ligare → to fasten or bind) to form a completed copy of the double-stranded DNA helix.

In DNA replication, the ends of chromosomes are of special importance. The ends of eukaryotic chromosomal DNA possess telomeres. **Telomeres** are repeated six nucleotide units from 100 to 1,000 units long that protect the ends of chromosomes. Telomeres can become shortened through repeated rounds of replication, a condition that has been linked to aging and disease. To somewhat counteract the shortening effect of replication on telomeres, *telomerase* catalyzes the lengthening of telomeres in eukaryotic organisms.

DNA replication is fast and accurate.

In order to complete a copy of an entire genome in a reasonable period of time, replication must be fast. The DNA polymerase shown in Figure 2.15 moves at over 500 nucleotides per second. DNA polymerase in humans moves much more slowly, at around 50 nucleotides per second. However, multiple origins of replication allow the over 6 billion base pairs that make up the 46 human chromosomes to be replicated quite quickly. Replication in a human cell requires about 8 hours.

In addition to being fast, it is also important that DNA replication be accurate. DNA replication includes a mechanism to ensure that a faithful copy of the genome is produced. Besides being a polymerase, one of the subunits in DNA polymerase is an exonuclease, that removes nucleotides from the strand. This enzyme automatically proofreads each new strand as it is synthesized and makes repairs when it discovers any mismatched nucleotides (e.g. thymine matched with guanine). DNA replication in eukaryotes is extremely accurate. Only one out of every 10^9–10^{11} base pairs is incorrectly incorporated.

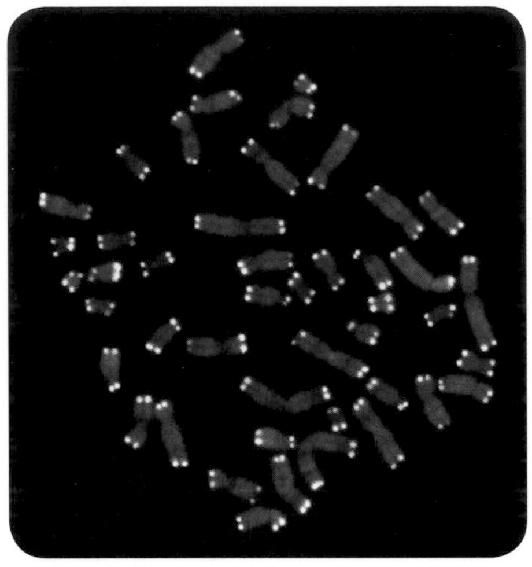

Shown here are human chromosomes with their telomeres labeled in white. Telomeres are like the plastic tips on shoelaces that prevent them from fraying.

Although there are some differences, replication in eukaryotes and prokaryotes is very similar. Except where specified, the process described above is accurate for both.

Mitosis

Mitosis is the process by which two cells are created that are identical to both each other and to the original cell. Once the genome is replicated, the copied chromosomes must be properly allocated to ensure that each daughter cell receives a complete copy of the genome during division. The large number of chromosomes in eukaryotic genomes makes the division of chromosomes between cells a potentially chaotic process. The cell requires a system of organization to divide the chromo-

FIGURE 2.16 Mitosis

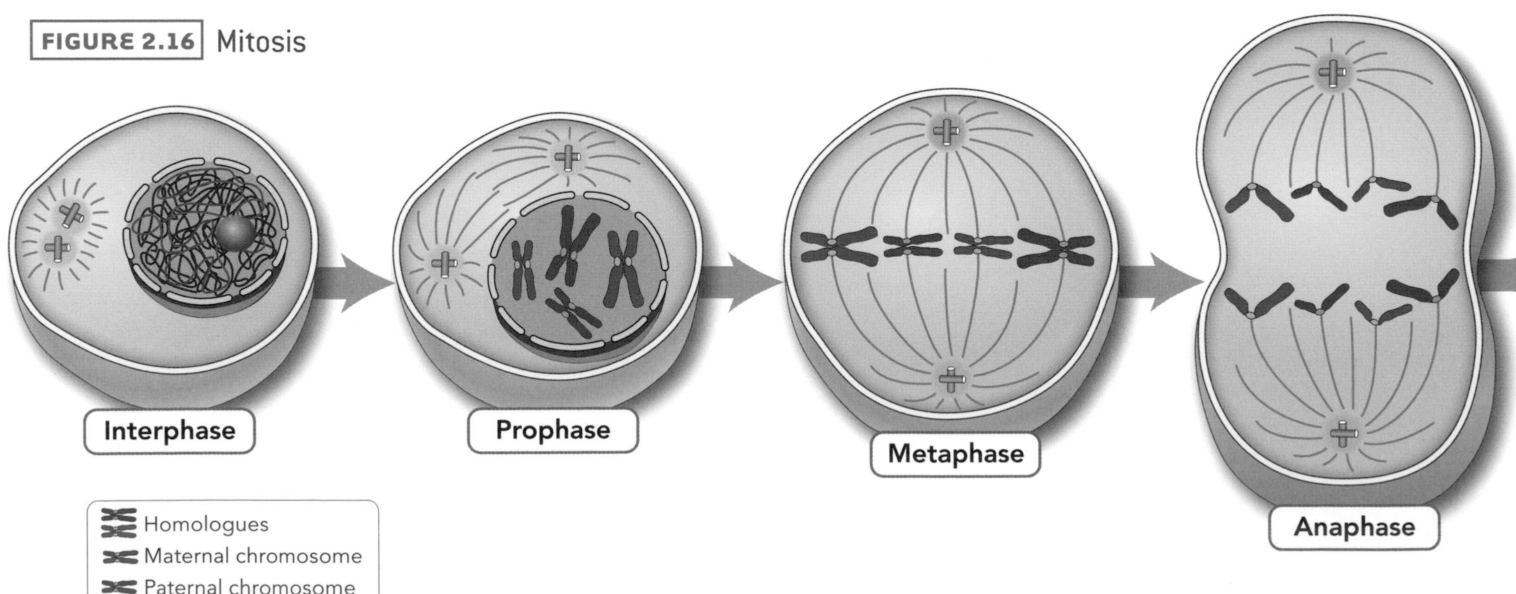

somes evenly between daughter cells and uses the machinery of mitosis to accomplish this division efficiently and accurately. **Mitosis** (Greek: mitos → cell) is nuclear division without genetic change. It consists of a series of steps that organize and divide replicated chromosomes. The four main stages of mitosis are prophase, metaphase, anaphase, and telophase (Figure 2.16). These stages in turn are divided into sub-stages, but these categories are beyond the MCAT®. Mitosis varies among eukaryotes. The following stages describe mitosis in a typical animal cell.

Prophase is characterized by the condensation of chromatin into chromosomes. The tightly coiled chromatin limits transcription, thus down-regulating gene expression during mitosis. The two identical copies of duplicated chromosomes, called sister **chromatids**, are joined together at groups of proteins near their centers called **centromeres**. Structures called **centrioles**, located in the **centrosomes**, move to opposite poles of the cell. First the nucleolus and then the defined nucleus disappear as the nuclear envelope breaks down. The **spindle apparatus** begins to form, consisting of **asters** (microtubules radiating from the centrioles), *kinetochore microtubules* growing from the centromeres, and **spindle microtubules** connecting the two centrioles. (The **kinetochore** is a structure of protein and DNA located at the centromere of the joined chromatids of each chromosome.)

In **metaphase** (Greek: meta → between), chromosomes align along the equator of the cell. This orderly lining up of the chromosomes ensures that they will be separated such that each daughter cell receives one of each chromosome.

During **anaphase** sister chromatids split at their attaching centromeres and segregate to opposite sides of the cell. Shortening of the kinetochore microtubules pulls the sister chromatids apart and moves them toward opposite poles. This split is termed *disjunction*. **Cytokinesis**, the actual separation of the cellular cytoplasm due to constriction of microfilaments around the center of the cell, may or may not commence toward the end of this phase.

In **telophase** (Greek: teleios → complete), the nuclear membrane reforms, followed by the reformation of the nucleolus. Chromosomes decondense and become difficult to see under a light microscope. Cytokinesis continues, resulting in two identical daughter cells that each contain one complete copy of the parent cell's genome.

FIGURE 2.17 Spindle Apparatus

Centrosome
Aster
Centrioles
Centromeres
Kinetochore
Spindle microtubules

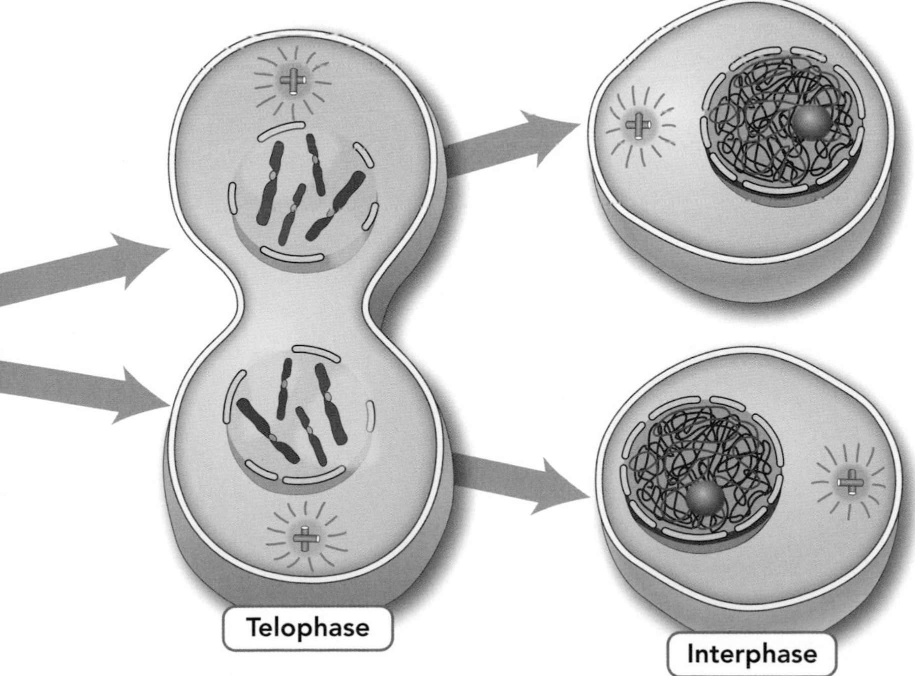

Remember the order of the stages of mitosis using the acronym PMAT.

Know the basic conditions that define each phase of mitosis. It is especially important to realize that mitosis results in genetically identical daughter cells.

These questions are NOT related to a passage.

Item 33

If each of the following mRNA nucleotide sequences contains three codons, which one contains a start codon?

- A) 3′-AGGCCGUAG-5′
- B) 3′-GUACCGAAC-5′
- C) 5′-AAUGCGGAC-3′
- D) 5′-UAGGAUCCC-3′

Item 34

Translation in a eukaryotic cell is associated with each of the following organelles or locations EXCEPT:

- A) the mitochondrial matrix.
- B) the cytosol.
- C) the nucleus.
- D) the rough endoplasmic reticulum.

Item 35

Which of the following is true concerning the genetic code?

- A) There are more amino acids than codons.
- B) Any change in the nucleotide sequence of a codon must result in a new amino acid.
- C) The genetic code varies from species to species.
- D) There are 64 codons.

Item 36

One difference between prokaryotic and eukaryotic translation is that:

- A) eukaryotic ribosomes are smaller.
- B) prokaryotic translation may occur simultaneously with transcription, while eukaryotic translation cannot.
- C) prokaryotes do not contain supra molecular complexes such as ribosomes.
- D) prokaryotic DNA is circular and thus does not require a termination sequence.

Item 37

An mRNA molecule being translated at the rough endoplasmic reticulum is typically shorter than the gene from which it was transcribed because:

- A) the primary transcript was cut as it crossed the nuclear membrane.
- B) normally multiple copies of the mRNA are produced and spliced.
- C) introns in the primary transcript are excised.
- D) several expressed regions of the primary transcript have equal numbers of base pairs.

Item 38

The gene for triose phosphate isomerase in maize (a corn plant) spans over 3400 base pairs of DNA and contains eight introns and nine exons. Which of the following would most likely represent the number of nucleotides found in the mature mRNA after post-transcriptional processing?

- A) 1050
- B) 3400
- C) 6800
- D) 13,600

Item 39

Eukaryotic mRNA production occurs in the following sequence:

- A) transcription from DNA in the cytoplasm followed by post transcriptional processing on the ribosome.
- B) transcription from DNA in the nucleus followed by post transcriptional processing in the nucleus.
- C) translation from DNA in the nucleus followed by posttranscriptional processing in the nucleus.
- D) translation from DNA in the cytoplasm followed by post-transcriptional processing on the ribosome.

Item 40

Which of the following statements regarding transcription is FALSE?

- A) The mRNA produced is complementary to the coding strand.
- B) Activators and repressors bind to DNA and affect the activity of RNA polymerase.
- C) The nucleotide sequence of the promoter region affects how often a region of RNA is transcribed.
- D) During transcription, RNA polymerase moves along the DNA strand in the 3’ → 5’ direction.

2.8 Mutations

Although the processes of DNA replication and mitosis are extremely accurate and efficient, the huge number of repetitions of these processes throughout the body ensures that mistakes do happen and that changes to the genome can occur. Any alteration in the genome that is not due to genetic recombination (which takes place in meiosis, described below) is called a **mutation**. Mutations are important not only for the individual carrier, but as a crucial source of genetic variation within populations, without which evolution could not occur. Mutations can be *spontaneous* (occurring due to **random errors** in the natural process of replication and genetic recombination) or *induced* (occurring due to physical or chemical agents called **mutagens**, which can damage DNA and increase the frequency of mutation above the baseline frequency of spontaneous mutations). The effects on the cell are the same in either case. The effect of a mutation on an organism's fitness may be **advantageous** or **deleterious**, or there may be no effect at all. Mutations may occur at the level of the nucleotide or the level of the chromosome.

Mutations are rare. Mutations in somatic cells are not passed to offspring; mutations in germ cells are.

A **gene mutation** is the alteration in the sequence of DNA nucleotides in a single gene. A **chromosomal mutation** occurs when the structure of a chromosome is changed. In multicellular organisms, a mutation in a somatic cell (Greek: soma → body) is called a *somatic mutation*. A somatic mutation of a single cell may have very little effect on an organism with millions of cells. In contrast, a mutation in a germ cell, from which all other cells arise, can have large consequences for the offspring produced. Under normal conditions, mutations are rare. Only about one out of every million gametes will carry a mutation for a given gene. Different types of mutations are categorized both by the effect of the change on the structure of the genetic sequence and by the effect on the sequence's function.

Categories of Mutations That Describe Structural Changes to the Gene

Mutations at the level of the gene most often change one nucleotide at a time. If a mutation changes a single nucleotide in a double strand of DNA, that mutation is called a **point mutation**. There are several known types of point mutations. One type, called a **base substitution mutation**, results when one nucleotide is swapped for another during DNA replication. A base substitution exchanging one purine for the other purine (A ↔ G) or one pyrimidine for the other pyrimidine (C ↔ T) is called a *transition mutation*. A base-pair substitution exchanging a purine for a pyrimidine or a pyrimidine for a purine is called a *transversion mutation*. Other types of point mutations include **addition mutations** (inserting a new nucleotide into the sequence) and **deletion mutations** (deleting a nucleotide from the sequence). Additions and deletions can have profound effects on the function of the affected gene.

FIGURE 2.18 Base-pair Substitutions

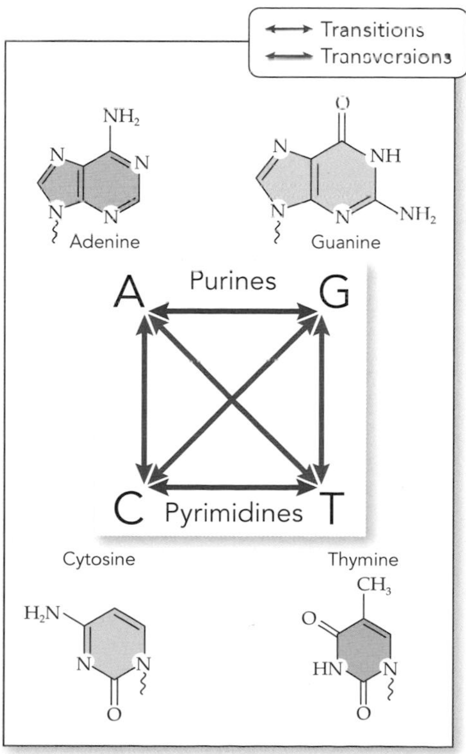

Categories of Mutations that Describe Functional Changes to the Gene

If a mutation has no effect on an organism's fitness, that mutation is said to be neutral. A neutral mutation could change the amino acid sequence of a protein without changing its function or could result in no change to an amino acid sequence (e.g. changing the codon AAA to AAG through a base substitution would still result in the amino acid lysine.) The type of neutral mutation in which the amino acid sequence is unchanged is called a **silent mutation**.

Some nucleotide mutations can cause significant changes to the function of a gene. A **missense mutation** occurs when a base substitution changes a codon (creating a **missense codon**) which results in the translation of a different amino acid. Missense mutations can be neutral and result in completely functional proteins. However, missense mutations can also significantly change a polypeptide's func-

Note that these categories of mutations are overlapping. There are multiple possible categories for any one change. For example, a base substitution could be silent, but could also be neutral and not silent. A base substitution can be a missense mutation if it changes a codon to code for a different amino acid, and this missense mutation may or may not neutral. A base substitution can also cause a nonsense mutation if it creates a stop codon. As you review the definitions of mutation categories, spend some time thinking through how a mutation may fit into more than one category at a time.

tion. Sickle cell anemia, for example, is a disease caused by a single amino acid difference in hemoglobin.

A **nonsense mutation** occurs when a change to the nucleotide sequence creates a stop codon where none previously existed. For example, a nonsense mutation could be caused by a base substitution changing the codon UCA, which codes for the amino acid serine, into the stop codon UAA. Nonsense mutations tend to have serious consequences for the cell because they terminate translation and usually create a truncated, non-functional protein.

The addition and deletion of nucleotides, which are also considered point mutations, can result in a frameshift mutation. A **frameshift mutation** occurs when the deletions or additions occur in multiples other than three. Because the genetic code is read in groups of three nucleotides, an addition or deletion of one or two nucleotides will change the *reading frame* of the code. An altered reading frame means that the entire sequence after the mutation will be shifted so that the three base sequences are grouped incorrectly. For instance, if a single T nucleotide were inserted into the series: AAA|GGG|CCC|AAA, so that it reads AAT|AGG|GCC|CAA|A, each 3-nucleotide sequence downstream from the mutation would be altered and therefore each amino acid coded for could change. On the other hand, if three T nucleotides were inserted randomly, the downstream sequence would not be shifted, and only one or a few 3-nucleotide sequences would be changed: AAT|TAG|GTG|CCC|AAA. This is a non-frameshift mutation. Non-frameshift mutations may still result in a partially or even completely active protein, while frameshift mutation most often result in completely non-functional proteins. Frameshifts may also result in nonsense mutations if the new reading frame includes a premature stop codon.

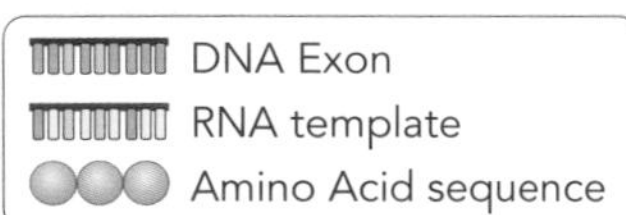

FIGURE 2.19 Mutations at the Level of the Gene

Changes in DNA caused by mutations are included in the RNA sequence through the process of transcription. These changes can have a variety of effects on the translated amino acid sequence and resulting protein function.

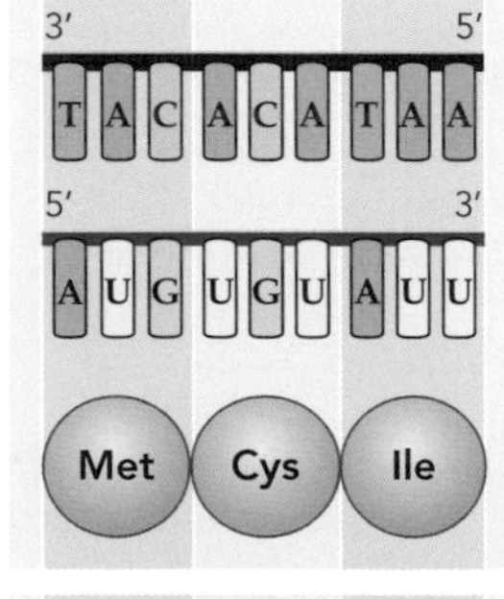

No mutation

This example illustrates the normal process of transcription and translation when no mutation has occurred. The amino acid sequence produced is intact and functional.

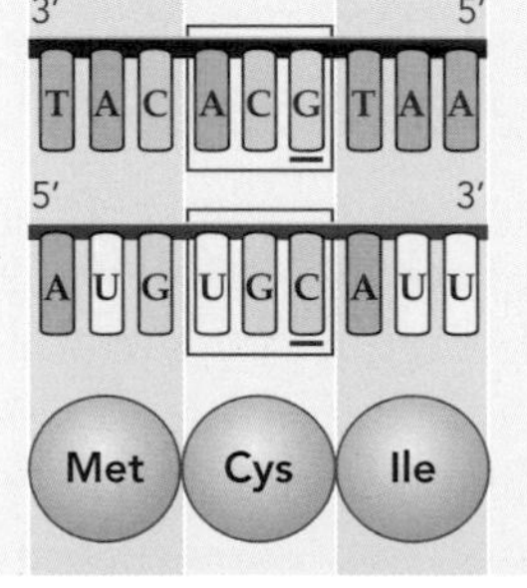

Base substitution - silent

A base-pair substitution has occurred, changing A to G on the DNA exon and thus changing U to C on the mRNA. Because the codons UGU and UGC both code for cysteine, the amino acid sequence remains unchanged and the protein is fully functional. This is an example of a silent mutation.

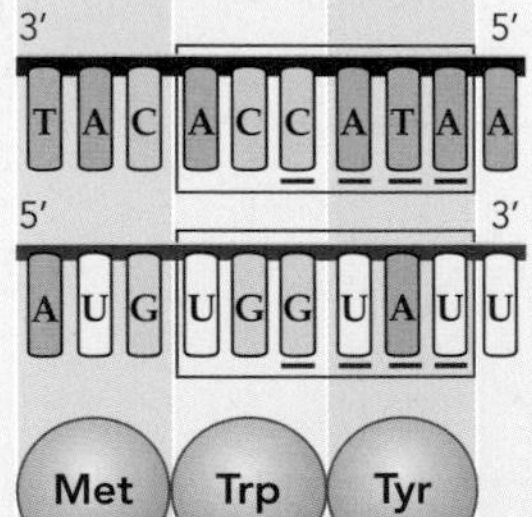

Addition - continuing protein

The addition (or deletion) of a single nucleotide causes a frameshift. From that point forward, the codons are translated on a different reading frame, resulting in a different string of amino acids. This type of mutation usually results in non-functional proteins.

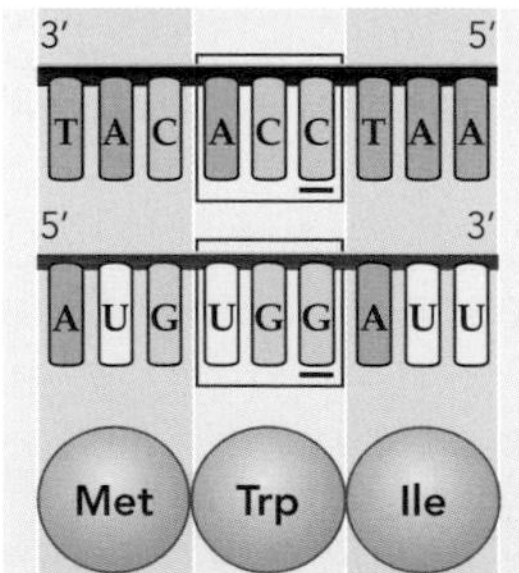

Base substitution - missense

A base-pair substitution has occurred, changing A to C on the DNA exon and thus changing U to G on the mRNA. A codon that used to code for cysteine (UGU) now codes for Tryptophan (UGG). This an example of missense mutation. Missense mutations may alter protein functionality, depending on the location and properties of the substituted amino acid.

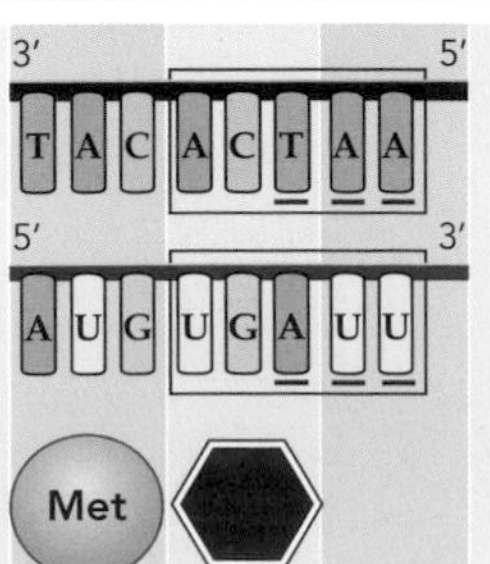

Addition - truncated protein (nonsense)

The addition (or deletion) of a single nucleotide causes a frameshift. From that point forward, the codons are translated on a different reading frame, resulting in a different string of amino acids. This type of mutation usually results in non-functional proteins.

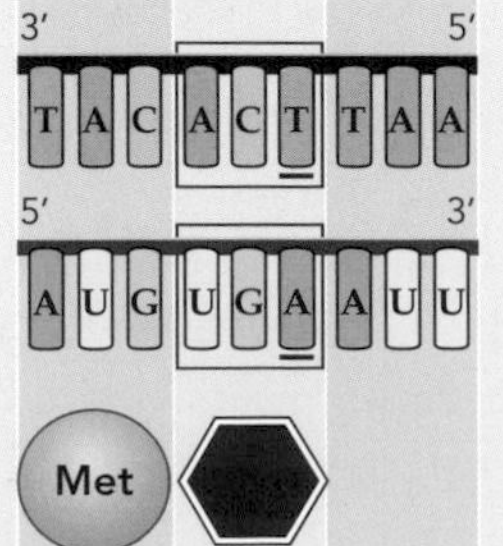

Base substitution - nonsense

A base-pair substitution has occurred, changing A to T on the DNA exon and thus changing U to A on the mRNA. A codon that used to code for cysteine (UGU) is now a stop codon (UGA). This is an example of a nonsense mutation. Transcription of the polypeptide chain ends prematurely, and the resulting protein is usually non-functional.

Mutations at the Level of the Chromosome

Changes at the chromosomal level often have serious consequences for the organism. Structural changes may occur to a chromosome in the form of deletions, duplications, translocations, and inversions. Chromosomal **deletions** occur when a portion of the chromosome breaks off, or when a portion of the chromosome is lost during homologous recombination and/or crossing over events. These topics will be discussed in greater detail later in this lecture. **Duplications** occur when a DNA fragment breaks free of one chromosome and incorporates into a homologous chromosome. **Gene duplication** (also called **gene amplification**) can increase the amount of a gene's product. Deletion or duplication can occur with entire chromosomes (*aneuploidy*) or even entire sets of chromosomes (*polyploidy*).

When a segment of DNA from one chromosome is exchanged for a segment of DNA on another chromosome, the resulting mutation is called a reciprocal **translocation**. In **inversion**, the orientation of a section of DNA is reversed on a chromosome. Translocation and inversion can be caused by transposition. Transposition takes place in both prokaryotic and eukaryotic cells. The DNA segments called **transposable elements** or **transposons** can excise themselves from a chromosome and reinsert themselves at another location. Transposons can contain one gene, several genes, or just a control element. A transposon within a chromosome will be flanked by identical nucleotide sequences. A portion of the flanking sequence is part of the transposon. When moving, the transposon may excise itself from the chromosome and move; copy itself and move; or copy itself and stay, moving the copy. Transposition is one mechanism by which a somatic cell of a multicellular organism can alter its genetic makeup without meiosis.

FIGURE 2.20 Transposons

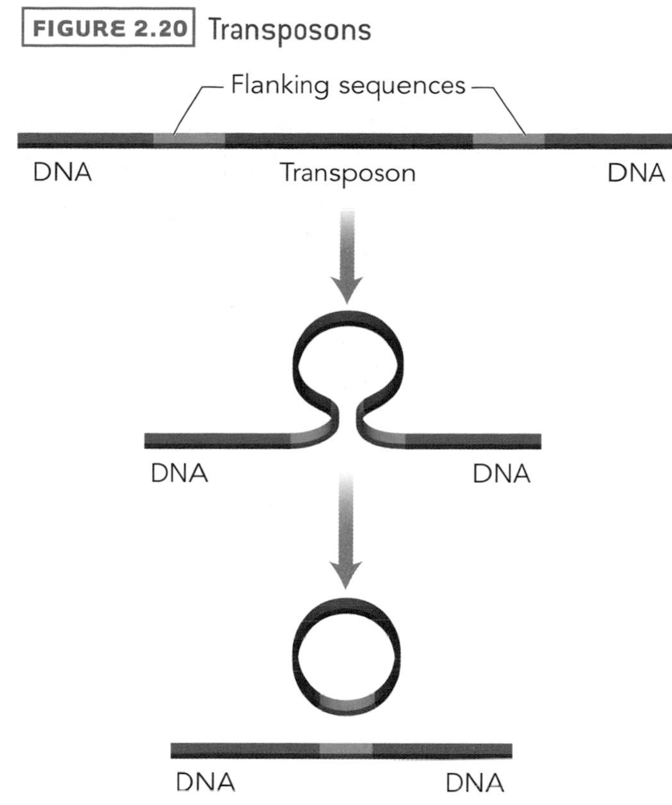

FIGURE 2.21 Mutations at the Level of the Chromosome

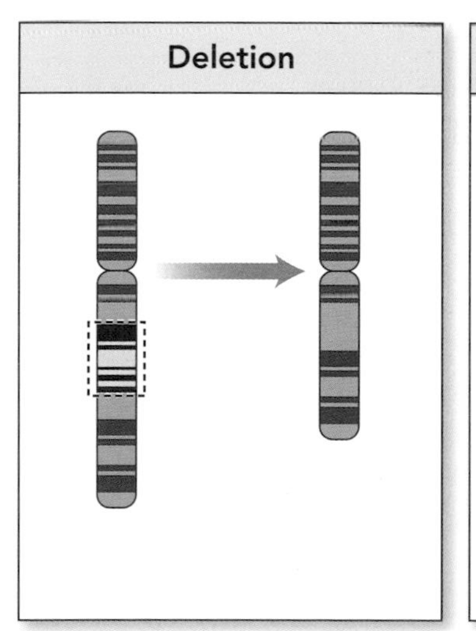

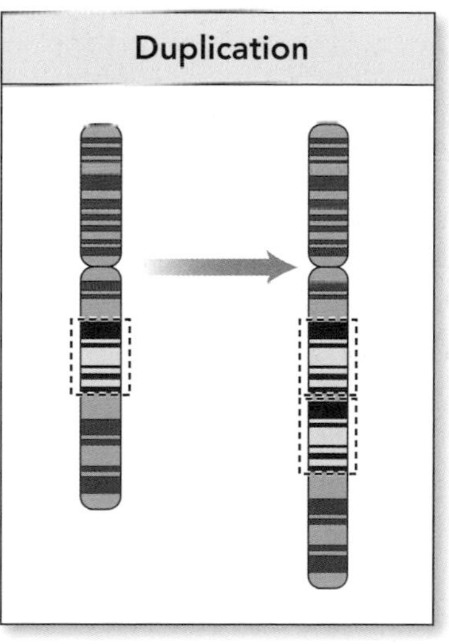

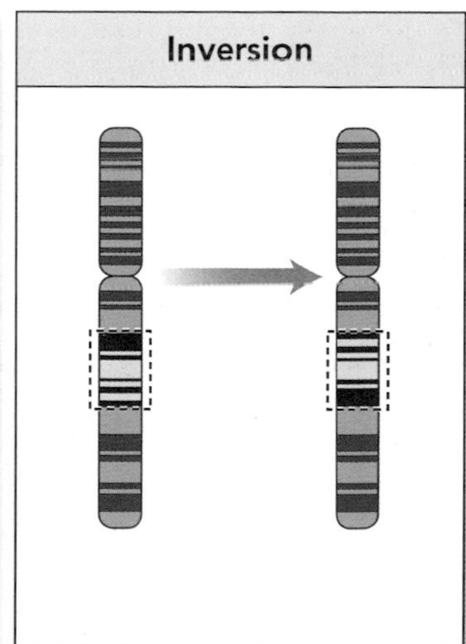

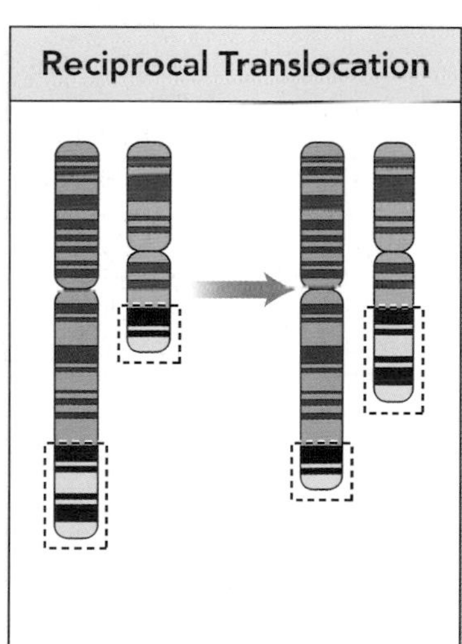

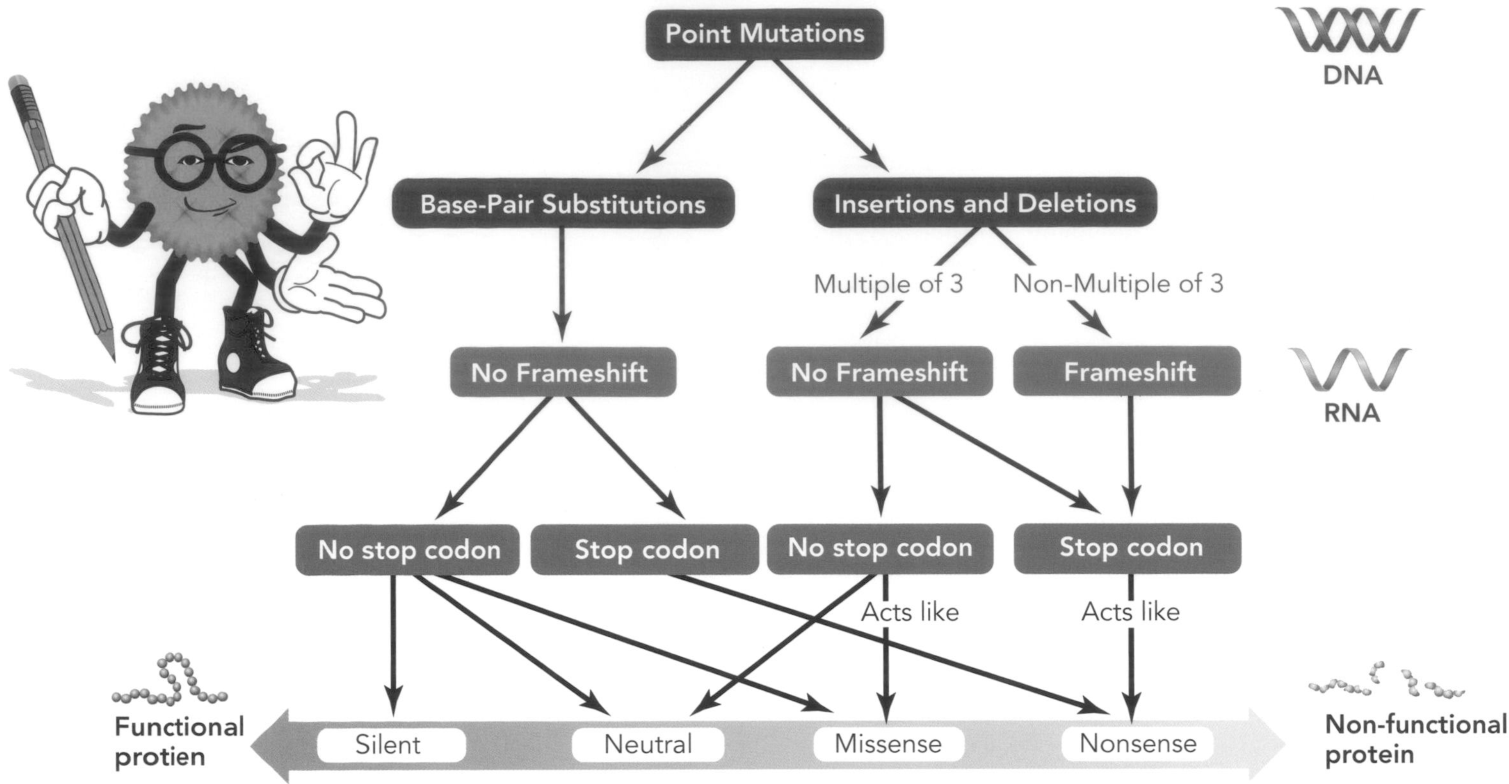

DNA Repair

The cell has several systems in place to repair mutated or damaged DNA. The role of DNA polymerase in correcting mismatched pairs of nucleotides in DNA replication has already been discussed. Damaged portions of DNA may also be altered through direct repair, in which damaged nucleotides are chemically changed back to their original structures, or through excision repair, in which damaged nucleotides are removed and replaced. However, despite the cell's repair mechanisms, damage to DNA can take place and can have serious consequences for cellular function and organismal health.

Cancer

As discussed in the Cell Lecture in *Biology 2: Systems*, cancer is the unrestrained and uncontrolled growth of cells that results when the regulation of the cell cycle has gone awry. However, cancer also has a genetic component that is related to mutation. Certain genes that stimulate normal growth in human cells are called *proto-oncogenes*. Proto-oncogenes can be converted to **oncogenes**, genes that cause cancer, by mutagens such as UV radiation or chemicals, or simply by random mutations. Mutagens that can cause cancer are called **carcinogens**. The genome also contains **tumor suppressor genes** that help regulate normal cell growth. When the normal functions of tumor suppressor genes are inactivated by mutation, cells growth may proceed uncontrolled.

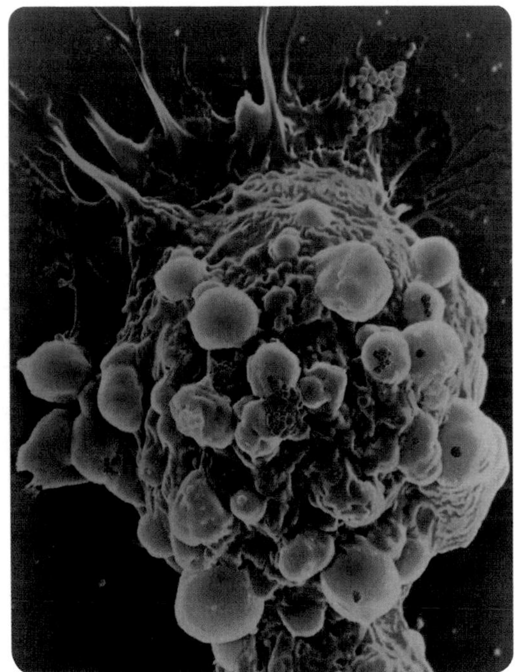

A single breast cancer cell has an uneven surface with blebs (blue) and cytoplasmic projections (red, at left). Clumps of cancerous (malignant) cells form tumors, which possess the ability to invade and destroy surrounding tissues and travel to distant parts of the body to seed secondary tumors. Malignant cells proliferate and grow in a chaotic manner, with defective cell division retained within each new generation of cells. Variations from the original cell type also occur in the size and structure of the cancer cell.

2.9 The Genome and Inheritance: Meiosis

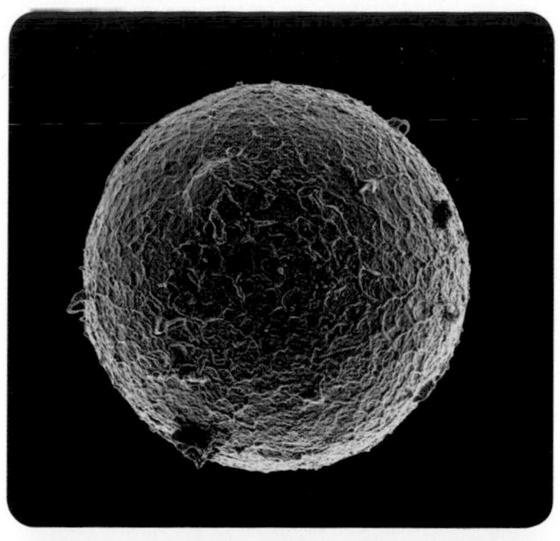

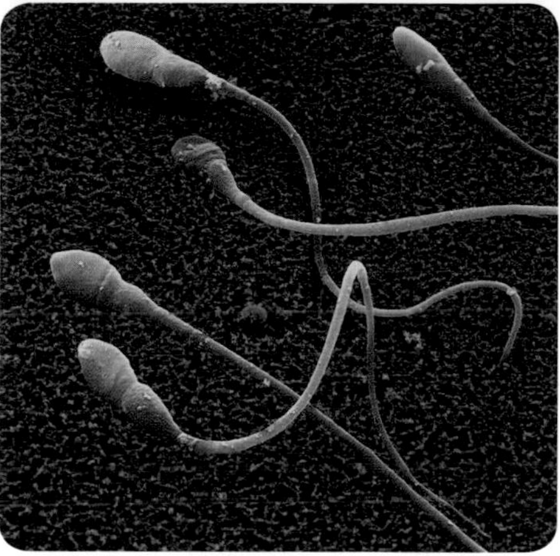

Electron micrographs of sperm and an egg. These two haploid cell types, formed by meiosis, join with each other to form a diploid zygote.

Even before the discovery of the existence of a genome and its role in directing the daily production of cellular products, scientists were aware of the concept of heritability. Certain traits seem to run in families, and children tend to look like their parents. Early experiments using bacterial genomes confirmed that DNA is the genetic material responsible for heritability rather than proteins or other cellular components that were contenders at the time. This section and the one that follows will explore the fundamental role of DNA in passing on traits from one generation to the next, first by examining meiosis, the process by which genetic material is apportioned to the next generation, and then through a review of the principles of inheritance and Mendelian genetics.

The Purpose and Products of Meiosis

Meiosis can be thought of as a special case of mitosis that takes place solely in the reproductive organs. Sexual reproduction takes place when genetic information from two individuals merge to produce offspring. For sexual reproduction to occur, reduction division of the genetic information is needed in order to create haploid reproductive cells, or **gametes**, from diploid parent cells. In humans, only the spermatogonium and the oogonium undergo meiosis. All other cells are somatic cells and undergo mitosis only. Meiosis is an important part of sexual reproduction and occurs only in eukaryotes. This section details the process of meiosis in animals, which is how it is most likely to be seen on the MCAT®.

While meiosis, like mitosis, is a form of cell division, the goals and end products of meiosis are different. The purpose of mitosis is to make exact copies of somatic cells in the body, whereas the purpose of meiosis is to create gametes that are suitable to be paired sexually with another gamete to contribute genetic information to the next generation. During mitosis, a cell undergoes one round of nuclear division to produce two diploid daughter cells, each bearing identical genetic information. In contrast, during meiosis, germ cells undergo two rounds of nuclear division to produce four haploid daughter cells, the gametes, each with a unique genetic makeup. The primary difference in the mechanisms of mitosis and meiosis can be found in metaphase of meiosis I in how the chromosomes align. Regulation of meiosis takes place in much the same way as that of mitosis.

The Mechanism of Meiosis

Cells that will undergo meiosis first go through replication of their chromosomes in the S phase of interphase so that at the beginning of meiosis, the chromosomes are duplicated and diploid. Meiosis consists of two rounds of division called meiosis I and meiosis II. Each round of meiosis consists of successive stages of prophase, metaphase, anaphase, and telophase.

The purpose of **meiosis I** is to separate homologous chromosomes to produce two haploid cells. Therefore meiosis I is known as a reduction division. Meiosis I proceeds similarly to mitosis, with differences described below. **Prophase I** is perhaps the most important stage of meiosis to understand. In prophase I homologous chromosomes line up alongside each other, matching their genes exactly. At this time, they may exchange sequences of DNA nucleotides in a process called **crossing over**. The **genetic recombination** that occurs in eukaryotes during crossing over is of critical importance for providing genetic variation in the genetic makeup of the gametes, and consequently, the offspring. Each of the duplicated chromosome in prophase I appears as an 'X' containing two sister chromatids. Therefore, the side by side homologues exhibit a total of four chromatids, and are called **tetrads** (Greek: tetras → four). If crossing over does occur, the two chromosomes are "zipped" along each other where nucleotides are exchanged, forming what is called the **synaptonemal complex**. Under the light microscope, a synaptonemal complex appears as a single point where the two chromosomes are attached, creating an 'X' shape called a **chiasma** (Greek: chiasmata → cross). When genes on the same chromosome are located close together, they are more likely to cross over together, and are said to be linked. This phenomenon is called **gene linkage**. In areas where crossing over occurs, the chromosomes may exchange sections of genetic information just once in a **single crossover**. Chromosomes may also trade a segment once and then trade back a sub-section of that segment so that each chromosome regains some of its own original genetic material. This phenomenon is called a **double crossover**. Examining the rates of single and double crossovers in a chromosome can indicate how closely two genes are linked and is the basis for the technique of **gene mapping**, which helps determine the locations and relative distances of genes on chromosomes.

In **metaphase I** the two homologues remain attached, and move to the metaphase plate. While in mitosis each chromosome lines up along the plate single file (46 chromosomes lined up in humans), in meiosis, the tetrads align on the metaphase plate (23 tetrads lined up in humans).

In **anaphase I** the homologous chromosomes each separate from their partner, independently assorting to create two haploid cells. This is in contrast to anaphase of mitosis, where identical sister chromatids segregate.

In **telophase I**, a nuclear membrane may or may not reform, and cytokinesis may or may not occur. In humans the nuclear membrane does reform and cytokinesis does occur. When cytokinesis occurs, the new cells are haploid with 23 replicated chromosomes and are called *secondary spermatocytes* or *secondary oocytes*. In the case of the female, one of the oocytes, called the first **polar body**, is much smaller and degenerates. This occurs in order to conserve cytoplasm, which is only contributed to the zygote by the ovum.

FIGURE 2.22 Meiosis

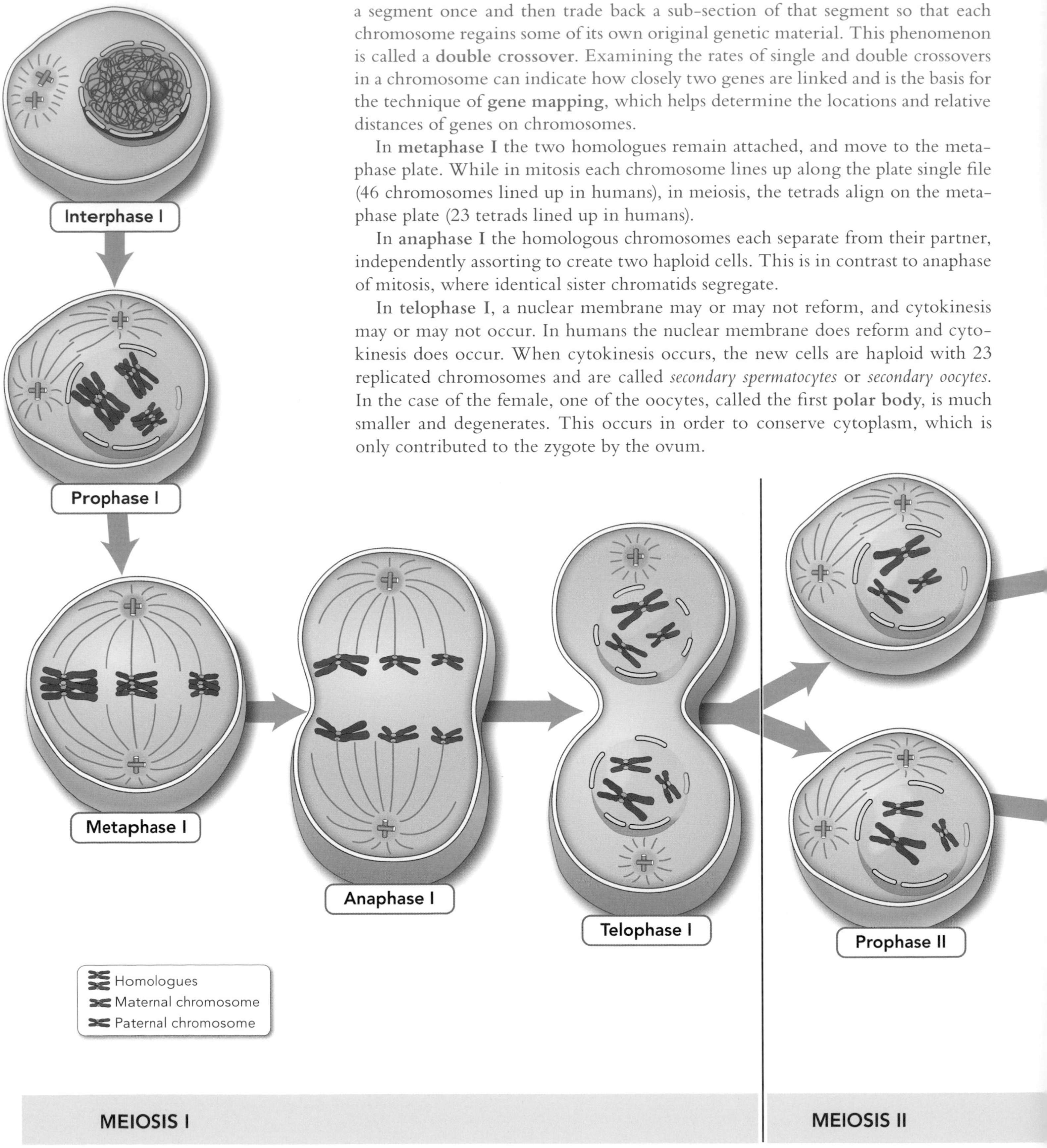

Interphase I

Prophase I

Metaphase I

Anaphase I

Telophase I

Prophase II

Homologues
Maternal chromosome
Paternal chromosome

MEIOSIS I

MEIOSIS II

Meiosis II proceeds through **prophase II**, **metaphase II**, **anaphase II**, and **telophase II**, appearing much like mitosis under the light microscope. The final products are haploid gametes, each with 23 chromosomes. In the case of the spermatocyte, four sperm cells are formed. In the case of the oocyte, a single ovum is formed after the degeneration of the polar bodies. (In the female, telophase II produces one gamete and a second polar body.)

If during anaphase I or II the centromere of any chromosome does not split, this is called **nondisjunction**. As a result of primary nondisjunction (nondisjunction in anaphase I), one of the cells will have two extra chromatids (a complete extra chromosome) and the other will be missing a chromosome. The extra chromosome will typically line up along the metaphase plate and behave normally in meiosis II. Nondisjunction in anaphase II will result in one cell having one extra chromatid and one cell lacking one chromatid. Nondisjunction can also occur in mitosis, but the ramifications are less severe because the genetic information in the new cells is not passed on to every cell in the body. One possible outcome of nondisjunction is having three copies of a single chromosome (a condition known as trisomy), which can have significant effects. For example, Down syndrome is caused by nondisjunction of chromosome 21.

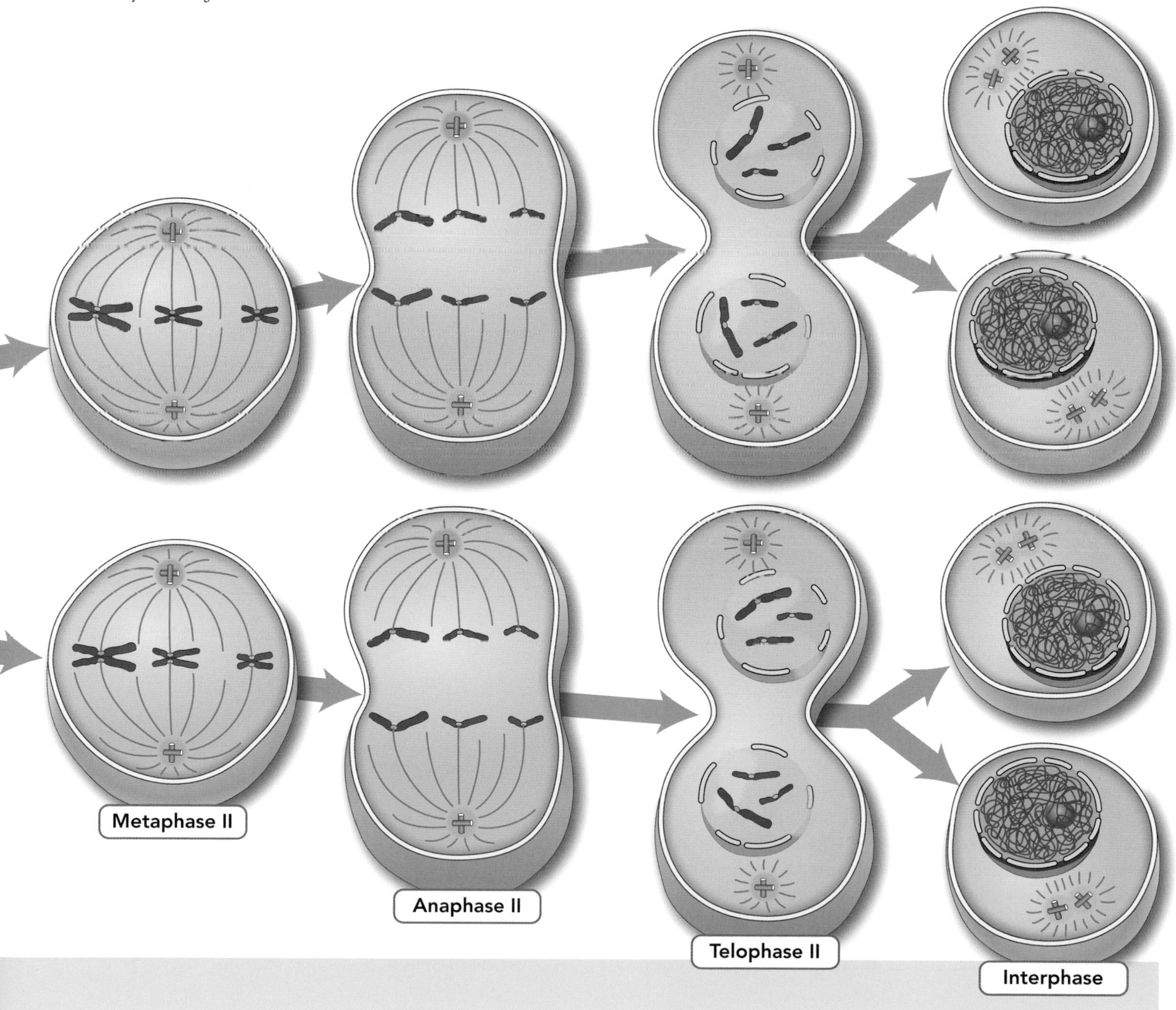

Meiosis as Gamete Production

The purpose of meiosis is to make haploid gametes that can be used in sexual reproduction. The production of gametes, or **gametogenesis**, occurs in several stages. Gametogenesis occurs via similar paths in males and females, with some key differences. The process in males is more straightforward. Once a male reaches sexual maturity, gametogenesis is ongoing, replenishing the body's supply of gametes as needed. In males, the diploid progenitor cells responsible for giving rise to gametes through the process of meiosis are called spermatogonia. A **spermatogonium** undergoes mitosis to produce two diploid copies known as *primary spermatocytes*. Each primary spermatocyte undergoes the reduction division of meiosis

FIGURE 2.23 Gamete Formation

A spermatogonium or oogonium undergoes DNA replication during the S phase of the cell cycle to become a primary spermatocyte or a primary oocyte. Primary spermatocytes and primary oocytes are still diploid, but contain replicated chromosomes with sister chromatids. The figure indicates the presence of sister chromatids with the subscript "s" for diploid primary spermatocytes and oocytes ($2n_s$) and for haploid secondary spermatocytes and oocytes (n_s), which have undergone a reduction division.

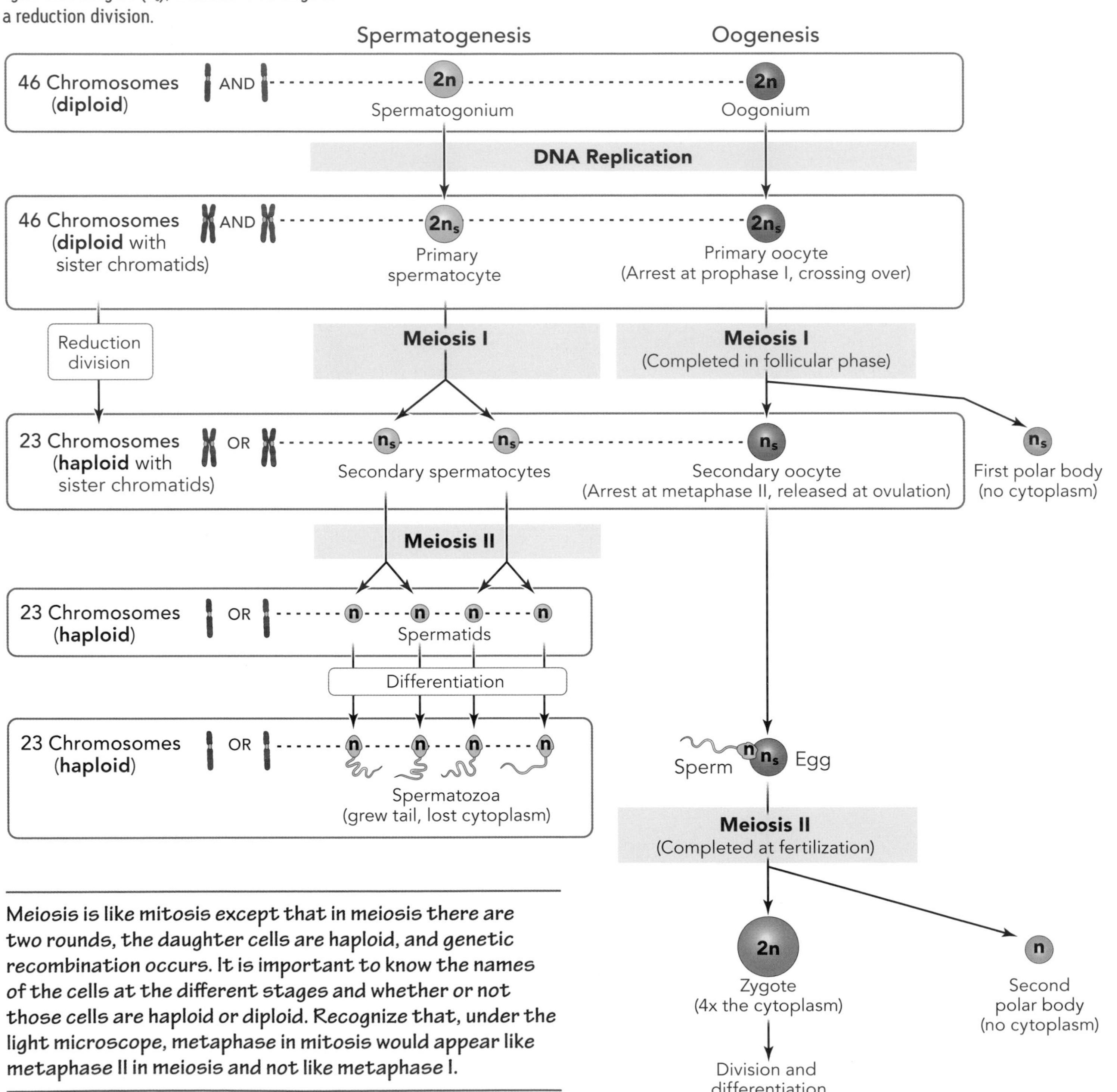

Meiosis is like mitosis except that in meiosis there are two rounds, the daughter cells are haploid, and genetic recombination occurs. It is important to know the names of the cells at the different stages and whether or not those cells are haploid or diploid. Recognize that, under the light microscope, metaphase in mitosis would appear like metaphase II in meiosis and not like metaphase I.

TABLE 2.3 > Stages of Development in Male and Female Gametes

Stages in Males	Stages in Females	Chromosomes	Stage is Reached
Spermatogonium	Oogonium	Diploid	Progenitor cell present at birth
Primary spermatocyte	Primary oocyte	Diploid	After mitosis
Secondary spermatocyte	Secondary oocyte	Haploid	After meiosis I
Spermatid	Ootid*	Haploid	After meiosis II
Sperm (or spermatozoa)	Ovum*	Haploid	After maturation process

* *Technically joined with a sperm by this stage to form a zygote, which is diploid*

I to become two haploid secondary spermatocytes. After the division of meiosis II, each secondary spermatocyte becomes two *spermatids*. A spermatid undergoes a process of maturation in which it loses its cytoplasm and gains a tail to become a mature male gamete known as **sperm**.

There are many parallels between the process of gamete production in males and females. In females, the diploid progenitor cell for gametogenesis is known as the **oogonium**. The oogonium undergoes mitosis to produce two *primary oocytes*. Unlike in males, this step in females primarily takes place before a female is born and the process does not proceed further until the female has reached puberty. Primary oocytes remain arrested in prophase I of meiosis until they receive the hormone signal to participate in the menstrual cycle (see the Endocrine System Lecture in *Biology 2: Systems* for more information on menstruation and ovulation). In preparation for ovulation, a primary oocyte completes meiosis I, producing a secondary oocyte. At this step, again, males and females differ. While meiosis I in males produces two secondary spermatocytes from each primary spermatocyte, the contents of a primary oocyte are not divided evenly among its daughter cells. One daughter cell receives all of the cytoplasm and becomes a secondary oocyte. The other daughter cell, which receives no cytoplasm, is the first polar body and is discarded. The resulting secondary oocyte, now haploid, begins the process of meiosis II but is arrested at the stage of metaphase II. In this arrested state, the secondary oocyte is released from the ovary and travels down the Fallopian tube. The secondary oocyte completes meiosis II only when penetrated by a sperm during the act of fertilization. The penetration of the sperm immediately initiates the completion of meiosis II, dividing the secondary oocyte into a second polar body, which is also discarded, and an ootid, which matures into an **ovum**. The joining of the genetic material of the sperm and the ovum produces a **zygote**.

Note that the process of gametogenesis in males produces four functional gametes (sperm) from each primary spermatocyte. In contrast, each primary oocyte in females results in only one functional ovum (the rest are polar bodies). The reason behind this has to do with conserving cytoplasm. Once an ovum is fertilized, the resulting zygote will need to undergo many rounds of division before it is able to implant on the uterine wall and establish a blood supply. The increased amount of cytoplasm present in an ovum provides the nutrients necessary to sustain a zygote as it becomes a blastula and travels from the Fallopian tube to the uterus. See the Endocrine System Lecture for more on development.

TABLE 2.4 > Summary of Chromosomes and Sister Chromatids

Process	Start	Finish
Replication	Diploid (46 chromosomes)	Diploid with sisters (46 chromosomes, 92 chromatids)
Mitosis	Diploid with sisters (46 chromosomes, 92 chromatids)	Diploid (46 chromosomes)
Meiosis I	Diploid with sisters (46 chromosomes, 92 chromatids)	Haploid with sisters (23 chromosomes, 46 chromatids)
Meiosis II	Haploid with sisters (23 chromosomes, 46 chromatids)	Haploid (23 chromosomes)

If you're having trouble keeping track of chromosome number in replication, mitosis, and meiosis, use this table to review what happens with the number of chromosomes and sister chromatids in each of these processes.

Note that meiosis only describes the process by which nuclear genetic information is passed from one generation to the next. For the MCAT®, know that genetic information can also be passed from organism to organism in other ways. Extranuclear inheritance, which is also called cytoplasmic inheritance (e.g. in the mitochondria and chloroplasts), takes place via its own mechanisms. *Genetic leakage*, the flow of genetic information from one species to another, can also take place under certain conditions.

2.10 The Genome and Inheritance: Mendelian and Population Genetics

Many ideas about the role of genetics in heritability were shaped by the early work of Gregor Mendel. Gregor Mendel was a 19th century monk who performed hybridization experiments using pea plants. The difference between Mendel and those who had come before him was that Mendel quantified his results, carefully counting and recording his findings. Mendel examined a variety of traits that naturally occur in pea plants and examined the heritability of these traits through controlled breeding of the plants. He found that when he crossed purple flowered plants with white flowered plants, the **first filial**, or **F1 generation**, included only purple flowers. He called the purple trait **dominant**, and the white trait **recessive**. Mendel examined seven traits in all, and each trait proved to have dominant and recessive alternatives. When Mendel self-pollinated the F1 generation plants, the F2 generation contained some plants that expressed the dominant trait and some that expressed the recessive trait in a ratio of 3:1 (which is now referred to as the

FIGURE 2.24 Mendelian Ratio: 3 to 1

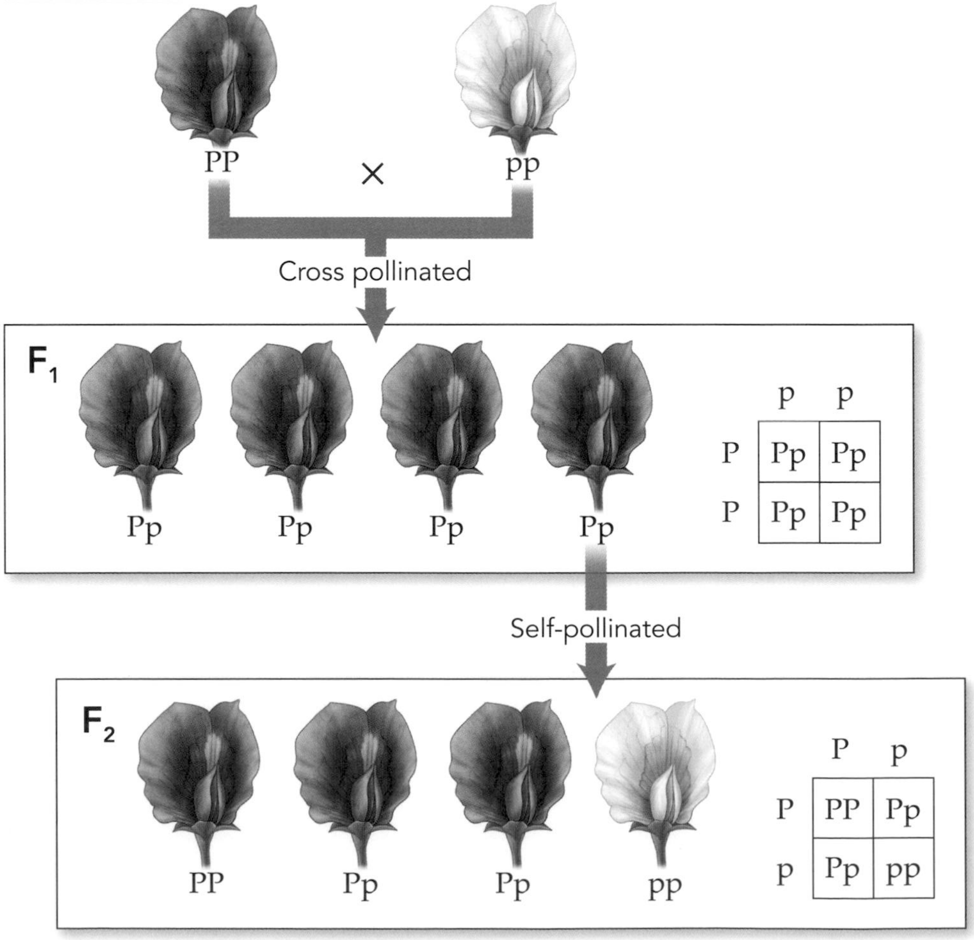

To test his model, Mendel performed a test cross, which is a cross between an unknown genotype and a known, recessive genotype. In his test cross, Mendel crossed the F1 generation of his flowers (purple) with a homozygous recessive parent plant (white). Because there were white offspring resulting from this cross of a purple F1 plant and a white parent plant, Mendel was able to prove that the F1 generation was heterozygous.

Mendelian ratio) (Figure 2.24). When the F2 generation was self-pollinated, 33% of the dominants produced only dominants, and the rest of the dominants produced the Mendelian ratio. The white flowered plants produced only white flowered plants. Mendel used this data to conclude that, even if plants expressed the dominant trait (purple), they might still retain latent information on the recessive trait (white) because they were able to produce white flowered plants in successive generations.

The key to understanding Mendel's experiments is to examine the alleles involved. For any one trait, a diploid individual will have two chromosomes containing separate genes that each code for that trait. These two chromosomes are homologous by definition. Their corresponding genes are located at the same **locus**, or position, on their respective chromosomes. Each gene contributes one **allele**, which codes for a specific outcome in that trait. There may be **single** or **multiple** allele types possible at each locus. For example, one chromosome may carry the allele coding for purple flowers (represented by P), while the other chromosome may carry the allele for white flowers (represented by p). The "normal" or most common allele type for a certain trait within a population is deemed the **wild type** allele. With regard to alleles for a certain trait, an individual's genetic makeup is called a **genotype** while the expression of the trait (i.e. the way the organism actually looks) is called the **phenotype**. In the example given, the possible genotypes are PP, Pp, and pp, while the possible phenotypes are purple and white. The phenotype is expressed through the action of enzymes and other structural proteins, which are encoded by genes. In **complete dominance**, as is the case with Mendel's purple and white flowers, the dominant allele masks expression of the recessive allele. This concept is demonstrated by the outcome that flowers with the genotype Pp appear purple. An individual with a genotype having two dominant (PP) or two recessive (pp) alleles is said to be **homozygous** for that trait. An individual with a genotype having one dominant and one recessive allele (Pp) is said to be **heterozygous** for the trait, and is called a **hybrid**.

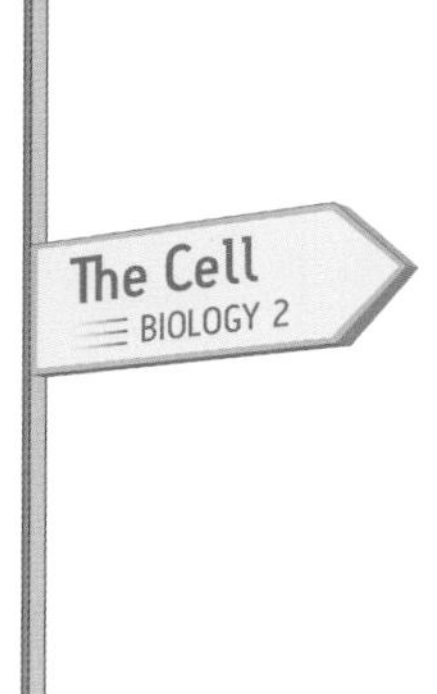

Mendel's First Law of Heredity, the **Law of Segregation**, states that alleles segregate independently of each other when forming gametes during meiosis. Any gamete is equally likely to possess any allele. Also, the phenotypic expression of the alleles is not a blend of the two, but an expression of the dominant allele (the principle of complete dominance).

Penetrance is the term used to refer to the probability of a gene or allele being expressed if it is present. In complete dominance, the penetrance of the dominant allele is 100%. A similar concept is that of **expressivity**, which is a measure of how much the genotype is expressed as a phenotype. Unlike penetrance, which is based on a binary condition (expressed vs. not expressed), expressivity describes the degree of expression of a certain trait. When a heterozygous individual exhibits a phenotype that is intermediate between its homozygous counterparts, the alleles are said to demonstrate **incomplete dominance**. By convention, alleles showing incomplete dominance are represented with the same capital letter, and distinguished with a prime or superscript. For instance, a cross between red flowered sweet peas and white flowered sweet peas may produce pink flowers. The genotype for the pink flowered individual would be expressed as either CC' or C^rC^w. If the heterozygote exhibits both phenotypes, the alleles are **co-dominant**. Human blood type alleles are co-dominant because a heterozygote exhibits A and B antigens on the blood cell membranes.

FIGURE 2.25 Dihybrid Cross

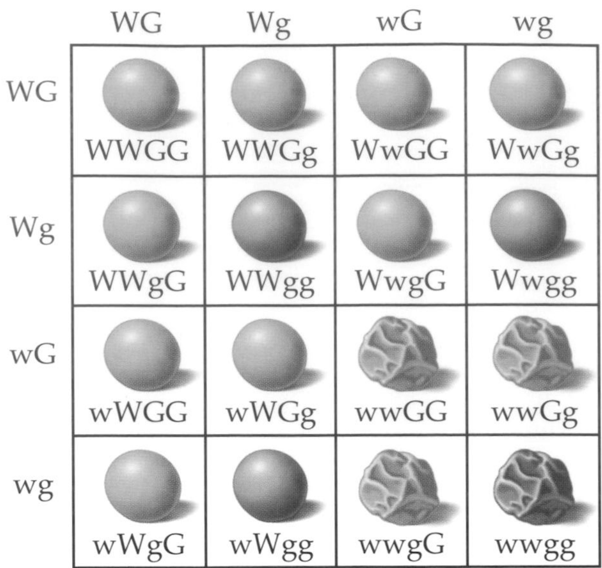

Figure 2.25 shows a helpful tool called a **Punnett square**, used for predicting genotypic ratios of offspring from parent genotypes. The genotypes of all possible gametes of one parent are displayed to the left of the column, and all possible gametes of the second parent are displayed above the first row. The alleles are then combined in the corresponding boxes to show the possible genotypes of the offspring. According to the law of segregation, each gametic genotype is equally likely. Therefore, each offspring genotype is also equally likely.

Mendel's Second Law of Heredity, the **Law of Independent Assortment**, states that genes located on different chromosomes assort independently of each other. In other words, genes that code for different traits (such as pea shape and pea color), when located on different chromosomes, do not affect each other during gamete formation. (Notice that the Law of Independent Assortment discusses different genes that code for different traits, in contrast to the law of Segregation, which instead discusses different alleles of a single gene.) If two genes are located on the same chromosome, the likelihood that they will remain together during gamete formation is indirectly proportional to the distance separating them. Thus, the closer they are on the chromosome, the more likely it is that they will not be separated by genetic recombination and instead will remain together. In Figure 2.25, we use a Punnett square to predict the phenotypic ratio of a **dihybrid cross**. 'W' is the allele for a round pea shape, which is dominant, and 'w' is the allele for wrinkled pea shape, which is recessive. 'G' is the allele for yellow color, which is dominant, and 'g' is the allele for green color, which is recessive. We make the assumption that the genes for pea shape and pea color are on separate chromosomes, and will assort independently of each other. Notice that the **phenotypic ratio of a dihybrid cross is 9:3:3:1**.

The expression of some traits is dependent on the sex of the individual. This is because the chromosomes of males and females differ. In humans, the 23rd pair of chromosomes establishes the sex of the individual, and each partner in the pair is called a **sex chromosome**. Sex chromosomes are designated as either X or Y. Human females usually carry two X chromosomes, while males usually have one X and one Y chromosome. In comparison to the X chromosome, the Y chromosome is greatly abbreviated and contains only a few genes. Genes located on the sex chromosomes are said to be **sex linked**. Generally, the Y chromosome does not carry the allele for the sex-linked trait; thus, the allele that is carried by the X chromosome in the male is expressed whether it is dominant or recessive. Because the female has two X chromosomes, her genotype is found through the normal rules of dominance. However, in most somatic cells, one of the X chromosomes will condense, and most of its genes will become inactive. The tiny dark object formed is called a **Barr body**. Barr bodies are formed at random, so the active allele is split approximately evenly among the cells. Nevertheless, in most cases, the recessive phenotype is only displayed in homozygous recessive individuals. Thus, the female may carry a recessive trait on her 23rd pair of chromosomes without expressing it. If she does, she is said to be a **carrier** for the trait. Such a recessive trait has a strong chance of being expressed in her male offspring regardless of the genotype of her mate.

FIGURE 2.26 Sex-linked Traits

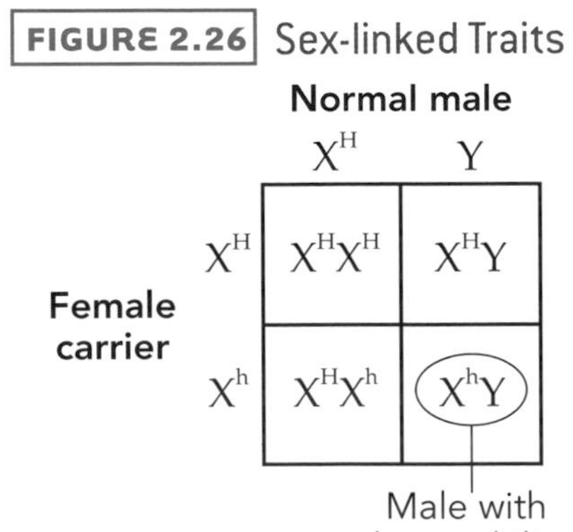

Hemophilia is one example of a sex-linked disease. The Punnett square shown in Figure 2.26 shows a cross between a female carrier for hemophilia and a healthy male. Since there are two possible phenotypes for the males, and one is the recessive phenotype, the male offspring from such a pairing have a 1 in 2 chance of having the disease.

The Hardy-Weinberg Principle

The Hardy-Weinberg Principle is a tool used to predict the probability of offspring genotypes in an entire population. By allowing an understanding of the probability across a population, the Hardy-Weinberg Principle can be an important clinical tool to predict the probability that an individual is a carrier for or will be affected by a certain disease when individual genotypes are unknown.

As discussed in the Cell Lecture in *Biology 2: Systems*, the **gene pool** is the total collection of all alleles in a population, and any change in the gene pool constitutes evolution. Hardy-Weinberg provides a snapshot of a population under the assumption that there is no net change happening in allelic frequencies over time. That theoretical state of suspended evolution is called **Hardy-Weinberg equilibrium.** Recall the conditions that a population must meet to be considered in Hardy-Weinberg equilibrium. They can be thought of as the inverse of the conditions under which evolution will occur.

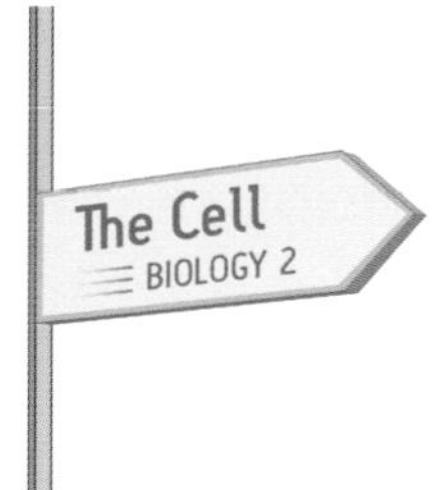

1. No selection for the fittest organism;
2. Random mating;
3. Large population;
4. Immigration or emigration must not change the gene pool; and
5. Mutational equilibrium.

No real population ever ceases to evolve, so no real population possesses these characteristics completely. However, if a population approximates Hardy-Weinberg equilibrium, the following equation can be employed to predict the frequencies of genotypes and phenotypes from allelic frequencies within a population:

$$\mathbf{p^2 + 2pq + q^2 = 1}$$

This equation predicts the genotype frequencies of a gene with only two alleles in a population in Hardy-Weinberg equilibrium. If p represents the frequency of dominant alleles and q represents the frequency of recessive alleles in the population, the first term in the equation (p^2) indicates the fraction of homozygous dominant genotypes in a population (like AA), the second term (2pq) indicates the fraction of heterozygotes (Aa), and the third term (q^2) indicates the fraction of homozygous recessive genotypes in the entire population (aa). The difference between the results here and those of Mendel for AA, Aa, and aa, are as follows: rather than having a 1 in 2 chance of inheriting an allele (A or a) from one of the two parents, as in Mendel's calculation, here the probability corresponds to the proportion of that allele (A or a) in the entire population.

To work through an example of using this equation, assume that 'A' is the dominant allele and 'a' is the recessive allele, and that they are the only alleles for a specific gene. Now imagine that 80% of the alleles are 'A'. This means that 80% of the gametes will be 'A' and 20% will be 'a'. The probability that two 'A's come together is simply $0.8^2 = 0.64$. The probability that two 'a's come together is $0.2^2 = 0.04$. Any remaining zygotes will be heterozygous, leaving 32% heterozygotes, ($2 \times 0.8 \times 0.2 = 0.32$). The fraction of heterozygotes can also be calculated by adding the probabilities of the two gametic combinations that result in heterozygotes – Aa and aA. Using the formula, we represent the frequency of 'A' as p and the frequency of 'a' as q. Because there are only two alleles, $\mathbf{p + q = 1}$.

Answer from page 42:

20 possible amino acids and 100 positions gives 20^{100} possible sequences.

These questions are NOT related to a passage.

Item 41

Which of the following is NOT true concerning DNA replication?

- A) DNA ligase links the Okazaki fragments.
- B) Helicase unwinds the DNA double helix.
- C) Only the sense strand is replicated.
- D) DNA strands are synthesized in the 5′ to 3′ direction.

Item 42

Translation, transcription, and replication take place in which of the following life cycle phases?

- A) G_1
- B) S
- C) G_2
- D) M

Item 43

A scientist monitors the nucleotide sequence of the third chromosome as a cell undergoes normal meiosis. What is the earliest point in meiosis at which the scientist can deduce with certainty the nucleotide sequence of the third chromosome of each gamete?

- A) Prophase I
- B) Metaphase I
- C) Prophase II
- D) Telophase II

Item 44

Radiation therapy is used to treat some forms of cancer by damaging DNA and thus killing the rapidly reproducing cancerous cells. Why might radiation treatment have a greater effect on cancer cells than on normal cells?

- A) Normal cells have more time between S phases to repair damaged DNA.
- B) Damaged DNA is more reactive to radiation.
- C) Cancer cells have lost the ability to repair damaged DNA.
- D) The effect of radiation is the same, but there are more cancer cells than normal cells.

Item 45

When a human female is born, the development of her oocytes is arrested in:

- A) prophase of mitosis.
- B) prophase I of meiosis.
- C) prophase II of meiosis.
- D) interphase.

Item 46

In the pedigree below, the darkened figures indicate an individual with hemophilia, a sex linked recessive disease. The genotype of the female marked A is:

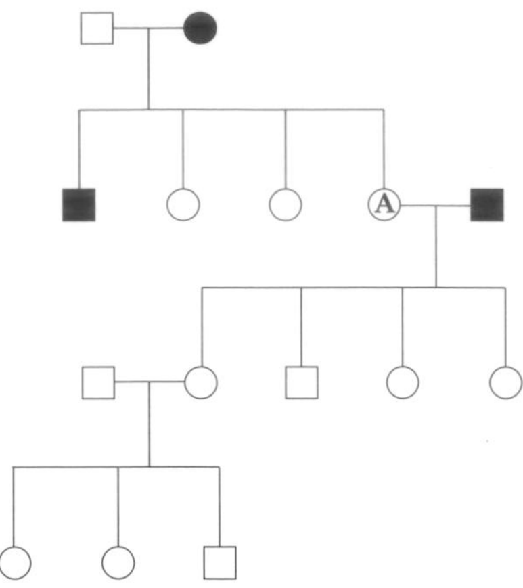

- A) X^HX^h
- B) X^HX^H
- C) X^hX^h
- D) X^hY

Item 47

Sickle cell anemia is an autosomal recessive disease. A male with the disease and a female that is not diseased, but carries the trait, produce two girls. What is the probability that neither girl carries a recessive allele?

- A) 0%
- B) 25%
- C) 50%
- D) 66%

Item 48

If, in a very large population, a certain gene possesses only two alleles and 36% of the population is homozygous dominant, what percentage of the population are heterozygotes?

- A) 16%
- B) 24%
- C) 36%
- D) 48%

EQUATION SUMMARY

Hardy-Weinberg equilibrium $p + q = 1$

$$p^2 + 2pq + q^2 = 1$$

TERMS YOU NEED TO KNOW

5' cap
A site
Activators
Addition mutation
Advantageous mutation
Allele
Alternative splicing
Anaphase
Anaphase I
Anaphase II
Anticodon
Aster
Barr body
Base substitution mutation
Bidirectional replication
Carcinogens
Carrier
Centrioles
Centromeres
Centrosomes
Chiasma
Chromatids
Chromatin
Chromosomal mutation
Chromosomes
Co-dominant
Codon
Complete dominance
Crossing over
Cytokinesis
Degenerative
Deleterious mutation
Deletion mutation
Deletions
Dihybrid cross
Dihybrid cross phenotypic ratio: 9:3:3:1
Diploid
DNA binding proteins
DNA helicase
DNA ligase
DNA methylation
DNA polymerase
Double crossover
DNA replication
Dominant
Duplications
E site
Elongation (in replication and translation)
Euchromatin
Exons
Expressivity
F1 Generation
First filial
Frameshift mutation
Gametes
Gametogenesis
Gene
Gene duplication (gene amplification)
Gene linkage
Gene mapping
Gene mutation
Gene pool
Genetic code
Genetic recombination
Gene repression
Genome
Genotype
Haploid
Hardy-Weinberg equilibrium
Heterochromatin
Heterozygous
Histones
Homologues
Homozygous
Hybrid
Incomplete dominance
Initiation (in replication and translation)
Initiation codon
Initiation complex
Initiation factors
Introns
Inversion
Jacob-Monod model
Kinetochore
Lac operon
Lagging strand
Large subunit
Law of Independent Assortment
Law of Segregation
Locus
Meiosis
Meiosis I
Meiosis II
Mendelian ratio: 3:1
Metaphase
Metaphase I
Metaphase II
Missense codon
Missense mutation
Mitosis
mRNA
Mutagens
Mutation
Non-coding RNA (ncRNA)
Nondisjunction
Nonsense mutation
Nucleolus

TERMS YOU NEED TO KNOW

Nucleosome
Okazaki fragments
Oncogenes
Oogonium
Operon
Origin of replication
Ovum
P site
Penetrance
Phenotype
Point mutation
Polar body
Poly A tail
Positive control
Post-translational modifications
Primary transcript
Primase
Promoter
Prophase
Prophase I
Prophase II
Punnett square
Random errors
Recessive
Release factors
Repetitive DNA
Repressors
Ribosome
Ribozyme
RNA polymerase
RNA primer
rRNA
Semiconservative
Semidiscontinuous
Sex chromosome
Sex linked
Signal peptide
Signal-recognition particle (SRP)
Silent mutation
Single copy DNA
Single crossover
Single or multiple
Small subunit
snRNA
snRNPs
Sperm
Spermatogonium
Spindle apparatus
Spindle microtubules
Splicing
Spliceosome
Stop codon (termination codon, nonsense codon)
Synaptonemal complex
Supercoils
Telomeres
Telophase
Telophase I
Telophase II
Termination (in replication and translation)
Test cross
Tetrads
The Central Dogma
Traits
Transcription
Transcription factors
Translation
Translocation
Transposable elements (transposons)
Triplet code
tRNA
Tumor suppressor genes
Wildtype
Wobble pairing
Zygote

DON'T FORGET YOUR KEYS

1. DNA is potential; RNA is regulation; protein is action.
2. Location matters – nucleus or cytoplasm?
3. See mitosis, think replication; see meiosis, think reproduction.

Metabolism

LECTURE 3

THE 3 KEYS

1. Metabolic pathways move toward either the storage or production of energy.
2. Blood glucose levels regulate systemic and intracellular pathways.
3. NADH and ATP are the cell's energy molecules.

3.1 Introduction

Organisms consume nutrients to satisfy their need for energy. Because food is not always readily available or constantly consumed, organisms must regulate the storage and use of energy so that they do not run out. When a cell uses a molecule for energy, it generally tries to turn it into acetyl-CoA or other Krebs cycle intermediates, which are then used to create ATP, the cell's primary energy molecule. When a cell stores a molecule, it polymerizes multiple monomers of the same kind, condensing their size and thus making it more convenient to store. Examples of this process include glycogenesis and fatty acid storage.

While some tissues can produce energy from a variety of molecules, other tissues rely almost exclusively on glucose to function. Because of this demand, it is the blood glucose level that regulates both intracellular and systemic pathways. This control comes from the hormones insulin and glucagon, which promote the storage and use of blood glucose, respectively. When a meal has been eaten recently, insulin directs tissues to use and store glucose that was absorbed in the intestines. When the body is in a fasting state, glucagon directs the liver to release glucose it has previously stored for use by other organs. The liver does not have enough glucose to supply the entire body, so other sources of energy such as fatty acids help to spare glucose for the brain and red blood cells, which depend on glucose.

The food humans consume contains energy from a number of sources, including carbohydrates, lipids, and proteins. To make this energy available to the cell, energy is stored in compounds such as NADH and ATP. NADH stores energy in the high-energy electrons of a hydride ion, and ATP stores it in high-energy phosphate bonds. NADH is primarily produced in the citric acid cycle and converted to ATP via the electron transport chain. The citric acid cycle and the electron transport chain make up a common final pathway of metabolism – the breakdown of many molecules leads here, where they are ultimately converted into ATP and carbon dioxide.

3.2 Use Versus Storage

The first part of this lecture focuses on the directionality of metabolic pathways toward either the use or storage of a molecule. Metabolic pathways proceed in one direction to store extra energy molecules after a meal if they are not immediately needed. Through the reversal of the same pathways, the stored energy molecules can be released many hours after a meal, when the intestines are empty of food.

The most important energy molecules on the MCAT® are carbohydrates and lipids. Proteins can also provide energy for the body, but this is mostly outside the scope of the MCAT®. Carbohydrates are stored primarily in the muscle and liver as glycogen. This storage process is called glycogenesis. Carbohydrates can be taken out of storage and broken down for energy. Processes that use carbohydrates include the breakdown of glycogen, or glycogenolysis, and the breakdown of glucose, or glycolysis.

Lipids, in the form of fatty acids, undergo roughly the same processes. They are primarily stored in adipocytes, or fat cells, in the form of triglycerides. They are also taken out of storage and broken down for energy. The chemical breakdown of a fatty acid is called beta-oxidation.

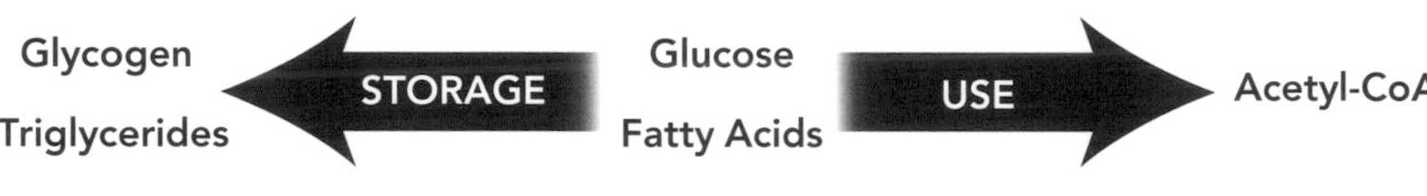

FIGURE 3.1 Use Versus Storage

Molecules have two metabolic fates: storage and use. Molecules can be brought out of storage and used to synthesize new molecules.

3.3 Glucose Metabolism

Use of Glucose

After a meal, the body uses newly absorbed glucose to satisfy its energy needs. The first step in this process is **glycolysis**, the breakdown of glucose into pyruvate. In this respect, glycolysis is a "use" pathway. Specifically, it describes the acquisition and use of glucose within a single cell. At the end of glycolysis, pyruvate can be turned into acetyl-CoA, which enters the citric acid cycle and the electron transport chain. A number of pathways feed into the citric acid cycle and electron transport chain. These final two pathways will be examined later in the lecture.

Glycolysis has traditionally been tested in some detail on the MCAT®.

Glycolysis is a series of reactions that converts a 6-carbon glucose molecule into two 3-carbon molecules of **pyruvate.** All living cells and organisms are capable of breaking down glucose to pyruvate; glycolysis is the most common chemical pathway for this process. Glycolysis is a particularly important metabolic pathway because it can occur with or without the presence of oxygen (**aerobic** or **anaerobic** conditions). Glycolysis occurs in the **cytosol** (fluid portion) of living cells.

The ten steps of glycolysis can be split into two equal halves. In the first half, two phosphate groups from two different ATP molecules are added to glucose. These phosphate groups are bulky and charged, and thus trap glucose inside the cell. They also prime the glucose, allowing the 6-carbon glucose to be split into two 3-carbon molecules (glycerol 3-phosphate and dihydroxyacetone phosphate). The first step of the first half of glycolysis occurs upon the entry of glucose into any human cell. Because this half requires the use of ATP, it is called the *energy input phase*. It is also called the *six carbon phase* because it is before glucose is split.

In the second half of glycolysis, the two newly created 3-carbon molecules are each converted to pyruvate. Through this process, two ATP are produced per 3-carbon molecule (four ATP total). In addition, one NADH is generated from NAD^+ per molecule (two NADH total). Because energy molecules are created in the second half of glycolysis, it is called the *energy output phase*. It is also called the *three carbon phase* because it is after the split of glucose. The net product of glycoly-

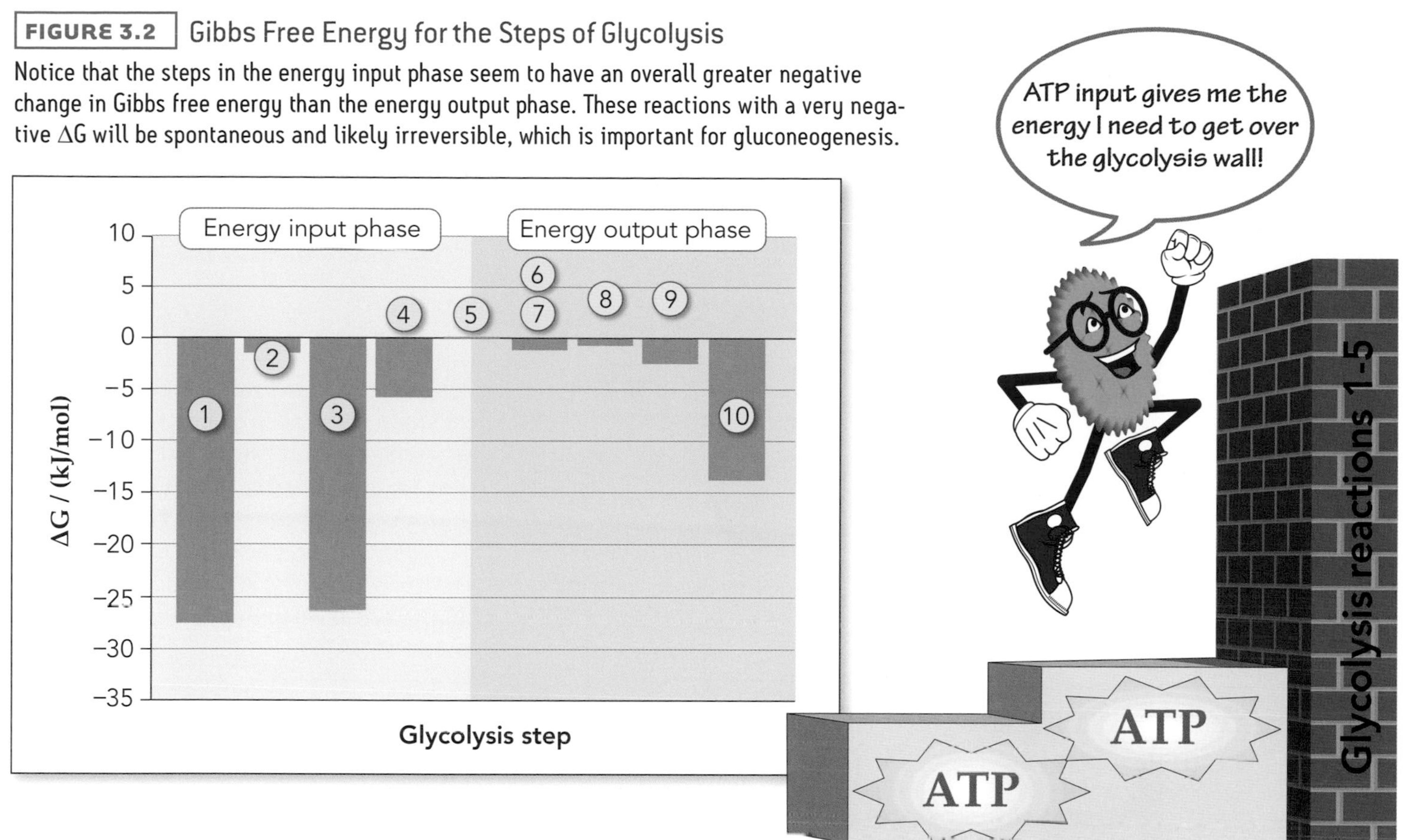

FIGURE 3.2 Gibbs Free Energy for the Steps of Glycolysis

Notice that the steps in the energy input phase seem to have an overall greater negative change in Gibbs free energy than the energy output phase. These reactions with a very negative ΔG will be spontaneous and likely irreversible, which is important for gluconeogenesis.

sis for each glucose molecule is two ATP and two NADH. The actual molecular steps of glycolysis can be seen in Figure 3.3.

The production of ATP in glycolysis is somewhat unusual. Most ATP in the cell is produced by the electron transport chain. The production of ATP by the transfer of a phosphate molecule from a molecule to an ADP, as in glycolysis, is called **substrate-level phosphorylation**.

The substrates of glycolysis include more than just glucose. Other monosaccharides such as fructose and galactose feed into glycolysis as well. Much of the fructose and galactose ingested by humans is converted into glucose by the liver; however, a fructose or galactose molecule can enter glycolysis as an intermediate of the six carbon phase.

Fermentation describes metabolism in the absence of oxygen; in other words, it is glucose undergoing anaerobic respiration. This process includes glycolysis as well as the reduction of pyruvate to ethanol or lactic acid and the oxidation of NADH back to NAD^+. Yeast and some microorganisms produce ethanol in fermentation, while human muscle cells and other microorganisms produce lactic acid. During fermentation, NAD^+ is restored from NADH for use in glycolysis, and the lactic acid or ethanol, along with carbon dioxide, is expelled from the cell as a waste product. Fermentation is not an optimal process, producing only 2 ATP per glucose molecule. By contrast, the Krebs cycle can produce as many as 36 ATP from one molecule of glucose, as discussed later in this lecture. However, without the regeneration of NAD^+ from NADH, ATP could not be generated at all.

There is also an alternative pathway to glycolysis – the **pentose phosphate pathway (PPP)**. This pathway diverges from glycolysis and eventually merges back with glycolysis at glyceraldehyde-3-phosphate (abbreviated as PGAL or G3P). Its purpose is to create NADPH and some five carbon sugars, including ribose. The first half of the pathway, referred to as the oxidative branch, generates NADPH. NADPH is used in various synthetic functions of the body, such as making cholesterol, and also acts as an antioxidant. The second, referred to as the

MCAT® THINK

We normally think about glycolysis as running forward, from glucose to pyruvate. Would glycolysis ever run backward? Under what conditions would this happen? (See answer on p. 88.)

FIGURE 3.3 Glycolysis

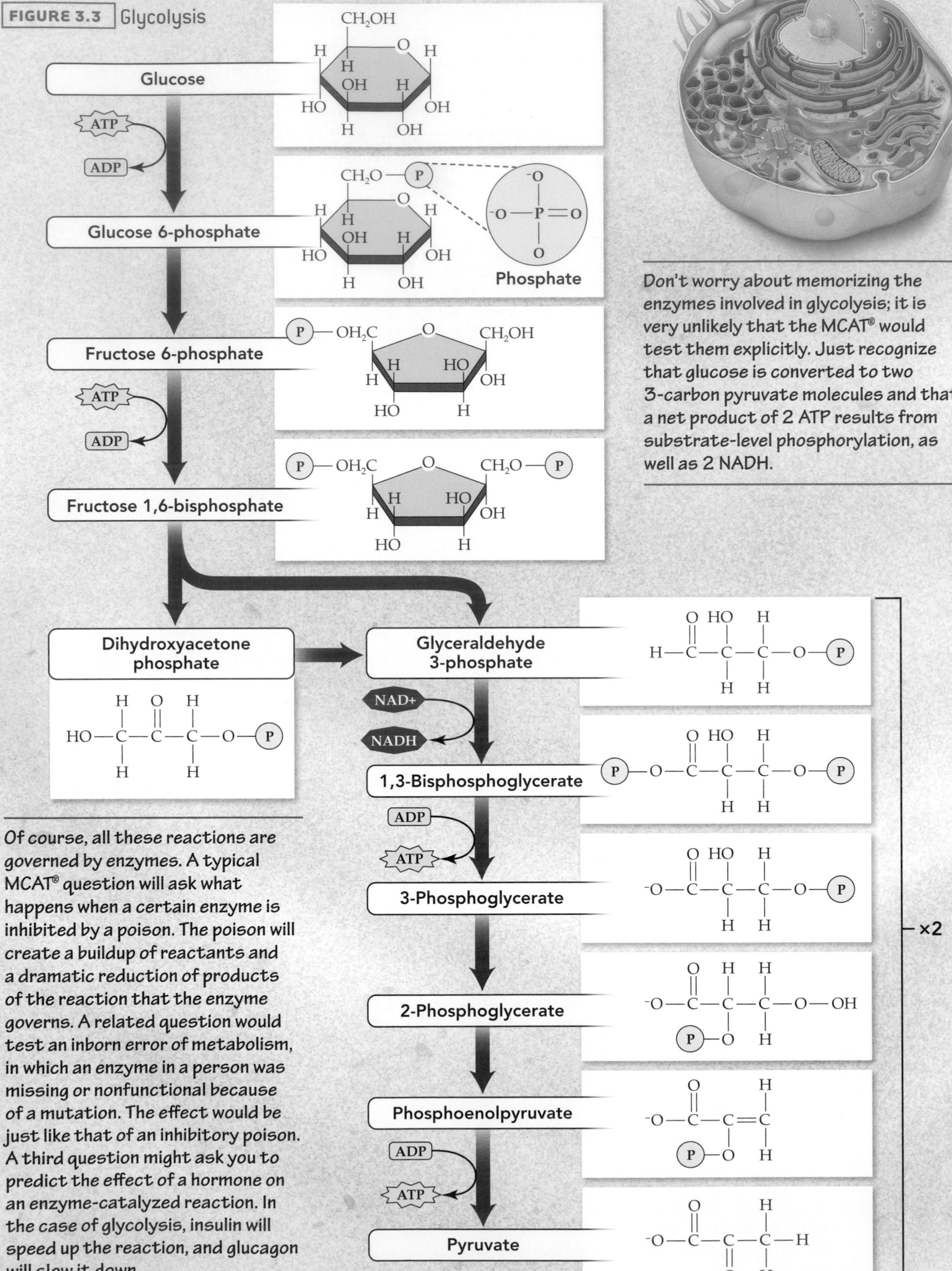

Don't worry about memorizing the enzymes involved in glycolysis; it is very unlikely that the MCAT® would test them explicitly. Just recognize that glucose is converted to two 3-carbon pyruvate molecules and that a net product of 2 ATP results from substrate-level phosphorylation, as well as 2 NADH.

Of course, all these reactions are governed by enzymes. A typical MCAT® question will ask what happens when a certain enzyme is inhibited by a poison. The poison will create a buildup of reactants and a dramatic reduction of products of the reaction that the enzyme governs. A related question would test an inborn error of metabolism, in which an enzyme in a person was missing or nonfunctional because of a mutation. The effect would be just like that of an inhibitory poison. A third question might ask you to predict the effect of a hormone on an enzyme-catalyzed reaction. In the case of glycolysis, insulin will speed up the reaction, and glucagon will slow it down.

non-oxidative branch, creates important five carbon sugars for the cell, like ribose for nucleotides. The pathway is constitutively active, or active at all times. While it occurs to some extent in all tissues, it occurs most commonly in tissues involved in lipid synthesis, such as in the liver and adipocytes. The pentose phosphate pathway is not regulated by an external hormone, but rather by NADPH, which inhibits the first step.

Storage and Release of Glucose

Glucose has the potential to be used by all cells via glycolysis. Some types of cells, such as muscle and liver cells, can also store glucose as glycogen for later use. Muscle cells store glucose for their own use. Liver cells store glucose so that they can later release it for use by other cells. The storage of glycogen is called **glycogenesis**, while the breakdown of glycogen is called **glycogenolysis**. Liver cells also have the unique property of being able to synthesize glucose from non-carbohydrate products, such as proteins and lactic acid, in a process called **gluconeogenesis**. Glucose produced by gluconeogenesis is also released for use by other cells.

Glycogen is a polymer of glucose molecules linked by α–1,4' glycosidic bonds. The primary substrate for glycogenesis is glucose 6-phosphate, the product of the first step of glycolysis. Glycogen synthesis uses one UTP, which is a triphosphate nucleotide that is energetically equivalent to ATP. Glycogenolysis does not require ATP. Instead an inorganic phosphate is enzymatically added to each α–1,4' bound glucose. Glycogen has occasional α–1,6' glycosidic bonds that create side chains. The metabolism of these side branches is more complicated, but is unlikely to be tested on the MCAT®.

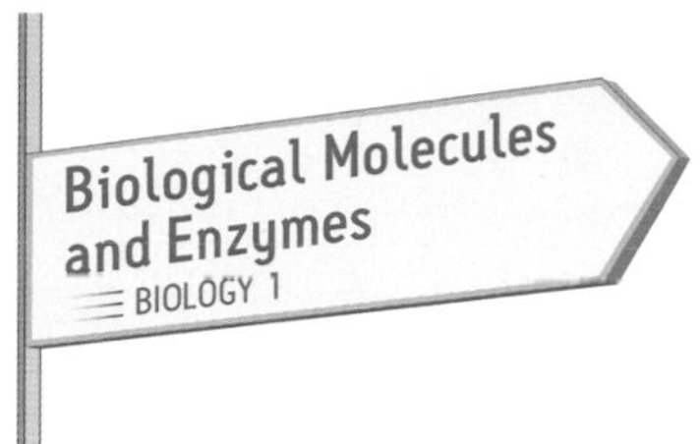

Synthesis of Glucose

In the fasting state, soon after glycogen breakdown begins, the liver begins the process of gluconeogenesis, synthesizing new glucose molecules out of materials that are not necessarily carbohydrates. Gluconeogenesis is important because it takes products that would otherwise be useless, such as lactic acid, and turns them into glucose. Gluconeogenesis, in conjunction with glycogenolysis, helps to maintain the blood glucose level many hours after a meal has been eaten. The pathway of gluconeogenesis is almost identical to the reversed pathway of glycolysis. Recall that enzymes catalyze both the forward and the backward reactions. A few of the reactions of gluconeogenesis with particularly large ΔG values have enzymes that are distinct from those of glycolysis. Gluconeogenesis produces free glucose that can be used by other organs.

To be a substrate for gluconeogenesis, the molecule must have a 3-carbon backbone. For example, fatty acids are catabolized two carbons at a time into acetyl-CoA, and therefore cannot act as substrates for gluconeogenesis. In contrast, glycerol, the three carbon backbone of a triglyceride, does have a three-carbon backbone and can be used for gluconeogenesis. Some, but not all, amino acids can be used for gluconeogenesis as well. Lactic acid can also be used as starting material for gluconeogenesis.

You can recognize the steps that have large ΔG values because they usually involve either ATP or NADH. If the MCAT® asks you to predict which reaction has the largest ΔG, or which would need a distinct enzyme to run in the reverse direction, you should pick the step that involves ATP or NADH.

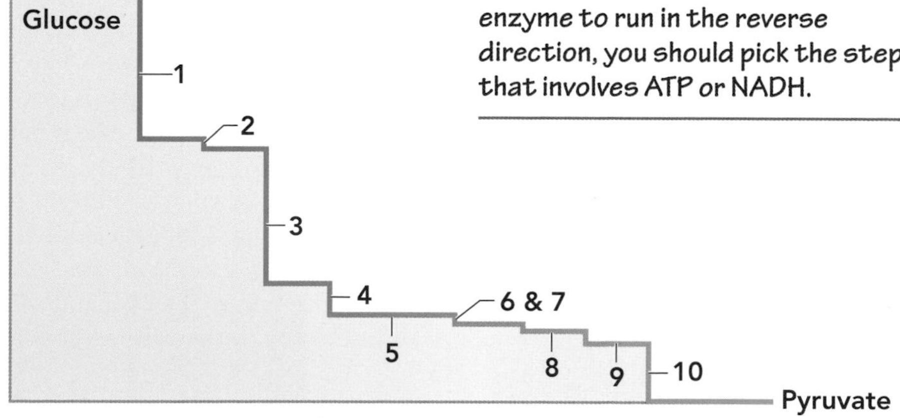

FIGURE 3.4 Glycolysis "Waterfall"

Each number represents the ΔG *in vivo* of a reaction of glycolysis. The steps with the largest ΔG are the primary control points of the pathway and therefore are not easily reversible. Notice these are also the reactions that involve ATP. Because the other reactions have relatively small ΔG values, they are more easily reversible, and their products and reactants are kept in a relatively constant proportion called a **dynamic steady state**.

Glycolysis and gluconeogenesis, like glycogenesis and glycogenolysis, are competing processes that are regulated by competing hormones. Prominent hormones for these reactions include insulin and glucagon. Like all hormones, their effects are widespread and diverse. In general, insulin promotes glycolysis and glycogenesis (decreasing glucose), while glucagon promotes gluconeogenesis and glycogenolysis (increasing glucose). Some exceptions to this rule will be discussed later.

All of these pathways – glycolysis, gluconeogenesis, glycogenesis, and glycogenolysis – intersect at a molecule called *glucose 6-phosphate*. For example, glucose 6-phosphate may be converted to *glucose 1-phosphate* and then to glycogen for storage if glucose is plentiful. If glucose 6-phosphate follows the glycolytic pathway, it is converted to *fructose 6-phosphate* in the second step of glycolysis.

FIGURE 3.5 Central Role of Glucose 6-Phosphate

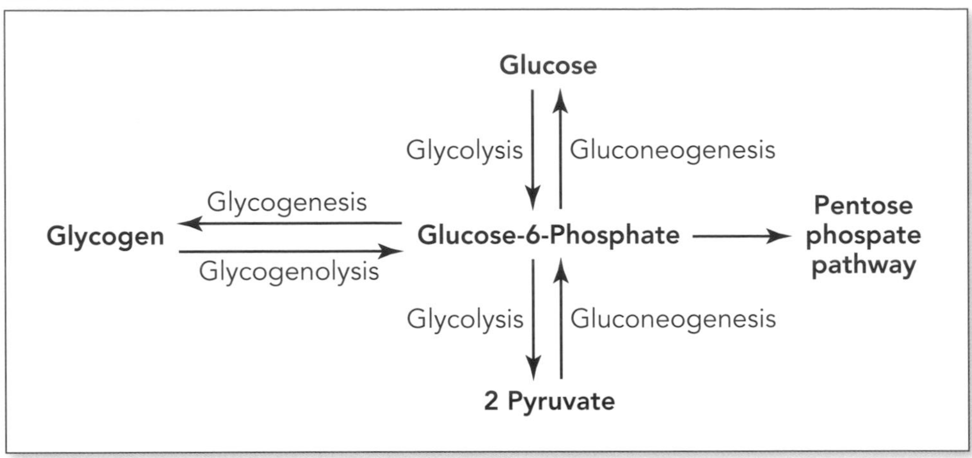

3.4 Fatty Acid Metabolism

Use of Fatty Acids

There are many types of lipids, as discussed in Lecture 1 of this manual. As far as metabolism is concerned, the MCAT® primarily tests fatty acids and triglycerides. These molecules store energy for the body. Because they contain long chains of alkanes, they are the most potent reducing agents in the body. Carbohydrates have alcohol groups that decrease the reducing potential of the carbons to which they are attached by partially oxidizing them. A similar comparison can be made between **saturated** and **unsaturated fats**. Because unsaturated fats have two fewer electrons for every double bond present, their reducing potential is decreased. Thus, unsaturated fats store less energy, measured as calories, in the body. This is part of the basis of recommendations to include more unsaturated fats in the diet than saturated fats. For a review of oxidizing and reducing agents, see the Solutions and Electrochemistry Lecture in the *Chemistry Manual.*

Fatty acids can be used in two different ways in the body. First, they can be used directly by the organ into which they diffuse. They are broken down into acetyl-CoA in a process called **beta-oxidation**. Second, in the liver, they can be converted into a new molecule, called a ketone body, which can be shared with other organs for energy. This process is called **ketogenesis**.

In the fasting state, beta-oxidation begins at about the same time that gluconeogenesis begins. Fatty acids are freed from adipocytes and travel in the bloodstream via lipoproteins to the liver and any other organs that can use them. The fatty acids diffuse through the cell membrane and enter into the mitochondria, where they

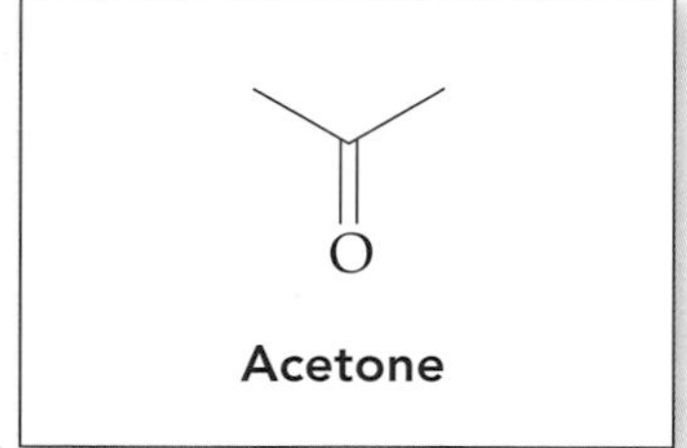

Acetone

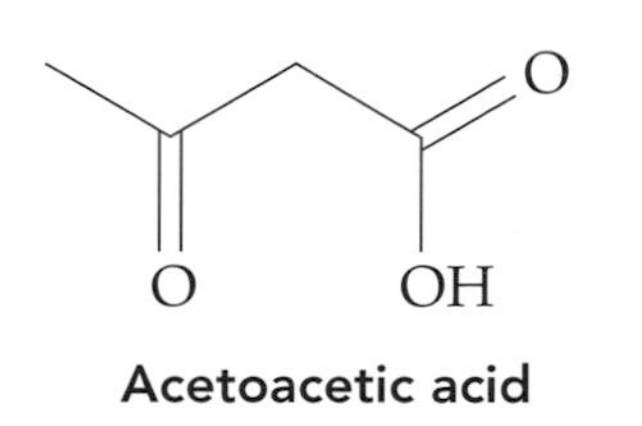

Acetoacetic acid

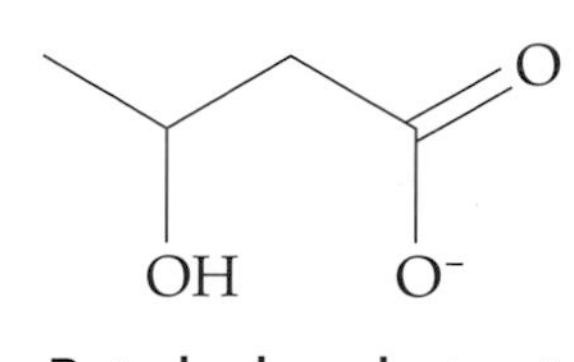

Beta-hydroxybutyrate

begin to undergo beta-oxidation. The process is called beta-oxidation because fatty acids are oxidized two carbons at a time.

Beta-oxidation occurs in two steps. Fatty acids are first converted into *acyl-CoA,* at the expense of 1 ATP, along the outer membrane of the mitochondrion. The acyl-CoA is then brought into the mitochondrial matrix, where it is cleaved two carbons at a time to make acetyl-CoA. This reaction also produces $FADH_2$ and NADH for every two carbons taken from the original fatty acid. Acetyl-CoA then enters into the citric acid cycle. The glycerol backbone of the triglyceride is converted into an intermediate of glycolysis.

Beta-oxidation works well for even-chain fatty acids, but odd-chain fatty acids end with a three carbon fatty acid. This three carbon molecule, as well as glycerol, can act as a substrate for gluconeogenesis. Because the single three carbon fatty acid makes up just a small fraction of any triglyceride molecule, it is occasionally said that lipids do not serve as a substrate for gluconeogenesis, even though that is not strictly true.

In addition to directly providing energy to cells via beta-oxidation, fatty acids can provide energy indirectly through **ketone bodies** produced by ketogenesis. There are three primary ketone bodies produced in humans: acetone, acetoacetic acid, and beta-hydroxybutyrate. Each of these is a small molecule with a carbonyl group. The carbonyl allows them to dissolve in the blood stream via hydrogen bonding, while also not adding charge, which would make crossing the cell membrane difficult. The biological purpose of ketone bodies is to spare glucose for the brain and red blood cells by providing an alternative source of energy for the other organs. However, if needed, the brain can use ketone bodies to supply a portion of its energy.

Ketogenesis takes place in the mitochondria of liver cells. The process is similar to gluconeogenesis, in that a substrate (fatty acid) enters the liver and is processed into a new molecule (ketone body) that can be sent to other organs. However, ketone bodies are *not* substrates for gluconeogenesis. During starvation, energy for the liver comes from fatty acids. In fact, fatty acids supply so much acetyl-CoA that the liver cannot use all of it. In the absence of insulin, some of the acetyl-CoA is converted to ketone bodies, which can travel to other organs, where they are converted back into acetyl-CoA and fed into the citric acid cycle.

The acetone produced in ketone body formation is the same acetone you might use as a solvent in organic chemistry labs or when removing fingernail polish. It smells fruity, and you can smell this on the breath of a person who is producing ketone bodies. Beta-hydroxybutyrate is not actually a ketone, but rather a carboxylic acid. For the purposes of biology and biochemistry, it is still called a ketone body.

Link gluconeogenesis, glycogenolysis, and beta-oxidation together in your mind as the processes that happen a few hours after you eat. In cases of extreme starvation, think of ketogenesis as well.

Storage and Release of Fatty Acids

Lipids are insoluble in the bloodstream, so they are transported in association with proteins. The entire complex of lipid and protein is known as a **lipoprotein**. Lipoproteins are produced primarily in the liver, intestines, and adipocytes, and are expelled from these cells via exocytosis. The intestines produce a special type of lipoprotein called a chylomicron, which contains a higher ratio of lipid to protein. Lipoproteins are the primary transport molecules that carry lipids from the intestines to the liver. The liver, in turn, repackages chylomi-

crons as *very low density lipoproteins (VLDL)* and *high density lipoproteins (HDL)*. VLDL transport lipids such as triglycerides, phospholipids, and cholesterol from the liver to other parts of the body, such as muscle and adipocytes. HDL, in contrast, picks up stray fatty acids and triglycerides from the periphery and brings them to the liver.

The liver also has the ability to generate fatty acids out of materials that are not lipids. After a meal full of carbohydrates, the excess of sugar produces too much acetyl-CoA for the liver to use. In the presence of insulin, the excess acetyl-CoA is converted into fatty acids in the cytosol. This process is in contrast to ketogenesis, which also begins with excess acetyl-CoA in the liver, but is associated with low insulin levels and takes place in the mitochondria.

Lipids are stored inside adipocytes as triglycerides. Triglycerides organize fatty acids in a condensed, organized way, just as glycogen organizes glucose molecules. Immediately after a meal, lipids are transported by VLDL to adipocytes and stored for future use. In a fasting state (around the time of gluconeogenesis), triglycerides are broken down in the cell by lipase. **Lipase** is an enzyme that hydrolyzes triglycerides and releases free fatty acids into the bloodstream. This lipase is very similar to the lipase that breaks down triglycerides in the intestines. The fatty acids released are then taken around the body to various tissues that use them for beta-oxidation. In times of extreme starvation, the body will also turn fatty acids into ketone bodies in the liver.

Intestinal lipase tries to get triglycerides into cells. Hormone sensitive lipase tries to get triglycerides out of cells.

FIGURE 3.6 Central Role of Acetyl-CoA

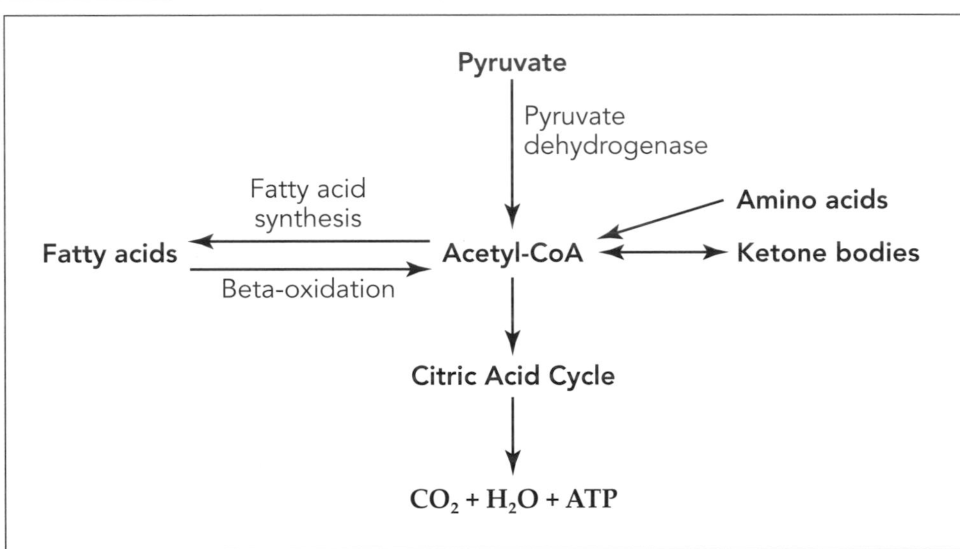

Link glycolysis, glycogenesis, and triglyceride storage together in your mind as defining the fed state. Glucose is used by all tissues for immediate energy needs, and any extra glucose and other high energy molecules are put into storage.

3.5 Protein Metabolism

Protein and amino acid metabolism includes protein formation and protein breakdown. Protein formation, or protein **anabolism**, occurs primarily during the fed state and should be associated with glycolysis, glycogenesis, and lipid storage. Protein breakdown, or protein **catabolism**, occurs primarily during the fasting state and should be associated with gluconeogenesis, glycogenolysis, beta-oxidation, and ketone body synthesis.

While protein formation occurs primarily in the fed state, recall that translation depends on mRNA and the ribosome, and that regulatory control has many levels beginning at the level of the DNA. (The structures of proteins and amino acids are discussed in the Biological Molecules and Enzymes Lecture, and translation is discussed in the Genetics Lecture.) Proteins are made from amino acids, and the bulk of a cell's amino acids are incorporated into proteins, which are constantly being synthesized and degraded. Aside from this pool of amino acids, there is no true storage form of amino acids analogous to glycogen or triglycerides.

Protein breakdown begins with the hydrolysis of amino acid chains in the small intestines. Recall that amino acids are connected by amide bonds, which can be hydrolyzed into an amine plus a carboxylic acid. Enzymes such as **trypsin**, **chymotrypsin**, and **carboxypeptidase** cleave proteins into small mono-, di-, and tri-amino acids. The final small amino acid chains are cleaved by enzymes of the brush border. They are then absorbed and released into circulation by intestinal epithelial cells. Amino acid breakdown begins with the removal of the nitrogen group, producing ammonia and a carbon chain. The ammonia is fed into the *urea cycle* to become urea, which is excreted in the urine. The carbon chain can then serve as a substrate for various stages of the citric acid cycle.

Amino acids can be used to synthesize a number of biological substances besides proteins. Some of them can be substrates for gluconeogenesis, while others are substrates for ketogenesis. They are also used to form neurotransmitters and hormones, as well as heme, the oxygen-carrying portion of hemoglobin. Amino acids can even be used to create other amino acids. Eleven of the twenty amino acids can be synthesized from other amino acids. The other nine are referred to as essential amino acids, which must be obtained from the diet.

For the MCAT®, understanding the nature of each metabolic pathway and how the pathways fit together will be rewarded over the memorization of individual molecules and steps. Read this lecture for the "main idea" of each metabolic pathway and how it contributes to the energetic needs of the body.

These questions are NOT related to a passage.

Item 49

VLDL is produced by which of the following organs?

- O A) The intestines
- O B) The liver
- O C) Adipocytes
- O D) Muscle

Item 50

Which of the following would be expected to cross a cell membrane without the aid of an accessory protein?

- O A) Glucose
- O B) Glycine
- O C) Ketone bodies
- O D) Triglycerides

Item 51

What is the net ATP production from fermentation?

- O A) 0 ATP
- O B) 2 ATP
- O C) 4 ATP
- O D) 8 ATP

Item 52

Which of the following produces the most ATP per unit mass?

- O A) Saturated fats
- O B) Unsaturated fats
- O C) Glucose
- O D) Protein

Item 53

Which of the following processes occurs under both aerobic and anaerobic conditions?

- O A) Electron transport chain
- O B) Krebs cycle
- O C) Glycolysis
- O D) Oxidative phosphorylation

Item 54

Glycolysis takes place in the cytoplasm of an animal cell. Which of the following is NOT a product or reactant in glycolysis?

- O A) Glucose
- O B) Pyruvate
- O C) ATP
- O D) O_2

Item 55

Heart and liver cells can produce more ATP for each molecule of glucose than other cells in the body. This is most likely due to:

- O A) a more efficient ATP synthase on the outer mitochondrial membrane.
- O B) an additional turn of the Krebs cycle for each glucose molecule.
- O C) a more efficient mechanism for moving NADH produced in glycolysis into the mitochondrial matrix.
- O D) production of additional NADH by the citric acid cycle.

Item 56

Which of the following is an example of substrate-level phosphorylation?

- O A) The phosphorylation of glucose by glucokinase
- O B) The reduction of NAD^+ by triosphosphate dehydrogenase
- O C) The removal of a phosphate group from glucose 6-phosphate by glucose 6-phosphatase
- O D) The addition of an inorganic phosphate to ADP by pyruvate kinase

3.6 Regulation of Metabolism

This section will describe the guiding principles of metabolic regulation. On the level of the organism, the primary source of energy is glucose. While nothing in biology is ever absolute, there are two rules that are almost always true in metabolism. The first is that blood glucose only can come from the intestines or the liver. The second is that red blood cells and the brain *always* require glucose.

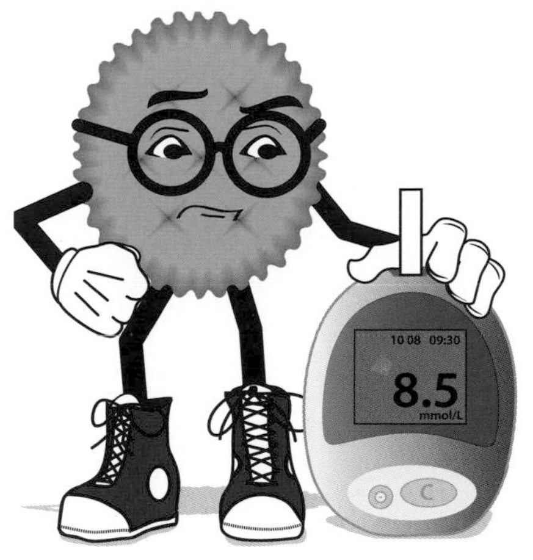

Physiologically normal individuals do not excrete glucose in their urine. However, people with diabetes, who have insufficient or ineffective insulin, do excrete glucose. One of the tests for diabetes is to check for glucose in the urine.

Glucose Supply

Immediately after a meal, the intestines are a source of abundant glucose. The amount of glucose presents a metabolic challenge – if the blood glucose level gets too high, some of the glucose will spill out in the urine. The kidney can only reabsorb glucose at a certain rate (see the Digestive and Excretory Systems Lecture in *Biology 2: Systems* for kidney physiology). In this state of glucose abundance, the body actively works to store glucose via glycogenesis. Extra glucose is also converted to fatty acids and stored as triglycerides in adipocytes. Thus, when there is a supply of glucose coming from the intestines, metabolic pathways tend to use glucose and store excess glucose as glycogen and triglycerides.

By contrast, a few hours after a meal, the liver becomes the primary supplier of blood glucose. The liver can make glucose in two different ways: it can break down its glycogen stores via glycogenolysis, and it can manufacture new glucose from non-carbohydrate molecules via gluconeogenesis. The glucose supply from the liver is nowhere near as abundant as that which comes from the intestines during and immediately after a meal. When glucose is being provided by the liver, metabolic pathways release glucose and fatty acids for use.

Glucose Demand

The brain and the red blood cells present a fixed glucose demand. Both require a steady supply of glucose to function. Glucose is one of the few molecules that can penetrate the protective barrier between the blood and the brain, known as the blood-brain barrier. Red blood cells require glucose because they do not have mitochondria; thus, their metabolism is limited to fermentation in the cytosol.

When glucose is abundant and coming mostly from the intestines, all organs will use blood glucose. However, when the glucose supply comes from the liver, it is limited. Most organs will begin to use fatty acids from adipocytes for their energy needs. The muscles are a special case in that they have their own internal glycogen supply. Muscles keep glucose produced from their glycogen stores for internal use rather than releasing it. They can use fatty acids as an energy source as well. All organs, except red blood cells, can also use ketone bodies for energy.

Hormones Communicate Glucose Levels

Blood glucose is primarily regulated by the hormones **insulin** and **glucagon**, although **epinephrine** and **cortisol** are also involved. Insulin is released from the pancreas in response to increased blood glucose levels and promotes glycolysis in all tissues, glycogenesis in the liver and muscle, fatty acid synthesis in the liver, and fatty acid storage in adipocytes. Glucagon is released from the pancreas in response to decreased blood glucose levels and promotes glycogenolysis in the liver and muscle, gluconeogenesis in the liver, fatty acid release in adipocytes, and beta-oxidation in almost all tissues. In late starvation, the absence of insulin promotes ketogenesis. Epinephrine is released in response to stress and, like glucagon, promotes glycogenolysis, the removal of glucose from storage. Cortisol is also released in response to stress, but promotes gluconeogenesis instead.

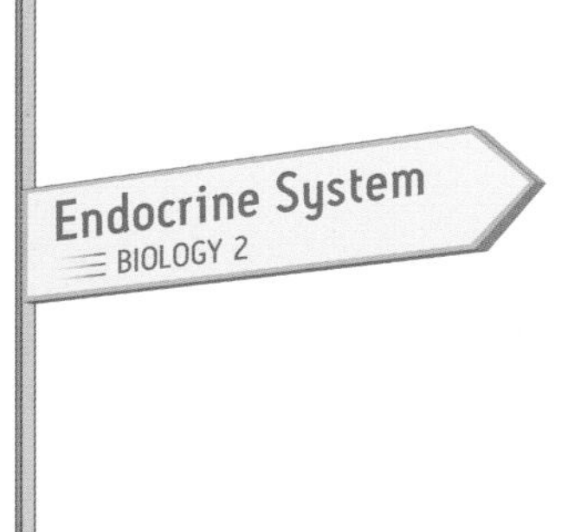

Chemical signals in the bloodstream control metabolic pathways by regulating the enzymes of metabolism. All biochemical signal molecules must have receptors in order to have an effect. Insulin, epinephrine, and glucagon are hydrophilic hormones and thus have receptors on the outside of the cell membrane. Cortisol, a glucocorticoid, is a hydrophobic hormone and has receptors in the nucleus. Hormones control metabolic enzymes in the same ways that all enzymes are controlled:

1. phosphorylation;
2. regulation of the synthesis of enzymes;
3. use of control enzymes; and
4. local metabolic effects.

Insulin and glucagon tend to exert their effects via reversible phosphorylation, though they can use any of the first three mechanisms above. Glycogen synthase, the enzyme that makes glycogen, is inactivated by phosphorylation. This process is mediated by insulin acting through a membrane protein. As another example, cortisol and glucagon regulate glucose 6-phosphatase, the last enzyme of gluconeogenesis, by increasing its synthesis. Control enzymes are perhaps the most complicated. An example is phosphofructokinase-2. The exact function of this enzyme is beyond the scope of the MCAT®, but it is activated by insulin and catalyzes the creation of a molecule that is a potent activator of glycolysis.

Thermodynamics
CHEMISTRY

Local metabolic effects occur in accordance with **Le Châtelier's principle**. Increasing substrate concentration causes an increase in the amount of product that is formed. This effect is not controlled by a hormone, but rather by local molecule concentrations. Ketogenesis provides an example of local metabolic effects When there is too much acetyl-CoA for the citric acid cycle in the liver to use, the liver begins to generate ketone bodies. Of course, insulin must also be absent for this to happen. However, the lack of insulin is simply permissive, or allows ketogenesis to happen. What truly starts the creation of ketone bodies is an excess of acetyl-CoA.

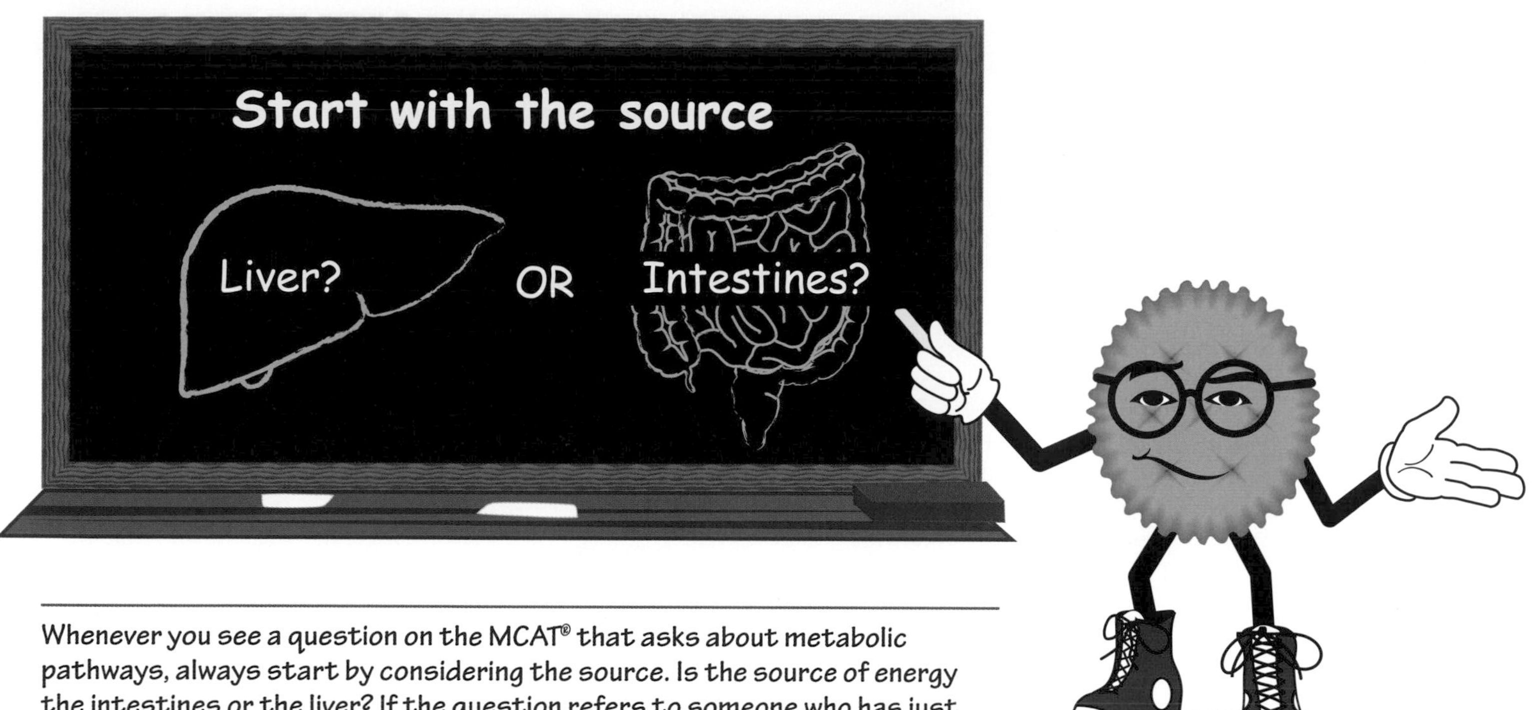

Whenever you see a question on the MCAT® that asks about metabolic pathways, always start by considering the source. Is the source of energy the intestines or the liver? If the question refers to someone who has just eaten a meal, or says that only one or two hours have passed since eating, the source is the intestines. In this case, you are in luck! All organs carry out glycolysis, the citric acid cycle, and the electron transport chain. Carbohydrates and lipids are stored as glycogen and triglycerides, respectively.

If more than two or three hours have passed since a meal, the source is the liver. Metabolism is more complex when this is the case. First, think about how the liver creates glucose for other organs – then you know that the liver is carrying out glycogenolysis and gluconeogenesis. Second, think about fixed demand. Ask yourself what parts of the body REALLY need the glucose – then you know that the red blood cells and the brain are carrying out glycolysis, the citric acid cycle, and the electron transport chain. Third, think about variable demand. Ask yourself how all of the other organs in the body get their energy – you know they obtain it from fatty acids, not glucose. Thus all other organs use beta-oxidation! There are only two exceptions to this rule that you must know. One is that muscles have their own supply of glycogen to use internally. The second is that many hours after eating a meal (approximately eight to twelve hours), the liver also makes ketone bodies, which can be used by all parts of the body except red blood cells.

Think about source, fixed demand, and variable demand when you answer any metabolism question on the MCAT®. The MCAT® will often give you one piece of information and require you to fill in another. Try two examples:

1) If the liver is undergoing gluconeogenesis, what is happening in an adipocyte?
In this scenario, the liver is behaving as a source of glucose. The fixed demand (the red blood cells and the brain) have priority for this supply. All other tissues use beta-oxidation. Thus adipocytes must be carrying out fatty acid breakdown. They can also use some fatty acids for beta-oxidation themselves.

2) If the liver is undergoing glycolysis, what is happening in the muscle?
In this scenario, the source must be the intestines. Thus all organs are undergoing glycolysis, including muscle. Since muscles also form their own glycogen stores, they are carrying out glycogenesis as well.

These questions are NOT related to a passage.

Item 57

If gluconeogenesis is occurring in the liver, which metabolic pathway will be happening in a red blood cell?

- O A) Gluconeogenesis
- O B) Glycogenolysis
- O C) The citric acid cycle
- O D) The pentose phosphate pathway

Item 58

Glucose 6-phosphatase is the enzyme that catalyzes the last step of gluconeogenesis, the formation of glucose from glucose 6-phosphate. If a child were born without a functional version of this enzyme, which of the following problems would be expected?

- O A) Decreased glycolysis in the liver during the fed state
- O B) Decreased glycogenesis in the liver during the fed state
- O C) Decreased exit of glucose from muscle cells during the fasting state
- O D) Decreased blood glucose levels during the fasting state

Item 59

When hormone-sensitive lipase is active during the fasting state, which of the following processes will not be active in a muscle cell?

- O A) Glycolysis
- O B) Gluconeogenesis
- O C) The citric acid cycle
- O D) The electron transport chain

Item 60

Which of the following cells does NOT produce carbon dioxide?

- O A) Red blood cells
- O B) Muscle
- O C) Liver
- O D) Adipocytes

Item 61

During the fasting state, and assuming that bloodstream oxygen levels are normal, which of the following does NOT serve as a substrate of gluconeogenesis in the liver?

- O A) Lactate
- O B) Glycerol
- O C) Odd chain fatty acids
- O D) Even chain fatty acids

Item 62

Which of the following organs CANNOT use fatty acids as an energy source?

- O A) The liver
- O B) Muscle
- O C) The brain
- O D) The kidney

Item 63

Which of the following does NOT represent a correct pathway for the control of metabolism at the biochemical level?

- O A) Insulin phosphorylates an enzyme to inactivate it.
- O B) Glucagon phosphorylates an enzyme to inactivate it.
- O C) An abundance of ATP in the cell slows glycolysis.
- O D) Epinephrine triggers the destruction of enzymes in the cell.

Item 64

One hour after a meal, which hormone would be expected to be elevated?

- O A) Insulin
- O B) Glucagon
- O C) Epinephrine
- O D) Cortisol

Questions 57-64 of 96

STOP

3.7 Energy: ATP and NADH

On the cellular level, the primary source of energy is the nucleotide **adenosine triphosphate (ATP)**, which contains three phosphate groups. Phosphate groups are very hydrophilic, and donation of these groups can change the conformation of proteins. For example, the addition of a phosphate group to Na^+/K^+ ATPase allows the enzyme to change configuration and pump Na^+ and K^+ against their concentration gradients. **NADH** is also an important source of cellular energy. It stores energy in the high energy electrons of its hydride and is used to drive ATP formation in the electron transport chain.

Note that a hydride ion is an H^- ion. It consists of a proton and two electrons. A hydride ion is not the same as a hydrogen proton, which has no electrons.

The phosphate groups of ATP contain phosphoanhydride bonds, or phosphoric acids that are linked at an oxygen atom. Their chemical reactivity is similar to that of the anhydrides discussed in the Oxygen Containing Reactions Lecture in the *Chemistry Manual*. Hydrolysis of phosphoanhydride bonds, which is spontaneous and exothermic, can provide the energy required for less energetically favorable reactions. For an exothermic reaction, ΔH, or the change in enthalpy, is negative. For a spontaneous reaction, ΔG, or the change in Gibbs free energy, is also negative.

Cells must constantly maintain functional levels of ATP to power metabolic reactions. ATP is synthesized by the addition of one phosphate group to adenosine *di*phosphate (ADP).

FIGURE 3.7 ATP and ADP

ATP

Phosphate groups

$-H_2O$
Energy input

$+H_2O$
Energy release

ADP

Phosphate groups

Know that
ATP → ADP + P_i has $\Delta G << 0$.

Since the hydrolysis of ATP has a negative ΔG, the synthesis of ATP has a positive ΔG of equal magnitude. The energy for this synthesis is extracted from the diet. All ATP is synthesized by the addition of a phosphate group to adenosine diphosphate; this addition is called phosphorylation. **Oxidative phosphorylation** occurs when oxidation reactions provide the energy for phosphorylation. In the mitochondria, a series of oxidation reactions results in the creation of a proton gradient that powers a turbine-like enzyme, ATP synthase, that catalyzes the synthesis of ATP. In substrate-level phosphorylation, oxidation and phosphorylation are not coupled. ADP is simply one of several substrates in an enzyme-catalyzed reaction that results in transfer of a phosphate group to ADP. There are enzymes in both glycolysis and the citric acid cycle that catalyze substrate-level phosphorylation.

ATP synthase operates by brute force. It forces the ADP and phosphate group to join by smashing them together.

The energy to run oxidative phosphorylation comes from NADH, which is the reduced form of nicotinamide adenine dinucleotide (NAD^+). NAD^+ consists of two nucleotides joined together by phosphate groups. Recall that a nucleotide consists of a base, a five carbon sugar, and at least one phosphate group. One of the base groups of one of the nucleotides in NAD^+ can exist in either an oxidized or reduced state. In the reduced state, NAD^+ has accepted a hydride ion (H^-) to become NADH. In other words, it has gained electrons. NADH carries electrons to the electron transport chain, acting as a **soluble electron carrier**. The hydride ion serves as the source of electrons passed down the electron transport chain to oxygen, powering the movement of three H^+ into the intermembrane space of the mitochondrion. By diffusing down their concentration gradient, these hydrogen ions power ATP synthase.

FIGURE 3.8 NAD^+ and NADH

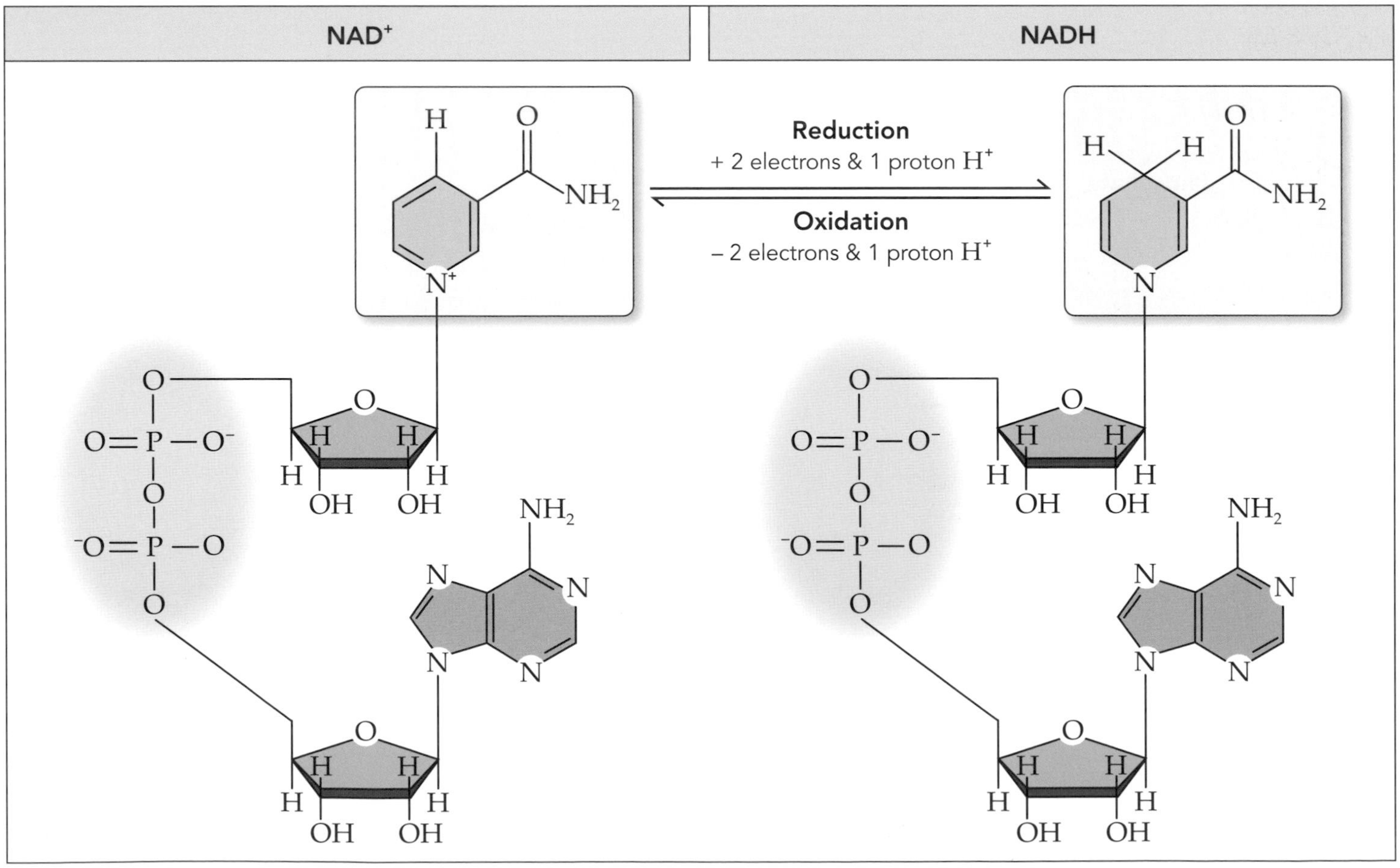

NAD^+	NADH

Reduction
+ 2 electrons & 1 proton H^+

Oxidation
– 2 electrons & 1 proton H^+

NADH and the Citric Acid Cycle

While NADH can be produced by a few different cellular processes (including glycolysis, as mentioned previously), most NADH in the cell comes from the citric acid cycle. Pathways that feed into the citric acid cycle include all of the previous pathways that produce acetyl-CoA, namely glycolysis (after pyruvate is converted into acetyl-CoA), beta-oxidation, and ketone body use. The citric acid cycle takes place in the **mitochondrial matrix**. The outer membrane of a mitochondrion is permeable to small molecules, and both pyruvate and NADH pass into the intermembrane space via facilitated diffusion through a large membrane protein. The inner **mitochondrial membrane**, however, is less permeable. Although pyruvate, fatty acids, and ketone bodies move into the matrix via facilitated diffusion, the hydrolysis of ATP is usually required to transport each NADH.

Acetyl-CoA is a coenzyme that transfers two carbons (from pyruvate) to the 4-carbon oxaloacetic acid to begin the **citric acid cycle** (also called the **Krebs cycle**). During the cycle, two carbons are lost as CO_2, and oxaloacetic acid is regenerated. The citric acid cycle is called a "cycle" because the end product, oxaloacetic acid, is combined with acetyl-CoA to restart the series of reactions. Each turn of the citric acid cycle produces **1 ATP, 3 NADH, and 1 $FADH_2$**. $FADH_2$ acts similarly to NADH, as will be described.

Notice that the output given above is per turn of the citric acid cycle. Since each glucose molecule is split in half, one glucose molecule powers two turns of the citric acid cycle. This means that 6 NADH are made per glucose in the citric acid cycle, compared to the 2 NADH made per glucose in glycolysis. A similar ratio exists for beta-oxidation, which produces 1 NADH per two carbons versus 3 NADH in the citric acid cycle. Only one ATP is made in the citric acid cycle, and it is made via substrate-level phosphorylation, just like in glycolysis.

Regulation of the citric acid cycle is tied to the amount of NAD^+ available. NAD^+ is generated by the oxidation of NADH by the electron transport chain. If the electron transport chain is inhibited, such as due to a lack of oxygen, NADH cannot be reduced to NAD^+. In this case, the citric acid cycle is inhibited and the cell shifts its energy production toward anaerobic pathways. This is an example

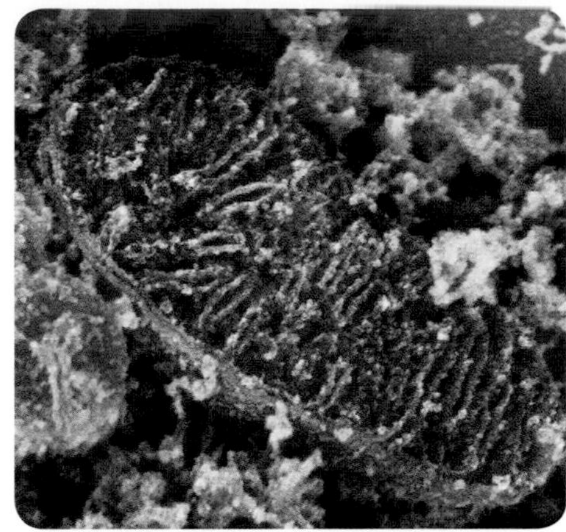

During aerobic respiration, most ATP is produced inside the mitochondrion.

Carbons are "lost as CO_2" in the citric acid cycle because a carboxylic acid is undergoing a decarboxylation reaction. This reaction is discussed in the Oxygen Containing Reactions Lecture in the Chemistry Manual.

FIGURE 3.9 Citric Acid Cycle

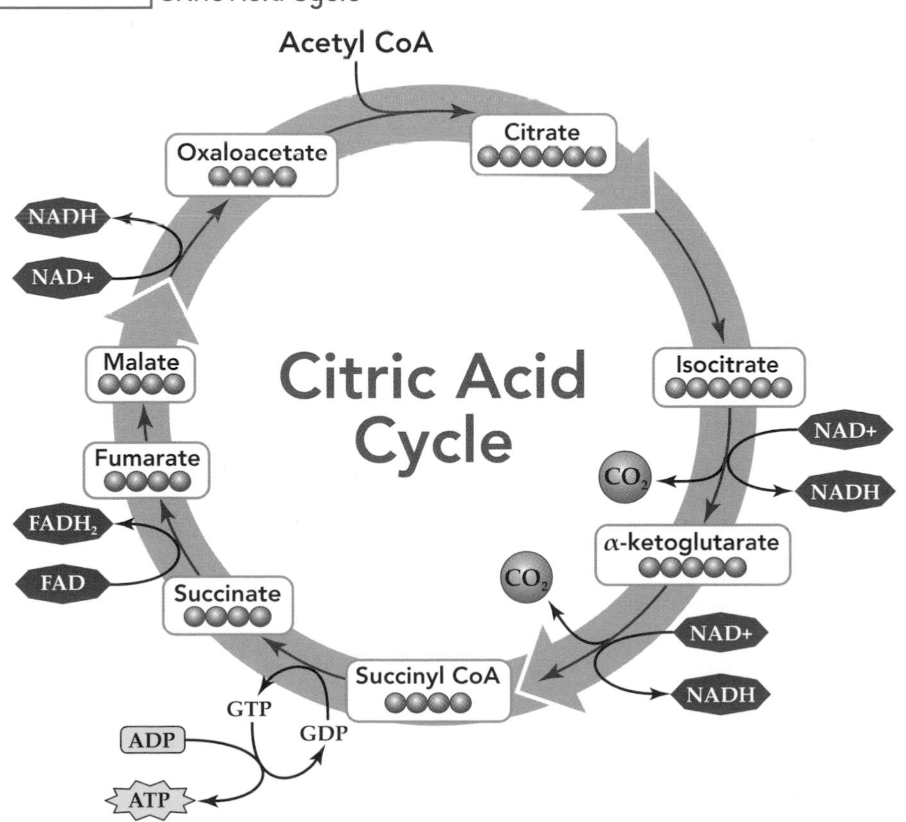

of the local metabolic effects discussed earlier in this lecture. Because of this close connection to the electron transport chain, the citric acid cycle is considered to be aerobic. NADH provides another source of regulation: the citric acid cycle produces NADH, so if an excess of NADH builds up, the reactions slow down.

Remember that the citric acid cycle occurs twice for each glucose; once for each pyruvate generated by glycolysis.

Note that acetyl-CoA is not the only substrate that can enter the citric acid cycle. Some molecules can be modified to various citric acid cycle intermediates that can then enter the cycle. For example, amino acids come with carbon backbones of varying lengths. After amino acids are deaminated in the liver, the deaminated product may be chemically converted to pyruvic acid or acetyl-CoA, or it may enter the citric acid cycle at various stages depending upon the length of the carbon backbone. Glutamic acid, for example, has a five carbon backbone and can be converted into the citric acid cycle intermediate α-ketoglutarate.

To be used for energy, amino acids must first be deaminated, after which they can enter the citric acid cycle as pyruvate or as one of the citric acid cycle intermediates. Nucleotides must also be deaminated before entering the vv cycle as an intermediate. Fats are converted to acetyl-CoA, which can then enter the citric acid cycle.

FIGURE 3.10 Metabolism of Proteins and Fats

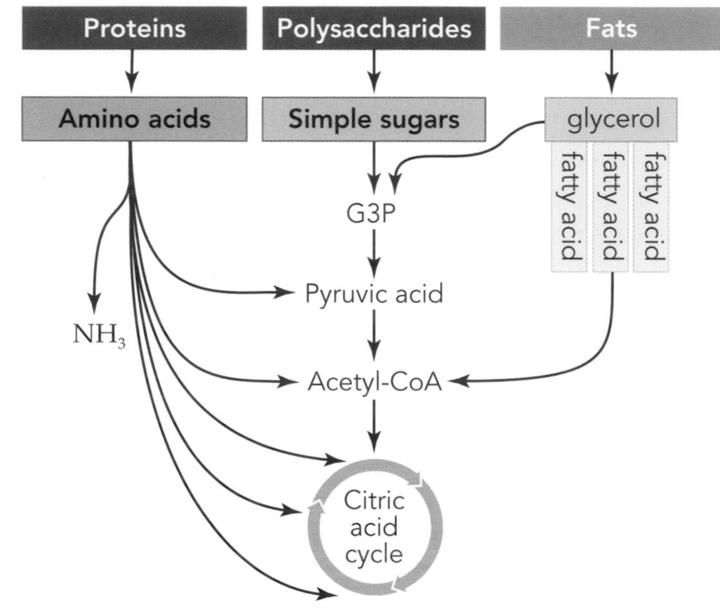

The electron transport chain can be thought of as an assembly line. Electrons are picked up at one end and handed down the line to oxygen.

ATP and the Electron Transport Chain

The **electron transport chain (ETC)** (Figure 3.11) is a series of proteins that carries electrons from NADH to O_2. These proteins include **ubiquinone** and **cytochromes**, which are intermediate electron carriers in the electron transport chain. They pick up electrons from NADH and transfer them to O_2, which is reduced to H_2O. Remember that when any molecule gains electrons, it is reduced. When that molecule gives them away, it is oxidized.

Another electron carrier, cytochrome c, has a second function – when it leaks out of the mitochondria in the event of cellular damage, it triggers apoptosis (cell death).

As electrons are passed along, protons are pumped into the intermembrane space, establishing a proton gradient called the **proton-motive force**. As the protons diffuse back into the mitochondrial matrix along their electrochemical gradient, they travel through **ATP synthase**, causing ATP to be generated. The horizontal flow of protons causes ATP synthase to turn. As it turns, it combines a phosphate group with an ADP to generate ATP. This mechanism of fueling ATP production is called **chemiosmotic coupling**, an example of oxidative phosphorylation in the body. A net product of 2 to 3 ATP is manufactured for each NADH, depending on whether an ATP was spent to transport NADH into the mitochondrial matrix. $FADH_2$ works in a similar fashion to NADH, except that $FADH_2$ reduces a protein further along in the ETC series, and thus only about 2 ATP are produced for each $FADH_2$.

The electron transport chain is fundamentally a reduction-oxidation reaction. NADH loses electrons (is oxidized) to become NAD^+. Oxygen gains electrons (is reduced) to form water. This is crucial to understand for the MCAT®.

Oxygen is a key regulator of the electron transport chain. When it is present, the electron transport chain runs as described above. When it is absent, there is no acceptor to which the final electron carrier of the chain can pass its electrons. As a result, the molecule remains in a reduced state. Eventually, the entire chain backs up and NADH has nowhere to pass its electrons, so the citric acid cycle slows, as discussed previously. The excess NADH also shifts the cell into anaerobic fermentation, so NADH is converted to NAD^+ by the conversion of pyruvate to lactate.

FIGURE 3.11 Electron Transport Chain

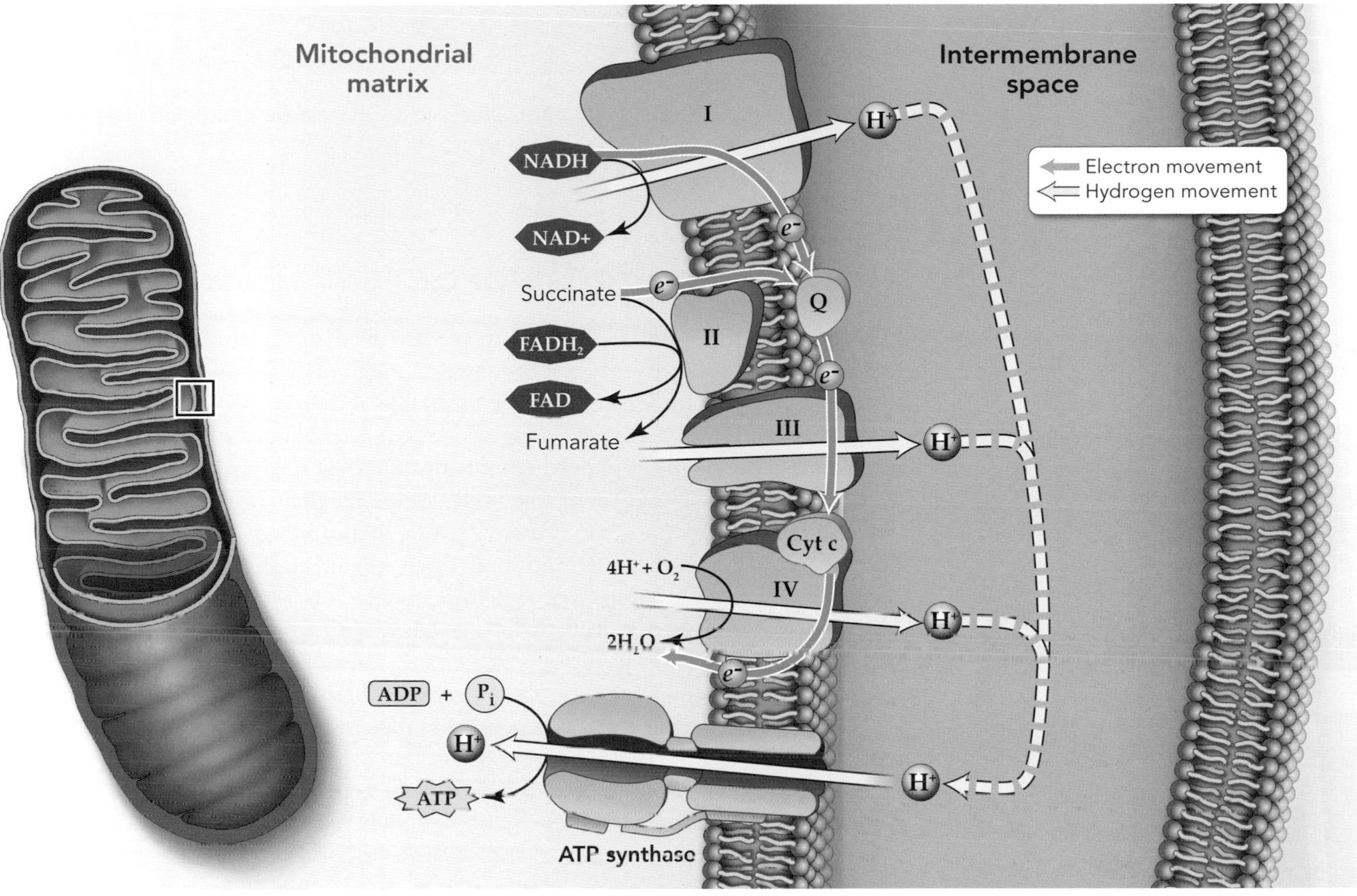

Notice that the intermembrane space has a lower pH than the matrix, due to the buildup of protons.

You don't have to memorize the names of the molecules or the enzymes of the citric acid cycle except for the ones that are red and bold; however, you should recognize them as being part of the citric acid cycle if they are presented in a diagram. Pay special attention to acetyl-CoA and ATP synthase. Also know the difference between oxidative phosphorylation and substrate-level phosphorylation.

Finally, you should definitely know the net products and reactants for respiration:

Glucose + $O_2 \rightarrow CO_2 + H_2O$

(This reaction is not balanced)

This is a combustion reaction. Notice that the oxygen you breathe in does not become CO_2, although it is exchanged for CO_2. Instead it becomes H_2O. Be sure you remember that the final electron acceptor is oxygen. This is why oxygen is necessary for aerobic respiration.

You should know that aerobic respiration, including glycolysis, produces about 36 net ATP. You should also know that 1 NADH produces 2 to 3 ATP and that 1 $FADH_2$ produces about 2 ATP. Know how many NADH, $FADH_2$, and ATP molecules are produced in each turn of the citric acid cycle, and that one glucose produces two turns.

TABLE 3.1 > Molecular Accounting

	Glycolysis	Pre-Krebs	Krebs	Total	ATP/mol	ATP total
ATP	2	0	2	4	1	4
NADH	2	2	6	10	3	30 - 2 = 28*
$FADH_2$	0	0	2	2	2	4
						NET 36

* The cost of transporting each glycolysis-produced NADH from the cytosol into the mitochondrion is one ATP.

3.8 Metabolic Disorders

Disruption of the regulatory mechanisms involved in metabolism can lead to a variety of metabolic disorders. **Obesity** is a metabolic disorder that has quickly become one of the important medical problems of the twenty-first century. Body mass index, or BMI, expresses weight compared to height and has traditionally been used to define obesity, although it is an imperfect measure. Obesity is defined as a BMI above 30. As of 2010, the CDC estimates that over one-third of adults in the United States are obese. Obesity has been associated with increased risk of heart disease, stroke, diabetes, and some types of cancer. The causes of and effective interventions for obesity remain elusive.

Over the past century, high-calorie foods have become more prevalent, and lifestyles have become increasingly sedentary. However, the source of obesity is more complicated than just eating more calories than are burned off during activity. Obesity is also influenced by genetics and the complex interaction of hormones and metabolites in the body.

One of the best studied hormones affecting appetite is leptin, which interacts with the hypothalamus to signal satiety, or a feeling of fullness. Obesity has been associated with deficiency or lack of response to leptin, but obesity should not be thought of as a leptin deficiency any more than it should be thought of as the result of greater calorie intake than expenditure. There are hundreds of hormones and molecules that regulate the drive to eat and the way the body processes food.

Weight loss is complex and involves multiple interrelated factors. Diets can be modified to include healthier and lower calorie food, and lifestyles can be modified to include more physical activity. However, sociological and psychological forces often pull a person back into old habits. In the clinic, the approach to weight loss is multifaceted, but usually centers on diet and exercise. Pharmaceutical companies have begun to create drugs that can modify metabolic pathways, but determining what pathways can be safely targeted with the result of meaningful weight loss has remained difficult. In the future, medications may play a larger role in treatment, but it is unlikely that they will ever be the entire solution.

The CDC recommends controlled calorie intake, increased physical activity, and improved eating behaviors. It looks like this shopper is making good food choices.

Questions 65 and 66 are based on the following information:

The first reaction of glycolysis converts glucose into glucose 6-phosphate at the expenditure of one ATP. The full reaction is shown, with thermochemical data below it.

Glucose + ATP → Glucose 6-phosphate + ADP

Glucose + Phosphate → Glucose 6-phosphate
$\Delta G = 20.9$ kJ/mol

ATP → ADP + P_i
$\Delta G = -48.1$ kJ/mol

Item 65

What is the ΔG of the conversion of one mole of glucose into glucose 6-phosphate?

- O A) -27.2 kJ
- O B) +27.2 kJ
- O C) -69.0 kJ
- O D) +69.0 kJ

Item 66

What is the expected range of the equilibrium constant, K?

- O A) $K > 1$
- O B) $K < 1$
- O C) $K = 1$
- O D) $K = 0$

Questions 67 - 72 are NOT based on a descriptive passage.

Item 67

Which of the following best describes the reaction of NAD^+ to NADH?

- O A) NAD^+ accepts a proton and is reduced to NADH.
- O B) NAD^+ donates a proton and is reduced to NADH.
- O C) NAD^+ accepts hydride and is reduced to NADH.
- O D) NAD^+ accepts hydride and is oxidized to NADH.

Item 68

The reaction that generates ATP from ADP and an inorganic phosphate would be expected to have which of the following values of ΔG?

- O A) $\Delta G > 0$
- O B) $\Delta G = 0$
- O C) $\Delta G < 0$
- O D) ΔG cannot be predicted without more information about the reaction.

Item 69

After electrons are passed from one protein complex to another, the final electron acceptor of the electron transport chain is:

- O A) ATP.
- O B) H_2O.
- O C) NADH.
- O D) O_2.

Item 70

In a human renal cortical cell, the Krebs cycle occurs in the:

- O A) cytosol.
- O B) mitochondrial matrix.
- O C) inner mitochondrial membrane.
- O D) mitochondrial intermembrane space.

Item 71

As electrons move within the electron transport chain, each intermediate carrier molecule is:

- O A) oxidized by the preceding molecule and reduced by the following molecule.
- O B) reduced by the preceding molecule and oxidized by the following molecule.
- O C) reduced by both the preceding and following molecules.
- O D) oxidized by both the preceding and following molecules.

Item 72

Assuming that 2 ATP are consumed in moving NADH from the cytosol to the mitochondrial matrix, and all other conditions are optimal, how many ATP are produced per glucose molecule?

- O A) 18
- O B) 32
- O C) 36
- O D) 38

TERMS YOU NEED TO KNOW

Acetyl-CoA
Adenosine triphosphate (ATP)
Aerobic
Anabolism
Anaerobic
Apoptosis
ATP synthase
Beta-oxidation
Carboxypeptidase
Catabolism
Chemiosmotic coupling
Chymotrypsin
Citric acid cycle (Krebs cycle)
Cortisol
Cytochrome
Cytosol
Dynamic steady state
Electron transport chain (ETC)
Epinephrine
Fermentation
Glucagon
Gluconeogenesis
Glycogenesis
Glycogenolysis
Glycolysis
Inborn error of metabolism
Insulin
Ketogenesis
Ketone bodies
Le Châtelier's principle
Lipase
Lipoproteins
Mitochondrial matrix
Mitochondrial membrane
Obesity
Oxidative phosphorylation
NADH
Pentose phosphate pathway (PPP)
Products of citric acid cycle: 1 ATP, 3 NADH, 1 $FADH_2$
Proton-motive force
Pyruvate
Saturated fats
Soluble electron carrier
Substrate-level phosphorylation
Trypsin
Ubiquinone
Unsaturated fats

MCAT® THINK ANSWER

When blood glucose is low, the body works to restore glucose to the blood. The blood serves all of the tissues in the body as a glucose bank account with a minimum balance requirement. When blood glucose levels drop, as when a person is exercising or fasting, the hormone glucagon is released and triggers both gluconeogenesis and glycogenolysis. Glycolysis backward is called gluconeogenesis - rebuilding glucose from pyruvate. Glycogen is broken down into glucose molecules in the process of glycogenolysis. Both processes recreate glucose and send it back to the blood. Gluconeogenesis (glycolysis backwards) occurs in any tissues where pyruvate is available to recreate glucose. Newly synthesized glucose enters the bloodstream to bring blood glucose back to homeostasis, making glucose available to other tissues that may need it.

DON'T FORGET YOUR KEYS

1. Metabolic pathways move toward either the storage or production of energy.
2. Blood glucose levels regulate systemic and intracellular pathways.
3. NADH and ATP are the cell's energy molecules.

Laboratory Techniques

THE 3 KEYS

1. Separation and purification techniques use chemical and physical properties to isolate compounds.
2. "Spec" techniques identify unknown features of compounds.
3. Genetic lab techniques identify or manipulate DNA to study or change healthy and pathological processes.

4.1 Introduction

Understanding laboratory techniques is vital to success on the MCAT® and as a physician. Physicians must be able to interpret studies that utilize such techniques in order to practice evidence-based medicine, and lab techniques are increasingly important in clinical practice as well. It is critical that physicians have the ability to explain these techniques to patients and determine when they should be used.

Succeeding on the MCAT® requires an understanding of the use and scientific principles of certain laboratory techniques, which can be divided into three categories:

1. Separations divide mixtures into their components based on intermolecular forces and can be used for purification, identification, or collection.
2. Spectroscopy and spectrometry provide structural information that can be used to identify compounds.
3. Genetic techniques have many clinical and research applications, including the isolation/identification of genes and the manipulation of DNA on the molecular level.

Familiarize yourself with lab techniques for two reasons. First, they may appear in questions testing basic scientific principles. Second, you will have a better understanding of the experiments and conclusions presented in passages when you understand the techniques used.

4.2 Separating Compounds

The sequence of an extraction is key to the separation of components. A weak acid or base will bind only strong complements, whereas a strong acid or base will react with all (weak and strong) complements. To separate multiple components, the first extraction uses a weak acid or base to extract only the strong complements. Then a strong acid or base is used to extract the remaining weak components. If the reverse order was used, a strong acid or base in the first separation would react with all - strong and weak - complements such that they would be extracted all at once from the organic to the aqueous layer, rather than being sequentially separated from one another.

Separations are a variety of lab techniques that use intermolecular forces to separate a mixture into its component parts. Certain separation techniques are better suited for certain mixtures based on the particular properties of the compounds in the mixture, and some techniques can provide quantitative information on a mixture's components. Compounds can be separated according to solubility, melting point, boiling point, or any other physical property that causes two substances in a mixture to behave differently from one another. Unique terminology is assigned to each type of separation: extraction, distillation, crystallization, and chromatography.

Extraction

Extraction is a separation technique based on solubility. The principle underscoring this technique is that "like dissolves like." Extraction involves two immiscible (not mixable) phases, most commonly an aqueous layer and a less dense organic mixture. As shown in Figure 4.1, these two layers have different polarities and thus are immiscible. The following steps are used to perform an extraction:

1. Add a weak acid and shake. The acid protonates strong bases in the organic layer, making them polar and thus causing them to move to the aqueous layer. The aqueous layer is separated and then washed with a base to neutralize the added acid, leaving only the strong organic base(s).

FIGURE 4.1 Extraction

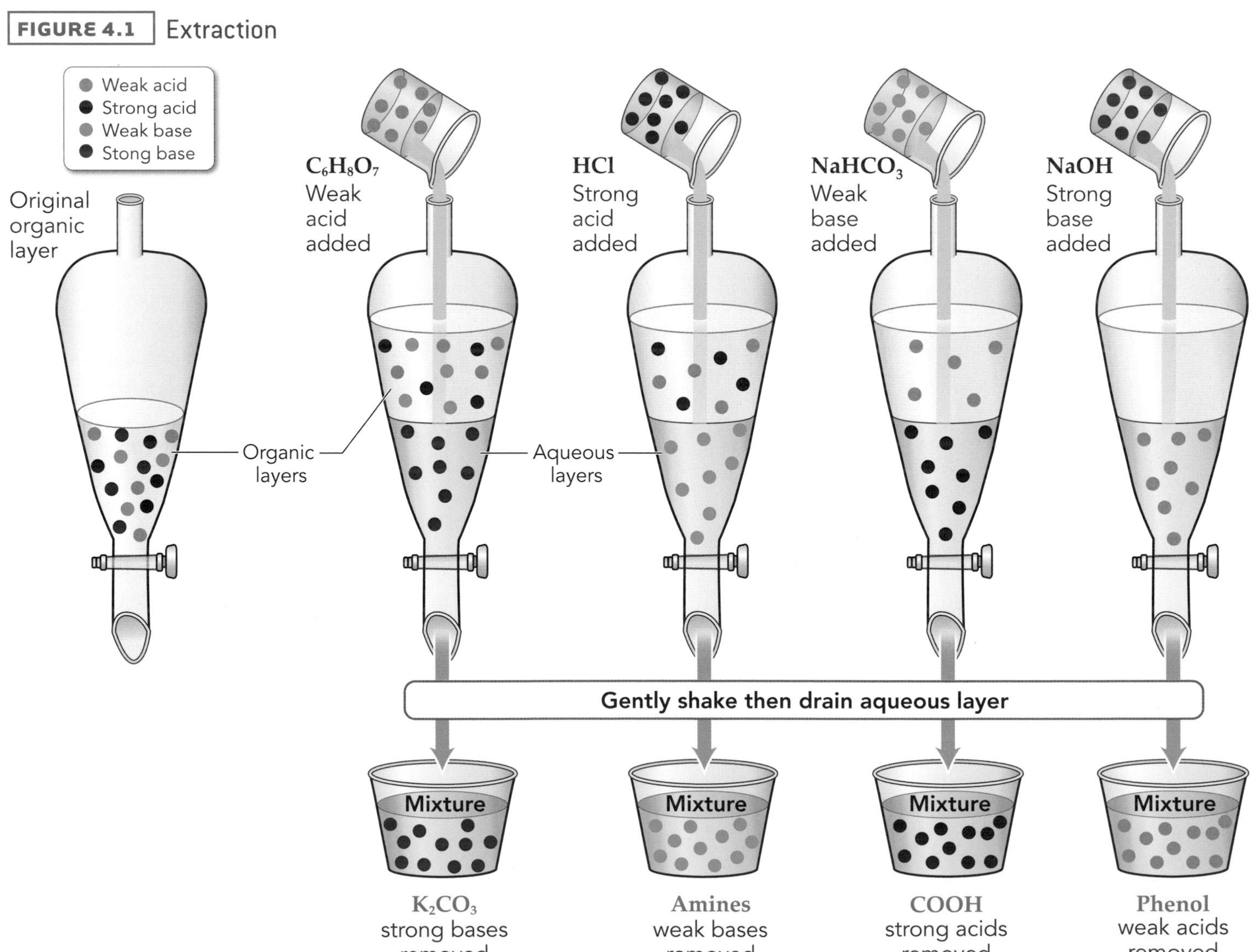

2. Add a strong acid and shake. The acid protonates weak bases in the organic layer, making them polar. The polar bases dissolve in the aqueous layer and are drained off. The separation is then washed with a base to neutralize the added acid, leaving only the organic weak base(s).
3. Add a weak base. The base deprotonates only the strongest organic acids, making them polar enough to dissolve in the aqueous layer. The polar acids are then drained off. The separation is washed with an acid to neutralize the added base, leaving only the strong organic acid(s).
4. Add a strong base. The strong base reacts with any weak acids that remain in the organic layer. The deprotonated acids dissolve in the aqueous layer and are drained off. Finally, this separation is washed with an acid to remove the added base, leaving only the weak organic acid(s).

One commonly used extraction technique is called a phenol-chloroform extraction, which can be used to separate nucleic acids from cellular proteins.

Distillation

Distillation is a technique used to separate compounds that have significantly different boiling points. A solution of two volatile liquids with boiling point differences of at least 20°C can be separated by slow boiling. The compound with the lower boiling point (and thus higher vapor pressure at a given temperature) will boil off first and can be captured and condensed in a cool tube. Distillation can be used to purify fresh water from salt water, or to increase the purity of an alcohol-water mixture, among many other uses.

If a solution of two volatile liquids exhibits a positive deviation to Raoult's law, the solution will boil at a lower temperature than either pure compound. The result will be a solution with an exact ratio of the two liquids. Such a solution cannot be separated by distillation.

Fractional distillation is a more precise method of distillation that can be used to separate liquids whose boiling points are fairly close together. In fractional distillation, the vapor is run through glass beads, allowing the compound with the higher boiling point to repeatedly condense and fall back into the solution.

FIGURE 4.2 Fractional Distillation

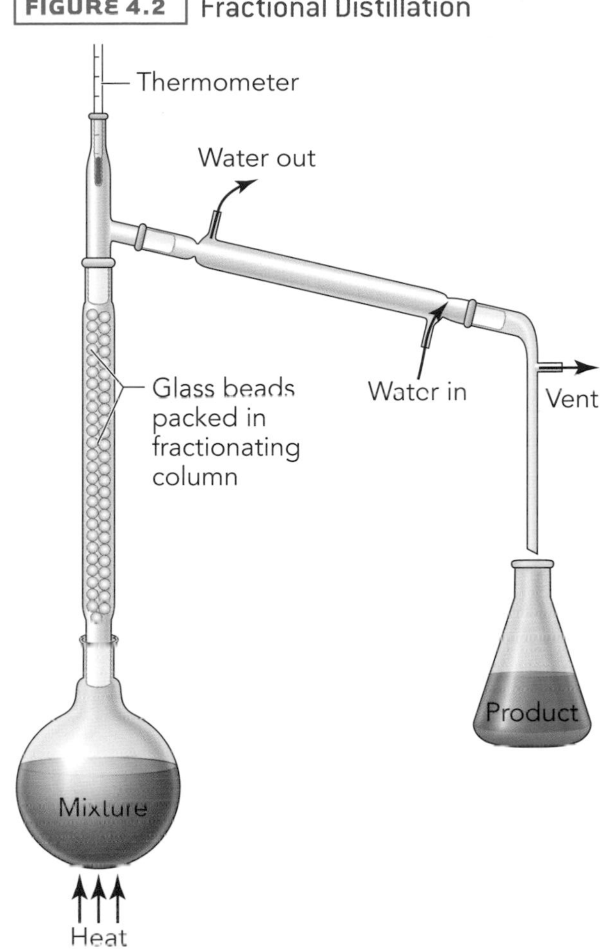

Crystallization

Crystallization is based on the principle that pure substances form crystals more easily than impure substances (i.e. pure substances have higher freezing/melting points). The classic example is an iceberg. An iceberg is formed from the ocean but is formed from pure water, not salt water. This is because pure water forms crystals more easily than salt water. Crystallization is a very inefficient method of separation; in other words, it is very difficult to arrive at a pure substance through crystallization. For most salts, crystallization is an exothermic process.

During the process of freezing, most of the salty impurities are frozen out of the iceberg. This is an example of crystallization.

Chromatography

Chromatography can be used to purify a compound from a mixture and/or to identify the ratio of compounds in a mixture. It is the separation of a mixture by passing it over or through a matrix that adsorbs (binds) different compounds more or less strongly according to their properties, ultimately altering the rate at which they lose contact with the matrix. The mixture is usually dissolved into a solution to serve as the mobile phase, while the matrix is often a solid surface. By adsorbing compounds from the mixture, the matrix surface establishes the stationary phase. The compounds in the mixture that have a greater affinity for the surface move more slowly. Typically the stationary phase is polar, causing more polar compounds to elute more slowly. Chromatography separates the mixture into separate and distinct layers, one pertaining to each component of the mixture.

Many of these chemistry techniques are also used in pharmaceutical and biomedical research, and therefore may appear on the biology section of the MCAT®.

In **column chromatography** (Figure 4.3), a solution containing the mixture is dripped down a column containing the solid phase (usually glass beads). The more polar compounds in the mixture travel more slowly down the column, creating separate layers for each compound. Each compound can be collected as it elutes with the solvent and drips out of the bottom of the column. In general, gravity drives the movement of the mixture in column chromatography. However, one variant of column chromatography is **high pressure liquid chromatography (HPLC)**, in which the column and solution use an apparatus that puts the system under high pressure.

FIGURE 4.3 Column Chromatography

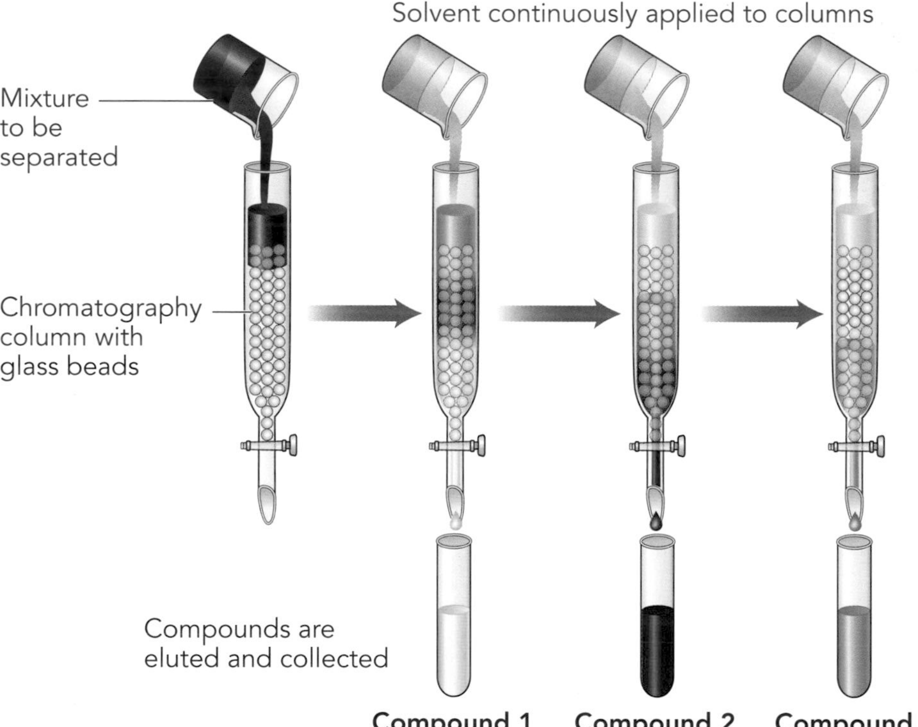

Column and thin layer chromatography separate compounds by exploiting differences in the polarity of their molecules.

In **paper chromatography** (Figure 4.4), a small portion of the sample to be separated is spotted onto paper. One end of the paper is then placed into a non-polar solvent. The solvent moves up the paper via capillary action and dissolves the sample as it passes over it. As the solvent continues to move up the paper, the more polar components of the sample move more slowly because they are attracted to the polar paper. The less polar components dissolve more easily to move up the paper with the solvent. The result is a series of dots representing the different components of the sample, with the most polar near the bottom and the least polar near the top. An *R_f factor* can be calculated for each component by dividing the distance traveled by the component by the distance traveled by the solvent. Non-polar components have an R_f factor close to one; polar components have a lower R_f factor. The R_f factor can be used to identify each component.

Thin-layer chromatography is similar to paper chromatography except that a coated glass or plastic plate is used instead of paper, and the results are visualized via an iodine vapor chamber.

FIGURE 4.4 Paper Chromatography

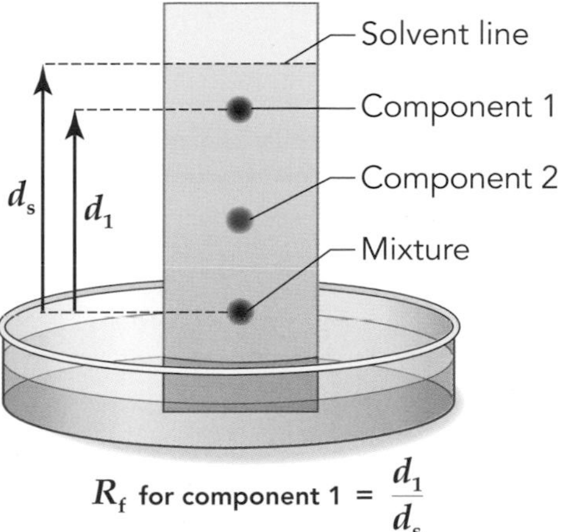

Gas chromatography is carried out to separate complex mixtures of compounds into individual components, allowing the composition to be analyzed and particular fractions to be isolated.

In **gas-liquid chromatography**, the liquid phase is the stationary phase. The mixture is dissolved into a heated carrier gas (usually helium or nitrogen) and passed over a liquid phase bound to a column. Compounds in the mixture equilibrate with the liquid phase at different rates and pass through an exit port as individual components.

Other types of chromatography are particularly well-suited for the separation of peptides and proteins. In **size-exclusion chromatography**, molecules are separated by their size and sometimes molecular weight, often through gel filtration. In **ion-exchange chromatography**, molecules are separated based on their net surface charge. This form of chromatography utilizes cationic or anionic "exchangers" that slow down the movement of charged molecules. Finally, **affinity chromatography** uses highly specific interactions to slow down select molecules, rather than simply separating out all molecules that have a particular property. Affinity chromatography can make use of receptor-ligand, enzyme-substrate, and antigen-antibody interactions, among others.

FIGURE 4.5 Gel Electrophoresis

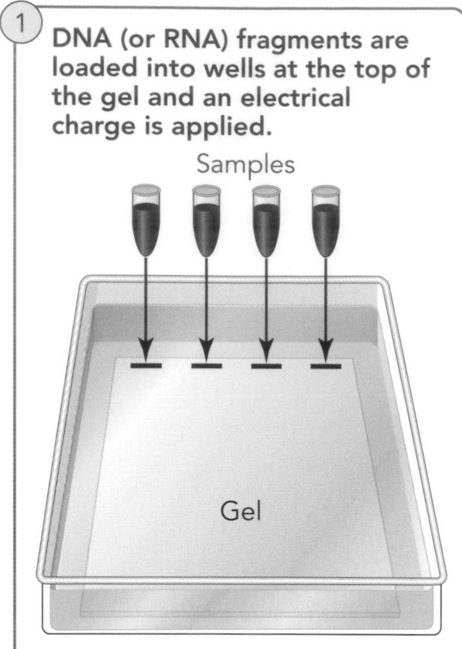

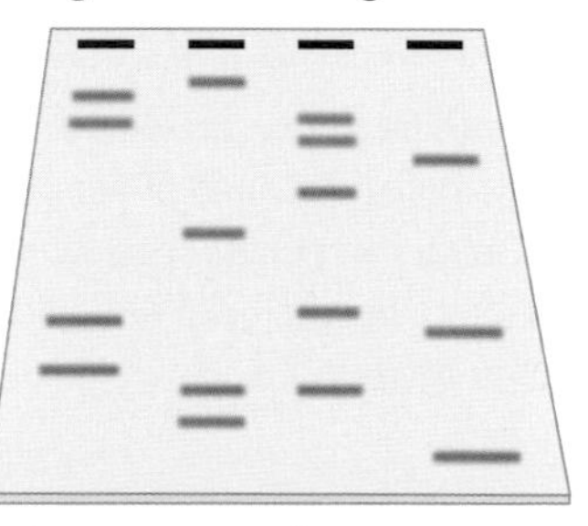

The recipe for finding a piece of DNA via gel electrophoresis and a Southern blot is:

1. **Chop up some DNA;**
2. **Use an electric field (gel electrophoresis) to spread out pieces according to size;**
3. **(Southern) blot it onto a membrane;**
4. **Add a radioactive probe made from DNA or RNA;**
5. **Visualize.**

Separation and Purification of Nucleic Acids and Peptides

So far, this lecture has focused on separations of molecules that are fundamentally different from one another, including separations of polar compounds from nonpolar compounds, volatile compounds from much less volatile ones, and so on. But there are also techniques that can be used to separate very similar compounds from one another, including different peptides or proteins, mixtures of nucleic acids of varying sizes, or mixtures of enantiomers.

Mixtures of nucleic acids (DNA and RNA fragments) or mixtures of proteins/polypeptides can be separated based on size and charge through **gel electrophoresis**. In gel electrophoresis, the molecular mixture is placed in a gel, and an electric field is applied.

Because nucleic acids are negatively charged, they migrate through the gel in response to the electric field. Larger particles move more slowly, since the agarose gel used for separation of nucleic acids forms a porous matrix and smaller pieces can more easily wind through the pores. After applying the electric field for an appropriate amount of time, nucleic acid fragments of different lengths will have migrated different distances, forming distinct "bands" that can be visualized, usually after blotting, which is discussed below.

Proteins are too large to be separated by pores, so a different type of gel is used. Normally, proteins in a mixture are denatured in the presence of a detergent before they are placed in the gel. The detergent coats each protein with negative charge proportional to its length. When an electric field is applied, proteins migrate at a rate proportional to their charge and length. Like nucleic acids, proteins of a distinct size will be visualized as a "band" in the gel. Proteins can also be separated via gel electrophoresis based on their **isoelectric points**, discussed in the Acids and Bases Lecture of the *Chemistry Manual*.

In order to identify the size or quantity of DNA, RNA, or polypeptide present in a band, gel electrophoresis is often performed with a "ladder" alongside. A ladder is a mixture of DNA, RNA, or polypeptide fragments of known sizes or quantities. The migration distances of the experimental mixture's bands can be compared against those of the ladder's bands to determine approximate size. Similarly, computerized visualization software can be used to compare the intensity of a band to the intensity of a known standard in order to approximate quantity. Bands from the gel can also be isolated and purified for further study or manipulation.

Once gel electrophoresis has been used to separate molecules according to their physical properties, particular nucleic acids or proteins can be visualized using "blotting." Blotting is a technique by which molecules are transferred from the gel onto a membrane, maintaining the same spatial relationship of bands based on size. This transfer to a membrane allows for easier manipulation or visualization of the molecules.

Southern blotting is a technique used to identify target fragments of a known DNA sequence in a large population of DNA. A Southern blot begins with DNA that has already been cleaved and then resolved (separated) by gel electrophoresis. The gel is first placed in a basic solution in order to denature the DNA fragments, meaning that the double-stranded structure separates into single strands. Next, a membrane, such as a sheet of *nitrocellulose*, is placed on top of or below the gel, and the resolved, single-stranded DNA fragments are transferred to the membrane. A labeled probe with a nucleotide sequence complementary to the target fragment is added to the membrane. The probe hybridizes with and marks the target fragment. The membrane is then visualized to reveal the location of the probe and the target fragment. Traditionally, a radiolabelled probe was used, which required membrane exposure to radiographic film. There are now other detection methodologies available, such as fluorescence.

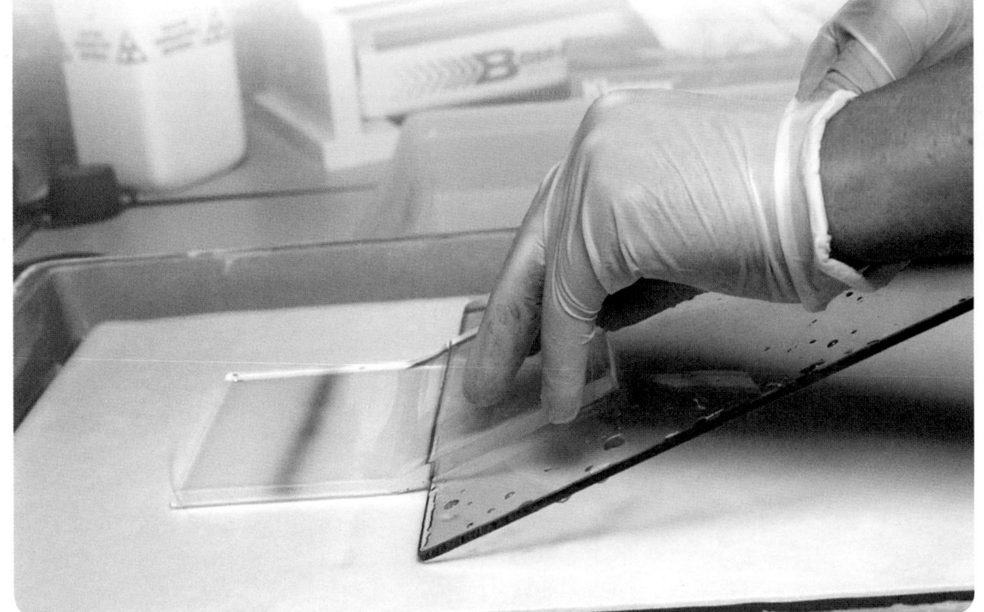

Southern blotting: A researcher transfers an electrophoresis gel containing DNA into a tray of salt solution prior to blotting the DNA onto nitrocellulose paper. The purple dye shows how far electrophoresis has progressed. Southern blotting is a technique used to reveal specific fragments of DNA (deoxyribonucleic acid) in a complex mixture. The total DNA is cut into fragments and separated by gel electrophoresis according to size. The DNA is then blotted onto a sheet of nitrocellulose, and a radioactive DNA is probe added to the nitrocellulose. The resulting banding pattern can be used to map the structure of particular genes.

A Southern blot identifies specific sequences of DNA by nucleic acid hybridization, and a Northern blot uses the same technique to identify specific sequences of RNA.

A *Northern blot* is just like a Southern blot, but it identifies RNA fragments, not DNA fragments.

A **Western blot** is used to detect a particular protein in a mixture of proteins. Although some of the specific steps are different, the basic process of transferring the resolved protein mixture from a gel to a separate membrane after electrophoresis is the same as in Southern and Northern blotting.

While there are numerous ways to visualize a protein following a Western blot, antibodies are commonly used. In this technique, an antibody (the *primary antibody*) specific to the protein in question is placed on the membrane. This primary antibody will only bind to the protein of interest. Next, a *secondary antibody-enzyme* conjugate is added. The secondary antibody recognizes and binds to the primary antibody and marks it with an enzyme for subsequent visualization. The reaction catalyzed by the enzyme attached to the secondary antibody produces a colored, fluorescent, or radioactive reaction product that can be visualized.

The **separation of enantiomers** from a **racemic mixture**, called chiral resolution, is a particular challenge because enantiomers have almost exactly the same physical and chemical properties. Generally speaking, there are three ways to resolve enantiomers. The first uses differences in crystallization of the enantiomers; in this case, direct visualization of the crystals can be used to separate enantiomers. Second, there are a number of stereospecific enzymes that can be added to a racemic mixture and will react with only one enantiomer in the mixture, creating a compound that can be separated using the types of techniques described previously. Once the altered enantiomer has been removed, the reaction can be reversed to produce the pure enantiomer. Finally, enantiomers in a racemic mixture can be converted into diastereomers, which have different physical and chemical properties that can be used for separation.

Don't let separation techniques scare you. Just remember that you can use the physical and chemical properties of different molecules to separate them from one another. Start by identifying which property is being used, and then apply what you know about those properties to help you answer the questions.

These questions are NOT related to a passage.

Item 73

Which of the following is NOT true concerning gel electrophoresis?

- O A) Nucleic acids can be separated by size based on migration through pores.
- O B) Nucleic acids migrate through gel in the presence of an electric field due to their negative charge.
- O C) Proteins can be separated by size based on migration through pores.
- O D) Proteins can be separated based on isoelectric point.

Item 74

Extraction is an effective method for separating compounds that can be treated with an acid or base and made to differ in:

- O A) boiling point.
- O B) molecular weight.
- O C) water solubility.
- O D) optical activity.

Item 75

In order to isolate insulin from a protein mixture taken from pancreatic beta cells of a mouse, scientists designed a column coated with antibodies against insulin. Isolation via this method can best be described as:

- O A) high pressure liquid chromatography.
- O B) ion exchange chromatography.
- O C) size exclusion chromatography.
- O D) affinity chromatography.

Item 76

In thin layer chromatography, polar compounds will:

- O A) rise more slowly through the silica gel than nonpolar compounds.
- O B) rise more quickly through the silica gel than nonpolar compounds.
- O C) move to the left through the silica gel.
- O D) move to the right through the silica gel.

Item 77

Which of the following statements is (are) true concerning separations?

I. Any two compounds with sufficiently different boiling points can be separated completely by distillation.
II. Crystallization is an efficient method of compound purification for most compounds.
III. Distillation is most effective when it is carried out slowly.

- O A) I only
- O B) III only
- O C) I and III only
- O D) II and III only

Item 78

Which of the following blotting techniques is (are) used for nucleic acids?

I. Southern
II. Northern
III. Western

- O A) I only
- O B) I and II only
- O C) II only
- O D) I, II, and III

Item 79

Which of the following is NOT a valid method for separation of a racemic mixture?

- O A) Visualization of crystals
- O B) Extraction via aqueous and polar phases
- O C) Utilization of stereospecific enzymes followed by separation
- O D) Conversion to diastereomers followed by separation

Item 80

In gel electrophoresis, DNA fragments are separated according to size. Which of the following is true of this process?

- O A) Positively charged DNA fragments move toward the cathode.
- O B) Positively charged DNA fragments move toward the anode.
- O C) Negatively charged DNA fragments move toward the cathode.
- O D) Negatively charged DNA fragments move toward the anode.

4.3 Identifying Molecules: Spec

Spectroscopy

Spectroscopy is the study of the interaction between matter and electromagnetic radiation (light). Different regions of the electromagnetic spectrum interact differently with matter, providing different information about the structures of molecules.

TABLE 4.1 > Spectroscopy Summary

Type of Spectroscopy	Region of Electromagnetic Spectrum	Structural Information Provided
Nuclear Magnetic Resonance (NMR)	Radio waves	Arrangement of carbon and hydrogen atoms
Infrared (IR)	Infrared light	Presence of functional groups
Ultraviolet-Visible (UV-Vis)	Ultraviolet light and visible light	Presence of conjugated π systems

Nuclear Magnetic Resonance (NMR) spectroscopy is the study of the interaction between atomic nuclei and radio waves. NMR is most commonly used to study hydrogen nuclei, but it can be used to study the nucleus of carbon-13 and other atoms as well.

Nuclei with odd atomic or mass numbers possess a mechanical property called *nuclear spin*. Hydrogen-1, for example, has an odd atomic and mass number. Carbon-13 has an even atomic number but an odd mass number. Both possess nuclear spin. A spinning proton, like any other rotating sphere of charge, generates a magnetic field, in this case around the nucleus.

When subject to an external magnetic field, the field of a nucleus aligns either with or against the external field. Nuclei whose fields align with the external field are said to occupy lower energy α spin states. Those whose fields are aligned against the external field are said to occupy higher energy β spin states. The stronger the magnetic field, the greater the difference in energy, ΔE, between the two states.

As discussed in Lecture 1 of the *Chemistry Manual*, the energy of a photon is equal to Planck's constant times the frequency of the associated electromagnetic wave: $\Delta E = hv$. Photons whose energies are equal to the ΔE between the two spin states can cause nuclei whose spins are aligned with the external field to flip and

The stronger the magnetic field, the greater the difference in energy between the α and β spin states.

FIGURE 4.6 α and β Spin States

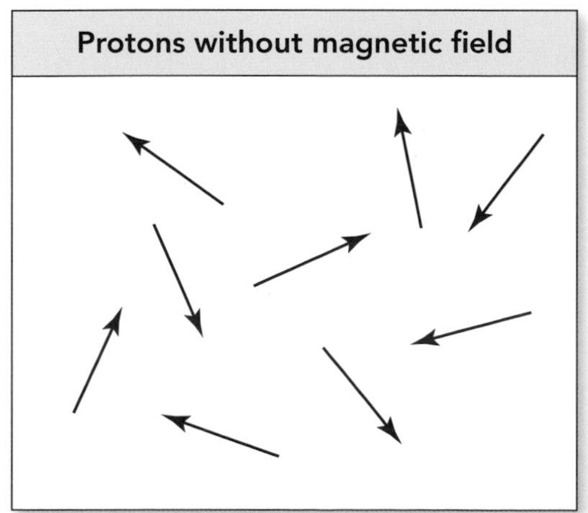

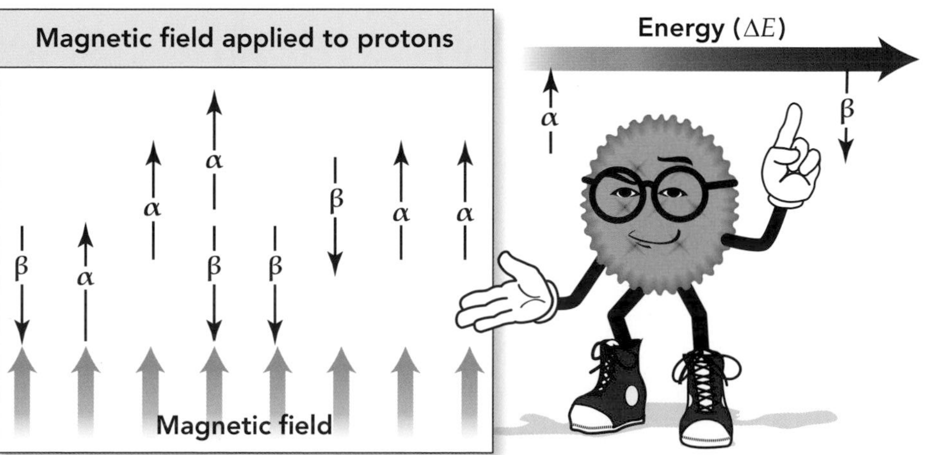

FIGURE 4.7 NMR and Magnetic Field Strength

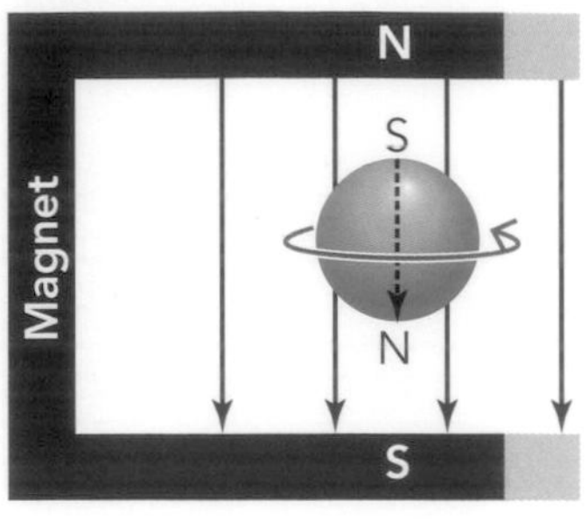

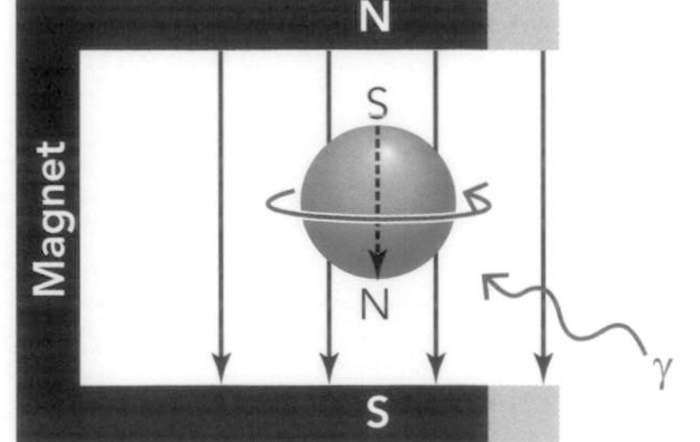

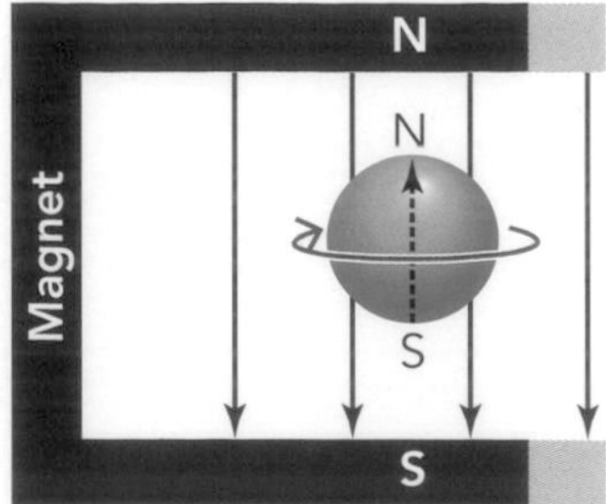

Low energy state

High energy state

align against it. Nuclei that have flipped to the β spin state are said to be in resonance with the external magnetic field. When protons return to their original spin states, they release electrical impulses that are detected by an NMR spectrometer.

In NMR, the frequency of the electromagnetic radiation is held constant while the magnetic field strength is varied. In the absence of any electrons, all protons absorb electromagnetic energy from a given magnetic field at the same frequency. However, hydrogen atoms within different compounds or functional groups experience different surrounding electron densities and are also uniquely affected by the magnetic fields of nearby protons. Electrons shield protons from the magnetic field, so the external field must be strengthened for a shielded proton to achieve resonance. Due to this effect, protons within a compound absorb electromagnetic energy of the same frequency at different magnetic field strengths.

Don't be intimidated by unfamiliar phrases like magnetic resonance and nuclear spin. Protons and electrons will behave just like any other type of moving charge.

An NMR spectrum is a graph of the magnetic field strengths absorbed by the hydrogen atoms of a specific compound at a single frequency. The field strength is measured in parts per million, ppm, and, despite the decreasing numbers indicated in the spectrum, increases from left to right. The leftward direction is called downfield and the rightward is called upfield. All the way to the right is a peak at 0 ppm. This peak represents the hydrogen atoms of *tetramethylsilane*, a reference compound that is used to calibrate the instrument.

FIGURE 4.8 NMR Spectrum

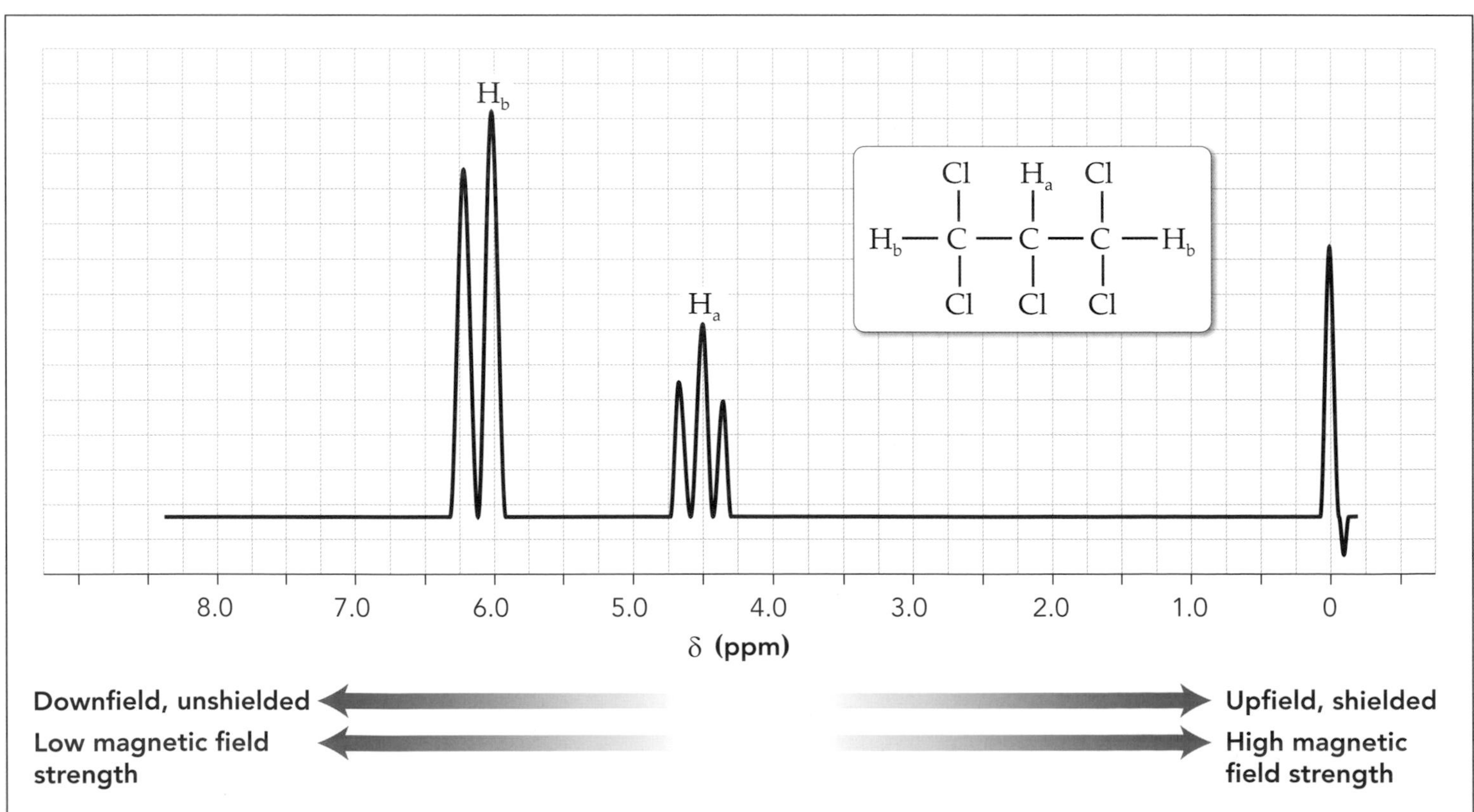

Very little specific information about NMR is required for the MCAT®. Most importantly, remember that unless otherwise indicated, NMR is concerned with hydrogen atoms. An MCAT® problem could provide an NMR spectrum and ask which peaks belong to which hydrogen atoms on a given compound, or which of four compounds would create the given spectrum. Answering this type of question requires an understanding of the following principles:

- Each peak represents chemically equivalent hydrogens;
- Splitting of peaks is caused by "neighboring hydrogens."

Each peak indicates one or a group of **chemically equivalent hydrogens**, meaning hydrogens whose positions on the compound are indistinguishable by NMR. Hydrogens that are chemically equivalent have the same chemical shift. **Chemical shift** is the difference between the resonance frequency of the chemically shifted hydrogens and the resonance frequency of hydrogens on a reference compound such as tetramethylsilane.

The area under a peak is proportional to the number of hydrogens represented by that peak. The more chemically equivalent hydrogens, the greater the area. The tallest peak does not necessarily correspond to the greatest area. The *integral trace* is a line drawn above the peaks that rises each time it goes over a peak. The rise of the integral trace is proportional to the number of chemically equivalent hydrogens in the peak beneath it. A newer instrument, called a digital trace, records numbers that correspond to the rise in the line. The exact number of hydrogens cannot be determined from the integral or digital trace. However, comparing the values assigned to different peaks provides the ratio of hydrogens between peaks.

The position of a peak on the NMR spectrum is dictated by electron shielding, so the positions of different groups of hydrogens can be predicted based on the presence of electron-withdrawing and electron-donating groups. Electron-withdrawing groups tend to lower shielding and thus decrease the magnetic field strength at which resonance takes place. This means that hydrogens adjacent to electron-withdrawing groups tend to have peaks downfield (to the left). Conversely, electron-donating groups tend to increase shielding and increase the field strength required for resonance.

Splitting (also called **spin-spin splitting**) of a peak into several smaller peaks is caused by neighboring hydrogens that are not chemically equivalent. A neighboring hydrogen is one that is bound to an atom adjacent to the atom to which the other hydrogen is connected. The number of peaks due to splitting for a group of chemically equivalent hydrogens is given by the simple formula n + 1, where *n* is the number of **neighboring hydrogens** that are not chemically equivalent. Thus, the number of neighboring hydrogens for a given peak can be determined by subtracting 1 from the number of smaller peaks into which the peak is split.

To interpret proton NMR spectroscopy, follow these steps:

- **Identify chemically equivalent hydrogens.**
- **Identify and count neighboring hydrogens that are not chemically equivalent. Use n + 1 to determine the number of peaks created by splitting for the chemically equivalent hydrogens.**
- **If necessary, identify electron withdrawing/donating groups near the chemically equivalent hydrogens. Withdrawing groups will move the signal to the left; donating groups will move the signal to the right.**

Aldehyde protons have a very distinctive shift at 9.5 ppm. Watch for it.

In a rare situation, carbon NMR may also appear on the MCAT®. Remember, the nucleus must have an odd atomic or mass number to register on NMR, so carbon-13 is the only carbon isotope that would register. Treat carbon NMR the same way as proton NMR, but ignore splitting.

Of course, NMR can be more complicated than is described here. However, the MCAT® would provide any additional information necessary to solve more complex problems. Figure 4.9 presents an additional NMR spectrum that can be used to test understanding. Before reading further, try to predict which hydrogens belong to which group of peaks (see answer on p. 118).

FIGURE 4.9 NMR Spectrum with Integral Trace

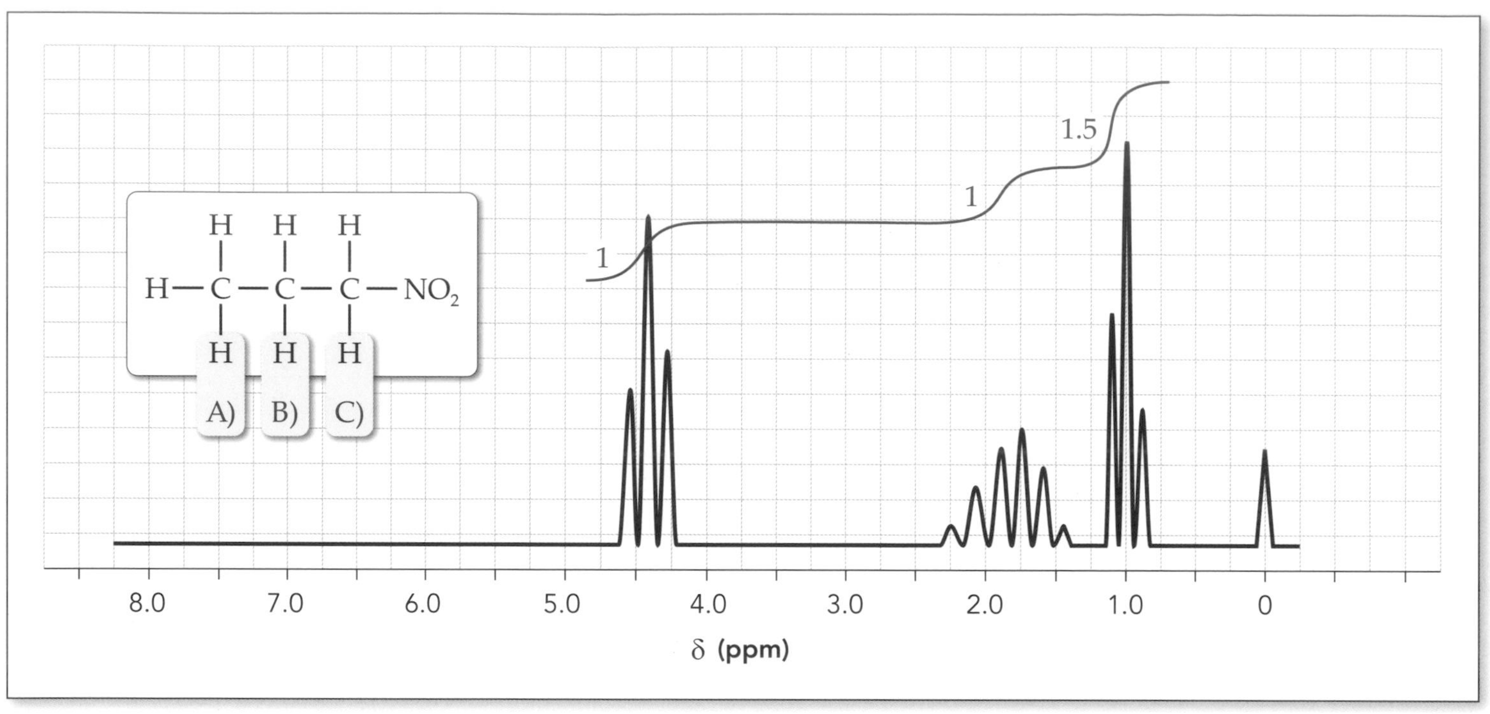

Another type of spectroscopy, IR spectroscopy, uses molecular dipoles to find information about functional groups. A dipole exists when the centers of positive and negative charge do not coincide. When exposed to an electric field, these oppositely charged centers move in opposite directions, either toward or away from each other. In infrared radiation, the direction of the electric field oscillates, causing the positive and negative centers within polar bonds to move toward each other and then away from each other. Thus, when exposed to radiation in the **infrared region** of the electromagnetic spectrum, the polar bonds within a compound stretch and contract, causing **intramolecular vibrations and rotations**.

Different bonds vibrate at different frequencies. When the resonance frequency of the oscillating bond is matched by the frequency of infrared radiation, the IR energy is absorbed. In **IR spectroscopy**, an infrared spectrometer slowly changes

FIGURE 4.10 Vibration of a Dipole

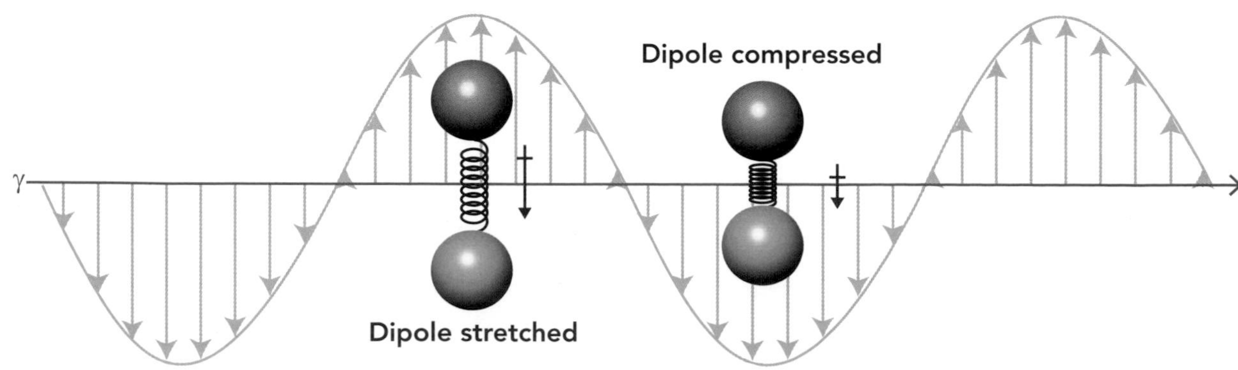

the frequency of infrared light shining on a compound and records the frequencies of absorption in number of cycles per centimeter, cm^{-1}. If a bond has no dipole moment, infrared radiation does not cause it to vibrate and no energy is absorbed.

The most predictable section of the IR spectrum is in the 1600 to 3500 cm^{-1} region. Figure 4.11 depicts the shapes and frequencies of absorption associated with common functional groups, which should be known for the MCAT®.

Limited predictions about the vibration of a bond can be made based on the masses of the atoms involved and the stiffness of the bond between them. Atoms with greater mass resonate at lower frequencies. Stiffer bonds, such as double and triple bonds, resonate at higher frequencies. Bond strength and bond stiffness follow the same trend: $sp > sp^2 > sp^3$.

An IR spectrum can help identify which functional groups are included in a compound, but it does not reveal the shape or length of the carbon skeleton. However, two compounds are very unlikely to have exactly the same IR spectrum. Thus the IR spectrum of a compound acts as a "fingerprint" for that compound.

The MCAT® may require knowledge of the IR spectra of certain functional groups. The most likely spectra that would be tested by MCAT® are C=O, a sharp dip around 1700 cm^{-1}, and O-H, a broad dip around 3200-3600 cm^{-1}.

FIGURE 4.11 IR Absorption of Common Functional Groups

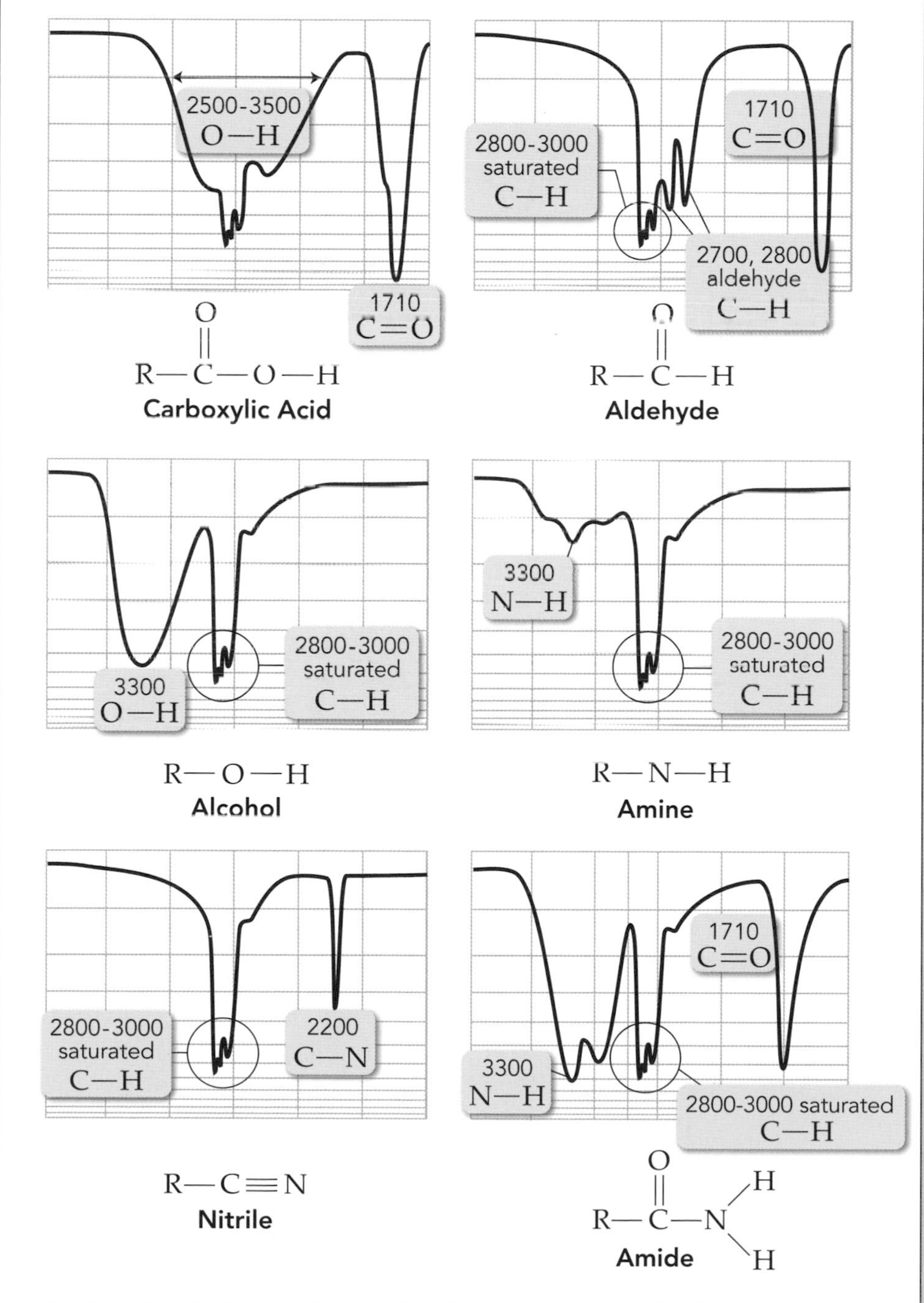

The fingerprint region of the IR spectrum is unique for nearly every compound, but it is very difficult to interpret. Know about the fingerprint region, but use IR to identify functional groups based on the region from 1600 to 3500 cm^{-1}.

Many of the complex vibrations that distinguish one compound from a similar compound are found in the 600 to 1400 cm^{-1} region, called the **fingerprint region**. Figure 4.12 shows three sample spectra that include the fingerprint region. Know where the fingerprint region is and why it is called the fingerprint region, but use the higher frequency range to identify functional groups.

FIGURE 4.12 Sample IR Spectra

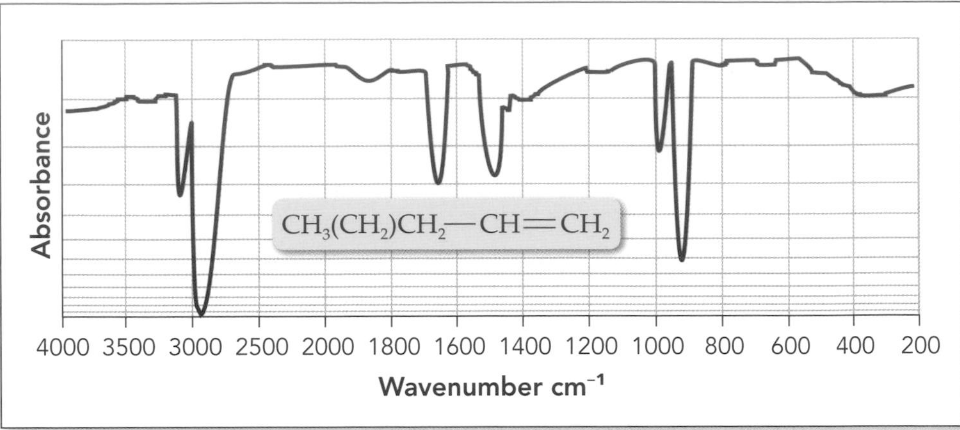

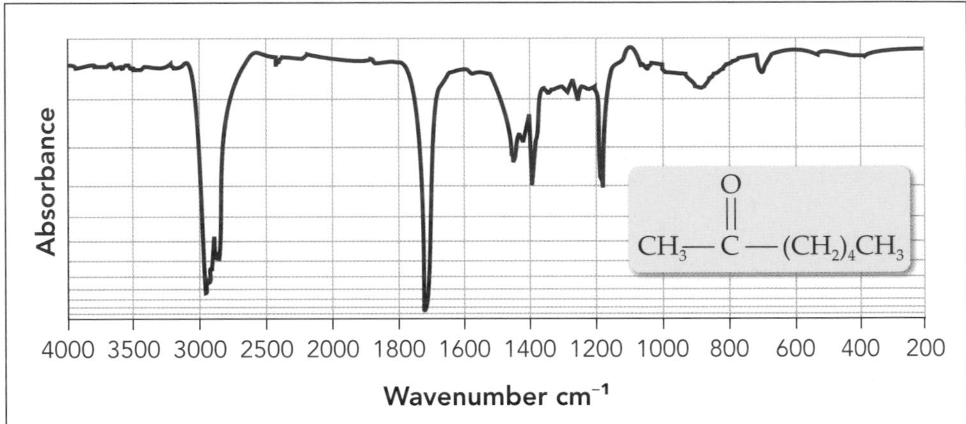

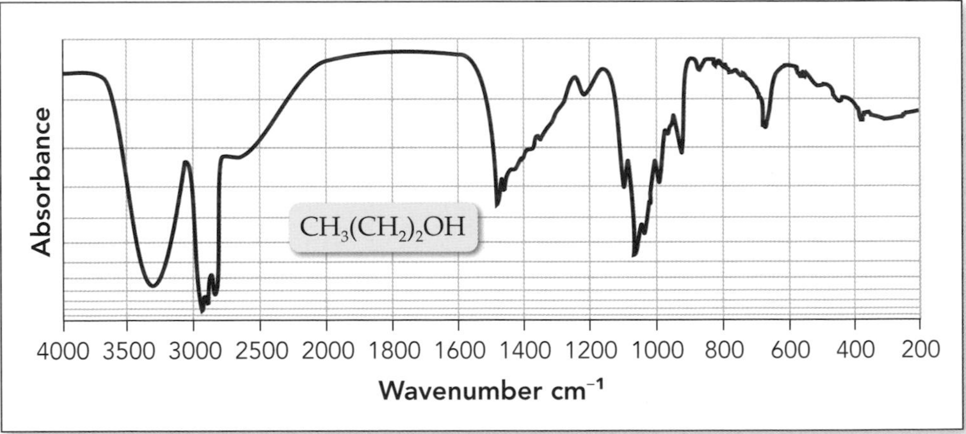

MCAT® THINK

So far, we've talked about how the bonds in molecules absorb infrared radiation of a characteristic frequency. However, bonds also emit radiation. The higher the temperature, the greater the amount of radiation emitted by bonds. Because cancerous tissue tends to be warmer than surrounding tissue, medical imaging professionals have suggested that infrared radiation detectors could be used to identify breast cancer. This still controversial method of detection is known as thermal imaging, or thermography.

The **ultraviolet region** of the electromagnetic spectrum is much shorter than infrared light, between 200 and 400 nm, and at a much higher energy level. **Ultraviolet (UV) spectroscopy** detects **conjugated systems** (double bonds separated by one single bond) by comparing the intensities of two beams of light from the same monochromatic light source. One beam is shone through a sample cell and the other is shone through a reference cell. The sample cell contains the sample compound to be analyzed dissolved in a solvent, while the reference cell contains only the solvent. The difference in energy absorbed by the sample and the reference is recorded as a UV spectrum of the sample compound.

The UV spectrum provides limited information about the length and structure of the conjugated portion of the molecule. When a photon collides with an electron in a molecule in the sample, the photon may be absorbed, bumping an electron up to a vacant molecular orbital. These are typically π-electron movements from bonding to nonbonding orbitals ($\pi \rightarrow \pi^*$). Electrons in σ-bonds usually require more energy to reach the next highest orbital, so they are typically unaffected by wavelengths greater than 200 nm. Conjugated systems with π-bonds, on the other hand, have vacant orbitals at energy levels close to their highest occupied molecular orbital (HOMO) energy levels. Such a vacant orbitals is called LUMO (lowest unoccupied molecular orbital). UV photons can momentarily displace electrons to the LUMO.

If a conjugated system is present in the sample, the measured intensity of the radiation after passing through the sample will be lower than that of the reference, due to absorption. The absorbance of the sample can be calculated as the logarithm of sample intensity divided by reference intensity. Absorbance also equals the product of concentration of the sample (c), the length of the path of light through the cell (l), and the molar absorptivity (ε):

The rule of thumb for UV absorption is a 30 to 40 nm increase for each additional conjugated double bond, and a 5 nm increase for each additional alkyl group.

$$A = \varepsilon cl$$

Molar absorptivity is a measure of how strongly the sample absorbs light at a particular wavelength. It can be thought of mathematically, as $\varepsilon = A/cl$.

The longer the chain of conjugated double bonds, the greater the wavelength of absorption. The rule of thumb is that each additional conjugated double bond increases the wavelength by about 30 to 40 nm. An additional alkyl group attached to any atom involved in the conjugated system increases the spectrum wavelength by about 5 nm. Isolated double bonds do not affect the absorption wavelength.

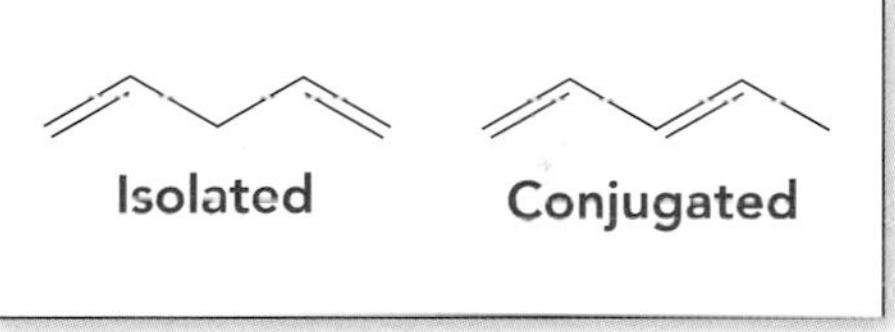

UV spectra lack detail. Samples must be extremely pure or the spectrum is obscured. Figure 4.13 shows the UV spectrum of 2-methyl-1,3-butadiene dissolved in methanol. The methyl group increases the absorption wavelength slightly. The methanol solvent makes no contribution to the spectrum. Spectra are typically represented by lists rather than being printed. The spectrum below would be listed as:

$$\lambda_{max} = 222 \text{ nm} \qquad \varepsilon = 20{,}000$$

Carbonyls, compounds with carbon-oxygen double bonds, also absorb light in the UV region. For example, acetone has a broad absorption peak at 280 nm. In this instance, unshared pairs of electrons are excited into a nonbonding π-orbital ($n \rightarrow \pi^*$).

FIGURE 4.13 UV Absorbance of 2-methyl-1,3-butadiene

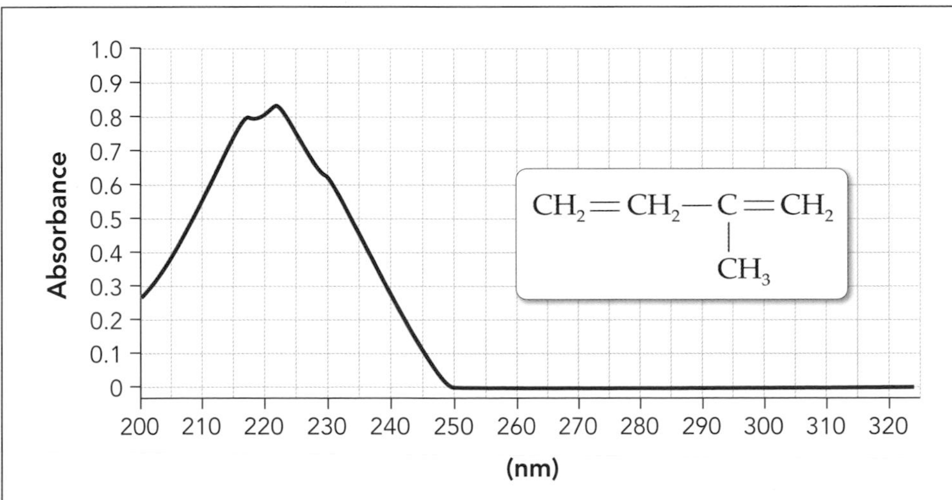

Keep your spectroscopies straight! NMR deals with the magnetic spin of hydrogen or carbon nuclei; IR spectroscopy deals with the way IR light causes bonds with dipoles to vibrate and rotate; and UV spectroscopy deals with the way UV light affects electrons in conjugated systems.

C=Ö: → C≐Ö:

$n \rightarrow \pi^*$

C=Ö: → C–̇Ö:

$\pi \rightarrow \pi^*$

If a compound has eight or more double bonds, its absorbance moves into the **visible region** of the electromagnetic spectrum. **β-carotene**, a precursor of vitamin A, has 11 conjugated double bonds. β-carotene has a maximum absorbance at 497 nm. Electromagnetic radiation of 497 nm has a blue-green color. Because carrots contain β-carotene, they absorb blue-green light, giving them the **complementary color** of red-orange. Structural changes in a compound can push its absorbance into the visible region; this is the mechanism behind the use of indicators in titrations.

Mass Spectrometry

By contrast to spectroscopy, which studies interactions between matter and electromagnetic radiation, spectrometry is the study of interactions between matter and energy sources other than electromagnetic radiation. **Mass spectrometry** is used to determine a compound's molecular weight, and, in the case of high resolution mass spectrometry, its molecular formula.

In a mass spectrometer, the molecules of a sample are bombarded with electrons, causing them to break apart and to ionize. The largest ion is the size of the original molecule but has one less electron. This cation is called the *molecular ion*. If methane were the sample, the molecular ion would be CH_4^+.

After a molecule is broken apart, the ions are accelerated through a magnetic field. The resulting force deflects the ions around a curved path. The radius of curvature of their path depends upon their *mass to charge ratio* (m/z). Most of the ions have a charge of 1+. The magnetic field strength is altered to allow the passage of differently sized ions through the flight tube.

A computer records the numbers of ions that arrive at the detector at different magnetic field strengths as peaks on a chart. The largest peak is called the *base peak*. The peak made by the molecular ions is called the *parent peak*. The parent peak is made by molecules that did not fragment. Look for the parent peak all the way to the right of the spectrum. Only heavy isotopes will be further right. All peaks are assigned *abundances* as percentages of the base peak. In Figure 4.14, the parent peak has an abundance of 10 because it is 10% as high as the base peak.

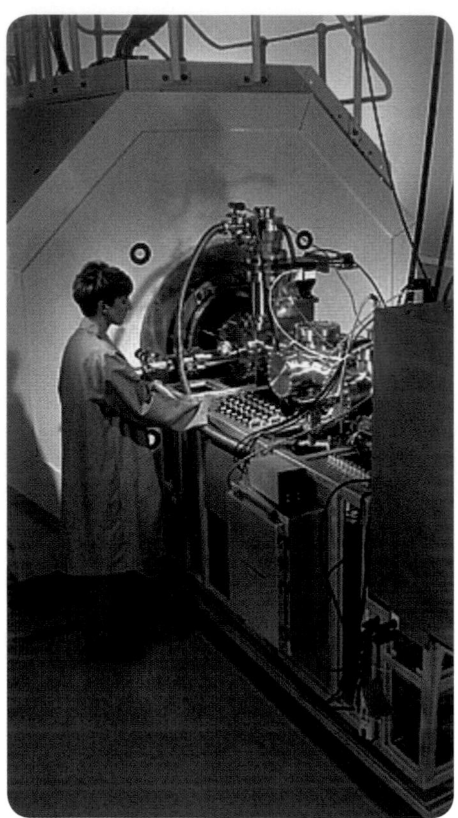

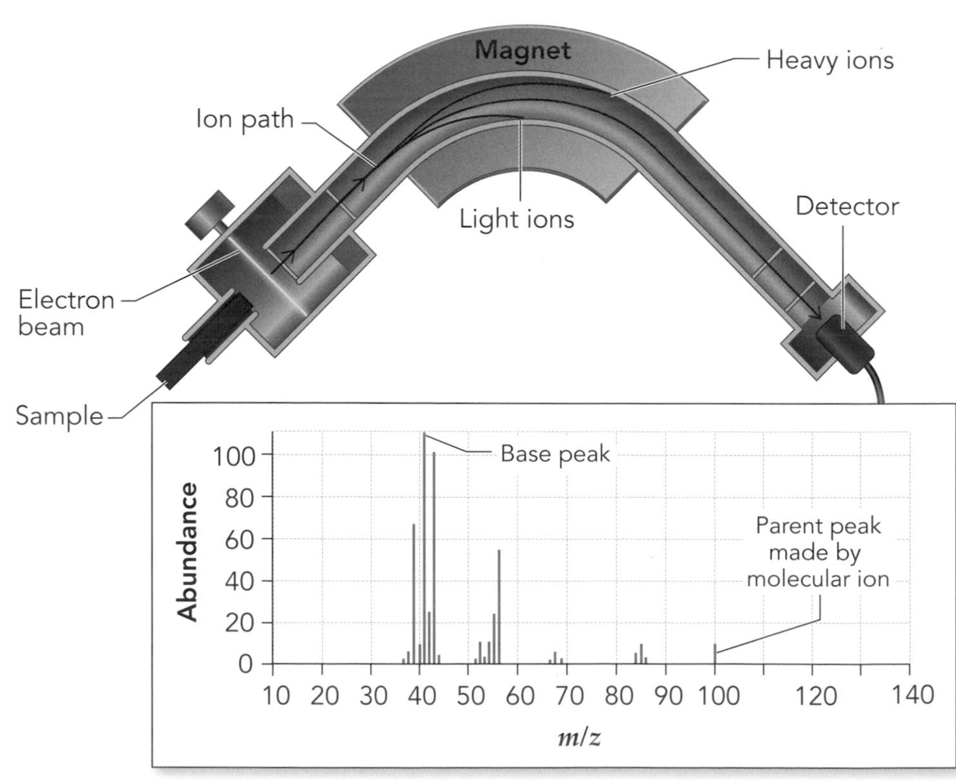

FIGURE 4.14 Mass Spectrometer

A mass spectrometer ionizes and fragments molecules in a sample, and then fires the fragments through a magnetic field. The amount that the fragments deviate is indicative of their mass and charge. This deviation provides detailed information about the sample's composition. A mass spectrometer is shown in the photo above.

These questions are NOT related to a passage.

Item 81

All of the following are true concerning NMR spectroscopy EXCEPT:

- ○ A) Protons are distinguished when they absorb magnetic energy at different field strengths.
- ○ B) "Downfield" is to the left on an NMR spectrum.
- ○ C) Functional groups are distinguished when they absorb magnetic energy at different field strengths.
- ○ D) Delocalized electrons generate magnetic fields that can either shield or deshield nearby protons.

Item 82

Which of the following structures is most likely to produce the infrared spectroscopy result depicted below?

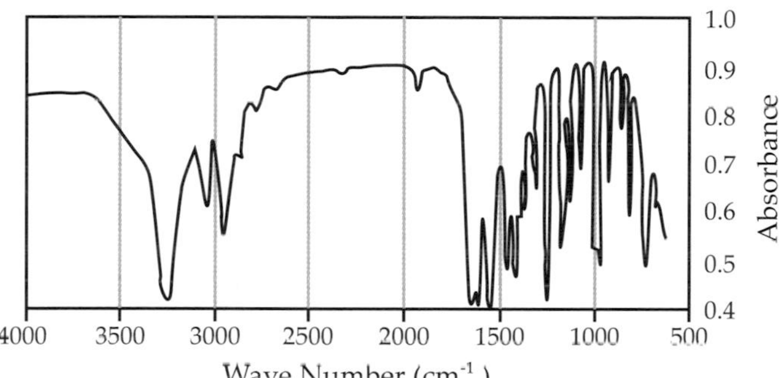

- ○ A) H_3C, O, CH_3
- ○ B) H_3C, O, CH_3, O, CH_3, O, O
- ○ C) O, CH_3, N, CH_3, H
- ○ D) H_3C, O, OH, CH_3

Item 83

A carbonyl group will absorb infrared radiation at a frequency of approximately:

- ○ A) 700 – 900 Hz.
- ○ B) 1630 – 1700 Hz.
- ○ C) 2220 – 2260 Hz.
- ○ D) 3300 – 3500 Hz.

Item 84

What are the predicted numbers of C^{13} NMR peaks for methylcyclopentane and 1,2-dimethylbenzene, respectively?

CH_3 — Methylcyclopentane

CH_3, CH_3 — 1,2-Dimethylbenzene

- ○ A) 2,3
- ○ B) 3,4
- ○ C) 4,4
- ○ D) 5,3

Item 85

Researchers used NMR spectroscopy in an attempt to characterize the molecule depicted in the inset below. Which of the following are represented by the peak at ~3.6 ppm?

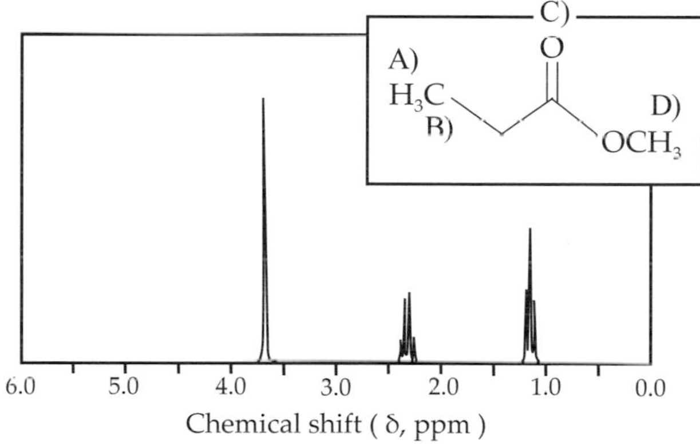

- ○ A) The "D" hydrogens
- ○ B) The "C" oxygen
- ○ C) The "B" carbon
- ○ D) The "A" hydrogens

Item 86

Which of the following must be FALSE concerning a molecule with a mass spectrometry parent peak of 134?

- ○ A) It normally carries no net charge.
- ○ B) It has a base peak at 15 m/z.
- ○ C) It has a molecular mass of 134 g/mol.
- ○ D) Its most abundant isotope has a mass of 160 g/mol.

Item 87

After analyzing both the products and reactants of a reaction, a chemist notices that a peak at roughly 3400 cm^{-1} has disappeared from the product reading. The reaction type was most likely:

- A) elimination.
- B) addition.
- C) hydration of an alkene.
- D) reduction of an aldehyde.

Item 88

Which of the following would show absorbance in the UV spectrum (200-400 nm)?

- A) 
- B) 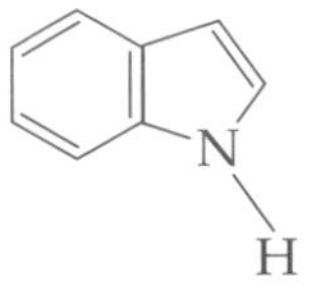 N H
- C)  CN
- D) 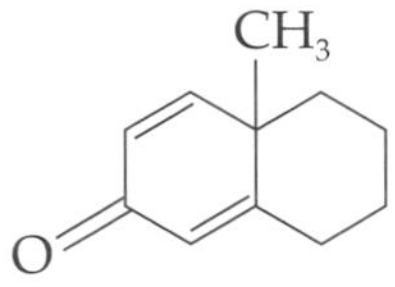 CH_3 O

4.4 Genetic Techniques

As noted in the Genetics Lecture, the scientific understanding of "genes" has evolved greatly over the last several decades. This is in part due to the use of genetic laboratory techniques. It is possible not only to isolate a gene and determine its function and origin, but also to manipulate it. A gene can be copied or altered, or we can cause it to be over- or under-expressed and observe the effects on the organism. Genetic techniques have a myriad of clinical, research, and ethical implications, and understanding them requires a strong grasp of basic biology and biochemistry.

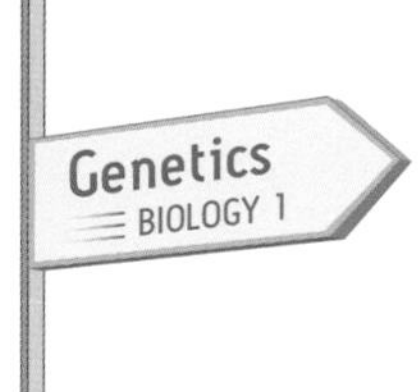

Broadly speaking, there are three types of genetic laboratory techniques:

1. Nucleic acid manipulation. DNA and RNA can be manipulated on a macro or micro level. Techniques can be used to join two strands together, pry two strands apart, chop one piece into smaller pieces, or join smaller pieces into a larger piece.
2. Recombination and cloning. Many copies of the same piece of genetic material can be created and put in new places or otherwise manipulated.
3. Sequencing and function. Techniques can be used to determine the exact nucleotide sequence of a piece of DNA or RNA. Additionally, a piece of nucleic acid that codes for a protein can be used to determine the function of that gene or protein.

You have to crawl before you can run – in other words, you need to understand basic manipulations before mastering complex techniques like PCR and cloning.

Nucleic Acid Manipulation

For a variety of reasons that will become clear later in this lecture, it is useful to know how to manipulate nucleic acids. More complicated lab techniques require the ability to convert DNA (or RNA) from 2 strands to 1 (and vice versa), as well as to chop up one big piece into many little pieces (and vice versa).

When heated or immersed in a high concentration salt solution or high pH solution, the hydrogen bonds connecting the two strands of a double-stranded DNA molecule are disrupted, and the strands separate; the DNA molecule is said to be **denatured** or *melted*. The temperature required to separate DNA strands is called the *melting temperature* (T_m). Since guanine and cytosine make three hydrogen bonds while thymine and adenine make only two, DNA with more G-C base pairs has a greater T_m. Heating to 95°C (just below the boiling point of water) is generally sufficient to denature any DNA sequence. Denatured DNA is less viscous, denser, and more able to absorb UV light than double-stranded DNA.

Separated strands will spontaneously associate with their original partner or any other complementary nucleotide sequence when not in a denaturing environment. Thus, the following double-stranded combinations can be formed: DNA-DNA, DNA-RNA, and RNA-RNA. This is called **nucleic acid hybridization**. Hybridization techniques allow scientists to identify nucleotide sequences by binding a known sequence with an unknown sequence.

Denaturing is going from 2 strands to 1 strand. Hybridization is going from 1 strand to 2 strands.

To denature DNA means to separate the two strands of the double helix.

DNA prefers to be double-stranded and will look for a complementary partner.

Recombination and Cloning

Recombination techniques take advantage of a method that bacteria use to defend themselves from viruses: cutting the viral DNA into fragments using restriction enzymes. Bacteria protect their own DNA from these enzymes through **DNA methylation** (adding a $-CH_3$ group). **Restriction enzymes** (also called restriction endonucleases) *digest* (cut) nucleic acid only at certain nucleotide sequences along the chain (see Figure 4.15). Such a sequence is called a *restriction site* or *recognition sequence*. Typically, a restriction site is a *palindromic* sequence four to six nucleotides long. (Palindromic means that it reads the same backwards as forwards.) Most restriction endonucleases cleave the DNA strand unevenly, leaving complementary single-stranded ends. These ends can reconnect through hybridization and are termed *sticky ends*. Once paired, the phosphodiester bonds of the fragments can be joined by DNA ligase.

There are hundreds of restriction endonucleases known, each attacking a different restriction site. Any sample of DNA of significant size is likely to contain a recognition sequence for at least one restriction endonuclease.

In the laboratory, scientists take advantage of the fact that two DNA fragments cleaved by the same endonuclease can be joined together regardless of the origins of the fragments. DNA created by this method is called **recombinant DNA**; it has been artificially recombined. Scientists can digest multiple pieces of DNA with the same restriction enzyme and then "paste" the pieces together to make a desired piece of recombinant DNA. This technology can be used to generate a DNA library for the purpose of DNA cloning.

FIGURE 4.15 Recombinant DNA

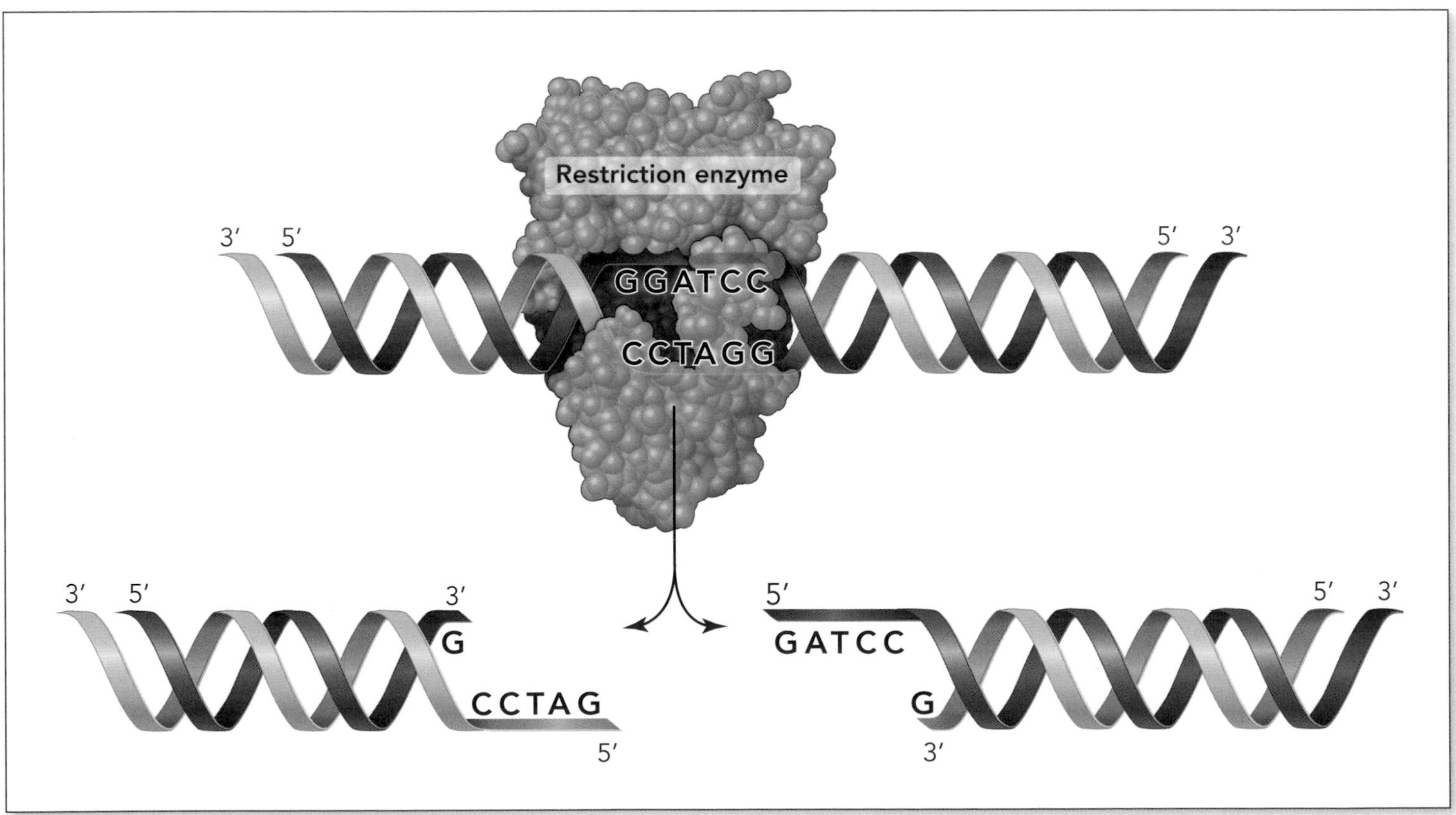

There are many reasons that it might be necessary to clone or amplify a piece of DNA. Generally speaking, one copy of a piece of DNA is too small to be useful in a laboratory. In order to sequence, recombine, or manipulate the DNA, it is necessary to have many copies, which is achieved by **gene cloning**. Cloning itself is accomplished either through bacteria and a cDNA library, or through polymerase chain reaction (PCR).

Recombinant DNA can be placed within a bacterial genome using a **vector**, typically a **plasmid** or sometimes an infective virus (Figure 4.17). The bacteria can then be grown in large quantities to form a **clone** of cells containing the vector with the recombinant DNA fragment. The clones can be saved separately to produce a **clone library**.

Not all bacteria will take up the vector, so a library may contain some clones that do not contain vectors. Including a gene in the original vector that lends resistance to a certain antibiotic makes it possible to screen the clone library for bacteria that did not take up the vector. The addition of the antibiotic eliminates clones without resistance, which must not have taken up the vector. Since some vectors will not take up the DNA fragment, some clones that do contain vectors will have vectors that lack the recombinant DNA. To allow screening for these clones, the *lacZ* gene, which enables the bacteria to metabolize the sugar X-gal, can be included in the original vector. An endonuclease with a recognition site that cleaves the *lacZ* gene can then be used to place the DNA fragment into the vector. Since the endonuclease cleaves the *lacZ* gene and the recombinant DNA is inserted in the middle of the *lacZ* gene, the *lacZ* gene will not work when the DNA fragment is placed in the vector. Clones with an active *lacZ* gene turn blue in the presence of X-gal, while clones with the cleaved form of the gene do not turn blue. Clones with the DNA fragment will therefore not turn blue when placed on a medium with X-gal.

Part of the screening process involves actually finding the desired DNA sequence from a library. **Hybridization** can be used as a technique to find a particular gene in a library. A fluorescently or radioactively labeled complementary sequence of the desired DNA fragment (called a **probe**) is used to search the library. The labeled clones are then identified. In the case of radiolabelling, the labeled clones expose photographic film while the non-radiolabeled clones do not.

Eukaryotic DNA contains introns. Since bacteria have no mechanism for removing introns, it is useful to clone DNA with no introns. In order to do this, the mRNA produced by the DNA is reverse transcribed using reverse transcriptase. The DNA product is called **complementary DNA** or **cDNA**. Adding DNA polymerase to cDNA produces a double strand of the desired DNA fragment.

To make a DNA library, take a DNA fragment, use a vector to insert it into a bacterium, and reproduce that bacterium like crazy. Now you have clones of bacteria with the DNA fragment.

cDNA is just DNA reverse transcribed from mRNA. The great thing about cDNA is that it lacks the introns that would normally be found in eukaryotic DNA.

FIGURE 4.16 cDNA Synthesis

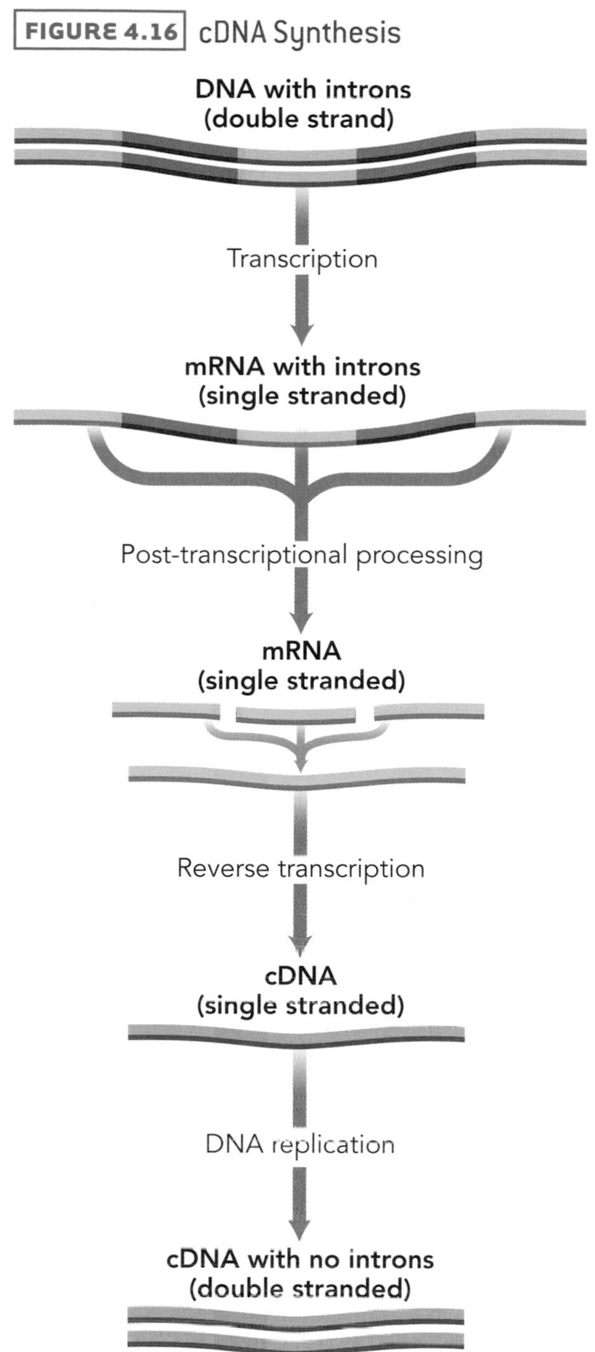

FIGURE 4.17 Clone Library

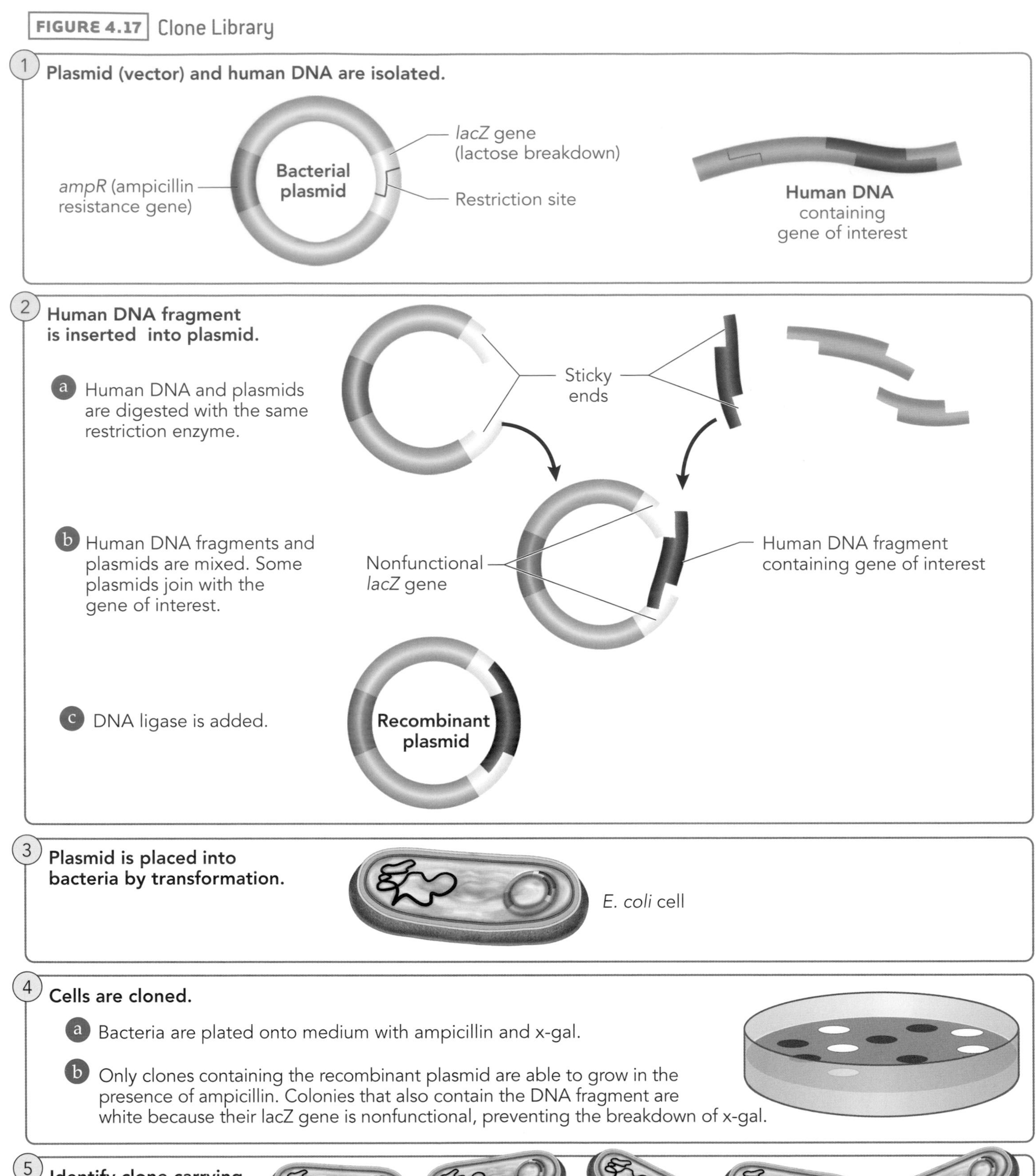

The cloning process isn't perfect, so some bacteria in a library won't have the vector and some vectors won't have the DNA fragment. To screen out these undesirable elements, the lacZ gene and an antibiotic resistant gene can be included in the preparation of the clone. Also, when preparing the clone, a restriction enzyme should be used that will insert the DNA fragment into the middle of the lacZ gene, causing it to be inactivated.

A much faster method of cloning, called **polymerase chain reaction (PCR)**, has been developed using a specialized polymerase enzyme found in a species of bacterium adapted to life in nearly boiling waters. In PCR, the double strand of DNA to be cloned is placed in a mixture with many copies of two DNA primers, one for each strand. The mixture is heated to 95°C to denature the DNA. When the mixture is cooled to 60°C, the primers hybridize (or **anneal**) to their complementary ends on the DNA strands. Next, the heat resistant polymerase is added with a supply of nucleotides, and the mixture is heated to 72°C to activate the polymerase. The polymerase amplifies the complementary strands, doubling the amount of DNA. The procedure can be repeated many times without adding more polymerase because the polymerase is heat resistant. By contrast, a heat sensitive polymerase would be denatured by the high temperature required to denature the DNA. The result is an exponential increase in the amount of DNA. Starting with a single fragment, over one million copies (2^{20}) can be produced by 20 cycles. What used to require days with recombinant DNA techniques can now be done in hours with PCR. Another advantage of PCR is that minute DNA samples can be amplified. In order to use PCR, the base sequence flanking the ends of the DNA fragment must be known so that the complementary primers can be chosen.

Because the amount of target DNA doubles in each cycle, PCR can be used to quantify the amount of DNA in each cycle (and thus the amount of starting DNA). This is called *quantitative PCR (qPCR)* or *real-time PCR*. Most commonly, qPCR uses a fluorescent dye or probe that binds to DNA and measures its concentration each cycle.

FIGURE 4.18 Polymerase Chain Reaction (PCR)

1 **Loading**
Target DNA, primers, and heat resistance polymerase are placed into a PCR thermal cycler.

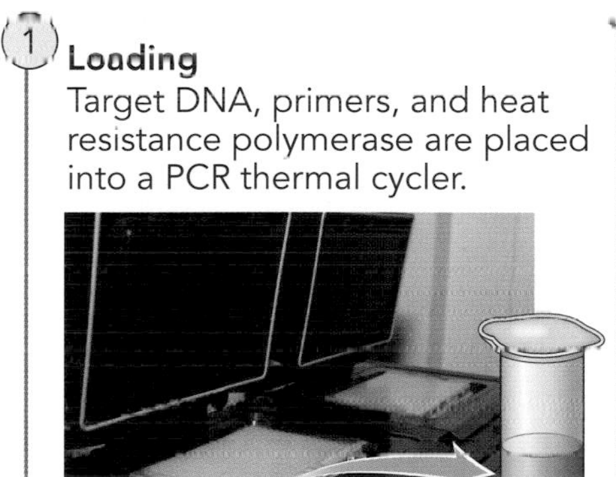

2 **Denaturing**
Temperature is increased to separate target DNA strands.

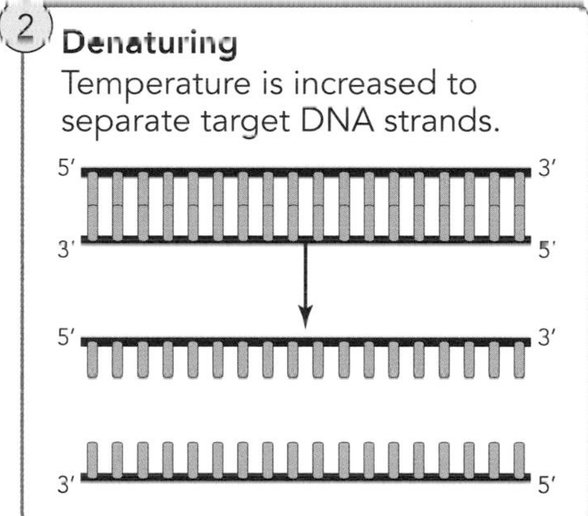

3 **Annealing**
Temperature is decreased and primers hybridize with target DNA.

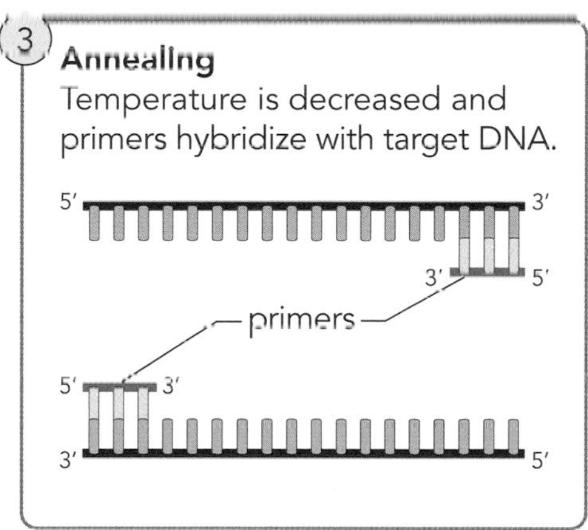

4 **Replication**
Heat resistant polymerase replicates target DNA.

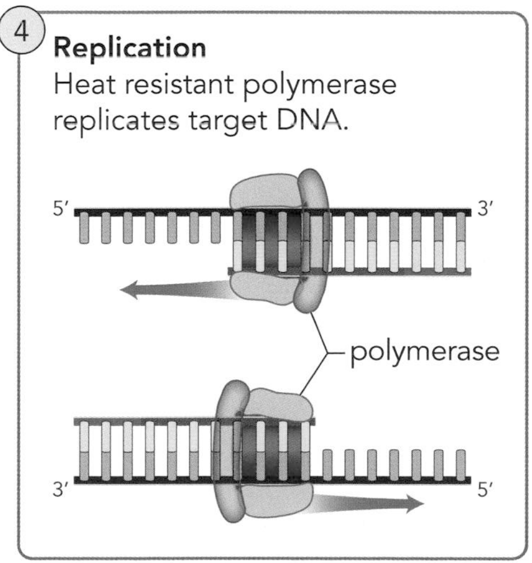

5 **Amplification**
Repeating the cycle exponentially amplifies the target DNA.

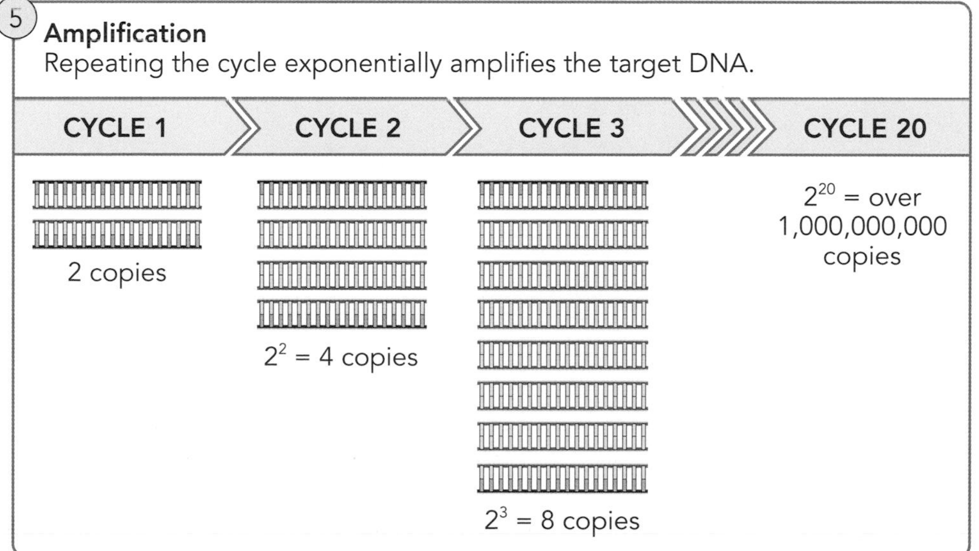

Sequencing and Function

Given a piece of DNA or RNA, genetic techniques can be used to determine its sequence, and correspondingly, what protein it will produce. It is also possible to determine the function of that protein.

Although **DNA sequencing** was first performed in the 1970s, it has become much more efficient and orders of magnitude faster. For many years, a *chain-termination method* called the *Sanger method* (Figure 4.19) was the main technique for sequencing. In this method, DNA is repeatedly replicated *in vitro*, with researchers providing all the necessary reagents, including all 4 nucleotides, primers, and enzymes. The researchers also add a small quantity of dideoxynucleotide (ddNTP) into the mix. Because of their structure, ddNTPs are incorporated into the growing DNA strand, but result in termination of replication ("chain-termination") once incorporated. The chain termination method involves setting up four replication tubes, each one containing one type of ddNTP (ddATP, ddTTP, ddCTP, and ddGTP).

For example, one tube would contain both adenine and ddATP. Each time the DNA replicated and attempted to incorporate an adenine, there would be a chance that it would instead choose ddATP, resulting in chain termination. If this replication cycle was repeated many times over (as in PCR), there would be some DNA strands that terminated at every adenine. Similarly, there would be strands terminating at every thymine in the ddTTP tube, every guanine in the ddGTP tube, and every cytosine in the ddCTP tube. Gel electrophoresis could then be used to compare the relative lengths of the strands. With this gel, it is relatively straightforward to determine the sequence of the replicated DNA segment.

More recently, rapid "next generation" DNA sequencing methods have been developed using automated systems. One such example utilizes fluorescence, with 4 differently colored molecules attached to each of the four nucleotides. DNA is replicated in vitro with these "colored" nucleotides. The new piece of DNA is thus color-coded, and can be passed through a computerized reader, which translates the sequence of colors into a DNA sequence.

FIGURE 4.19 Sanger Method

Template strand	ddGTP	ddCTP	ddATP	ddTTP
3′ T	A A	A A A	A A A	A A A A
G	C C	C C C	C C	C C C C
T	A A	A A	A A	A A A A
G	C C	C C	C	C C C C
A	T T	T	T	T T T T
A	T T	T	T	T T T
T	A A	A	A	A A
A	T T	T		T T
C	G G	G		G
A	T	T		T
C	G	G		
5′ G		C		

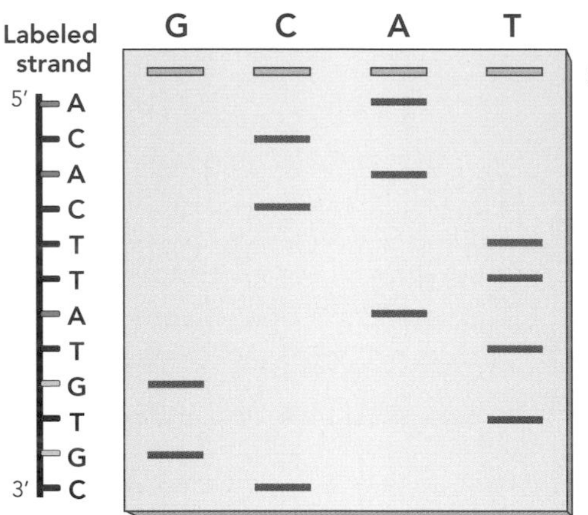

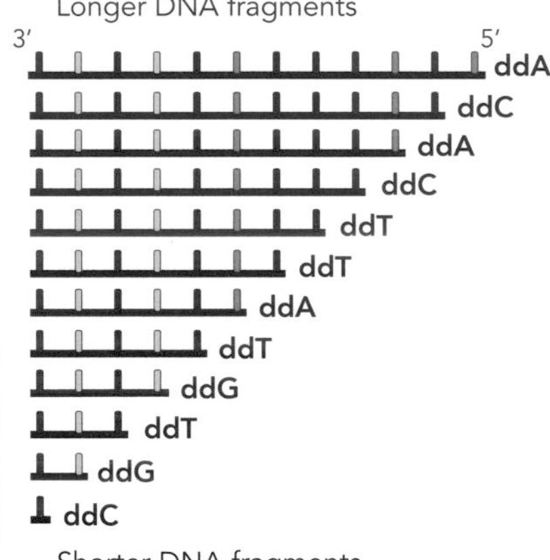

FIGURE 4.20 Automated Sequencing

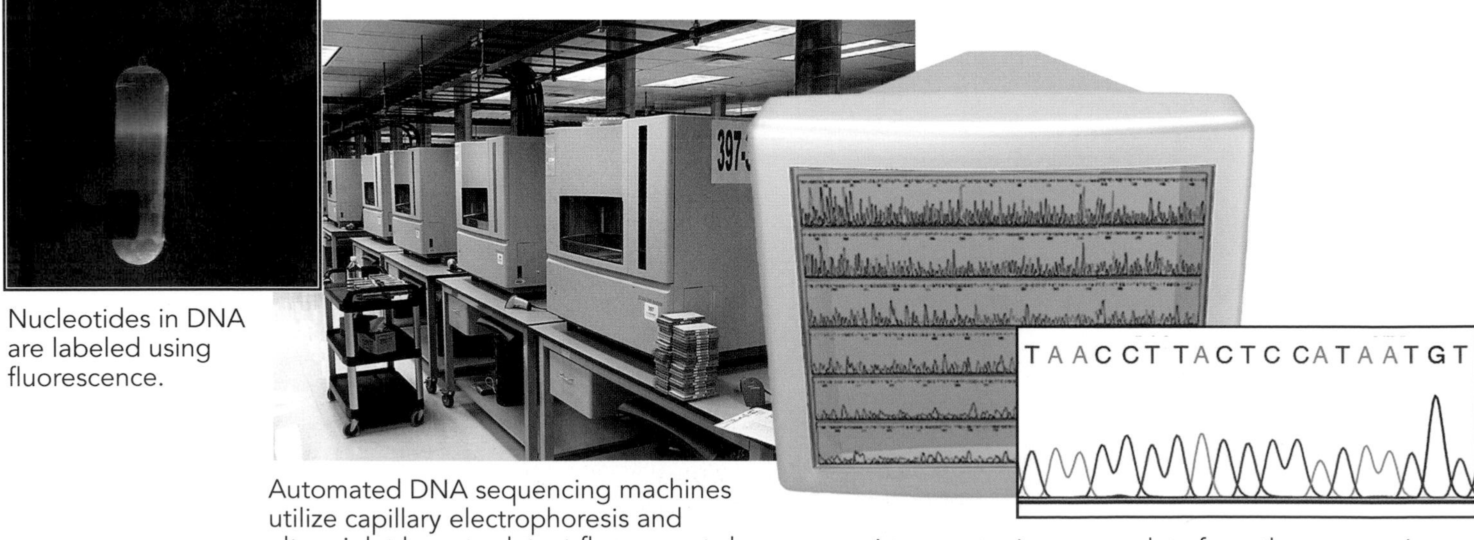

Nucleotides in DNA are labeled using fluorescence.

Automated DNA sequencing machines utilize capillary electrophoresis and ultra-violet laser to detect fluorescent dyes.

A computer interprets data from the sequencing machines and determines the exact sequence of nucleotides.

Gene expression levels for any given DNA sequence can vary greatly depending on cell type as well as intracellular and extracellular conditions. **Analyzing gene expression** requires measuring the gene's downstream mRNA or protein product. This can be done on a large scale through a *DNA microarray* or *gene chip*. A gene chip compares the levels of mRNA between two different cells and/or conditions. One of these microarrays may contain probes (small DNA sequences complimentary to mRNA) for hundreds or thousands of genes.

To run a gene chip, mRNA from two different conditions (often the same cell type before and after a stimulus) must be isolated. mRNA from the first situation is labeled in red, while mRNA from the second is labeled in green. Both sets of mRNA are then incubated with the same gene chip. Genes that are down-regulated from situation 1 to 2 appear as red dots in the appropriate area of the gene chip, since more red-labeled mRNA is present to bind to the probes. Likewise, genes that are up-regulated appear green. If a gene's expression level remains unchanged, there will be an equal amount of green and red mRNA, creating a yellow spot on the microarray.

FIGURE 4.21 Gene Chip

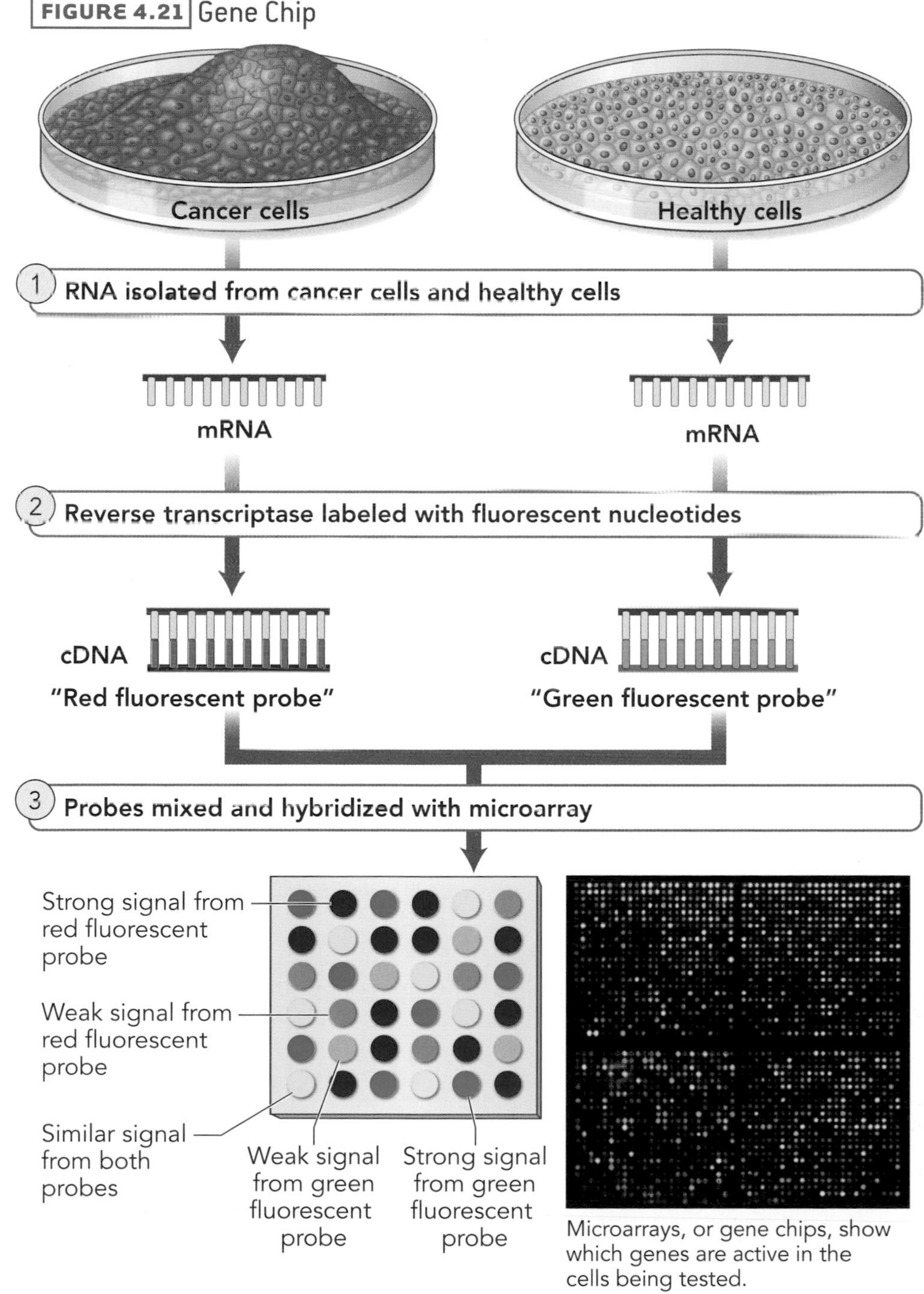

Microarrays, or gene chips, show which genes are active in the cells being tested.

In addition to examining gene sequence and expression, researchers are often interested in **determining gene function**. There are a variety of ways that the function of a gene can be determined. One method is to observe gene conservation or evolution among different species. However, more modern techniques involve direct manipulation of genes. Some of these techniques involve observing the results of a reduction or elimination of gene expression. Others allow observation of the results when a gene is over-expressed, or when the gene is expressed in a cell, tissue, or organism in which it is not normally expressed.

Endocrine System
BIOLOGY 2

A common method used to examine gene function is to create a genetic *knockout*, in which a target gene is deleted from the genome. Once the gene is knocked out, cells can be analyzed for phenotypic changes, providing information about the function of the gene that was removed. A knockout can refer to a cell line or to an entire organism; the latter is termed a knockout animal. In order to make a knockout animal, it is necessary to knock out the genes from gametes or from embryonic **stem cells** and to grow the animal from a zygote. (Note that if the gene to be knocked out is necessary for embryonic development, it will be impossible to generate a true knockout animal.) As an example, a mouse model of diabetes can be generated by knocking out the gene that codes for the insulin receptor.

Alternatively, gene expression can be reduced by the use of *RNA interference*, or *RNAi*. RNAi is a naturally occurring biological process in which small pieces of RNA bind to mRNA molecules, preventing their translation and/or marking them for degradation. Scientists can exploit this process to block expression of specific genes.

It is also possible to examine a gene's function by causing it to be overexpressed. One method is to alter the sequence of the gene's surrounding DNA, such as by increasing the strength of the promoter before a gene and thus increasing the expression of that gene. Another method is to express the gene in a new cell line or organism. For example, the gene that codes for the green fluorescent protein in jellyfish can be placed in the genome of an organism from another species, which then produces the protein and glows green.

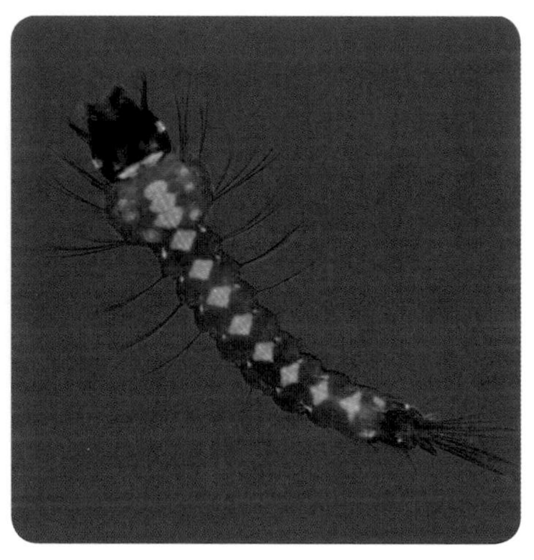

This photo shows a mosquito larva which has had a green fluorescent protein (GFP) gene, from a jellyfish, inserted into its genome.

MCAT® THINK

Manipulating genes in animals is one of the most common ways to create animal models of human diseases. For example, deletion of certain genes involved in cell cycle checkpoints can result in animals that are more prone to cancer. These animals can be studied to help us better understand the disease pathogenesis and treatment options.

Practical Applications of Genetic Techniques

All of the aforementioned genetic lab techniques have a host of practical applications in medicine and research. They can be used to identify individuals by their genetic code, treat genetic diseases, screen for carriers of genetic disorders, and much more.

Restriction fragment length polymorphism (RFLP) analysis identifies individuals, rather than identifying specific genes. The genomes of different individuals possess different restriction sites and varying distances between restriction sites. In other words, the human population is *polymorphic* for their restriction sites. After fragmenting the DNA sample with endonucleases, a band pattern unique to an individual is revealed on radiographic film via Southern blotting techniques. RFLPs (pronounced "riflips") are the DNA fingerprints used to identify criminals in court cases.

The genome of one human differs from the genome of another at about one nucleotide in every 1000. These differences have been called *single nucleotide polymorphisms* (SNPs). Like RFLPs, SNPs can serve as a fingerprint for an individual's genome.

One of the "holy grails" of medical research is curative treatment of genetic diseases. One method used by researchers is **human gene therapy**. Gene therapy involves genetic manipulation of an affected individual's DNA, in which the defective allele of the gene is replaced by the wildtype, or correctly functioning, allele. Theoretically, gene therapy can be accomplished by recombining the DNA in all defective cells, such as with a viral vector, or by altering the genome of a stem cell and letting it replicate in order to correct the deficit. Although there have been some successes with gene therapy, it remains highly experimental and at times has had dangerous side effects.

Genetic laboratory techniques can be also used for screening. Patients can be screened to see if they have certain genetic disorders, and newborns are routinely screened for a panel of genetic conditions. Potential parents can be screened to see if they are carriers of a genetic disorder and if their offspring could therefore be afflicted with the disease. A different type of screening involves antibiotic resistance in bacteria, allowing for treatment with the proper antibiotics. Traditionally, bacterial resistance screening was carried out by growing bacteria in a culture and exposing them to antibiotics. However, genetic screening techniques are becoming increasingly more common, as they are faster, cheaper, and at times more accurate.

Another significant application of genetic techniques is in **biometry**, the use of statistical methods to understand biological data. Biostatistical analysis can be applied to a wide variety of biological inquiries. Currently, one of the major uses of statistical analysis in biology is the attempt to better understand population genetics. With the wide variety of genetic data now available, it is possible to study population genetics on a large scale. The analysis of this data has had a powerful impact on the field of medicine, allowing researchers to identify genes correlated with certain medical conditions, as well as to better understand global health and epidemiology.

Safety and Ethics of Genetic Techniques

New scientific advances have raised issues around the **safety and ethics of DNA technology**. Some wonder whether it is ethical to alter the DNA of agricultural plants, other animals, and even ourselves. One contentious issue is the use of genetic modifications in agriculture, such as to produce a crop that is resistant to environmental hazards. Others think it might be a "slippery slope" from genetic screening of offspring to "designer babies," where parents could choose the sex and desirable physical or mental attributes of their offspring. Many of the lab techniques involve manipulation of embryonic stem cells, which leads to issues surrounding the purported origins of life. There are also controversial discussions related to gene patenting, biological warfare, and more. Modern advancements in genetic techniques have come with a whole host of complex ethical implications.

It is important to understand how every technique is done, which requires an understanding of the basic science behind it, as well as why it is being done or how it fits into the larger picture of a complex technique. On the MCAT®, many of these techniques, especially ones involving genetics, may be involved in questions about other topics, such as ethics, biostatistics, or safety.

These questions are NOT related to a passage.

Item 89

In PCR amplification, a primer is hybridized to the end of a DNA fragment and acts as the initiation site of replication for a specialized DNA polymerase. The DNA fragment to be amplified is shown below. Assuming that the primer attaches exactly to the end of the fragment, which of the following is most likely the primer? (Note: The N stands for any nucleotide.)

5′-ATGNNNNNNNNNNNNNGCT-3′

- O A) 5′-GCT-3′
- O B) 5′-TAC-3′
- O C) 5′-TCG-3′
- O D) 5′-AGC-3′

Item 90

Which of the following regarding restriction enzymes, such as EcoRI and HindIII, is most likely FALSE?

- O A) They are made by bacteria as a defense against viruses.
- O B) EcoRI is synthesized in the cytosol.
- O C) They recognize sequences that read the same forward and backwards.
- O D) DNA cut by EcoRI easily joins to DNA cut by HindIII.

Item 91

Which of the following best describes the molecule shown and its effect on replication?

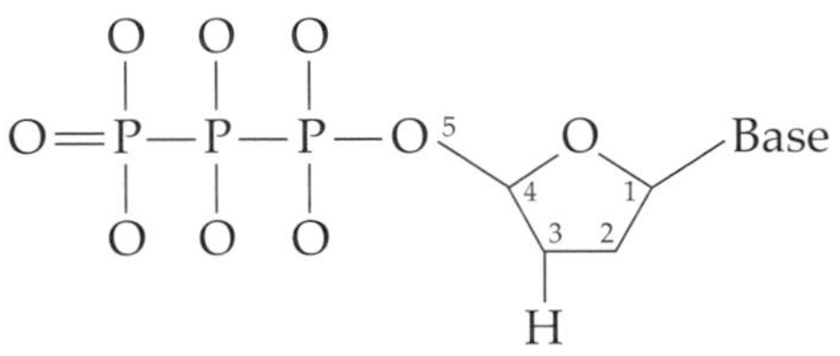

O O O
O=P—P—P—O 5 O Base
4 1
3 2
O O O
H

- O A) There is no 3’ hydroxyl group, so a phosphodiester bond will be unable to form and replication will terminate.
- O B) There is no 3’ hydroxyl group, so replication will continue as normal.
- O C) There is no 5’ phosphate group, so replication will continue as normal.
- O D) There is no 5’ phosphate group, so a phosphodiester bond will be unable to form and replication will terminate.

Item 92

Cystic fibrosis is an autosomal recessive trait resulting from the dysfunction of a sodium chloride transporter protein. Which of the following describes the best experimental approach to developing a mouse model of cystic fibrosis?

- O A) Take the human protein encoding the sodium chloride transporter and express it in mice.
- O B) Identify the mouse homologue of the sodium chloride transporter and develop a knockout mouse.
- O C) Identify the mouse homologue of the sodium chloride transporter and feed the mice food laced with RNAi for that protein.
- O D) Identify the promoter for the mouse homologue of the sodium chloride transporter and change it to a weaker one.

Item 93

Starting with *n* copies of a gene, *x* cycles of PCR are performed. How many copies of the gene result from this procedure?

- O A) n^x
- O B) n^{2x}
- O C) $n(2^x)$
- O D) x^n

Item 94

Pancreatic beta cells were isolated from a mouse after a fast. The same mouse was then fed, followed by another round of beta cell collection. If samples from both groups of cells were run on the same DNA microarray, what color would be seen on the region of the chip containing probes for the insulin gene?

- O A) Green
- O B) Yellow
- O C) Red
- O D) No color

Item 95

Suppose a forensic scientist is trying to prove that a criminal defendant was at a crime scene. Which of the following would be the LEAST useful piece of evidence?

- O A) Blood found at the scene showing signs of a rare disorder with which the defendant also suffers
- O B) Blood found at the scene that is the same blood type as that of the defendant
- O C) RFLP analysis of DNA found at the crime scene that was identical to DNA taken from the defendant
- O D) SNP analysis of DNA found at the crime scene that was identical to DNA taken from the defendant

Item 96

Developmental biologists have developed inducible knockout mice for certain genes. In these animals, an enzyme responsible for excising the gene of interest is only active after treatment with certain pharmaceuticals. This development would be most useful for the study of which of the following genes?

- A) The *LacZ* gene
- B) A telomerase gene that is active in many cell types during old age
- C) A dopamine transporter gene that becomes active during puberty in certain brain regions
- D) A *Hox* family gene necessary for proper embryonic neurulation

Question 96 of 96

STOP

TERMS YOU NEED TO KNOW

Affinity chromatography
Analyzing gene expression
Anneal
β-carotene
Biometry
Chemical shift
Chemically equivalent hydrogens
Chromatography
Clone
Clone library
Column chromatography
Complementary color
Complementary DNA (cDNA)
Conjugated systems
Denatured
Determining gene function
Distillation
DNA methylation
DNA sequencing
Extraction
Fingerprint region
Gas-liquid chromatography
Gel electrophoresis
Gene cloning
High pressure liquid chromatography (HPLC)
Human gene therapy
Hybridization
Infrared region
Infrared (IR) spectroscopy
Intramolecular vibrations and rotations
Ion-exchange chromatography
Isoelectric points
Mass spectrometry
Neighboring hydrogens
Nuclear Magnetic Resonance (NMR) spectroscopy
Nucleic acid hybridization
Paper chromatography
Plasmid
Polymerase chain reaction (PCR)
Probe
Racemic mixture
Recombinant DNA
Restriction enzymes
RFLP
Safety and ethics of DNA technology
Separation of enantiomers
Separations
Size-exclusion chromatography
Southern blotting
Splitting (spin-spin splitting)
Stem cells
Thin-layer chromatography
Ultraviolet region
Ultraviolet (UV) spectroscopy
Vector
Visible region
Western blot

FIGURE 4.9 NMR Spectrum Answers

Each letter, *a*, *b*, and *c*, represents a group of chemically equivalent hydrogens. The groups of peaks from left to right correspond to the *c*, *b*, and *a* hydrogens respectively. Since NO_2 is electron-withdrawing, the *c* hydrogens are further downfield. The *b* hydrogens have 5 neighbors, so their peak has 6 smaller peaks. The digital trace shows that the peak furthest upfield has 1.5 times as many hydrogens as each of the other peaks. The ratio of a hydrogens to *b* or *c* hydrogens is 3 to 2, so this peak must represent the *a* hydrogens.

DON'T FORGET YOUR KEYS

1. Separation and purification techniques use chemical and physical properties to isolate compounds.
2. "Spec" techniques identify unknown features of compounds.
3. Genetic lab techniques identify or manipulate DNA to study or change healthy and pathological processes.

STOP!

DO NOT LOOK AT THESE EXAMS UNTIL CLASS.

30-MINUTE IN-CLASS EXAM FOR LECTURE 1

Passage I (Questions 1-7)

The three dimensional shape of a protein is ultimately determined by its amino acid sequence. The folding pattern itself is a sequential, cooperative process where initial folds assist in aligning the protein properly for subsequent folds. Proteins that provide assistance in the folding process by stabilizing partially folded intermediates are called chaperones.

Folding of myosin (the thick filament involved in muscle contraction) in striated muscle is mediated by the chaperone Hsp90. Newly synthesized myosin forms a transient complex with Hsp90 in which the myosin motor domain is partially folded. Myosin transits through this chaperone complex on the pathway to myofibril assembly. This pathway appears to involve an Hsp90 co-chaperone, Unc45b. Unc45b has a region that is conserved among proteins that interact with myosin. Mutations in this domain result in decreased accumulation of striated muscle myosin filaments and disruption of contractile ring formation, both processes that are dependent on myosin function.

Analysis of synthesized myosin subfragments has shown that folding of the myosin motor domain is the rate limiting step and may require folding factors. If Unc45b is indeed a striated myosin specific chaperone, it might be expected to target the myosin motor domain. To test this hypothesis, scientists synthesized full-length myosin (MHC) and two subfragments, one including the myosin motor domain (S1) and one without (S2). They also isolated the native (fully formed and functioning) myosin motor domain subfragment (HMM) from chicken muscle. Unc45b was tagged with an epitope coding sequence to create Unc45b^{Flag}, which was then bound to radioactively tagged anti-Flag antibody. The subfragments and native protein were incubated with either Unc45b^{Flag}/Hsp90 complex or purified Unc45b^{Flag}. Binding of Unc45b^{Flag} or the Unc45b^{Flag}/Hsp90 complex was visualized by autoradiography as a dark band at a characteristic position for each protein or fragment. The results are shown in Figure 1.

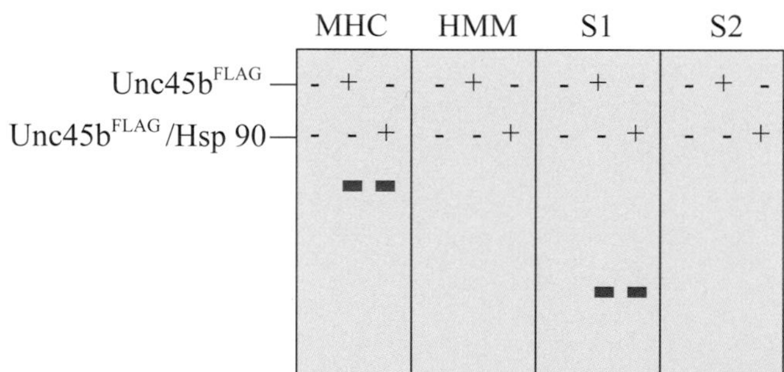

Figure 1 Binding of synthesized myosin heavy chain and its subfragments to Unc45b^{Flag} and Unc45b^{Flag}/Hsp90 complex, visualized by tagged Anti-Flag antibody

1. Do the results of this experimental setup allow the conclusion that Unc45b acts as a co-chaperone for the folding of the myosin motor domain?

- **A.** Yes, because they show that the Unc45b^{Flag}/Hsp90 complex binds to the synthesized subfragment myosin motor domain.
- **B.** Yes, because they show that mutations in Unc45b result in decreased accumulation of type II striated muscle myosin filaments.
- **C.** No, because they do not show that the Unc45b^{Flag}/Hsp90 complex enhances the folding of the myosin motor domain.
- **D.** No, because they show that the Unc45b^{Flag}/Hsp90 complex does not bind to the native conformation of the myosin motor domain.

2. Which of the following is the best explanation for why attempts at predicting protein configuration based upon amino acid sequence have been unsuccessful?

- **A.** It is impossible to know the amino acid sequence of a protein without knowing the DNA nucleotide sequence.
- **B.** Chaperones help to determine the three dimensional shape of a protein.
- **C.** The three dimensional shape of a protein is based upon hydrogen and disulfide bonding between amino acids, and the number of possible combinations of bonding amino acids makes prediction difficult.
- **D.** The amino acid sequence of the same protein may vary slightly from one sample to the next.

3. Chaperones assist in the formation of a protein's:

- **A.** primary structure.
- **B.** secondary structure.
- **C.** tertiary structure.
- **D.** quaternary structure.

4. The scientists first incubated each protein fragment with Anti-Flag antibody only because:

- **A.** they wanted to ensure that the Anti-Flag antibody was visualizable by autoradiography.
- **B.** if the Anti-Flag antibody bound to any of the proteins, it could not be used to assess whether the protein bound to Unc45b^{Flag} or the Unc45b^{Flag}/Hsp90 complex.
- **C.** they wanted to ensure that the Anti-Flag antibody bound to the Unc45b^{Flag}.
- **D.** each protein fragment had a different tertiary structure.

GO ON TO THE NEXT PAGE.

5. Natural selection has resulted in increased chaperone synthesis in the presence of elevated temperatures. How might increased chaperone production in the presence of heat be advantageous to a cell?

   A. Heat destabilizes intermolecular bonds, making protein configuration more difficult to achieve. Chaperones counteract this effect by stabilizing the partially folded intermediates.
   B. Increased temperatures increase reaction rates, creating an excess of fully formed proteins. Chaperones stabilize the partially folded intermediates and slow this process.
   C. Increased chaperone production requires energy. This energy is acquired from the kinetic energy of molecules and thus cools the cell.
   D. Elevated temperatures result in increased cellular activity, requiring more proteins. Chaperones increase the rate of polypeptide formation.

6. Which of the following bonds in a protein is likely to be LEAST stable in the presence of heat?

   A. A disulfide bond
   B. A hydrogen bond
   C. A polypeptide bond
   D. The double bond of a carbonyl

7. Suppose that the folding of the myosin motor domain is also assisted by an enzyme that non-selectively assists in the creation of disulfide bonds. This enzyme most likely:

   A. lowers the activation energy of the formation of cystine.
   B. raises the activation energy of the formation of cystine.
   C. lowers the activation energy of the formation of proline.
   D. raises the activation energy of the formation of proline.

Passage II (Questions 8-14)

Galactose is normally metabolized via the Leloir pathway to produce glucose-6-phosphate for glycolysis. The first step of this pathway is the phosphorylation of galactose, catalyzed by galactokinase. A common cause of galactosemia, the inability to digest galactose, is deficiency of the next enzyme in the pathway, galactose-1-phosphate uridyl transferase (GALT). The associated symptoms are believed to result from the buildup of the toxic metabolite galactose-1-phosphate. It has been suggested that the inhibition of galactokinase might be a useful treatment for GALT-deficient patients.

Scientists explored a possible site of inhibition by mutating the residue glutamate-43 in the sugar binding site of human galactokinase and assessing the kinetic consequences. Mutating the glutamate side chain to alanine (creating the mutant E43A) caused no major changes in the kinetic parameters. In contrast, altering this residue to glycine (creating the mutant E43G) caused a substantial drop in the turnover number (the number of substrate molecules converted to product per active site in a solution saturated with substrate, also called k_{cat}) with no corresponding drop in the specificity constant.

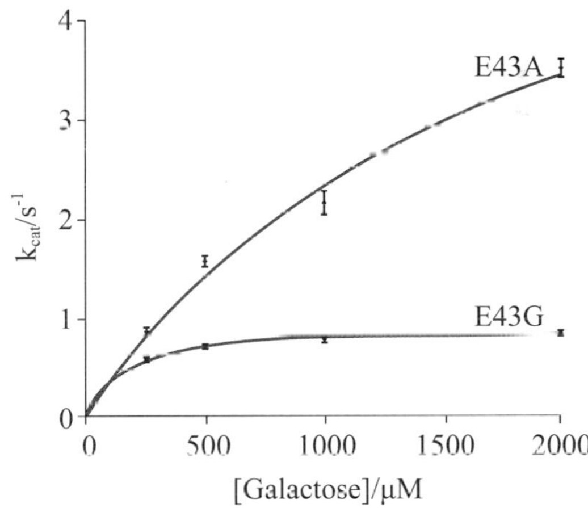

Figure 1 Turnover number as a function of galactose concentration for mutant proteins E43A and E43G

The specificity constant is related to Km as follows:

$$\textit{specificity constant} = \frac{k_{cat}}{K_m}$$

While K_m is a summed measure of the interaction between the substrate and the enzyme across all stages of the catalytic cycle, the specificity constant reports on the initial enzyme-substrate encounter. In the case of E43G, the kinetic changes show that the mutation causes little or no change in the rate of interaction between galactose and the enzyme but that the overall rate of catalysis is reduced.

GO ON TO THE NEXT PAGE.

8. The activity of galactokinase causes a buildup of galactose-1-phosphate when the GALT enzyme is deficient because:

A. galactokinase lowers the energy of activation for the forward reaction in the phosphorylation of galactose and does not affect the energy of activation for the reverse reaction.
B. galactokinase lowers the energy of activation for both the forward and reverse reactions in the phosphorylation of galactose.
C. galactokinase lowers the energy of activation for the forward reaction in the phosphorylation of galactose and raises the energy of activation for the reverse reaction.
D. galactokinase alters the relative amounts of reactant and product at equilibrium, causing the galactose-1-phosphate product to be favored.

9. Which type of inhibition might be expected to lead to a decreased specificity constant?

A. Noncompetitive, because K_m would stay the same and the turnover number would decrease.
B. Noncompetitive, because K_m would increase and the turnover number would decrease.
C. Competitive, because K_m would stay the same and the turnover number would decrease.
D. Competitive, because K_m and the turnover number would both increase.

10. Which of the following is the most likely explanation for the finding that the E43G mutant protein demonstrated a decreased turnover number while the specificity constant was unaffected?

A. The E43G mutant showed no enzymatic function.
B. K_m changed by a factor approximately equal to the factor by which k_{cat} changed.
C. Glycine is a nonpolar amino acid, while glutamate is basic.
D. The E43G mutant protein had an increased K_m compared to the native galactokinase.

11. Suppose that the scientists used an uncompetitive inhibitor to inhibit galactose, rather than mutating a side chain. What would be the expected effect on K_m and V_{max}?

A. K_m would increase or decrease, depending on the specific inhibitor used, and V_{max} would decrease.
B. K_m would increase and V_{max} would stay the same.
C. K_m would stay the same and V_{max} would decrease.
D. K_m and V_{max} would both decrease.

12. Catalysis of the first step of the Leloir pathway, phosphorylation of galactose, requires energy input from an associated cosubstrate. Which of the following is most likely to be the cosubstrate?

A. ADP
B. A heme group
C. Glucose
D. ATP

13. Which of the following describes a general feature of proteins that makes them well suited to be enzymes?

A. Proteins have large variability in structure, allowing for lock-and-key specificity with different substrates.
B. Proteins are defined by their amphipathic nature, which allows them to assemble into membranes that isolate substrates from the watery environment of the cell.
C. Proteins cannot be denatured even in extreme environmental conditions.
D. Proteins have high regularity in structure, allowing for lock-and-key specificity with different substrates.

14. The structure of α-D-Galactose is shown.

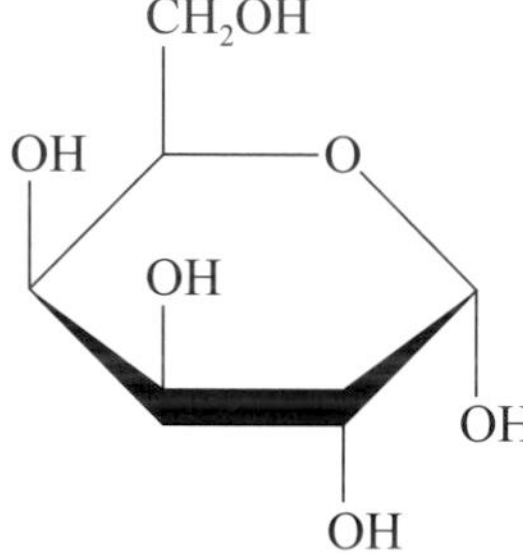

What type of reaction would allow α-D-Galactose molecules to join together to form polysaccharides?

A. Nucleophilic addition
B. Peptide bond formation
C. Dehydration
D. Hydrolysis

GO ON TO THE NEXT PAGE.

Passage III (Questions 15-20)

Hepatitis C virus (HCV) frequently causes chronic infection that can lead to cirrhosis and liver cancer. The density of circulating hepatitis C virus (HCV) particles in the blood of chronically infected patients is quite heterogeneous. The very low density of some particles has been attributed to an association of the virus with triglyceride rich lipoproteins (TRL), namely the low, intermediate and very low density lipoproteins (LDL, IDL and VLDL, respectively) and chylomicrons, as well as apolipoprotein B (apoB) positive lipoproteins. This association likely results in hybrid lipoproteins known as lipoviro-particles (LVP), containing the viral envelope glycoproteins E1 and E2. (Glycoproteins are composed of a protein with a short chain of monosaccharides attached.) The specific infectivity of these particles is higher when the ratio of lipids to proteins is greater. The mechanism of the association of HCV particles with lipoproteins remains elusive, and the role of apolipoproteins in the synthesis and assembly of the viral particles is unknown.

Microsomal triglyceride transfer protein (MTP) is an essential protein in the synthesis and assembly of TRL in the liver and intestine. To evaluate the role of MTP in the synthesis and assembly of lipoviro-particles, the human intestinal cell line Caco-2 was infected with the E1E2 lentiviral vector and then incubated with an MTP inhibitor (Cp 346086). MTP activity was measured one and two days later. The results are shown in Figure 1.

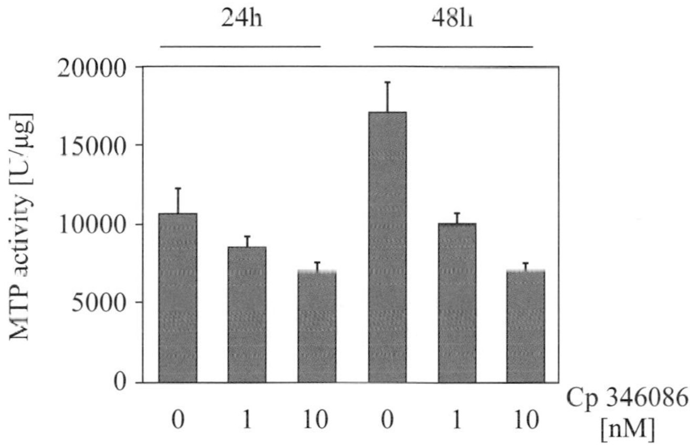

Figure 1 MTP activity in the basal medium, measured in enzyme activity units U per µg, at 24 and 48 h after addition of 1 or 10 nM Cp 346084

The secretions of apoB, E1, and E2 were also measured one and two days later. The quantity of E1 and E2 secreted into the basal medium after 24h or 48h incubation with 1 and 10 nM inhibitor was greatly reduced and correlated with the concentration of secreted apoB (data not shown). The effects on apoB concentration are shown in Figure 2.

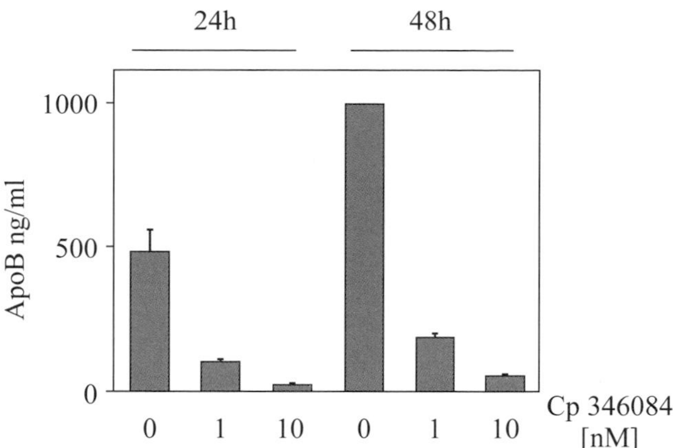

Figure 2 Concentrations of secreted apoB in the basal medium at 24h and 48h after addition of 1 or 10 nM Cp 346084

This passage was adapted from "Secretion of Hepatitis C Virus Envelope Glycoproteins Depends on Assembly of Apolipoprotein B Positive Lipoproteins." Icard V, Diaz O, Scholtes C, Perrin-Cocon L, Ramie`re C, et al. *PLoS ONE*. 2009. 4(1) doi:10.1371/journal.pone.0004233 for use under the terms of the Creative Commons CCBY 3.0 license (http://creativecommons.org/licenses/by/3.0/legalcode).

15. Which of the following accurately describes the structure of triglycerides?

A. Two fatty acids and a polar group attached to a glycerol backbone
B. Three fatty acids attached to a glycerol backbone
C. A long-chain alcohol and long-chain fatty acid attached by an ester linkage
D. A four ringed structure

16. The association of HCV with which of the following TRL would create the most infectious lipoviro-particle?

A. Very low density lipoprotein (VLDL)
B. Low density lipoprotein (LDL)
C. Intermediate density lipoprotein (IDL)
D. High density lipoprotein (HDL)

GO ON TO THE NEXT PAGE.

17. Which additional finding would support the conclusion that apoB lipoproteins contribute to lipoviro-particle formation?

- **A.** Infected patients lacking apoB lipoproteins had lower levels of circulating VLDL.
- **B.** A line of apoB negative epithelial cells was found to secrete HCV envelope proteins.
- **C.** Inhibition of MTP did not lead to reduced secretions of any proteins other than apoB.
- **D.** A line of liver cells infected with the E1E2 lentiviral vector did not produce significant co-precipitation of apoB and HCV envelope proteins.

18. Which of the following findings is supported by the experimental data?

- **A.** The doses of 1 nM and 10 nM Cp 346086 have the same effect on MTP activity.
- **B.** Secretion of apoB is directly correlated with MTP activity.
- **C.** Secretion of E1 and E2 is inversely correlated with MTP activity.
- **D.** The presence of Cp 346086 did not cause decreased MTP activity.

19. According to the passage, which of the following would most likely be found as a component of glycoproteins like E1 and E2?

- **A.** Starch
- **B.** Glycogen
- **C.** Glucose
- **D.** Cellulose

20. Phospholipids are well suited to be components of a lipoprotein membrane because they are:

- **A.** polar.
- **B.** nonpolar.
- **C.** amphipathic.
- **D.** hydrophobic.

Questions 21 through 23 are **NOT** based on a descriptive passage.

21. Which type of forces holds together complementary strands of DNA?

- **A.** Polar covalent bonds
- **B.** Nonpolar covalent bonds
- **C.** Hydrogen bonds
- **D.** Van der Waals forces

GO ON TO THE NEXT PAGE.

22. Lineweaver-Burk plots, where the reciprocal of reaction velocity is plotted as a function of the reciprocal of substrate concentration, are commonly used to demonstrate enzyme kinetics.

Which of the following Lineweaver-Burk plots demonstrates the effects of a competitive inhibitor?

A.

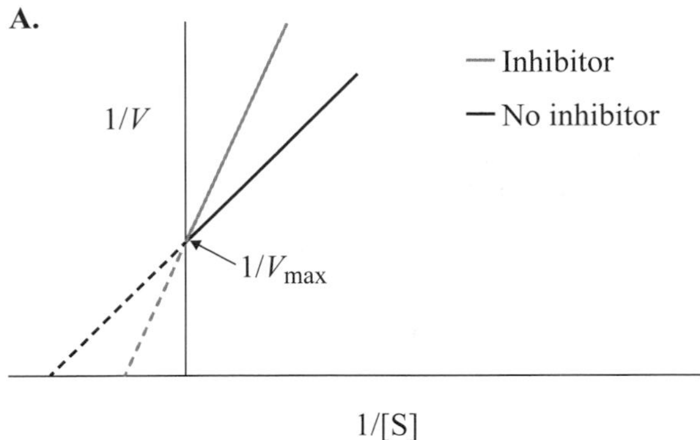

B.

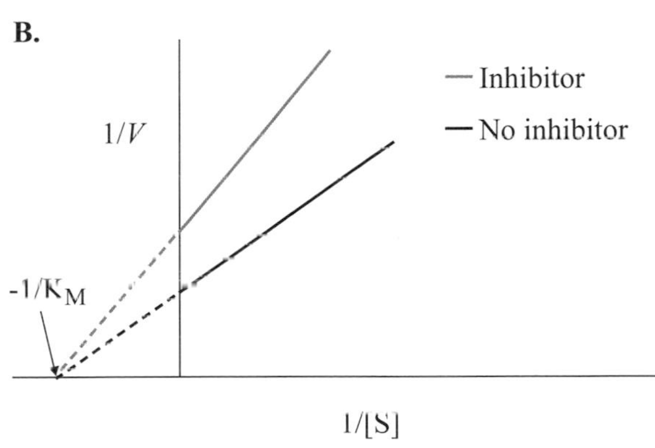

C.

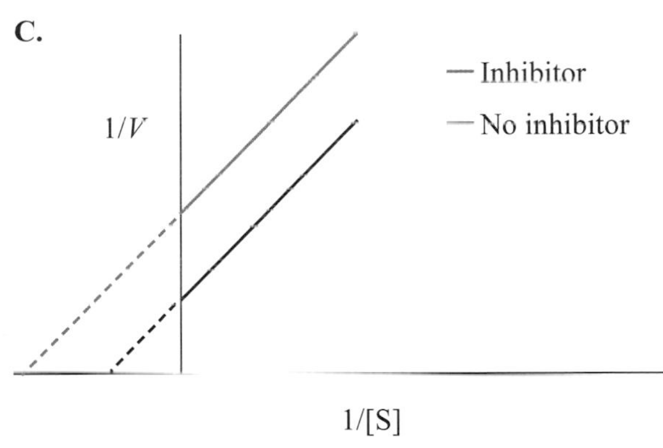

D.

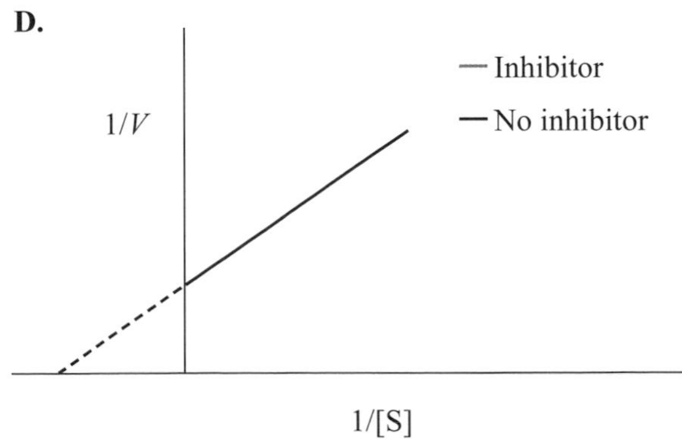

23. All of the following accurately describe differences between RNA and DNA EXCEPT:

A. In general, DNA is double-stranded and RNA is single-stranded.
B. In a eukaryotic cell, DNA is found in the nucleus; RNA can be found in both the cytosol and nucleus.
C. On one of the carbons of the pentose sugar, there is a hydroxyl group in DNA but only a hydrogen in RNA.
D. RNA contains uracil where DNA contains thymine.

STOP. IF YOU FINISH BEFORE TIME IS CALLED, CHECK YOUR WORK. YOU MAY GO BACK TO ANY QUESTION IN THIS TEST BOOKLET.

STOP.

30-MINUTE IN-CLASS EXAM FOR LECTURE 2

Passage I (Questions 24-29)

The primary abnormality in Down syndrome (DS), trisomy 21, is well known; but how this chromosomal gain produces a complex variety of DS phenotypes, including immune system defects that make DS individuals particularly susceptible to autoimmune disease and recurrent infection, is not well understood. It is postulated that epigenetic effects may contribute to development of the DS immune system phenotype, with altered DNA methylation acting in response to changes in gene dosage.

Experiment 1:

Using microarray analysis, scientists profiled DNA methylation in total peripheral blood leukocytes (PBL) and T-lymphocytes from adults with DS and a population of control adults and found gene-specific abnormalities of CpG methylation in DS. Many of the differentially methylated genes have known or predicted roles in lymphocyte development and function. Strong differences ($p<0.0001$) were found between DS and control groups for each of the eight genes tested: *TMEM131, TCF7, CD3Z/CD247, SH3BP2, EIF4E, PLD6, SUMO3*, and *CPT1B*. The differentially methylated genes were found on various autosomes with no specific enrichment on chromosome 21. Results from the *TMEM131* gene are shown in Figure 1.

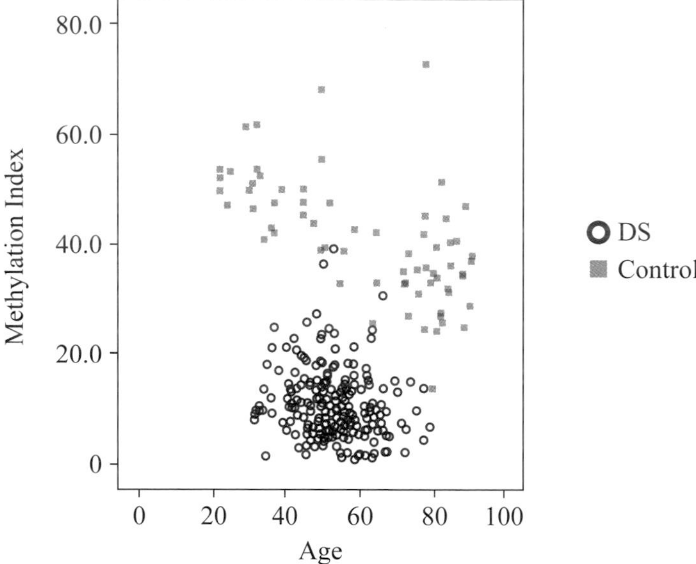

Figure 1 *TMEM131* methylation in DS and control subjects

Experiment 2:

Some, but not all, of the differentially methylated genes showed different mean mRNA expression in DS versus control PBL. These five differentially expressed genes (*TMEM131, TCF7, CD3Z, NOD2*, and *NPDC1*) were examined in normal lymphocytes before and after exposure to the demethylating drug 5-aza2'deoxycytidine (5aza-dC) plus mitogens. Results for *TMEM131* expression are shown in Figure 2.

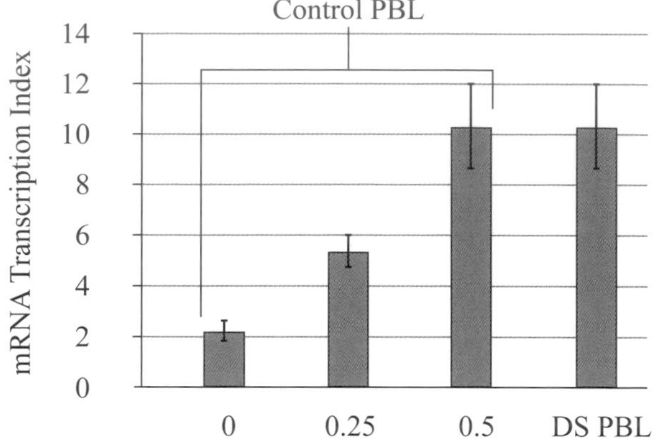

Figure 2 *TMEM131* gene expression in DS subjects and in control subjects after 0, 0.25, and 0.5 μM 5aza-dC

This passage was adapted from "Altered DNA Methylation in Leukocytes with Trisomy 21." Kerkel K, Schupf N, Hatta K, Pang D, Salas M, et al. *PLoS Genetics*. 2010. 6(11) doi:10.1371/journal.pgen.1001212 for use under the terms of the Creative Commons CCBY 3.0 license (http://creativecommons.org/licenses/by/3.0/legalcode).

24. Which of the following conclusions is supported by the findings of Experiment 1?

A. Immune deficiency in DS individuals is due to hypermethylation at chromosome 21.
B. Immune deficiency in DS individuals is due to hypomethylation at chromosome 21.
C. Immune deficiency in DS individuals is due to altered multi-chromosomal methylation.
D. Immune deficiency in DS individuals is sex-linked.

25. CpG methylation refers to methylation at a region of DNA where the linear order of base pairs includes a cytosine nucleotide directly followed by a guanine nucleotide. Which of the following regions is complementary to a possible CpG methylation site?

A. 3' – TAGCT – 5'
B. 3' – ACGTC – 5'
C. 5' – TGCTG – 3'
D. 5' – CAGCT – 3'

GO ON TO THE NEXT PAGE.

26. The combined evidence of Experiments 1 and 2 suggests that which of the following might be a possible chain of cause and effect?

A. DNA methylation→ aneuploidy → differential gene expression
B. Aneuploidy → DNA methylation → differential gene expression
C. Aneuploidy → differential gene expression → DNA methylation
D. DNA methylation → differential gene expression → aneuploidy

27. The highest densities of DNA methylation are likely to be found in:

A. heterochromatin.
B. euchromatin.
C. histones.
D. non-coding RNA.

28. Which of the following is/are true regarding the *TMEM131* gene?

I. Increased methylation results in altered expression in DS individuals.
II. Decreased methylation alters normal PBL to DS levels of gene expression.
III. In control individuals, gene expression should be expected to decrease with age.

A. I only
B. II only
C. I and III only
D. II and III only

29. The researchers repeat the Experiment 2 protocol to explore the effect of 5aza-dC on *CD3Z* gene expression in control PBL. They find that higher doses of 5aza-dC produce lower levels of *CD3Z* gene expression. These results are best explained by which of the following?

A. Increased methylation caused by 5aza-dC decreases gene expression.
B. Methylation sites of the *CD3Z* gene are located in the promoter region.
C. *CD3Z* is an autosomal gene.
D. Increased methylation in repressor regions leads to increased expression.

Passage II (Questions 30-35)

For many genes in eukaryotes, the mRNA initially transcribed is not translated in its entirety. Instead, it is processed in a series of steps occurring within the nucleus. The 5′ end of the pre-mRNA is capped with GTP, forming a 5′–5′ triphosphate linkage. Several adenosine residues are added to the 3′ end to form a poly-A tail.

During processing, as much as 90% of the pre-mRNA is removed from the nucleotide sequence as introns and the remaining exons are spliced together into a single mRNA strand (Figure 1).

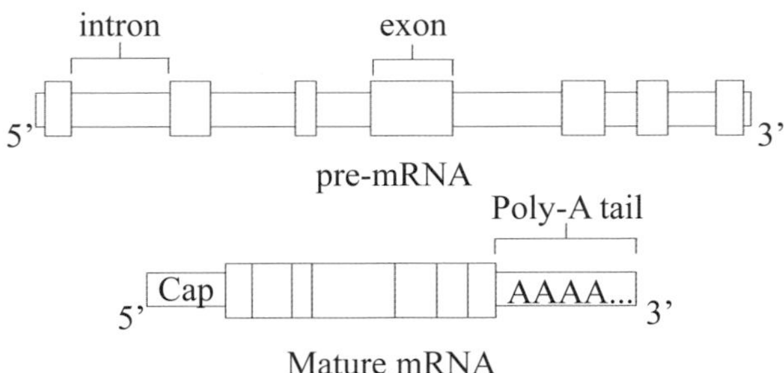

Figure 1 Post-transcriptional processing of mRNA

A recent study showed that Alus, which are retrotransposed elements, may be important in determining the splicing patterns of pre-mRNA in humans. A large fraction of Alus are found in intronic sequences. The study showed that more Alus flank alternatively spliced exons than constitutively spliced ones; this effect is especially notable for those exons that have changed their mode of splicing from constitutive to alternative during human evolution. In one experiment, two Alu elements that were inserted into an intron in opposite orientations underwent base-pairing and affected the splicing patterns of a downstream exon, shifting it from constitutive to alternative.

As their functions become better understood, intronic sequences are becoming of greater interest to scientists. In R looping, a technique used to identify introns, a fully processed mRNA strand is hybridized with its double stranded DNA counterpart under conditions that favor formation of hybrids between DNA and RNA strands. In this process, the RNA strand displaces one DNA strand and binds to the other DNA strand along complementary sequences. The results can be visualized through electron microscopy, as shown in Figure 2.

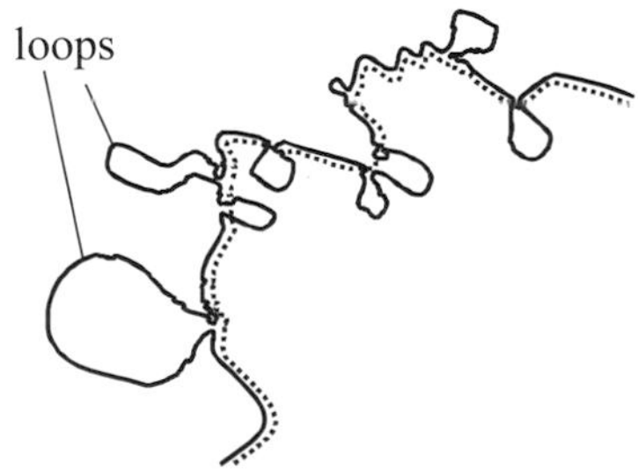

Figure 2. R looping formed by hybridization between DNA and the resultant mRNA sequence

GO ON TO THE NEXT PAGE.

30. Which of the following would most strongly indicate that the poly-A tail is added after transcription rather than during transcription?

  A. Evidence of an enzyme in the nucleus that catalyzes the synthesis of a sequence of multiple adenosine phosphate molecules
  B. A sequence of multiple thymine nucleotides following each gene in eukaryotic DNA
  C. A sequence of multiple uracil nucleotides following each gene in eukaryotic mRNA
  D. A sequence of multiple adenosine nucleotides following each gene in eukaryotic DNA

31. Small nuclear ribonucleoproteins (snRNPs) catalyze the splicing reaction in the post transcriptional processing of RNA. Based upon the information in the passage, in which of the following locations would snRNPs most likely be found?

  A. The cytosol of a prokaryotic cell
  B. The cytosol of a eukaryotic cell
  C. The lumen of the endoplasmic reticulum
  D. The nucleus of the eukaryotic cell

32. The loops in Figure 2 represent:

  A. DNA introns.
  B. DNA exons.
  C. RNA introns.
  D. RNA exons.

33. If true, which of the following would cast the greatest doubt on the findings of the Alus experiment described in the passage?

  A. Constitutive splicing evolved before alternative splicing.
  B. Exons evolved before introns.
  C. Alternative splicing evolved before introns.
  D. Introns evolved before alternative splicing.

34. Why might alternative splicing be beneficial?

  A. Alternative splicing creates more copies of a protein
  B. Alternative splicing creates a wider variety of proteins
  C. Alternative splicing removes retrotransposable elements
  D. Alternative splicing encourages base-pair matching

35. All of the following are associated with the process of eukaryotic mRNA splicing EXCEPT:

  A. snRNP.
  B. snRNA.
  C. rRNA.
  D. the lariat.

Passage III (Questions 36-43)

In the life cycle of sexual organisms, a specialized cell division—meiosis—reduces the number of chromosomes from two sets (2n, diploid) to one set (n, haploid), while fertilization restores the original chromosome number. However, deregulation of meiosis has been observed in a number of plant species.

Apomixis, or asexual clonal reproduction through seeds, is of immense interest due to its potential application to agriculture. One key element of apomixis is apomeiosis, a deregulation of meiosis that results in a mitotic-like division. Scientists isolated and characterized a novel gene, *osd1*, which is directly involved in controlling entry into the second mitotic division in the sexually reproducing plant *Arabidopsis thaliana*. The *osd1* gene contains three exons and two introns and encodes a protein of 243 amino acids with particularly high conservation among various species observed in the central *osd1*-motif. Two other mutations that affect key meiotic processes in *A. thaliana* were already known – one that eliminates recombination and pairing (*Atspo11-1*) and another that modifies chromatid segregation (*Atrec8*).

In A*tspo11-1/Atrec8* double mutants, the first meiotic division is replaced by a mitotic-like division, followed by an unbalanced second division that leads to unbalanced spores and sterility. By combining the *osd1* mutation with *Atspo11-1* and *Atrec8*, the researchers created a new genotype called *MiMe*. The presence of the *Atspo11-1* and *Atrec8* mutations leads to a mitotic-like first meiotic division, while the presence of the *osd1* mutation prevents the second meiotic division from occurring. In *MiMe*, meiosis is totally replaced by a mitotic-like division without affecting subsequent sexual processes. The obtained plants produce functional gametes that are genetically identical to their mother.

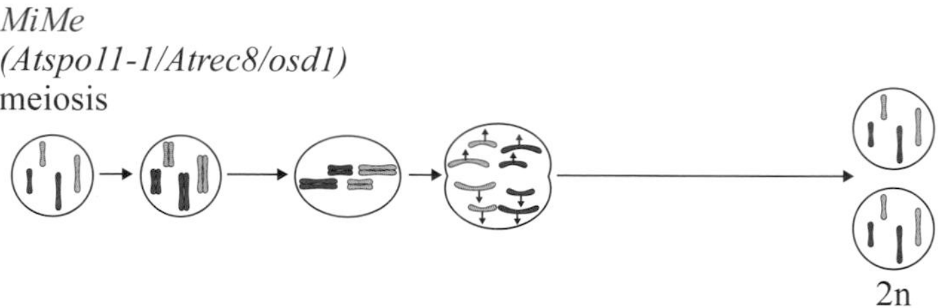

Figure 1. Summary of gamete formation through apomeiosis in the *MiMe* genotype

36. What is the most likely reason that apomixis might be important for agricultural improvement?

  A. It creates genetically stronger plants that are resistant to disease.
  B. It allows for the propagation of plants with predictable characteristics.
  C. It allows for viable seeds to develop more quickly.
  D. It creates plants that need less time input from humans to thrive.

GO ON TO THE NEXT PAGE.

37. During mitosis, the nuclear envelope of a plant cell:

A. disintegrates during replication of the chromosomes.
B. disintegrates while crossing over is taking place.
C. disintegrates while the chromosomes condense.
D. remains intact.

38. All of the following characteristics distinguish meiosis from mitosis EXCEPT:

A. a succession of two rounds of division following a single replication.
B. pairing and recombination between homologous chromosomes.
C. co-segregation of sister chromatids at the first division.
D. replication of chromosomes during interphase.

39. Suppose that to test the viability of the gametes produced in the experiment described in the passage, scientists combined a female *MiMe* gamete produced through apomeiosis with a male wild-type gamete. The resultant plant would be:

A. haploid.
B. diploid.
C. triploid.
D. tetraploid.

40. All of the following might describe events occurring in prophase I of normal meiosis EXCEPT:

A. tetrad formation.
B. spindle apparatus formation.
C. chromosomal migration.
D. genetic recombination.

41. Suppose scientists perform a related experiment on a different plant species and find that the resultant plants produce female gametes that are all haploid and male gametes that are all diploid. Which of the following must be true?

A. Female germ cells are not undergoing recombination.
B. Male germ cells are not undergoing recombination.
C. Female germ cells are not undergoing meiosis I.
D. Male germ cells are not undergoing meiosis I.

42. When combined with the information in the passage, which finding would challenge the applicability of apomixis to crop improvement?

A. Plant fertility decreases as ploidy increases.
B. Apomeiosis results in diploid gametes.
C. Meiosis results in a greater rate of mutation than mitosis.
D. *A. thaliana* is a non-edible plant.

43. Which of the following could illustrate the process of meiosis in an *Atspo11-1/Atrec8* double mutant?

A.

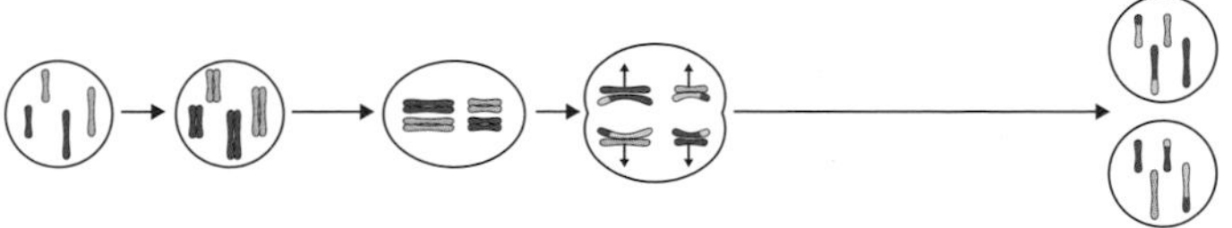

B.

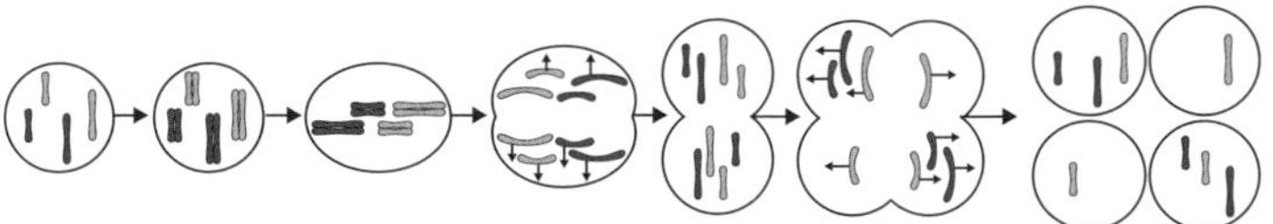

C.

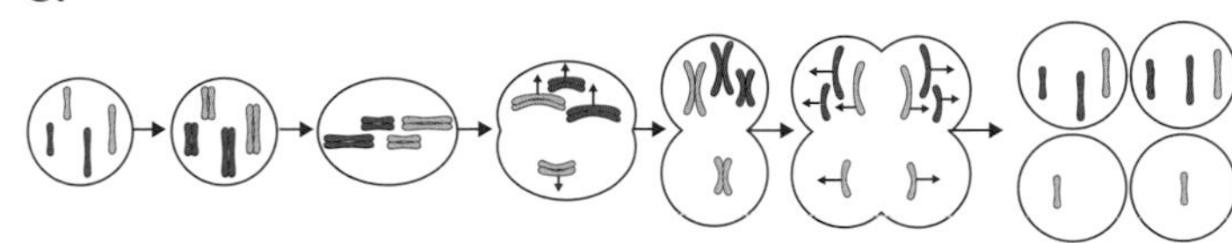

D.

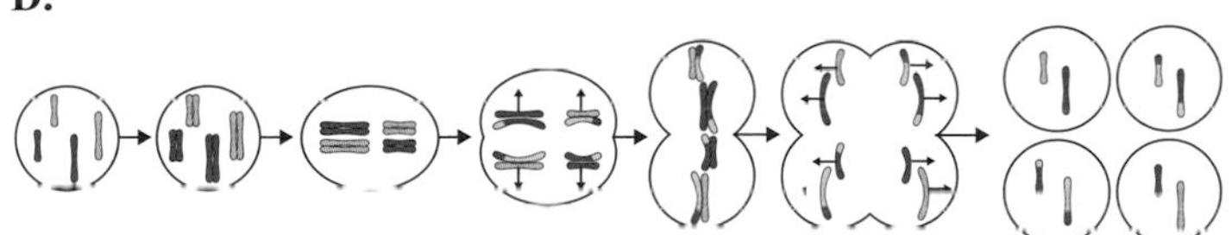

In-Class Exams

GO ON TO THE NEXT PAGE.

Questions 44 through 46 are **NOT** based on a descriptive passage.

44. Which of the following is true concerning the genetic code?

A. There are more amino acids than there are codons.
B. Any change in the nucleotide sequence of a codon must result in a new amino acid.
C. The genetic code varies from species to species.
D. There are 64 codons.

45. Turner syndrome occurs due to nondisjunction at the sex chromosome resulting in an individual with one X and no Y chromosome. Color-blindness is a sex-linked recessive trait. A color-blind man marries a healthy woman. They have two children, both with Turner syndrome. One of the children is color-blind. Which of the following is true?

A. Nondisjunction occurred in the father for both children.
B. Nondisjunction occurred in the mother for both children.
C. Nondisjunction occurred in the mother for the colorblind child and in the father for the child with normal vision.
D. Nondisjunction occurred in the father for the colorblind child and in the mother for the child with normal vision.

46. A primary spermatocyte is:

A. haploid and contains 23 chromosomes.
B. haploid and contains 46 chromosomes.
C. diploid and contains 23 chromosomes.
D. diploid and contains 46 chromosomes.

STOP. IF YOU FINISH BEFORE TIME IS CALLED, CHECK YOUR WORK. YOU MAY GO BACK TO ANY QUESTION IN THIS TEST BOOKLET.

STOP.

30-MINUTE IN-CLASS EXAM FOR LECTURE 3

Passage I (Questions 47- 53)

Acute lung injury (ALI) is an inflammatory disease of the lungs that is characterized by hypoxemic respiratory failure with bilateral pulmonary infiltrates. Sites of acute inflammation are frequently characterized by considerable shifts in the supply and demand of metabolites.

In vivo analysis of ^{13}C-glucose metabolites utilizing liquid-chromatography tandem mass-spectrometry demonstrated that increases in glycolytic capacity, improvement of mitochondrial respiration, and concomitant attenuation of lung inflammation during ALI were specific for alveolar-epithelial expressed hypoxia-inducible factor 1A (HIF1A).

Scientists hypothesized that HIF1A in alveolar epithelial cells dampens lung inflammation by enhancing glycolysis and optimizing mitochondrial respiration during ALI.

Experiment 1

This experiment used *Hif1A$^{f/f}$* SurfactantCre$^+$ mice with induced deletion of HIF1A in their alveolar epithelial cells; mice lacking HIF1A were found to experience profound lung inflammation during ALI.

Some of the *Hif1A$^{f/f}$* SurfactantCre$^+$ mice were exposed to ventilator induced lung injury (VILI). Elevations of transcript levels of glycolytic enzymes were found to be attenuated in *Hif1A$^{f/f}$* SurfactantCre$^+$ mice compared to wild-type mice.

Measured [^{13}C6] Glucose and Glut1 transcript levels are shown in Figure 1.

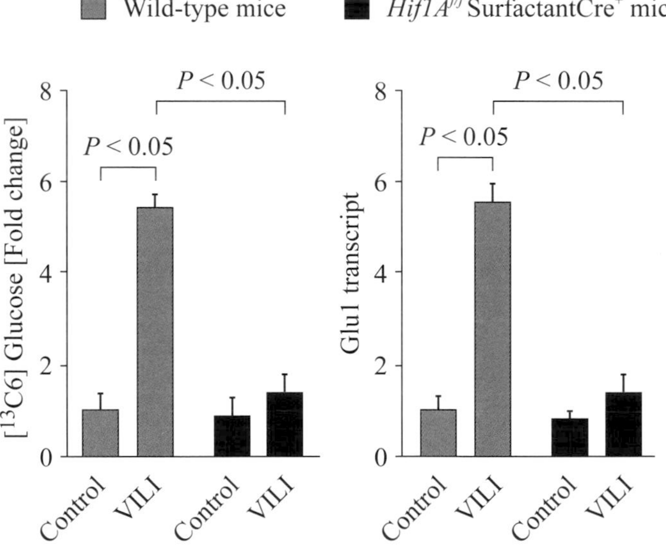

Figure 1 Effect of induced deletion of alveolar epithelial HIF1A on glycolysis during ALI

Experiment 2

Wild-type and *Hif1A$^{f/f}$* SurfactantCre$^+$ mice treated with the glycolysis inhibitor 2-deoxy-D-glucose (2-DG) were exposed to VILI. Survival times are shown in Figure 2.

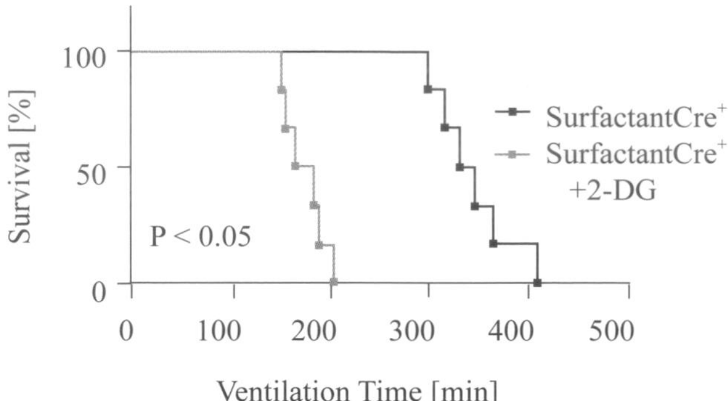

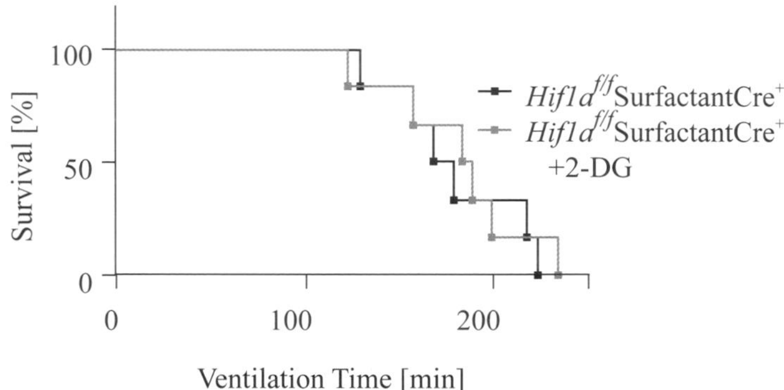

Figure 2 Effect of inhibition of glycolysis on survival time during VILI

47. Which of the following shows the net reaction for the glycolysis of glucose?

A. Glucose + 4 ADP → pyruvate + 2 ATP
B. Glucose + 2 ADP + 2 P_i + 2 NAD^+ → 2 pyruvate + 2 ATP + 2 NADH
C. Glucose + O_2 → CO_2 + H_2O + 2 ATP
D. Glucose + O_2 → 2 pyruvate + 2 ATP + 2 NADH

48. What is the most likely reason that 2-deoxy-D-glucose was used in Experiment 2?

A. 2-deoxy-D-glucose is implicated in the development of acute lung injury.
B. 2-deoxy-D-glucose is expressed in alveolar epithelial cells.
C. 2-deoxy-D-glucose, like HIF1A, inhibits alveolar epithelial glycolysis.
D. 2-deoxy-D-glucose inhibits glycolysis, and glycolysis is mediated through alveolar epithelial HIF1A.

GO ON TO THE NEXT PAGE.

49. The substrates of glycolysis include which of the following monomers?

I. Monosaccharides
II. Fatty acids
III. Amino acids

A. I only
B. I and II only
C. I and III only
D. I, II and III

50. Which of the following describes the most likely effect of an increased ratio of insulin to glucagon on glycolytic rate and overall metabolism?

A. Increased glycolytic rate and net anabolism
B. Increased glycolytic rate and net catabolism
C. Decreased glycolytic rate and net anabolism
D. Decreased glycolytic rate and net catabolism

51. Based on passage information, which of the following is likely to have the highest glycolytic rate?

A. Wild-type without VILI
B. Wild-type with VILI
C. $Hif1A^{f/f}$ SurfactantCre^{+} without VILI
D. $Hif1A^{f/f}$ SurfactantCre^{+} with VILI

52. Cancer cells are known to display increased expression of hypoxia-inducible transcription factor (HIF-1). Based on passage information, cancer cells are LEAST likely to exhibit increased expression of:

A. glycolytic enzymes.
B. glucose transporter GLUT1.
C. glucose transporter GLUT3.
D. gluconeogenic enzymes.

53. Each reaction in the glycolytic pathway is governed by an enzyme. Phosphofructokinase, which catalyzes the conversion of fructose 6-phosphate to fructose 1,6-biphosphate, is allosterically regulated. What is the most likely mechanism of regulation?

A. ADP activates the enzyme by decreasing its affinity for fructose 6-phosphate.
B. ADP inhibits the enzyme by increasing its affinity for fructose 6-phosphate.
C. ATP inhibits the enzyme by decreasing its affinity for fructose 6-phosphate.
D. ATP activates the enzyme by increasing its affinity for fructose 6-phosphate.

Passage II (Questions 54- 60)

In the fed state, under the influence of insulin, white adipose tissue (WAT) stores excess energy as triacylglycerols. Lipolysis is the process by which stored triacylglycerols are released as nonesterified fatty acids.

Enzymatic breakdown of triacylglycerols is initiated by adipose triglyceride lipase (ATGL) and leads to the formation of diacylglycerols that are in turn hydrolyzed by hormone-sensitive lipase (HSL). The final step of this catabolic process is the hydrolysis of monoacylglycerols by monoglyceride lipase, leading to the release of one molecule of glycerol and three fatty acids.

Fatty acids have been postulated to play a critical role in the development of insulin resistance. In the two experiments below, researchers investigated the role of WAT lipolysis, including the specific contribution of HSL, in the control of insulin sensitivity and glucose metabolism.

Experiment 1

Researchers investigated the relationship between WAT lipolysis and insulin sensitivity in humans. As shown in Figure 1, a positive association was found between spontaneous glycerol release, measured ex vivo on WAT explants, and insulin resistance, as measured by the homeostasis model of indirect assessment of insulin resistance (HOMA-IR).

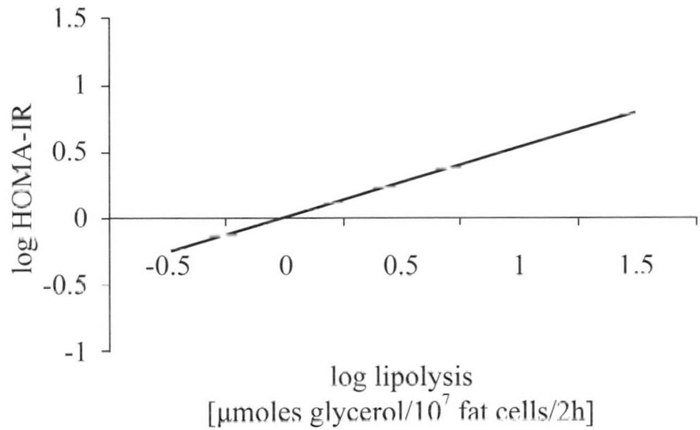

Figure 1 Relationship between WAT lipolysis and insulin resistance in human subjects

GO ON TO THE NEXT PAGE.

Experiment 2

Mice haploinsufficient for HSL were generated by mating wild-type (WT) and $HSL^{-/-}$ mice. Resultant $HSL^{+/-}$ mice showed reduced lipolytic capacities without alteration of fat mass. Both WT and $HSL^{-/-}$ mice underwent insulin tolerance tests, where higher insulin tolerance corresponds to a greater decrease from basal glucose levels. The results are shown in Figure 2.

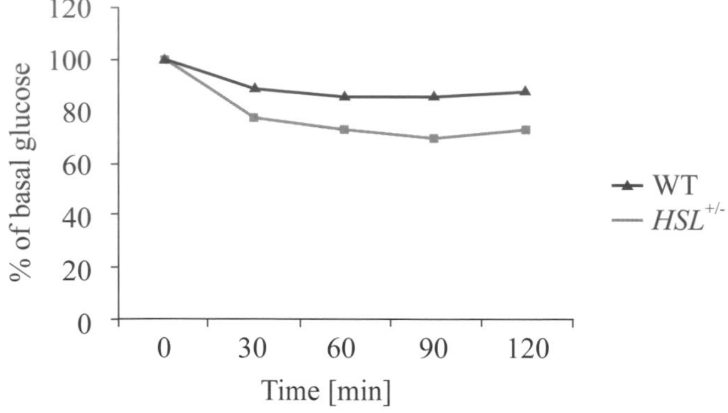

Figure 2 Results of insulin tolerance tests performed on wild type and $HSL^{+/-}$ mice fed a high fat diet for 12 weeks

54. Which type of linkage is broken when a diacylglycerol molecule is hydrolyzed by HSL?

A. Glycosidic
B. Ester
C. Ether
D. Phosphodiester

55. Insulin activates enzymes involved in which of the following metabolic processes?

I. Glycogenesis
II. Gluconeogenesis
III. Lipolysis

A. I only
B. I and II only
C. I and III only
D. I, II, and III

56. What is the most likely reason that mice haploinsufficient for HSL were used in experiments designed to assess the role of WAT lipolysis in the control of insulin sensitivity?

A. HSL expression promotes insulin resistance.
B. HSL initiates enzyme breakdown of triacylglycerols.
C. HSL level is a determinant of lipolytic capacity in WAT.
D. HSL level is an indirect measure of glucose metabolism.

57. Based on passage information, what would be the most likely effect of a drug designed to inhibit HSL expression on insulin resistant individuals?

A. Increased insulin sensitivity and increased fat mass
B. Decreased insulin sensitivity and increased fat mass
C. Increased insulin sensitivity and no change in fat mass
D. Decreased insulin sensitivity and no change in fat mass

58. Once inside the mitochondria, fatty acids are metabolized by which of the following cellular processes?

A. Deamination
B. Glycolysis
C. Lipolysis
D. Beta-oxidation

59. Is it reasonable to expect that diminished lipolytic capacity would be associated with improved insulin and glucose tolerance?

A. Yes, because, like glucose, the products of lipolysis are homeostatically regulated.
B. Yes, because, like glucose, the products of lipolysis can be oxidized and enter the citric acid cycle.
C. No, because the regulation of lipolysis is distinct from that of glucose uptake, storage, and metabolism.
D. No, because in the absence of lipolysis, increased protein metabolism compensates for decreased glucose metabolism.

60. Which finding would provide the strongest support for the passage assertion that, compared to WT mice, $HSL^{+/-}$ mice exhibited diminished lipolytic capacities?

A. HSL mRNA expression was reduced by 50% in $HSL^{+/-}$ mice.
B. HSL protein expression was reduced by 50% in $HSL^{+/-}$ mice.
C. ATGL protein expression was not significantly altered in $HSL^{+/-}$ mice.
D. Adipocytes in $HSL^{+/-}$ mice had reduced in vitro response to stimulation by lipolytic agents.

GO ON TO THE NEXT PAGE.

Passage III (Questions 61- 66)

Blood glucose levels are under the control of two hormones released from the pancreatic islets of Langerhans. When glucose is high, islet β cells secrete insulin, which promotes glucose storage in multiple tissues and inhibits glucose production by the liver. By contrast, when glucose is low, islet α cells secrete glucagon, which promotes gluconeogenesis and liver glycogen breakdown.

The mechanism regulating glucagon secretion is poorly understood. Glucagon release may be inhibited by paracrine signals, including γ-aminobutyric acid (GABA) and Zn^{2+}. In addition, glucose may suppress glucagon secretion by inhibiting ATP-dependent K^+ (K_{ATP}) channels expressed by α-cells.

In the two experiments below, researchers observed the effects of paracrine signals, glucose, and K_{ATP} channel activity on glucagon release.

Experiment 1

To determine whether glucose suppresses glucagon release independently of paracrine signals mediated by Zn^{2+} or GABA, glucagon secretion by isolated, intact mice islets was measured under conditions of Zn^{2+} chelation and $GABA_A$ receptor antagonism. The results are shown in Figure 1.

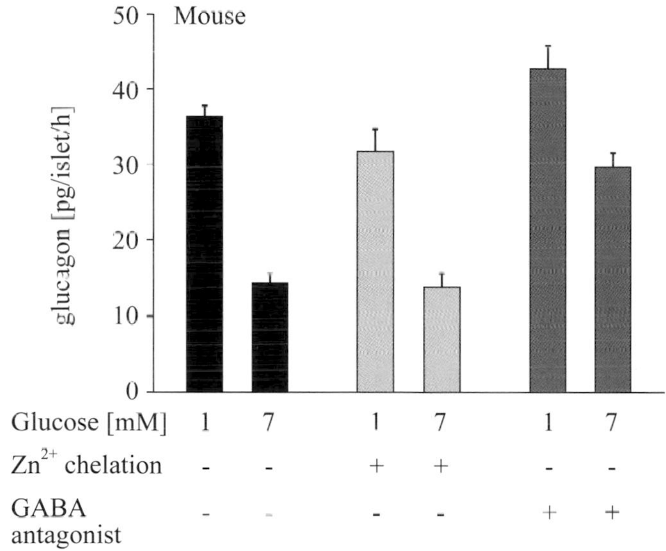

Figure 1 Effect of glucose on glucagon secretion in the absence of paracrine Zn^{2+} or GABA signaling

Experiment 2

To observe the effect of K_{ATP} channel activity on glucagon release, isolated, intact human islets were treated with the K_{ATP} channel blocker tolbutamide.

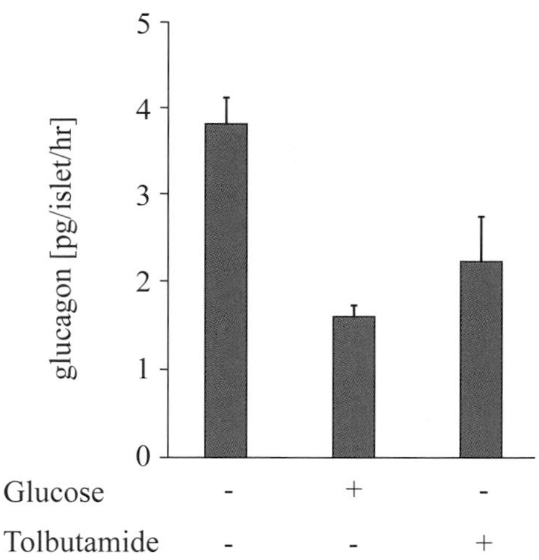

Figure 2 Effect of K_{ATP} channel activity on glucagon release

This passage was adapted from "A K_{ATP} Channel-Dependent Pathway within α Cells Regulates Glucagon Release from Both Rodent and Human Islets of Langerhans." MacDonald PE, De Marinis YZ, Ramracheya R, Salehi A, Ma X, et al. *PLoS Biology*. 2007. 5(6) doi:10.1371/journal.pbio.0050143 for use under the terms of the Creative Commons CCBY 3.0 license (http://creativecommons.org/licenses/by/3.0/legalcode).

61. Insulin is most likely to promote which of the following cellular processes?

A. Glycogenolysis
B. Lipolysis
C. Gluconeogenesis
D. Glycogenesis

62. The results presented in Figure 1 suggest that glucose suppresses glucagon secretion:

A. only in the presence of Zn^{2+} or GABA paracrine signaling.
B. only in the absence of GABA paracrine signaling.
C. only in the presence of GABA paracrine signaling.
D. both in the presence and absence of Zn^{2+} and GABA paracrine signaling.

63. The K_{ATP} channels that regulate glucagon secretion can be closed by ATP. ATP is produced by each of the following cellular processes EXCEPT:

A. chemiosmotic coupling.
B. oxidative phosphorylation.
C. the pentose-phosphate pathway.
D. the citric acid cycle.

GO ON TO THE NEXT PAGE.

64. The structure of ATP is shown.

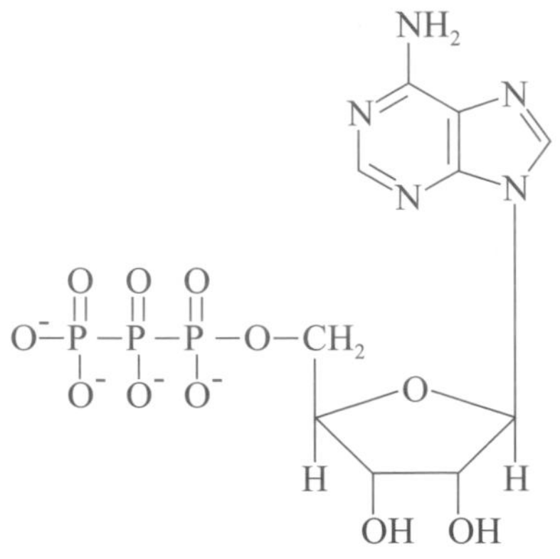

Through which reaction does ATP release the free energy required for less energetically favorable reactions?

A. Hydrolysis of phosphoanhydride bonds
B. Transfer of high potential electrons
C. Uncoupled oxidative phosphorylation
D. Conversion of ribose to deoxyribose

65. Glucagnoma, a rare tumor of the islet α cells, leads to an excess of the hormone glucagon in the blood. A patient with glucagnoma would most likely experience which of the following symptoms?

A. Increased glucogenesis
B. Hyperglycemia
C. Hypoglycemia
D. Increased glycolysis

66. Following Experiments 1 and 2, researchers proposed the existence of an α-cell glucose-sensing pathway involving closure of ATP-dependent K^+ channels in the presence of glucose. Which of the following findings would make the existence of such a pathway LEAST likely?

A. In the presence of a maximally inhibitory tolbutamide concentration, glucose was unable to produce any further inhibition of glucagon release.
B. In the presence of an insulin agonist, increased glucose concentration was not associated with suppression of glucagon release.
C. The K_{ATP} channel opener diazoxide reversed glucose-dependent suppression of glucagon release.
D. Glucose-dependent suppression of glucagon release persisted when paracrine GABA or Zn^{2+} signaling was blocked.

Questions 67 through 69 are **NOT** based on a descriptive passage.

67. In aerobic respiration, the energy from the oxidation of NADH:

A. directly synthesizes ATP.
B. passively diffuses protons from the intermembrane space into the matrix.
C. establishes a proton gradient between the intermembrane space and the mitochondrial matrix.
D. pumps protons through ATP synthase.

68. The net result of aerobic respiration can be summarized most accurately as:

A. the oxidation of glucose.
B. the reduction of glucose.
C. the elimination of glucose.
D. the lysis of glucose.

69. The process of synthesis of ATP in the glycolytic reaction governed by *phosphoglycerate kinase* is called:

A. oxidative phosphorylation.
B. substrate-level phosphorylation.
C. exergonic phosphate transfer.
D. electron transport.

STOP. IF YOU FINISH BEFORE TIME IS CALLED, CHECK YOUR WORK. YOU MAY GO BACK TO ANY QUESTION IN THIS TEST BOOKLET.

STOP.

30-MINUTE IN-CLASS EXAM FOR LECTURE 4

Passage I (Questions 70- 75)

In 1951 a chemist made $C_{10}H_{10}Fe$ by reacting two moles of cyclopentadienylmagnesium bromide (a Grignard reagent) with anhydrous ferrous chloride. The planar structure of the resulting stable solid was uncertain and became an area of great interest in the following years. The structure proposed by the original chemist is shown in Figure 1.

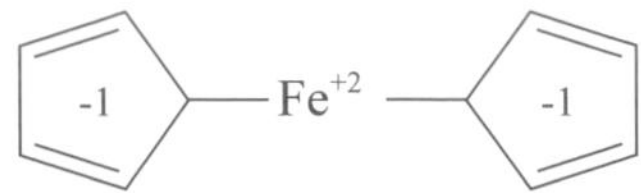

Figure 1 Proposed structure 1

Chemists later proposed a new planar structure called a "sandwich" complex, which is shown in Figure 2.

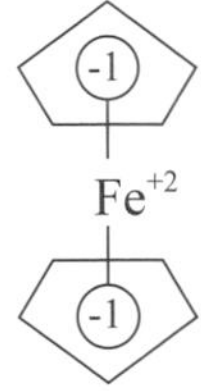

Figure 2 Proposed structure 2

The spectroscopy for $C_{10}H_{10}Fe$ is shown in Tables 1 and 2.

Chemical Shift	Coupling Pattern	Integral Value
4.12 ppm	singlet	10

Table 1 Proton NMR data

Frequency	Description of Peak
2900 cm^{-1}	very strong

Table 2 IR peaks at frequencies greater than 1500 cm^{-1}

When $C_{10}H_{10}Fe$ is reacted with acetic anhydride in the presence of an acid as shown in Reaction 1, a dark orange solid is formed with the molecular formula $C_{12}H_{12}OFe$. The reaction of $C_{10}H_{10}Fe$ with the anhydride helped scientists to confirm which structure was valid.

Reaction 1

A summary of the spectroscopy for the product shown in Reaction 1 is given in Tables 3 and 4.

Chemical Shift	Coupling Pattern	Integral Value
2.30 ppm	singlet	3
4.20 ppm	singlet	5
4.50 ppm	doublet	2
4.80 ppm	doublet	2

Table 3 Proton NMR data

Frequency	Description of Peak
2900 cm^{-1}	very strong
1700 cm^{-1}	very strong

Table 4 IR peaks at frequencies greater than 1500 cm^{-1}

70. What is the other product that is produced in Reaction 1 but not shown?

A. A carboxylic acid
B. A ketone
C. An aldehyde
D. An ester

71. The new peak in the IR data after the reaction with acetic anhydride comes from:

A. a carbonyl stretch.
B. a C-H stretch.
C. the coupling of two protons.
D. a C-C-H bend.

72. The NMR peak at 2.30 ppm in Table 3 is from protons:

A. on the carbon of the double bonds in the cyclopentadiene ring.
B. on the carbon of the methyl group attached to the cyclopentadiene ring.
C. on the carbon of the methyl group attached to a carbonyl carbon.
D. on the carbon of the cyclopentadiene ring, not in a double bond.

73. Why is it important that the ferrous chloride be anhydrous in the reaction to form $C_{10}H_{10}Fe$?

A. The cyclopentadienylmagnesium bromide will react with water.
B. The ferrous chloride will turn to ferric chloride.
C. Ferrous chloride will not dissolve in water.
D. The water would catalyze the reaction and it would erupt.

GO ON TO THE NEXT PAGE.

74. In Figure 2, the five-membered rings are:

A. aromatic.
B. antiaromatic.
C. nonaromatic.
D. Aromaticity cannot be determined for any structures that do not contain benzene.

75. How does the spectroscopy done before the reaction indicate that structure 1 is not the true structure?

A. If structure 1 were the true structure, there would be 3 chemical shifts in Table 1.
B. If structure 1 were the true structure, there would be 4 chemical shifts in Table 1.
C. If structure 1 were the true structure, there would be a frequency of 1700 cm^{-1} and not a frequency at 2900 cm^{-1} in Table 2.
D. If structure 1 were the true structure, there would be a frequency of 1700 cm^{-1} as well as the frequency at 2900 cm^{-1} in Table 2.

Passage II (Questions 76- 81)

Researchers used the following microscale extraction protocol to isolate the three compounds shown in Figure 1, each of which has a pharmaceutical application. Benzoic acid is used in fungal treatments, while 9-fluorenone is a component of some antimalarial drugs. Ethyl 4-aminobenzoate can be used in oral anesthetics. The physical properties of these molecules are shown in Table 1.

O
C
NH_2
$COOC_2H_5$
COOH

9-Fluorenone
Ethyl 4-aminobenzoate
Benzoic Acid

Figure 1. Chemical structures of the compounds separated by extraction protocol

Compound	mp(°C)	bp(°C)	Specific gravity
9-Fluorenone	82	342	1.13
Ethyl 4-aminobenzoate	89	310	1.17
Benzoic acid	122	249	1.27
Diethyl ether	-116	35	0.713

Table 1. Physical properties of pharmaceutical compounds and solvent in extraction protocol

50 mg of each compound was dissolved in 4 mL of diethyl ether. 2 mL of 3 M HCl was added to create a two phase system. The system was mixed thoroughly and then allowed to separate. After removal of the aqueous layer, the extraction was repeated with the remainder of the mixture. 6 M NaOH was then added to the extracted aqueous solution. The solution was cooled in an ice bath, and the resulting precipitate was collected and washed with distilled water.

The remaining organic layer was then extracted with two 2 mL portions of 3 M NaOH. 6 M HCl was added to the alkaline solution, which was cooled to form a precipitate.

The remaining organic component was washed with distilled water and then 250 mg of Na_2SO_4 were added. After two minutes, the Na_2SO_4 was removed using a filter pipet and the remaining solution was transferred to an Erlenmeyer flask placed in a warm sand bath, resulting in the formation of a precipitate.

The precipitate formed in each step of the protocol described was weighed, and the melting points were determined using the capillary method.

GO ON TO THE NEXT PAGE.

76. What is the function of the Na_2SO_4 when added to the ether solution?

A. Na_2SO_4 catalyzes the separation of the 9-fluorenone and ether.
B. Na_2SO_4 catalyzes the separation of the benzoic acid and ether.
C. Na_2SO_4 removes the remaining impurities of the solution.
D. Na_2SO_4 acts as a drying agent.

77. Which compound comes out in the aqueous layer of the first extraction with 3 M HCl?

A. 9-fluorenone
B. Ethyl 4-aminobenzoate
C. Benzoic acid
D. Diethyl ether

78. What is the expected molecular weight of the compound extracted by NaOH?

A. 117 g/mol
B. 122 g/mol
C. 165 g/mol
D. 180 g/mol

79. In the last extraction, the aqueous layer will be:

A. below the organic layer, because it has a lower density than the organic layer.
B. below the organic layer, because it has a greater density than the organic layer.
C. above the organic layer, because it has a lower density than the organic layer.
D. above the organic layer, because it has a greater density than the organic layer.

80. What is the purpose of the warm sand bath?

A. Heat evaporates the ether, concentrating the 9-fluorenone.
B. Heat evaporates the ether, concentrating benzoic acid.
C. Heat accelerates the endothermic precipitation process.
D. Heat accelerates the exothermic precipitation process.

81. Suppose that the researchers instead wanted to separate several peptides. Which technique would they most likely use?

A. Gel electrophoresis
B. Distillation
C. Southern blotting
D. Northern blotting

Passage III (Questions 82- 88)

Plasmids are often used as vectors in genetic engineering because of their ability to introduce new genetic information into an organism. Scientists investigating a new technique to produce human insulin using *Escherichia coli* have found that the genes that code for insulin production can be incorporated into the plasmid R388 and, once introduced into *E. coli,* the R388 plasmid can be passed from bacterium to bacterium through conjugation. The researchers wanted to investigate whether the stability of the plasmid (meaning how well the plasmid is maintained during cell division) and rate of conjugation between *E. coli* are sufficient to allow for large-scale production of insulin.

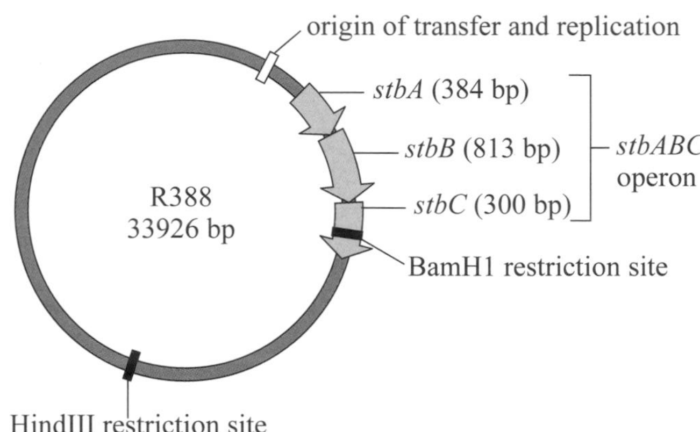

Figure 1 Plasmid R388 containing the *stbABC* operon.

Plasmid R388 contains an operon, *stbABC*, adjacent to the origin of conjugative transfer. With the aim of maximizing the presence of R388 in their E. coli populations, scientists investigated the effects of three stbABC genes (*stbA, stbB,* and *stbC*) on plasmid stability and conjugation.

GO ON TO THE NEXT PAGE.

Experiment 1:

To study the role of *stb* genes in R388 prevalence, scientists compared stability and transfer frequencies between wild-type plasmids and those with site-specific deletions including *stbA* deletion (R388Δ*stbA*), *stbB* deletion (R388Δ*stbB*), *stbC* deletion (R388Δ*stbC*), and deletion of the entire *stbABC* operon (R388Δ*stbABC*). The results of this experiment are shown below:

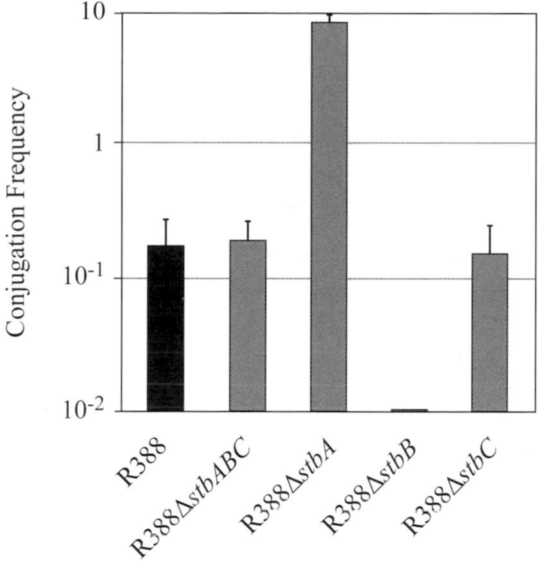

Figure 2 Conjugation frequencies of plasmid R388 derivatives.

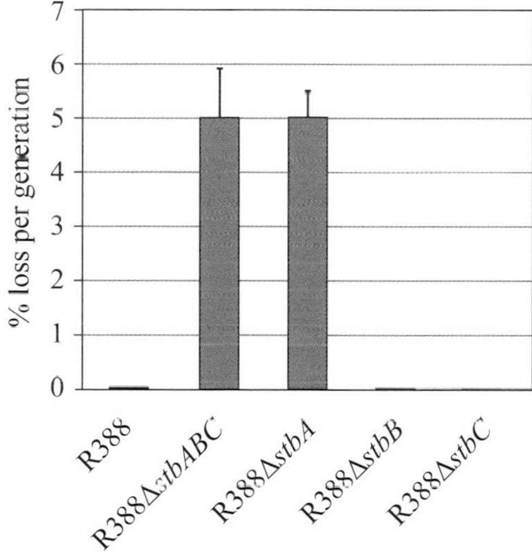

Figure 3 Stability of plasmid R388 derivatives.

This passage was adapted from "The stb Operon Balances the Requirements for Vegetative Stability and Conjugative Transfer of Plasmid R388". Guynet C, Cuevas A, Moncalián G, de la Cruz F. *PLoS Genetics*. 2011. 7(5) doi:10.1371/journal.pgen.1002073 for use under the terms of the Creative Commons CCBY 3.0 license (http://creativecommons.org/licenses/by/3.0/legalcode).

82. Which of the following best describes the effects of deleting the *stbA* gene from the operon?

A. It affects both conjugation and stability
B. It affects conjugation but does not affect stability
C. It does not affect conjugation but does affect stability
D. It affects neither conjugation nor stability

83. If the researchers had only investigated the deletion of the entire *stbABC* operon rather than the effect of individual gene deletion, which of the following might they have incorrectly concluded?

A. The *stb* genes have no effect on stability or conjugation.
B. The *stb* genes have no effect on stability.
C. The *stb* genes have no effect on conjugation.
D. The effects of *stbA* on conjugation balance the effects of *stbB*.

84. In a follow-up experiment, the scientists removed each of the *stb* genes from the plasmid and separated them through gel electrophoresis. In this experiment, which gene travels farthest through the gel?

A. *stbA*
B. *stbB*
C. *stbC*
D. All three genes share the same polarity and travel equal distances.

85. The researchers have found that they can incorporate a gene codes for human insulin production (*ins236*) into the R388 plasmid using restriction enzymes to produce recombinant DNA. Which of the following is NOT a possible product of a mixture of R388 and *ins236* after they are cut by the restriction enzyme HindIII?

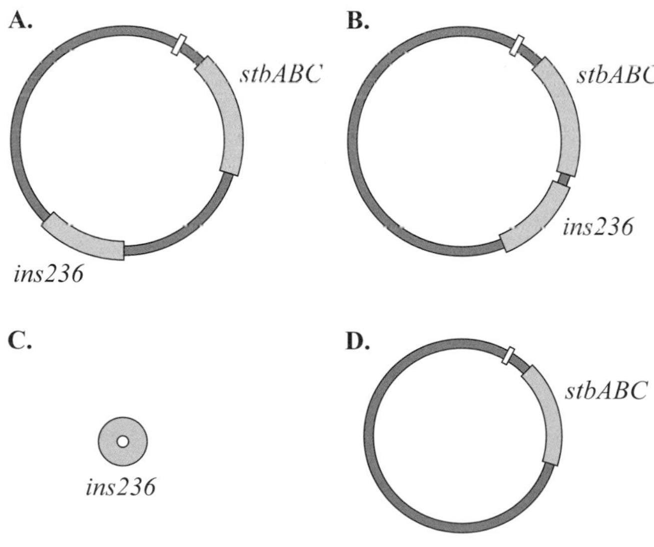

GO ON TO THE NEXT PAGE.

In-Class Exams

86. If, instead of using HindIII, scientists used BamHI to insert *ins236* into plasmid R388, what would be the most likely effect?

- **A.** Increased conjugative rate and decreased stability
- **B.** Increased stability only
- **C.** Increased conjugative rate only
- **D.** Conjugative rate and stability identical to wild-type plasmids

87. Horizontal gene transfer is the transmission of genetic material between organisms in ways other than reproduction. Which of the following is NOT an example of horizontal gene transfer?

- **A.** Transmutation
- **B.** Transduction
- **C.** Transformation
- **D.** Conjugation

88. Why can conjugation be beneficial to bacteria?

- **A.** It allows for the transfer of advantageous genes between organisms.
- **B.** Plasmids obtained through conjugation can be incorporated into the host genome.
- **C.** It allows bacteria to replace old DNA with new DNA.
- **D.** Plasmids can be passed from one generation to the next .

Questions 89 through 92 are **NOT** based on a descriptive passage.

89. IR spectroscopy is normally used to distinguish between:

- **A.** neighboring protons on different compounds.
- **B.** neighboring protons on the same compound.
- **C.** different functional groups on the same compound.
- **D.** acids and bases.

90. The chart below contains information regarding two non-polar compounds, compound A and compound B.

	Compound A	**Compound B**
Molar mass (g/mol)	92.14	78.16
Vapor pressure at 25° C (mm Hg)	38.95	101.24
Boiling point (°C)	110.63	80.12
$\Delta H^\circ_{f,gas}$ (kJ/mol)	+50.00	+82.93

What is the most efficient way to separate these two compounds?

- **A.** Extraction
- **B.** Distillation
- **C.** Column chromatography
- **D.** Crystallization

91. Using a nucleic acid hybridization technique, scientists created a double-stranded combination of DNA and RNA. Scientists most likely employed this technique in order to:

- **A.** amplify a DNA sequence.
- **B.** create a recombinant DNA sequence.
- **C.** locate recognition nucleotide sequences known as restriction sites.
- **D.** identify DNA or RNA molecules with sequences similar to those of a labeled probe.

92. A chemist used paper chromatography in order to determine the relative polarities of four unknown compounds. His results are shown in the table below. Which of the four compounds is the most polar?

	R_f
Compound A	0.92
Compound B	0.76
Compound C	0.78
Compound D	0.54

- **A.** Compound A
- **B.** Compound B
- **C.** Compound C
- **D.** Compound D

STOP.

ANSWERS & EXPLANATIONS

FOR

30-MINUTE IN-CLASS EXAMINATIONS

ANSWERS TO THE 30-MINUTE IN-CLASS EXAMS

Lecture 1	Lecture 2	Lecture 3	Lecture 4
1. C	24. C	47. B	70. A
2. C	25. A	48. D	71. A
3. C	26. B	49. A	72. C
4. B	27. A	50. A	73. A
5. A	28. B	51. B	74. A
6. B	29. D	52. D	75. A
7. A	30. A	53. C	76. D
8. B	31. D	54. B	77. B
9. A	32. A	55. A	78. B
10. B	33. C	56. C	79. B
11. D	34. B	57. C	80. A
12. D	35. C	58. D	81. A
13. A	36. B	59. B	82. A
14. C	37. C	60. D	83. C
15. B	38. D	61. D	84. C
16. A	39. C	62. D	85. B
17. C	40. C	63. C	86. D
18. B	41. D	64. A	87. A
19. C	42. A	65. B	88. A
20. C	43. B	66. B	89. C
21. C	44. D	67. C	90. B
22. A	45. C	68. A	91. D
23. C	46. D	69. B	92. D

MCAT® BIOLOGICAL SCIENCES

Raw Score	Estimated Scaled Score
22-23	132
20-21	131
19	130
18	129
17	128
15-16	127
14	126
12-13	125

MCAT® BIOLOGICAL SCIENCES

Raw Score	Estimated Scaled Score
11	124
9-10	123
8	122
6-7	121
5	120
3-4	119
1-2	118

EXPLANATIONS TO IN-CLASS EXAM FOR LECTURE 1

Passage I

1. **C is correct.** Any answer choice that does not accurately describe the results of the experiment can be eliminated. Choice B can be eliminated because this result was part of the background research rather than being a result of the experiment. Choice A describes the results accurately but overstates the evidence; the results described show that the Unc45b^{Flag}/Hsp90 complex binds selectively to the myosin motor domain, which in turn supports the co-chaperone function, but is not conclusive. C is a better answer because it points out an experimental setup and result that would provide stronger support for a co-chaperone function. Choice D is wrong because it describes the results accurately but does not answer the question. The result indicated actually provides support (but not conclusive evidence) for the co-chaperone function, since a chaperone should not bind to the native protein, which is already fully folded.

2. **C is correct.** Process of elimination is the best technique for this question. To help clarify a question, it is sometimes helpful to restate the question as a statement with "because," and then add the answer choices. For example, "Attempts at predicting protein configuration based upon amino acid sequence have been unsuccessful because:..." Even if choice A were true, it does not answer the question. Choice B is false because chaperones do not determine the product; they only stabilize intermediates. Choice D is generally false except in rare cases of neutral mutation. Choice C is a direct response to the question and is also true.

3. **C is correct.** The folding of a peptide chain is called the tertiary structure of a protein. The passage states that chaperones assist in the "folding process." This is the best answer.

4. **B is correct.** This question requires an understanding of the experimental methodology. The Anti-Flag antibody is used to visualize the binding of Unc45b^{Flag} or the Unc45b^{Flag}/Hsp90 complex to the protein subfragments. If the antibody itself bound to any of the subfragments, it would be impossible to address the hypothesis that Unc45b^{Flag} will selectively bind to the non-native myosin motor domain. Choice A is incorrect because it is not implied in the passage and is not the purpose of this experimental step. Choice C is incorrect because the Anti-Flag antibody is already bound to the Unc45b^{Flag} in each other trial; even if this were a concern of the researchers, it could not be addressed when only the Anti-Flag antibody is present. Choice D is true but does not answer the question that was asked.

5. **A is correct.** Choice A describes the role of chaperones as explained in the passage. A cell with more chaperones can synthesize proteins more easily, giving it a selective advantage. Choice B is incorrect because chaperones don't slow the process of protein folding. C is wrong for a number of reasons. For one, the energy for protein synthesis comes from ATP, not heat. As for choice D, chaperones don't affect the rate of polypeptide synthesis; they affect polypeptide folding.

6. **B is correct.** Why does a protein denature in the presence of heat? The hydrogen bonds and other non-covalent interactions in the secondary and tertiary structure are disrupted. Another way to answer this question is to notice that all the bonds are covalent except hydrogen bonds. Although hydrogen bonds are the strongest type of intermolecular bond, they are much weaker than covalent bonds, and will be disrupted before covalent bonds when heat is applied.

7. **A is correct.** Disulfide bond formation occurs in the synthesis of cystine, not proline, and that an enzyme lowers the activation energy of a reaction. Knowledge of the role that proline and cystine play in forming the tertiary structure of proteins is required for the MCAT®.

Passage II

8. **B is correct.** An enzyme (like any type of catalyst) lowers the energy of activation of both the forward and reverse reactions, as stated in answer choice B. This means that choices A and C can be eliminated. Choice D is incorrect because a catalyst does NOT alter the equilibrium mix of reactants and products. The reason that lowering the energy of activation for both the forward and reverse reactions can cause a buildup of the product is that in the absence of the enzyme, the forward rate would be so low that no significant amount of product would be formed.

9. **A is correct.** The correct answer to this question has to accurately describe the effects of the type of inhibition named and describe an effect that would decrease the specificity constant. Recall from the passage that the specificity constant is found by dividing the turnover number, k_{cat}, by K_m. A decrease in turnover number or an increase in K_m would decrease the specificity constant. Also notice that turnover number must be proportional to V_{max}. Replacing "turnover number" in each answer stem with "V_{max}" makes it possible to answer the question based on background knowledge of the types of inhibition. Competitive inhibition increases K_m but does not change V_{max}. Choices C and D both describe competitive inhibition incorrectly and can be eliminated. Also, the effect of the scenario described in choice D on the specificity constant cannot be predicted; it would depend on the exact amount of change in each parameter. Choice B is incorrect because noncompetitive inhibition does not change K_m. Choice A describes the effect of noncompetitive inhibition correctly and describes a scenario that would lead the specificity constant to decrease.

10. **B is correct.** This question requires reasoning about the equation given for the specificity constant in the passage. If the turnover number (the denominator) decreases, K_m (the denominator) must decrease by the same amount for the overall value of the fraction to stay the same. Choice A must be incorrect - as described in the passage and demonstrated in Figure 1, E43G does show some enzymatic activity, although the catalytic efficiency is reduced. Choice C is true but does not answer the question. (Choice C also probably goes beyond the knowledge of amino acids required for the MCAT®. Glutamate is the name for the amino acid glutamic acid in its anion form.) Finally, choice D is a tempting answer, since increased K_m reflects decreased enzymatic affinity for the substrate. However, notice that according to the equation given in the passage, an increase in K_m along with the decrease in turnover number would cause the specificity constant to decrease, not stay the same.

11. **D is correct.** It is the only answer choice that correctly describes the effect of an uncompetitive inhibitor on K_m and V_{max}. Choice A describes a mixed inhibitor (recall that some mixed inhibitors preferentially bind to the enzyme prior to formation of the enzyme-substrate complex and thus raise K_m, while others preferentially bind to the enzyme-substrate complex and thus lower K_m). Choice B describes a competitive inhibitor. Choice C describes a noncompetitive inhibitor, which has no preference between the enzyme alone or enzyme-substrate complex and thus does not change K_m.

12. **D is correct.** ATP is a source of readily available energy and can act as a cosubstrate (a type of coenzyme). It would be easy to mistakenly choose A, but ADP is the byproduct that remains when a phosphate group has been removed from ATP, rather than being the source of energy. As this example shows, it is important to always quickly look at all of the answer choices even after choosing one that seems to be correct. A heme group is a prosthetic group rather than a cosubstrate; furthermore, choice B can be eliminated because a heme group does not provide energy as ATP does. Although glucose is ultimately metabolized to produce ATP, it cannot itself be coupled to a reaction to provide energy. This means that choice C is incorrect.

13. **A is correct.** One of the key characteristics of proteins is that they can have a huge variety of structures due to the multitude of possible combinations of R groups with differing chemical properties. As a result, the active site of each type of enzyme can be precisely fitted to a particular substrate (enzyme specificity). In contrast, choice D describes the characteristics of proteins incorrectly. Choice B describes a characteristic feature of lipids, not proteins. Choice C is incorrect, since extremes of pH and temperature can denature proteins.

14. **C is correct.** The structure of α-D-Galactose is unnecessary information intended to confuse the test-taker. The question could be restated as "What reaction allows carbohydrate molecules to join together to form polysaccharides?" It is important to know that bonds between carbohydrates are formed by dehydration. In fact, most macromolecules are formed by dehydration reactions. This includes peptide bond formation, but peptide bonds are formed between amino acids, not carbohydrates, so choice B is incorrect. Choice A might sound promising because of the word "addition," but nucleophilic addition is not involved in polysaccharide formation. Choice D must be wrong because hydrolysis corresponds to bond breaking, not bond formation.

Passage III

15. **B is correct.** This question is a straightforward test of knowledge of the structures of different types of fats. It is important to be familiar with the general structure of triglycerides, phospholipids (described by A), waxes (described by C), and steroids (described by D). Even without remembering the structure of a triglyceride, it would be possible to find the answer to this question by reasoning from the name: "tri-" means 3, and "glyceride" refers to the glycerol backbone.

16. **A is correct.** The passage states that LVP with a greater ratio of lipids to proteins have greater infectivity than those with a lower ratio of lipids to proteins. Thus the question can answered with the knowledge that lipids are less dense than proteins. This makes sense because of their structure: fatty acids are composed of a long chain of carbons with attached hydrogens, which have a very low molar mass, while proteins also have a carbon backbone but have a variety of side chains with heavier elements. The lipoprotein with the highest ratio of lipids to proteins will have the lowest density. Even without remembering that lipids are less dense than proteins, it would be possible to at least eliminate choices B and C. Since the question calls for the HIGHEST infectivity (which is dependent on density), the correct answer must be one of the two extremes described by choices A and D.

17. **C is correct.** The MCAT® is likely to ask questions asking for the interpretation of additional findings, but this is a particularly difficult example. It is best answered by process of elimination. Choice A can be eliminated because it does not refer to lipoviro-particles at all. This answer might be chosen by a test-taker who was reading too quickly and thought it referred to lipoviro-particles rather than VLDL. Choice B contradicts the conclusion: if a cell line with no apoB lipoproteins was able to secrete the HCV envelope proteins, an alternative mechanism would have to be considered. Choice C directly relates to the experimental design described in the passage. If MTP inhibition reduced the secretion of multiple proteins other than apoB, it would be possible that the effect on E1 and E2 secretion was due to one of those other proteins. The fact that only apoB was reduced supports the conclusion that apoB is involved in the secretion of these glycoproteins and ultimately lipoviro-particle formation. The finding described in D does not provide firm support for or against the conclusion described in the question stem. Choice C is a better answer.

18. **B is correct.** This question requires interpretation of the graphical data and the findings described in the passage. Choice B is correct because Figure 2 shows a significant decrease in secreted apoB in the presence of Cp 346086, and Figure 1 shows that Cp 346086 did in fact inhibit MTP. Thus apoB secretion decreases when MTP activity decreases, a direct correlation. If choice A were true, Figure 1 would show no difference between the two doses of MTP inhibitor, but the data indicate a difference at both 24h and 48h. Choice C can be eliminated because the passage states that the secretion of these glycoproteins was greatly decreased when MTP was inhibited. This finding suggests a direct correlation rather than an inverse correlation. Choice D is incorrect: as shown in Figure 1, MTP activity was significantly lower in the presence of Cp 346086.

19. **C is correct.** The passage says that a glycoprotein is composed of a protein and a short chain of monosaccharides. Choices A, B, and D are all polysaccharides used for long-term energy storage or structural material; only glucose is a monosaccharide.

20. **C is correct.** Phospholipids are amphipathic, meaning that one end is polar (the phosphate group) and the other end is nonpolar (the fatty acid tails). Choices B and D mean the exact same thing, so neither can be the correct answer. Choice A could be eliminated even without the knowledge that phospholipids are amphipathic; by definition, no fat is completely polar, although a polar group may be attached.

Stand-alones

21. **C is correct.** Recall that hydrogen bonds are critical to the structure of DNA. Purine-pyrimidine base pairs from complementary DNA strands are held together by hydrogen bonds. Choices A and B can be eliminated because covalent bonds are not involved in holding together complementary DNA strands; although hydrogen bonds are the strongest of the intermolecular bonds, they are not as strong as covalent bonds. Van der Waals forces exist between all molecules, but they are not the major forces behind complementary base pairing. Choice C is a better answer.

22. **A is correct.** This question is a good example of one that appears much more difficult than it actually is. The MCAT® probably would not require knowledge of Lineweaver-Burk plots; the question simply requires application of knowledge about the different types of inhibition. Choices B and C can be eliminated because they both demonstrate a change in V_{max}, whereas competitive inhibition does not change V_{max}. Choice D can be eliminated because it does not show a change in K_m, unlike in competitive inhibition.

23. **C is correct.** This answer choice describes a difference between the two types of nucleic acids but switches RNA and DNA. It is RNA that contains the hydroxyl group and DNA that contains only a hydrogen at the same carbon. This difference can be remembered by thinking of the full names of RNA and DNA: ribonucleic acid and *deoxygenated* ribonucleic acid. The other answer choices correctly describe differences between RNA and DNA that must be known for the MCAT®.

EXPLANATIONS TO IN-CLASS EXAM FOR LECTURE 2

Passage I

24. **C is correct.** The passage states that there was no specific enrichment of DNA methylation on chromosome 21, eliminating choices A and B. It also states that enrichment occurred on various autosomes, so the effects are not sex-linked; D can be eliminated.

25. **A is correct.** DNA is read in the 5' to 3' direction, so at a CpG site, C should be 5' to G. The complement A would be 5' – ATCGA – 3'. All other choices have complementary sequences in which C is 3' to G. The fastest way to answer this question would be to look only at the "CG" combinations in each answer choice and realize that the one from the other three has to be correct.

26. **B is correct.** Aneuploidy is the term used to describe the condition of having one or more extra or missing chromosomes, such as trisomy 21 (DS). Aneuploidy is a major chromosomal mutation that generally results from nondisjunction during meiosis. The results of Experiment 1 suggest that altered DNA methylation may be a response to trisomy 21. The results of Experiment 2 indicate that altered DNA methylation affects gene expression. Also, recall that the background prior to the experiments describes the hypothesis that DNA methylation is altered in response to changes in gene dosage, which must occur due to an alteration of ploidy. According to this hypothesis, which is supported by the results of the experiments, aneuploidy would have to precede DNA methylation, which means choices A and D can be immediately eliminated. The results of Experiment 2 indicate that DNA methylation precedes differential gene expression, so choice C is incorrect.

27. **A is correct**. Choices C and D can be eliminated because histones (proteins) and non-coding RNAs will not contain any DNA methylation. DNA methylation represses gene expression by making DNA inaccessible to transcription factors. Heterochromatin, which consists of genes that are not currently being transcribed, is associated with higher levels of DNA methylation than euchromatin, which is chromatin that is actively being transcribed.

28. **B is correct.** The graph from Experiment I shows that DS individuals have DECREASED methylation compared to the control group, so choice I is false. Choices A and C can be eliminated. Option II appears in both of the remaining answer choices, so it is only necessary to determine whether III is true to answer the question. The graph from Experiment I shows that methylation of *TMEM131* DECREASES with age, so gene expression should INCREASE with age in control individuals. Therefore, option III is incorrect, making B the correct answer. It is also possible to determine that option II is true. The passage states that the drug 5aza-dC causes decreased methylation. The graph from Experiment 2 shows that increased doses of the drug (decreased methylation) cause gene expression of *TMEM131* in control cells to mimic that of DS individuals. Therefore, DNA methylation inhibits *TMEM131* gene expression, and option II is correct:

29. **D is correct.** If it is true that increased methylation in repressor regions increases gene expression, decreasing the methylation of repressor regions on CD3Z with 5aza-dC could decrease gene expression. Choice A is incorrect because 5aza-dC DECREASES methylation rather than increasing it. Choice B is wrong because if most methylation sites were located on the promoter region, demethylation would cause INCREASED gene expression. Choice C is irrelevant since all of the genes explored were autosomal.

Passage II

30. **A is correct.** Choice A indicates that the poly-A tail is not coded for by DNA, but is synthesized separately. It offers a mechanism by which synthesis may take place other than transcription. Choice B indicates that the poly-A tail is transcribed from DNA at the end of the gene. Even if choices C and D made sense, they would indicate that the poly-A tail was transcribed from a gene.

31. **D is correct.** The question is really asking, "Where does post-transcriptional processing take place?" The answer is in the nucleus. Post-transcriptional processing of rRNA and tRNA commonly takes place in prokaryotes, but the post-transcriptional processing of mRNA described in the passage takes place in eukaryotes. Furthermore, snRNPs are not found in prokaryotes. The "sn" stands for "small nuclear" and prokaryotes do not have nuclei.

32. **A is correct.** Figure 2 is an electron micrograph of R looping. The passage explains that R looping is a technique where DNA and mature RNA are hybridized. Mature RNA has no introns, so choice C is wrong. The loops are parts of the DNA that correspond to the removed sections of the RNA and thus have no complementary RNA sequence; the loops are DNA introns.

33. **C is correct.** The outcome of the experiment described indicates that intronic sequences (the inserted Alus) control the changeover of splicing from constitutive to alternative. If alternative splicing existed before introns evolved, factors other than intronic sequence would have had to be controlling alternative splicing mechanisms, contradicting the study's findings of intronic control.

34. **B is correct.** Alternative splicing allows for flexibility in the inclusion or exclusion of exons, which is not possible with constitutive splicing. As a result, many different proteins can be synthesized from a single gene. Therefore, alternative splicing increases the diversity of the proteins that can be produced from the genome, without expanding the genome itself.

35. **C is correct.** Splicing in eukaryotes is carried out by the spliceosome complex. A spliceosome is composed of snRNPs which, in turn, are made up of snRNA and a variety of proteins. The spliceosome brings the ends of an intron together to form a loop known as a lariat, excises the intron, and joins the ends of the two exons together. Splicing takes place in the nucleus. By contrast, rRNA is located in the cytoplasm of the cell and in translation not splicing.

Passage III

36. **B is correct.** Apomixis creates plants with identical genotypes to the mother plant. Choice A is incorrect because lack of genetic variability actually makes the population of plants more susceptible to disease. Choices C and D can be eliminated because the passage does not provide any information about the speed or input of resources necessary to create seeds through apomixis.

37. **C is correct.** Prophase is the stage in which the nuclear membrane begins to disintegrate and chromosomes condense. Replication occurs during the S phase, so A is wrong. Choice B is incorrect because there is no crossing over in mitosis. The nuclear membrane does disintegrate to allow chromosomal movement via the spindle apparatus, so D is wrong. Note that even without remembering the phase in which the nuclear membrane disintegrates, B and D could be eliminated based on general knowledge of mitosis.

38. **D is correct.** Replication of the chromosomes during interphase characterizes both mitosis and meiosis.

39. **C is correct.** The passage states that the *MiMe* mutant plants create gametes that are genetically identical to the maternal plant, which means they must be diploid. A wild-type (non-mutant) gamete is haploid. Therefore a plant produced by a cross between the two should be triploid.

40. **C is correct.** In prophase I, a tetrad will form, genetic recombination will occur, and a spindle apparatus will form. Chromosomal migration describes anaphase.

41. **D is correct.** Choices A and B can immediately be eliminated because recombination affects the genetic material of each participating chromosome but does not change the number of chromosomes. The change from diploid to haploid takes place during meiosis I. The best way to remember that the change from diploid to haploid must occur in meiosis I is to recall that meiosis II is basically the same as mitosis, and the number of chromosomes does not change in mitosis. Since the male gametes are diploid, the male germ cells must not be undergoing meiosis I, making choice D correct.

42. **A is correct.** Gametes produced through apomixis are diploid, so ploidy is expected to double every generation using this technique. If increased ploidy decreases fertility, crops produced by apomixis will have a limited number of productive generations before becoming infertile. Choice B is a true statement but does not answer the question. Since the goal of apomixis is genotype perpetuation, lower mutation rates in mitotic-like division would be desirable, so C is false. Choice D is a distractor. The fact that the process of engineering apomixis might work in a non-edible plant does not indicate that it could not work in an edible plant.

43. **B is correct.** The passage states that *Atspo11-1/Atrec8* double mutants have unbalanced gametes, causing sterility. Just by looking at the end products of the answer choices, it is possible to narrow the possible correct answers to choices B and C. The passage also states that in *Atspo11-1/Atrec8* double mutants, the first meiotic division is replaced by a mitotic-like division. In B, the first division is mitotic-like with the separation of sister chromatids. In choice C, the first division is unlike mitosis because sister chromatids do not separate and chromosomes divide unevenly between the daughter cells.

Stand-alones

44. **D is correct.** There are 4^3 possible different codons. There are more codons than there are amino acids used to produce proteins. This means that an amino acid could be coded for by several codons. The genetic code is evolutionarily very old, and is almost universal. Only a few species use a slightly different genetic code.

45. **C is correct.** Both children are female because the genotype of Turner syndrome, according to the information provided, must be XO. The O reflects the lack of a chromosome from the parent within whom nondisjunction occurred; the X came from the other parent. In the scenario described in the question stem, the mother only has healthy X chromosomes to pass on, while the father has only one colorblind X chromosome to pass on. Thus the colorblind child got her X chromosome from the father and no chromosome from the mother, and the healthy child got her X chromosome from the mother and no chromosome from the father.

46. **D is correct.** The primary spermatocyte is the spermatogonium just after DNA replication. Humans never have more than 46 chromosomes. The primary spermatocyte has 92 chromatids but only 46 chromosomes.

EXPLANATIONS TO IN-CLASS EXAM FOR LECTURE 3

Passage I

47. **B is correct.** Choices C and D are wrong because glycolysis is independent of oxygen. The products of choice A include only one pyruvate and no NADH, and the equation is not balanced.

48. **D is correct.** As is often the case on the MCAT®, the correct answer choice may not seem to be the best possible answer to the question asked. Nonetheless, it may be the best among the four available answer choices. No pre-existing knowledge of experimental design is required to answer this question, since only one of the answer choices can be identified as factually accurate based on information presented in the passage. 2-deoxy-D-glucose is a known glycolysis inhibitor. There is no indication that it is implicated in the development of acute lung injury (ALI). In fact, ALI is associated with an increased rate of glycolysis. Choice A can be eliminated. Similarly, the passage gives no indication that 2-deoxy-D-glucose is expressed in alveolar epithelial cells. It says only that mice were treated with 2-deoxy-D glucose. Therefore, choice B is also incorrect. Choice C can be eliminated because it contradicts passage information. The passage suggests that HIF1A promotes glycolysis rather than inhibiting it. This leaves choice D. It may not be altogether satisfying, but the passage does state that 2-deoxy-D-glucose is a glycolysis inhibitor and suggests that glycolysis is mediated through alveolar epithelial HIF1A. Be careful! Often there will be two or more answer choices that are factually correct based on information presented in the passage. If so, choose the one that best answers the question.

49. **A is correct.** The substrates of glycolysis are monosaccharides—including glucose, fructose, and galactose— and the glycerol backbones of triglycerides, which are converted into intermediates of the glycolysis pathway. Glycolysis produces pyruvate, which is converted into acetyl-CoA, a substrate of the citric acid cycle. Fatty acids are broken down into acetyl-CoA via beta-oxidation. They enter the citric acid cycle but do not undergo glycolysis. The carbon chains of amino acids also serve as substrates for the citric acid cycle,but not glycolysis.

50. **A is correct.** Insulin promotes cellular uptake and use of glucose. Therefore, an increased ratio of insulin to glucagon is most likely to lead to an increased glycolytic rate. The choices can be narrowed down to A or B. Insulin also promotes storage of glucose and inhibits breakdown of glycogen and fats, so an increased insulin to glucagon ratio is most likely to lead to net anabolism.

51. **B is correct.** According to Figure 1, wild-type mice exposed to VILI have the highest glucose and Glut1 transcript levels. Therefore, wild-type with VILI would have the highest glycolytic rate. Given that "elevations of transcript levels of glycolytic enzymes were found to be attenuated in *Hif1A*$^{f/f}$ SurfactantCre^{+} mice," it is unlikely that *Hif1A*$^{f/f}$ SurfactantCre^{+} mice would have the highest glycolytic rate.

52. **D is correct.** The hypoxia-inducible factor described in the passage promotes glucose uptake and usage, so it can be inferred that hypoxia-inducible transcription factor (HIF-1) does the same. Thus, increased expression of HIF-1 should lead to increased expression of transporters and glycolytic enzymes. Choices A, B, and C can be eliminated, leaving D as the correct answer. Glycolysis and gluconeogenesis are reciprocally regulated, meaning that when one is occurring relatively frequently, the other is occurring relatively infrequently. For this reason, cancer cells, which display increased expression of HIF-1 and thus increased expression of glycolytic enzymes, would be least likely to exhibit increased expression of gluconeogenic enzymes.

53. **C is correct.** Decreasing an enzyme's affinity for its substrate inhibits that enzyme, so choice A can be eliminated. Conversely, increasing an enzyme's affinity for its substrate activates that enzyme, so choice B can be eliminated. Because glycolysis produces ATP, it makes sense that ATP would inhibit and ADP would activate phosphofructokinase. Therefore, choice D can be eliminated, and choice C is correct.

Passage II

54. **B is correct.** The passage states, "Lipolysis is the process by which stored triacylglycerols are released as nonesterified fatty acids." Hormone sensitive lipase (HSL) hydrolyzes one of the two ester bonds that exist between the glycerol backbone and each of the two fatty acid chains of a diacylglycerol. In general, hydrolysis of an ester linkage produces an alcohol—for example, glycerol— and an acid—for example, a fatty acid. Ester linkages are of the form RCOOR', whereas ether linkages are of the form ROR.' Carbohydrates form glycosidic linkages and nucleic acids form phosphodiester linkages.

55. **A is correct.** Insulin promotes use and storage of glucose, and therefore activates enzymes for glycogenesis (glycogen synthesis). It concurrently inhibits enzymes for gluconeogenesis (glucose synthesis) and lipolysis (fat breakdown).

56. **C is correct.** According to the passage, HSL hydrolyzes diacylglycerols, so HSL level is a determinant of lipolytic capacity. HSL promotes lipolysis, which is positively associated with insulin resistance, but HSL does not directly promote insulin resistance; choice C is a better answer. It is ATGL that initiates enzymatic breakdown of triacylglycerols, not HSL, so choice B is wrong. While it may be the case that higher levels of HSL tend to be associated with lesser metabolism of glucose, HSL level is more appropriately a measure of lipid metabolism rather than glucose metabolism, making choice D incorrect.

57. **C is correct.** As shown in Figure 1, reduced HSL activity is associated with increased insulin sensitivity; that is, *HSL*$^{+/-}$ mice had lower percentages of basal glucose in their plasma. Therefore, choices B and D, which suggest that reduced HSL activity would decrease insulin sensitivity, must be incorrect. The passage states that *HSL*$^{+/-}$ mice did not experience a change in fat mass, so a drug that inhibits HSL would not be expected to increase fat mass. Choice A can be eliminated. The most likely outcome would be an increase in insulin sensitivity and no change in fat mass, making C the correct answer.

58. **D is correct.** Once inside the mitochondria, fatty acids undergo beta-oxidation to form acetyl CoA, which enters the citric acid cycle. Proteins and carbohydrates undergo deamination and glycolysis, respectively. Lipolysis is the process by which a triacylglycerol is broken down into one glycerol and three fatty acid molecules.

59. **B is correct.** Figure 2 shows that *HSL*$^{+/-}$ mice, which have diminished lipolytic capacity, have higher insulin tolerance than WT mice. This suggests that the answer will be either A or B. While it is true that fatty acids and glucose are homeostatically regulated, the mere fact that they are regulated does not allow for a prediction of the relationship between lipolytic capacity and glucose and insulin tolerance. Choice A can be eliminated. Both products of lipolysis—namely, fatty acids—and glucose can be oxidized to acetyl CoA and enter the citric acid cycle. When lipolytic capacity is high, fatty acids are in plentiful supply and are prone to be oxidized and enter the citric acid cycle. However, when lipolytic capacity is low, the cell will increasingly draw upon other precursors to acetyl CoA, including glucose. Therefore, it is reasonable to expect that diminished lipolytic capacity would be associated with improved glucose and insulin tolerance, and choice B is the best answer. As stated in answer choice C, the regulation of lipolysis is distinct from that of glucose uptake, storage and metabolism. Nonetheless, the two are closely related and the existence of distinct regulatory pathways does not preclude changes in one pathway from impacting another. In the absence of glucose, amino acids in the muscle are metabolized, but glucose metabolism is preferred to protein metabolism, and protein metabolism does not fully compensate for diminished lipid and glucose metabolism. Thus choice D can be eliminated.

60. **D is correct.** Choices A, B, C and D all provide support for the assertion that *HSL*$^{+/-}$ mice exhibited diminished lipolytic capacities. However, choice D provides the strongest support. The findings presented in choices A and B confirm that *HSL*$^{+/-}$ mice are haploinsufficient for hormone sensitive lipase, but they do not rule out the existence of a compensatory mechanism occurring as a result of the reduction in HSL expression. The finding presented in answer choice C does rule out one potential compensatory mechanism, but it does not, in and of itself, suggest diminished lipolytic capabilities. Only answer choice D confirms that reduced lipolytic response was actually observed in *HSL*$^{+/-}$ mice.

Passage III

61. **D is correct.** When glucose concentrations are relatively high, insulin promotes cellular use and storage of glucose. This means that choice D, glycogenesis (the creation of glycogen), is the best answer. When glucose concentrations are relatively low, glucagon—not insulin— promotes glycogenolysis (the breakdown of glycogen) and gluconeogenesis (synthesis of glucose from non-carbohydrate sources). Therefore, choices A and C are incorrect. Finally, insulin promotes fat synthesis, so choice B, lipolysis (the breakdown of lipids) is incorrect.

62. **D is correct.** Zn^{2+} chelation and $GABA_A$ receptor antagonism block paracrine signaling by Zn^{2+} and GABA, respectively. The first and second columns show that glucose suppresses glucagon secretion in the presence of both Zn^{2+} and GABA paracrine signaling. The third and fourth columns show that glucose suppresses glucagon secretion in the absence of Zn^{2+} paracrine signaling. The fifth and sixth columns show that glucose suppresses glucagon secretion in the absence of GABA paracrine signaling. Therefore, glucose suppresses secretion both in the presence and absence of Zn^{2+} and GABA paracrine signaling, making choice D correct.

63. **C is correct.** The pentose-phosphate pathway does not produce ATP. Instead, it produces NADPH and five carbon sugars, including ribose. Chemiosmotic coupling, an example of oxidative phosphorylation, produces NAD^+, FAD, ATP and water. The citric acid cycle produces CO_2, ATP, NADH and $FADH_2$.

64. **A is correct.** Hydrolysis of phosphoanhydride bonds in ATP is exergonic ($\Delta G < 0$). Following input of the small amount of energy required to break the bonds comes a large output of energy associated with the formation of new bonds. It is the electron carriers NADH and $FADH_2$ that carry high potential electrons, so choice B is incorrect. Uncoupled oxidative phosphorylation generates heat by uncoupling oxidative phosphorylation from ATP synthesis. It is used by animals to maintain body temperature and is not the reaction through which ATP releases energy needed to drive less energetically favorable reactions. Therefore, choice C is incorrect. Finally, the ribose sugar of ATP is converted to deoxyribose when ATP is used in DNA synthesis. It is not necessary to be familiar with the use of ATP in DNA synthesis. Just know that ATP stores energy in its phosphate bonds. Any other answer, including answer choice D—conversion of ribose to deoxyribose— is not the best answer to the question of how ATP acts as an energy source.

65. **B is correct.** Glucagon tends to increase blood levels of glucose. Glucagon promotes glycogenolysis and gluconeogenesis, both of which increase the concentration of glucose in the blood, resulting in a state of hyper- rather than hypoglycemia. It is insulin that promotes glucogenesis and glycolysis.

66. **B is correct.** The question stem explains that researchers think that glucose causes the ATP-dependent K^+ channels in α-cells to close. It asks the test-taker to identify which finding would make it least likely that glucose has this effect. The passage indicates that the closing of K_{ATP} channels inhibits glucagon release. The first finding, choice A, is that glucose cannot inhibit glucagon release above and beyond the inhibition caused by the K_{ATP} channel blocker tolbutamide. Because glucose has a similar inhibitory effect to tolbutamide, it makes sense that glucose might not be able to affect any additional inhibition, even if the hypothesis given in the question stem were true. Therefore, choice A is not the best answer. Choice C supports the question stem: if glucose suppresses glucagon release by closing K_{ATP} channels, it makes sense that opening those channels might reverse glucose-dependent suppression. Choice C can be eliminated. Choice D states that glucose continued to suppress glucagon release even when paracrine signaling was blocked. If glucose regulates glucagon release independently of paracrine signaling, as the findings described in the passage suggest, it makes sense that glucose would continue suppressing release even in the absence of paracrine signaling. Thus, choice D does not challenge the hypothesis given in the question stem and is not the best answer. Answer choice B states that glucose cannot inhibit glucagon release in the presence of an insulin agonist. In general, insulin and glucagon have opposing effects on metabolism, and it makes sense that the release of one would be inhibited in the presence of the other. In the presence of a substance that mimics the action of insulin, glucose should inhibit glucagon release. This finding challenges the hypothesis presented in the question stem, making B the best answer.

This is a very difficult question. The best answer choice does not disprove the existence of an α-cell glucose-sensing pathway involving closure of ATP-dependent K^+ channels in the presence of glucose. It just challenges the existence of the pathway in a way that the other answer choices do not.

Stand-alones

67. **C is correct.** The high-energy electrons from NADH drive protons outward across the inner mitochondrial membrane. Even without remembering the role that NADH plays in aerobic respiration, it would be possible to eliminate choice B because energy is not required for passive diffusion.

68. **A is correct.** Aerobic respiration is the oxidation of glucose to carbon dioxide and water. The overall net reaction for aerobic respiration is: Glucose + $O_2 \rightarrow CO_2 + H_2O$. Oxygen, not glucose, is reduced in this reaction. The terms "elimination" and "lysis" are not applied to the breakdown of glucose.

69. **B is correct.** Substrate-level phosphorylation is a reaction through which an energy-rich intermediate transfers its phosphate group to ADP, forming ATP. Glycolysis produces ATP through substrate-level phosphorylation. Therefore, a glycolytic reaction that produces ATP would do so through substrate-level phosphorylation. Note that the reference to phosphoglycerate kinase is not relevant to answering the question. Substrate-level phosphorylation should be distinguished from oxidative phosphorylation, which is the production of ATP via the electron transport chain and ATP synthase.

EXPLANATIONS TO IN-CLASS EXAM FOR LECTURE 4

Passage I

70. **A is correct.** Anhydrides can participate in an acylation reaction in which half of the anhydride adds to another molecule and the other half yields a carboxylic acid. Simply counting the total atoms of the reactants and subtracting the total atoms of the product shown for Reaction 1 gives a clue to the answer of this question.

71. **A is correct.** Remember that IR spectroscopy is used to identify the functional groups present in a compound. The IR spectra of carbonyl compounds contain a sharp dip around 1700 cm^{-1}.

72. **C is correct.** Table 3 shows that the integral value for the peak with a chemical shift of 2.30 ppm is three. The integral value indicates the number of protons that give rise to the signal. Because three chemically equivalent protons gave rise to this signal, it must be due to the protons on the carbon atom of the methyl group attached to the carbonyl carbon. This is the only carbon atom that is bonded to three protons.

73. **A is correct.** The passages states that cyclopentadienylmagnesium bromide is a Grignard reagent. Grignard reagents are strong bases and will react with water.

74. **A is correct.** A compound is considered aromatic if it satisfies two criteria. First, the compound must contain a ring comprised of continuous, overlapping *p* orbitals. The passage states that the compound has a planar structure. Therefore, its *p* orbitals are continuous and overlapping. Second, the number of electrons in that ring must be a Hückel number; that is, the number of π electrons must be equal to $4n+2$, where n is a whole number. The iron atom in the compound is assigned the oxidation state +2, and each ring is considered to have a single negative charge. Therefore, in isolation, each ring has six π electrons; think of each carbon as contributing one π electron to the ring. The sixth π electron comes from the negative charge. $4(1) + 2 = 6$. Each ring has a Hückel number of electrons, so the compound is aromatic.

75. **A is correct.** If structure 1 were the correct structure, signals would arise from three groups of chemically equivalent protons. The first would be from the protons on the carbons attached to the iron atom. The second would be from the protons on the carbons attached to the carbons that are attached to the iron. Finally, the third would be from the protons on the remaining carbon.

Passage II

76. **D is correct.** Water has some slight solubility in organic extracts. Inorganic anhydrous salts such as magnesium, sodium, and calcium sulfate readily form insoluble hydrates, removing the water from wet organic phases. Choice A is wrong because 9-fluorenone is neutral; there is no reason that Na_2SO_4 would cause it to separate from the ether. Choice B must be wrong because the benzoic acid has already been extracted by the time Na_2SO_4 is added. (Benzoic acid was extracted after deprotonation by HCl.) Finally, Choice C is also incorrect because there is no basis for thinking sodium sulfate could remove impurities.

77. **B is correct.** The acid protonates the basic amino group on ethyl 4-aminobenzoate, making it soluble in the aqueous solution. The other compounds are not basic, and would not be made soluble by the acid.

78. **B is correct.** The benzoic acid will be deprotonated by NaOH, making it soluble in the aqueous layer. The MW of benzoic acid can be calculated by looking at the structure as shown in Figure 1, and is equal to 122 g/mol. Choice A is the molar mass that would be calculated if you forgot that each carbon of the aromatic ring, other than the one attached to the side chain, has a hydrogen attached. Choice C is the molar mass of ethyl 4-aminobenzoate, and choice D is the molar mass of 9- fluorenone.

79. **B is correct.** This question requires the organic layer is made up mostly of diethyl ether. From the table, we see that diethyl ether has a specific gravity of less than one and is thus less dense than water; this means that the organic layer will float on top of the aqueous layer. However, this is NOT always true for extractions; sometimes the aqueous layer is less dense than the organic layer and will therefore float on top of the organic layer. Refer to the specific gravities of the given compounds to determine which will be on top and which will be below. Also, for this question, notice that you could immediately eliminate choices B and D because they describe the effects of differing densities inaccurately.

80. **A is correct.** Ether has a low boiling point compared to the only compound that remains after the previous extractions, 9-fluorenone. As the ether evaporates, 9-fluorenone is concentrated. Even the purpose of the heat is to evaporate the ether. Choice D can be eliminated because heat would not accelerate an exothermic process. Choice C can also be eliminated because precipitation is exothermic, not endothermic.

81. **A is correct.** This question requires knowledge of techniques commonly featured on the MCAT®. Gel electrophoresis is commonly used to separate peptides based on charge. Distillation is not used for the separation of peptides. Southern blotting is used for DNA fragments and Northern blotting is used for RNA fragments.

Passage III

82. **A is correct.** Compare the relevant bars on the graphs between the results for wild-type and R388Δ*stb*A plasmids. The graphs show that deletion of the *stb*A gene dramatically increases the rate of conjugative transfer and increases the rate of plasmid loss from generation to generation (decreases stability). Therefore, both stability and conjugation differ from the wild-type, making A the best choice.

83. **C is correct.** The R388Δ*stb*ABC plasmid differs from the wild-type in stability but not in rate of conjugation. Looking only at these two results, the scientists would conclude that the *stb* genes affect stability (eliminating choices A and B), but have no effect on conjugation (making C the best answer). Choice D is true, but scientists would have no way of deducing this information without testing each *stb* gene individually.

84. **C is correct.** Gel electrophoresis separates DNA fragments by size. The gene *stbC*, at only 300 base pairs, is the smallest of the three genes, and small fragments travel more quickly than large fragments through the agarose gel. Even if you were unsure whether smaller or larger fragments traveled farther in a given amount of time, you should be able to limit the answer choices to either B or C. This is a question of extremes, so either the largest (*stbB*) or smallest (*stbC*) fragment would have to be the correct answer.

85. **B is correct**. Site-specific restriction with the enzyme HindIII creates "sticky ends" on the cut DNA that can reconnect with any other site that has been cut by the same enzyme. The sticky ends on the *ins236* may join the sticky ends of the cut R388 plasmid (as in choice A), may join with each other (as in choice C), or the sticky ends of the cut R388 plasmid may join with each other (as in choice D) creating a product identical to the wild-type R388. In any restriction assay, a combination of these product types will occur. However, restriction enzymes can only act at specific restriction sites, so insertion of the *ins236* cannot take place where a HindII restriction site is not present (as would have to happen to produce choice B).

86. **D is correct.** The BamHI restriction site is located within the *stbC* gene, so restriction at this site would likely interrupt the function of this gene and mimic the deletion of *stbC*. The question is simply asking to determine how *stbC* deletion affects the function of the plasmid. The graphs in Experiment 1 show that *stbC* deletion affects neither stability nor conjugation, producing results identical to wild-type plasmids.

87. **A is correct.** Transduction (movement of DNA between bacteria via a virus), transformation (uptake of genetic information from the environment), and conjugation (transfer of genetic material between bacteria via direct contact) are all examples of ways a bacterium can obtain genetic information other than from the mother cell during reproduction (vertical transfer). Transmutation is not a form of genetic transfer.

88. **A is correct.** Conjugation permits the spread of genetic information from one bacterium to another. Such genetic information often can confer benefits (such as antibiotic resistance). Choices B and D are true; under some circumstances, plasmids can be incorporated into the host genome and plasmids can be passed to daughter cells. However, these two choices do not directly answer the question of how conjugation BENEFITS the bacterium, making A the best answer. Choice C is incorrect because conjugation does not replace DNA, but adds new genetic information to the bacterium.

Stand-alones

89. **C is correct.** Infrared spectroscopy is used to distinguish functional groups.

90. **B is correct.** Compounds with boiling points differing by more than 20°C can be separated by distillation, a separation technique made possible by differences in vapor pressure. Compound A has a boiling point of 110.63° whereas compound B has a boiling point of 80.12°. Both extraction and column chromotography rely on difference in polarity. The question stem states that both compounds are non-polar. Crystallization is a very inefficient method of separation.

91. **D is correct.** Nucleic acid hybridization techniques are used to identify DNA or RNA molecules with sequences similar to those of a labeled probe. For example, a fluorescently or radioactively labeled complementary RNA sequence (called a probe) might be used to identify a target DNA sequence among a library of DNA sequences.

92. **D is correct.** R_f = length traveled by the component divided by length traveled by the mobile phase. Because polar compounds are attracted to the polar paper on which they travel, their movement is slowed. Therefore, they have R_f values lower than those of nonpolar compounds. The most polar compound is the compound with the lowest R_f value.

ANSWERS & EXPLANATIONS

FOR

QUESTIONS IN THE LECTURES

Lecture Question Expls.

ANSWERS TO THE LECTURE QUESTIONS

Lecture 1	Lecture 2	Lecture 3	Lecture 4
1. B	25. C	49. B	73. C
2. B	26. D	50. C	74. C
3. A	27. A	51. B	75. D
4. D	28. D	52. A	76. A
5. C	29. B	53. C	77. B
6. A	30. A	54. D	78. B
7. C	31. C	55. C	79. B
8. C	32. C	56. D	80. D
9. B	33. B	57. D	81. C
10. C	34. C	58. D	82. C
11. B	35. D	59. B	83. B
12. C	36. B	60. A	84. C
13. C	37. C	61. D	85. A
14. B	38. A	62. C	86. D
15. C	39. B	63. D	87. A
16. B	40. A	64. A	88. B
17. C	41. C	65. A	89. D
18. B	42. B	66. A	90. D
19. A	43. A	67. C	91. A
20. D	44. A	68. A	92. B
21. C	45. B	69. D	93. C
22. C	46. A	70. B	94. A
23. B	47. A	71. B	95. B
24. B	48. D	72. B	96. D

EXPLANATIONS TO QUESTIONS IN LECTURE 1

1. **B is correct.** Fundamentally, catabolic reactions break down molecules while anabolic reactions build up molecules. Hydrolysis is used to break down triglycerides, proteins, and carbohydrates, and is involved in nucleotide catabolism, making choice B. For the MCAT®, choices A and C are synonymous and both describe anabolic reactions: dehydration and condensation reactions link together two monomers, releasing a water molecule in the process. Choice D is a distractor: elimination describes a class of reactions within organic chemistry, but this question is written from a biological/biochemical perspective. Given the presence of choice B, which answers the question on a biochemical level, choice D can be eliminated.

2. **B is correct.** DNA is a nucleotide polymer. A nucleotide is comprised of a ribose sugar, a phosphate group, and a nitrogenous base. The nucleotides in DNA are held together by phosphodiester bonds, eliminating choices A, C, and D. Peptide bonds link amino acids together to make polypeptides or proteins, making choice B correct.

3. **A is correct.** Plants store carbohydrates as starch. Starch is a polymer that is able to be digested by animals, so choice A is correct. Animals, not plants, store carbohydrates as glycogen, ruling out choice B. Glucose is not a polymer, making choice D incorrect. Cellulose is a polysaccharide found in plant cell walls but is not digestible by humans, so choice C is incorrect.

4. **D is correct.** Fats are a more efficient form of energy storage than carbohydrates and proteins, making choice C incorrect and choice D correct. The phospholipid bilayer membrane is a component of cell structure that is made up of fat, making choice A incorrect. Fats, such as prostaglandins, behave as hormones, making choice B incorrect.

5. **C is correct.** DNA is double stranded with A, C, G, and T, while RNA is single stranded with uracil (U) replacing T. The 'D' in DNA stands for deoxy-, meaning that DNA lacks a hydroxyl group possessed by RNA at its second pentose carbon atom. Thus, RNA contains an additional hydroxyl group, making choice C correct. Thymine is found in DNA, but not RNA, ruling out choice A. A double helix is the characteristic shape of DNA, not RNA, making choice B incorrect. Both DNA and RNA are capable of hydrogen bonding, making choice D incorrect.

6. **A is correct.** Though this question presents with a lot of distracting information, it is merely asking what reactant is necessary to break a glycoside linkage. Both alpha and beta linkages in polysaccharides are hydrolyzed by adding water, making choice A the correct answer. The question asks for a reactant; choices C and D are enzyme catalysts which are never reactants, eliminating them as possible answer choices. Choice B is also incorrect.

7. **C is correct.** Since A always binds with T and G always binds with C, both the ratio of A/T and the ratio of G/C equal one, making choice C correct. In a single strand of DNA, there is no pairing between adenine and thiamine and guanine and cytosine. Therefore it cannot be expected that the number of adenine residues equals the number of thymine residues (in biochemistry, residues refer to monomers), making choice A incorrect. Likewise, there is no reason to believe that the number of adenine residues should equal the number of guanine residues, eliminating choice B. While the ratio of A/T and G/C both equal one because there is one purine for every pyrimidine in double stranded DNA, there is no reason to believe that the sum of adenine and thymine residues equals the sum of cytosine and guanine residues, making choice D incorrect.

8. **C is correct.** Prostaglandins are lipids that act as hormones, and hormones are secreted into the circulatory system and allow for communication with different organs or tissues. Hydrophobic hormones bind with receptors intracellularly. As such, prostaglandins would not be able to achieve their end effect if they were embedded in membranes, making choice C correct. Glycolipids, sphingolipids, and steroids are all major components of the cell membrane.

9. **B is correct.** Proteins are the only major nutrient containing nitrogen. The body begins breaking down its proteins during times of fasting and starvation. Glycogenolysis is the breakdown of glycogen which does not contain nitrogen so choice A can be eliminated. Similarly, lipolysis is the breakdown of lipids; lipids do not contain nitrogen, choice C can be eliminated. Excess ADH secretion would result in decreased urine production. Though this may increase the concentration of nitrogenous waste products because they will be dissolved in less water, this would not result in excessive amounts of nitrogen. Also note that the question asks what the most likely cause is. It is far more likely that one has a breakdown in bodily proteins rather than a tumor in that specific location. Choice D can be eliminated.

10. **C is correct.** The bending of the polypeptide chain is the tertiary structure of a protein, so choice C is correct. The primary structure describes only the amino acid sequence of the protein, ruling out A. Secondary protein structure refers to the formation of α-helices and β-pleated sheets. As the question states that proline cannot participate in the α-helices, it does not participate in secondary structure, eliminating choice B. Quaternary structure describes the union of multiple peptide chains, which is not described in this question, eliminating choice D.

11. **B is correct.** Enzymes function by binding the substrates on their surfaces in the correct orientation to lower the energy of activation. The change in free energy for the reaction, ΔG, is the difference in energy between reactant and products and is not changed by enzymes, eliminating choice A. Enzymes do not affect the temperature of number of reacting molecules, eliminating choices C and D.

12. **C is correct.** Decreasing the temperature always decreases the rate of any reaction, and has the ability to bring the enzyme either closer or farther from its optimal temperature, eliminating choice B. Lowering the concentration of a substrate will only lower the rate of an enzymatic reaction if the enzyme is not saturated, making choice C the correct answer. Adding a noncompetitive inhibitor will definitely lower the rate of a reaction because it lowers V_{max}, eliminating choice D. Changing the pH will increase or decrease the rate of an enzymatic reaction depending upon the optimal pH for that enzyme, eliminating choice A.

13. **C is correct.** A high temperature would denature the enzyme, rendering it ineffective. This precludes all other answers from being true: without a functioning enzyme, an enzyme-catalyzed reaction would not proceed to completion, eliminating choices A, B, and D.

14. **B is correct.** The amino acid bias and shapes of the secondary structures (α-helices and β pleated sheets) are partially explained by the rigid structure of the peptide bond, whose double bond character prevents rotation and makes the amide group planar. This rigidity provides steric constraints on hydrogen bond formation for some amino acids that prevents them from participating in some secondary structural elements. This structural feature does not affect the sequence of amino acids, eliminating choice A. Secondary structure is a better answer than tertiary structure: secondary structure is defined by hydrogen bonding along the protein's backbone, while tertiary structure is defined by interactions between side groups. The partial double bond character of the peptide bond is a characteristic of the backbone, so it more logically affects secondary structure, eliminating choice C. For the same reasoning, choice B is a better answer than D, which can be eliminated.

15. **C is correct.** Heat of combustion is one means of assessing energy storage potential. Saturated fats have the greatest energy storage potential, about twice that of carbohydrates and proteins, eliminating choices A and B. The highly reduced nature of fatty acids is what allows them to be such an efficient energy storage molecule. Saturated fats are more highly reduced than unsaturated fats, resulting in a higher energy storage potential, eliminating choice D and making C correct.

16. **B is correct.** Enzymes function by aiding in the breaking of bonds in the substrate and making the bonds in the product, eliminating choice A. Choice C is true: this is a description of the induced-fit model, eliminating it. Enzymes are more effective catalysts than non-biological catalysts, eliminating D. Choice B is a false statement: at equilibrium there is no net change in the concentration of products and reactants, making it the right answer.

17. **C is correct.** Feedback inhibition works by inhibiting enzyme activity and preventing the buildup and waste of excess nutrients, making both I and II correct and eliminating choices A and B. Non-enzymatic feedback mechanisms also exist, like the action potential in the neuron. This makes III incorrect, eliminating D and making C the correct answer.

18. **B is correct.** Noncompetitive inhibition changes the configuration of the enzyme. In competitive inhibition, an inhibitor binds to the active site, preventing the substrate from binding. The shape of the enzyme is not altered, eliminating A. Both positive inhibition and feedback inhibition can occur via competitive or noncompetitive means, eliminating choices C and D.

19. **A is correct.** The implanted, fertilized embryo produces human chorionic gonadotropin (HCG), which stimulates the corpus luteum to continue producing progesterone in a positive feedback mechanism. Negative feedback would result in stable, rather than increasing levels of progesterone, eliminating choice B. Feedback inhibition describes the process by which a molecule binds to an enzyme, decreasing its activity, eliminating choice C. Feedback enhancement is a made up term and a distractor, eliminating choice D.

20. **D is correct.** The small intestine is more basic than the stomach, meaning that there is a decreased hydrogen ion concentration, eliminating choices A and B. Peptidases that function in the stomach must work at a low pH. Because enzymes are only active across a narrow pH range, the movement from a high pH environment to a low pH environment would decrease the enzymes' activity, eliminating C and making D the correct answer.

21. **C is correct.** A competitive inhibitor may be overcome by increasing the concentration of substrate. With a sufficiently large concentration of substrate, the substrate will outnumber the competitive inhibitor and outcompete it. Choices A and D can be eliminated. Increasing temperature would not allow the substrate to outcompete the inhibitor, eliminating choice B.

22. **C is correct.** Noncompetitive inhibitors lower V_{max} and have no effect on K_m. V_{max} is a measure of the velocity, or speed at which the enzyme can catalyze the reaction. Because there is less enzyme available as it becomes unable to bind to the substrate once it binds to the inhibitor, V_{max} decreases. Noncompetitive inhibitors have no effect on K_m, which indicates the concentration of substrate needed to saturate the enzyme. This is generally used as a measure of the enzyme's affinity for the substrate. In this case, the active sites of uninhibited enzymes are unaffected, resulting in no effect on K_m. Uncompetitive inhibitors decrease both V_{max} and K_m, eliminating A. Proteolytic enzymes are those that catalyzes the hydrolysis of peptide bonds, eliminating B. Mixed inhibitors share characteristics of both noncompetitive and competitive inhibitors. They decrease V_{max} and have the ability to either increase or decrease K_m, eliminating D.

23. **B is correct.** Cooperativity occurs in enzymes when the binding of one substrate either increases or decreases the affinity of the enzyme for another substrate. Thus, cooperativity requires multiple binding sites on the enzyme, making choice B correct. A mixed inhibitor binds to both the substrate and enzyme-substrate complex. This is unrelated to cooperativity, eliminating choice A. Likewise, a high concentration of substrate and positive or negative feedback are not necessary for cooperativity, eliminating choices C and D.

24. **B is correct.** K_m indicates the concentration of substrate needed to saturate the enzyme. Uncompetitive inhibitors only bind to the enzyme-substrate complex but do not bind to free enzyme. K_m is decreased because the binding of the uncompetitive inhibitor prevents the enzyme and substrate from dissociating. Because the substrate cannot dissociate from the enzyme, it takes a lower concentration of substrate to saturate the enzyme, lowering the K_m. This makes choice B correct and eliminates choices A and D. C is incorrect: uncompetitive inhibitors bind to the enzyme-substrate complex; this complex does not exist until the enzyme binds substrate.

EXPLANATIONS TO QUESTIONS IN LECTURE 2

25. **C is correct.** All of the answer choices are important functions of genetic information. However, choice C is not necessary for the survival of an individual organism (although it is necessary to the survival of a species). Choices A, B, and D all act within, and are important for, an individual lifetime.

26. **D is correct.** Choice A is incorrect because environmental factors can play a role in gene regulation at nearly every step of the process of expression. Gene expression is often regulated by environmental factors at the level of transcription, for example, through epigenetic changes. In choice B, environmental effects select for certain phenotypic differences, but do not produce them. Additionally, even though living organisms share many of the same gene sequences necessary for supporting life, it is inaccurate to say that genetic differences are negligible. Choice C is true but does not directly address the question of the interplay between genes and the environment. Choice D is the best answer because environmental factors affect where and how a genome is read, which can result in differing products or differing amounts of products.

27. **A is correct.** Epigenetic alterations change the way the genome is read by the cellular machinery, but they do not change the genome itself, making choice A false and the right answer.. Choice C is true and incorrect because, while most organisms have DNA genomes, some viruses do contain genomes made from RNA. For choices B and D, it is true that the genome can be read differently under different circumstances. Notice that choices B and D are essentially saying the same thing – that it is possible for the genome to be read differently. The repetitiveness of these two choices prevents either from being the correct answer.

28. **D is correct.** Epigenetic changes help control gene expression by regulating the access of cellular machinery to certain areas of the genome through their effects on chromatin structure. Choices A, B, and C all affect chromatin structure and are examples of epigenetic changes. Epigenetic changes do NOT change the sequence of the genome's nucleotides (only the way the genome is read), making choice D the correct answer.

29. **B is correct.** Increased DNA methylation generally blocks cellular machinery from transcribing the highly methylated area. This results in inactivation of Section X. Without the up-regulation from Section X, Gene Y will produce fewer products which will result in decreased disease symptoms. This chain of logic makes B the correct answer. Choices A and D can be eliminated because activation of Section X would not result in decreased symptoms and inactivation of Section X will not result in increased symptoms.

30. **A is correct.** In order to fit large amounts of genetic material into a small volume, the genome is tightly wound around a series of proteins. The DNA is wrapped around histone proteins. Eight wrapped histones in conjunction form a nucleosomes. The nucleosomes wind into complexes to form chromatin. When cellular division takes place, chromatin is further condensed into chromosomes that can be split between the two daughter cells.

31. **C is correct.** Nucleosomes are the structural level that allows the DNA/protein complex to form tightly organized spirals called solenoids and supercoils, eliminating choice A. Choice B is true and incorrect. Histone proteins do contain basic functional groups that give them a net positive charge at normal body pH, which encourages interaction with the negatively charged phosphates groups on DNA. By mass, chromatin is approximately one-third DNA and two-thirds protein, eliminating choice D. Choice C is untrue and correct because heterochromatin is too tightly wound to be accessed by cellular machinery. Before transcription can take place, heterochromatin must first be unwound, but constitutive heterochromatin is permanently wound and, therefore, is not transcribed.

32. **C is correct.** Homologous chromosomes contain information coding for the same traits, but each chromosome may contain different alleles coding for different phenotypes for each trait, making choice C the correct answer. Choice A is false because the number of chromosomes in a human cell prior to replication is 46 (23 homologous pairs) and the number following replication is also 46 (with sister chromatids). Choice B is also false. Diploid cells have homologous chromosomes; haploid chromosomes lack homologues. Choice D is incorrect because the tightly wound structure of chromosomes inhibits the process of transcription which can only take place on relatively unwound genetic material.

33. **B is correct.** The start codon is AUG. It is good to know that mRNA is translated 5′—›3′ but that information is not necessary to answer this question. The correct answer will contain AUG reading in the 5′—›3′ direction. Only choices A, B and C have an AUG sequence, so choice D can be eliminated. However, if there are three codons in choice C, they must be: AAU, GCG, and GAC. The three in A must be: GAU, GCC, and GGA, leaving B as the correct answer.

34. **C is correct.** In eukaryotes, transcribed mRNA leaves the nucleus prior to translation and the processes of transcription and translation are spatially separated by the nuclear membrane. No translation takes place within the nucleus, making C the correct answer. The other organelles mentioned are associated with translation. Mitochondria contain their own ribosomes which create proteins through translation. Other ribosomes are responsible for translation of mRNA products from the nuclear genome and are present in the cytosol and at the rough endoplasmic reticulum.

35. **D is correct.** There are $4^3 = 64$ possible different codons, making choice D correct. There are more codons than amino acids (used in proteins), making choice A incorrect. This means that any amino acid could have several codons, eliminating choice B. Choice C is not accurate because the genetic code is evolutionarily very old, and almost universal. Only a few species use a slightly different genetic code.

36. **B is correct.** Only choice B is both true and concerns translation. Choice A is incorrect because eukaryotic cells contain some ribosomes that are larger than those of prokaryotes. Prokaryotes do contain ribosomes, so choice C is wrong. Translation does not concern DNA, so choice D is incorrect.

37. **C is correct.** Choice A would be a reasonable explanation for the reduced length of mRNAs, but it does not take place. The production of multiple copies of an mRNA discussed in choice B does not address the questions stem and can be eliminated. Choice D is likewise irrelevant to the difference in length between a gene and its associated mRNA. Introns make up a large component of gene sequences. During posttranscriptional modification, the introns (intervening sequences) are removed from a pre-mRNA sequence, which makes the mRNA shorter than the corresponding gene.

38. **A is correct.** Introns are removed from the primary transcript during posttranscriptional processing. The number of nucleotides in the mature mRNA would have to be less than the number of base pairs of the gene. Choices B, C, and D all have an equal or greater number of nucleotides than the original gene. Only choice A contains a decreased number of nucleotides to allow for the removal of the introns.

39. **B is correct.** To accomplish gene expression, transcription always occurs before translation; choices C and D can be eliminated. To choose between choices A and B, recall that a gene is transcribed into mRNA in the nucleus. The mRNA then leaves the nucleus in its finished form and can be transcribed into protein in the cytoplasm.

40. **A is correct.** Both the mRNA produced through transcription and the coding strand are complementary to the template strand, making choice A false and the correct answer. Choices B, C, and D are all true. Activators and repressors bind to the DNA close to the promoter region and either activate or repress the transcription activities of RNA polymerase. The nucleotide sequence of the promoter region affects the likelihood and frequency of transcription – sequences which more exactly estimate the consensus sequence are more likely bind RNA polymerase and are more likely to be transcribed. During the elongation phase of transcription, the RNA polymerase moves along reading the antisense DNA strand in the 3′ —› 5′ direction and synthesizes the new mRNA strand in the 5′ —› 3′ direction.

41. **C is correct.** Okazaki fragments are joined together by DNA ligase, so choice A is true and can be eliminated. Choice B is also true and incorrect; the function of DNA helicase is to unwind DNA so that replication can occur. New DNA strands are synthesized in the 5′ to 3′ direction making choice D true and incorrect. DNA replication is semiconservative, which means that both the sense and antisense strands are replicated, and each old strand is combined with a new strand. Thus, choice C is false and the correct answer.

42. **B is correct.** The point of this question is to choose the phase of the life cycle in which all three processes (replication, transcription, and translation) take place. Transcription and translation can take place throughout most of the lifecycle. However, replication only takes place only during the synthesis (S) phase, making B the correct answer.

43. **A is correct.** In normal meiosis, the only change in the nucleotide sequence of the third chromosome will occur during crossing over. Crossing over occurs in prophase I. Even though the cells remain diploid with sister chromatids at this point in meiosis, by the end of prophase I, crossing over has finished and the genetic sequence of each future gamete should be established with certainty, making choice A the best answer.

44. **A is correct.** Choice A gives the most logical explanation. Often, DNA damage is not permanent if it is repaired before replication. The time between S phases (when replication takes place) is shorter for rapidly reproducing cells. Cancer cells reproduce rapidly; thus, cancer cells cannot repair the damage as thoroughly as normal cells. Choices B and C are not true. Choice D is very unlikely as normal cells are necessary for proper functioning and the continuation of life. Choice A is best supported by the information presented in the book about the cellular life cycle.

45. **B is correct.** It is worth memorizing that in humans, the life cycle of all oocytes is arrested at the primary oocyte stage (prophase I) until puberty. Therefore, choice B is the only correct answer. Even without knowledge of the oocyte life cycle, be aware that oocytes are gametes and therefore produced through meiosis, not mitosis. Choice A can be readily eliminated.

46. **A is correct.** Choice D has a Y chromosome and is a male. Therefore, it can be eliminated. For female A, since her mother had hemophilia, the mother must have been homozygous recessive for the disease. The father could not have been a carrier. Thus, female A received an X^h from her mother and an X^H from her father and is heterozygous for the disease. Since she is only a carrier, it is possible that she passed on only her good X and that all her children are healthy.

47. **A is correct.** If the father is homozygous recessive and the mother is heterozygous, their daughters MUST carry at least one recessive allele. The offspring of this couple could either be homozygous recessive and develop sickle cell anemia or be heterozygous carriers for the disease. Both girls must at least be carriers for the trait because definitely they receive their father's recessive chromosome.

48. **D is correct.** This is an application of the binomial theorem under Hardy Weinberg Equilibrium. $p^2 + 2pq + q^2 = 1$ and $p + q = 1$. The question stem states that $p^2 = 0.36$. Therefore, $p = 0.6$. Using subtraction, $q = 0.4$. Therefore the number of heterozygotes, $2pq = 0.48$, making choice D correct.

EXPLANATIONS TO QUESTIONS IN LECTURE 3

49. **B is correct.** VLDL is produced by the liver and used to transport lipids to other parts of the body. The lipoproteins produced by the intestines are called chylomicrons. Adipocytes and skeletal muscle are examples of peripheral tissue which rely on lipoproteins for triglycerides, which they use as an energy source. Neither type of tissue produces lipoproteins.

50. **C is correct.** Small, nonpolar molecules are most easily able to cross the cell membrane through simple diffusion because of the hydrophobic interior of the membrane. Oxygen is a small and nonpolar molecule. Therefore, it can diffuse across the cell membrane without the assistance of an accessory protein. Glucose and glycine are too polar to cross unassisted. Triglycerides, while nonpolar, are too large to cross the cell membrane without being broken down first.

51. **B is correct.** Fermentation consists of two steps: glycolysis and the reduction of pyruvate into either lactic acid or ethanol. Glycolysis produces four ATPs and consumes two ATPs, yielding a net of two ATPs. The production of both lactic acid and ethanol is used to regenerate NAD^+ and does not produce ATP.

52. **A is correct.** Fatty acids, as the least oxidized of the macronutrients, contain greater reducing potential per unit mass than carbohydrates, which are glucose polymers, and proteins. The double bonds in unsaturated fats lowers their reducing potential compared to saturated fats of similar mass.

53. **C is correct.** Glycolysis is the first step of both aerobic and anaerobic respiration. The Krebs cycle, oxidative phosphorylation, and the electron transport chain only occur under aerobic conditions.

54. **D is correct.** ATP is a product. Two ATPs enter the reaction to "prime the pump", and four ATPs are produced. Glucose is a reactant and pyruvate is a product. Oxygen plays no role in glycolysis.

55. **C is correct.** This answer can most easily be found by process of elimination. Choice A is incorrect because ATP synthase is on the *inner* mitochondrial membrane. Choice B and D are poor answers because they mention the specific processes, Glycolysis and Krebs cycle, with which you should be familiar. A change in these processes would indicate a completely different process. Choice C, on the other hand, refers to membrane transport in a more general way allowing for the possibility that a specific mechanism of transport may differ in heart and liver cells.

56. **D is correct.** Substrate-level phosphorylation reactions are characterized by the direct transfer of a phosphate group from a reactive intermediate onto an ADP or GDP molecule. The addition of an inorganic phosphate to ADP, facilitated by pyruvate kinase, is an example of this. Glucokinase catalyzes the phosphorylation of glucose, not ADP. Triosephosphate dehydrogenase catalyzes an oxidation-reduction reaction, not a phosphorylation. Glucose-6-phosphatase catalyzes a dephosphorylation, not a phosphorylation.

57. **D is correct.** The pentose phosphate pathway is used to generate NADPH, which will be used to reduce glutathione in red blood cells. In the fasting state, red blood cells rely upon liver gluconeogenesis for their glucose supply. They do not have the enzymes necessary to produce glucose themselves. Red blood cells do not store glycogen, so they cannot have glyocogenolytic pathways active. The citric acid cycle occurs in mitochondria, which red blood cells do not possess.

58. **D is correct.** Glucose 6-phosphatase catalyzes the conversion of glucose-6-phosphate to glucose. Glucose 6-phosphate cannot easily cross cell membranes because of its charged phosphate group. Without glucose-6-phosphatase, there would be a buildup of glucose-6-phosphate at the site of gluconeogenesis: the liver. Gluconeogenesis occurs during the fasting state. At this time, the liver is the primary supplier of blood glucose. If it cannot export glucose, blood glucose levels will be low. Choices A and B are incorrect because loss of this enzyme should not affect glycolysis or glycogenesis. Choice C is incorrect because muscle tissue is not a major source of blood glucose even when this enzyme is functional.

59. **B is correct.** Gluconeogenesis occurs in the liver, not in muscle. The activation of hormone-sensitive lipase indicates that glucose produced by the liver will be preferentially used by the brain and red blood cells, but muscle has its own store of glycogen which it can use. This glycogen will be broken down into glucose, which can then enter glycolysis. Both the pyruvate produced by glycolysis and the acetyl-CoA from fatty acids can enter aerobic respiration.

60. **A is correct.** Carbon dioxide is produced by oxidative decarboxylation of pyruvate and by the citric acid cycle. Both of these processes occur in the mitochondria. Red blood cells do not contain mitochondria. All of the other cell types do.

61. **D is correct.** The precursor for gluconeogenesis that is derived from fatty acids, propionyl-CoA, contains a three carbon backbone. Since beta-oxidation occurs in two carbon steps, only odd-numbered fatty acids can produce this molecule. When even-chain fatty acids are broken down, they only produce acetyl-CoA. Propionyl-CoA participates in gluconeogenesis by first being converted to pyruvate. Lactate can also undergo this conversion. Glycerol, which also has a three carbon backbone, can enter gluconeogenesis by being converted to glyceraldehyde 3-phosphate.

62. **C is correct.** The brain cannot directly use fatty acids for energy, they must first be converted to ketone bodies.

63. **D is correct.** Enzymes can be either activated or inactivated by phosphorylation. Both insulin and glucagon control metabolic enzymes by phosphorylation. ATP slows down glycolysis by phosphorylating fructose 6-phosphate, which allosterically regulates phosphofructokinase. Epinephrine works by utilizing a cAMP cascade. This can result in enzymes being inactivated through phosphorylation, but it doesn't destroy them.

64. **A is correct.** One hour after a meal, the primary source of energy is the intestines. In the fed state, blood glucose levels are high. Hormones respond to environmental conditions. Insulin levels would rise in response to high blood glucose levels. Glucagon and epinephrine promote glycogenolysis and cortisol promotes gluconeogenesis. They are all catabolic hormones. Their levels should be low while blood glucose is high.

65. **A is correct.** The conversion of one mole of glucose into glucose-6-phosphate requires the breakdown of one mole of ATP into ADP + P_i and the addition of these phosphate groups onto glucose. ΔG = -48.1 kJ/mol for the breakdown of ATP and ΔG=20.9 kJ/mol for the addition of phosphate onto glucose. Adding these numbers together gives ΔG = -27.2 kJ/mol.

66. **A is correct.** The equilibrium constant, K, gives the ratio of products to reactants for a given reaction. Since this reaction is exergonic overall, it should heavily favor products.

67. **C is correct.** NAD^+ is an oxidizing agent and will get reduced during conversion of NAD^+ to NADH. Protons do not have an available electron pair to donate in order to reduce NAD^+. The hydride ion has an electron pair which can be used to reduce NAD^+. Since the product of this reaction is NADH, the hydride ion must be transferred onto the NAD^+ ring.

68. **A is correct.** ATP stores energy to be used at a later time. This means that producing it must require energy and be an endergonic process. The energy input that is required to produce ATP is provided by dietary intake.

69. **D is correct.** Oxygen accepts the electrons (along with protons) to form water. ATP and NADH are not electron acceptors. H_2O is the product of the electron transport chain.

70. **B is correct.** The Krebs cycle occurs within the mitochondrial matrix in all eukaryotic cells. Glycolysis occurs in the cytosol and the electron transport chain occurs in the inner mitochondrial membrane of eukaryotes. The intermembrane space is located on the opposite side of the inner mitochondrial membrane from the mitochondrial matrix. Protons are pumped into the intermembrane space from the matrix during oxidative phosphorylation. The specific location of the cell is extraneous information.

71. **B is correct.** As electrons flow, the carriers pass along one or two electrons, and are reduced (gain electrons) then oxidized (lose electrons) until the last carrier donates electrons to oxygen.

72. **B is correct.** The net product of glycolysis for one glucose molecule is 2 ATP and 2 NADH. The additional steps of aerobic respiration produce 34 ATP. This is a net of 36 ATP without accounting for the NADH. Since 2 ATP are used to move each NADH in, this results in the loss of 4 ATP and net product of 32 ATP.

EXPLANATIONS TO QUESTIONS IN LECTURE 4

73. **C is correct.** Gel electrophoresis is a process that uses an electric field to separate nucleic acids or peptides based on size or charge. Since nucleic acid phosphate groups give each nucleotide a uniform negative charge, all strands of nucleic acid would migrate the same distance in an electric field if they encountered no resistance; this makes choice B true and incorrect. During electrophoresis, however, the strands must migrate through a porous agarose gel, which impedes the progress of larger segments and separates the strands by size. For this reason, choice A is true and can be eliminated. Proteins are large enough that they cannot be separated using pores, making choice C untrue and the correct answer. Proteins are also unique in that they can be separated by isoelectric point, often in the same gel that was used to separate them based on size; choice D is incorrect.

74. **C is correct.** Extraction is separation based upon solubility differences between molecules in a mixture. A strong acid or base is often used to make certain molecules more polar and thus more likely to dissolve in the aqueous phase. Separations based on boiling point are known as distillations, so choice A is incorrect. A researcher trying to separate compounds based on molecular weight would likely use size-exclusion chromatography and gel filtration, making answer choice B incorrect. Separation based on optical activity, also known as chiral resolution, can be accomplished in multiple ways, none of which require extraction. Choice D can also be eliminated.

75. **D is correct.** There are several different types of chromatography that could be tested on the MCAT®. High performance liquid chromatography (sometimes called HPLC) involves using high pressure to force the elution mixture through a column. There is no indication in the question stem that this experiment is being done under pressure, making answer choice A incorrect. Both ion exchange and size exclusion chromatography are effective at separating proteins and peptides, but neither of these methods utilize an antibody-antigen interaction – choices B and C can be eliminated. Using an antibody to separate some antigen from a mixture is an example of affinity chromatography, making choice D the correct answer. This type of experiment can also utilize the high affinity binding between receptors and their ligands or enzymes and their substrates.

76. **A is correct.** Thin layer chromatography (TLC) uses a silica gel, which is highly polar. Polar compounds are strongly attracted to the polar silica, and have a more difficult time moving up the gel. Nonpolar substances, which are not attracted to the gel, will move further. This makes choice A correct and choice B incorrect. There is no lateral movement in TLC, making choices C and D distractor answers that can be eliminated.

77. **B is correct.** Crystallization is a very inefficient method for separating compounds, and it is extremely difficult to arrive at a pure substance with only this method, so II is false, which makes answer choice D incorrect. Distillation, while generally an effective method, cannot completely separate two compounds. At some level of purity an azeotrope will form which has a boiling point higher or lower than either of the pure compounds being separated. This makes I false, eliminating choices A and C. Only choice B remains. Distillation is more effective when done slowly, as this gives the compound with a lower boiling point time to completely boil off.

78. **B is correct.** It is important to know what each of the blotting techniques discussed in the lecture are used for. Southern blots use hybridization of small probes to identify specific segments of DNA. Northern blots are similar, but are used to detect RNA. Western blots are used to identify specific proteins or protein fragments, usually using antibodies. Only answer choice B, which includes both Northern and Southern blots, can be correct.

79. **B is correct.** Chiral resolution, which separates racemic mixtures, is a difficult task that can performed in three different ways. The first involves differences in crystals formed by enantiomers. Through visualization of crystals, researchers can sometimes identify specific stereoisomers, making choice A incorrect. The second method uses stereospecific enzymes to modify only one enantiomer in a way that makes it susceptible to physical separation techniques; choice C can be eliminated. Finally, chemists can use reactions that convert enantiomers into diastereomers, which can be separated based on physical properties. They can be converted back into their enantomeric forms. Choice D can also be eliminated. Enantiomers have identical physical properties, including solubility, meaning an extraction would be not be effective in separating them.

80. **D is correct.** This is a question whose answer choices have two parts – a common MCAT® occurrence. It can be helpful to focus on one portion of each answer at a time when answering these questions. The first part of each answer choice here calls DNA either positively or negatively charged. Because of its phosphate groups, DNA always has a negative charge. This eliminates choices A and B. The second part of each answer choice describes the direction DNA migrates during gel electrophoresis. Answering this portion requires some physics and inorganic chemistry knowledge. Anions are the source of electrons in an electrically charged device, which means they are the point that positive electrical charge enters the device. This flow of positive charge makes them attractive to anions, which have a negative charge. Thus, negatively charged DNA will migrate toward the positively charged anode, making choice D correct and C incorrect. It is easiest to remember this simply as "***an****ions* flow toward the ***an****ode*."

81. **C is correct.** NMR Spectroscopy identifies unique atoms with odd mass numbers (usually protons) by measuring their spin states when different external magnetic field strengths are applied. The technique does not identify whole functional groups. This makes choice A true – it can be eliminated – and choice C untrue. The field strength is measured in parts per million (ppm) and displayed along the x-axis of an NMR readout. Peaks that occur farther right on the x-axis are considered more "upfield" whereas peaks farther to the left are "downfield." Answer choice B can also be eliminated. Although it is not necessary to know many of the specifics of NMR spectroscopy, it is helpful to know that delocalized electrons can shield or deshield nearby protons from the external magnetic field, thus shifting their peaks upfield or downfield. Choice D is true for this reason, and thus incorrect.

82. **C is correct.** The first thing worth noting in this spectrum is the sharp peak at roughly 1,700 cm^{-1}, which is indicative of one or more carbonyl groups. Unfortunately, every answer choice involves a carbonyl group, so none can be eliminated using this peak. The next region of interest occurs between 3,000 and 3,500 cm^{-1}. The peak here indicates the presence of an –OH or –NH group. Neither answer choices A nor B have these groups, so both can be eliminated. The –OH peak from the carboxylic acid in choice D would be very broad and span the region from 3,300 to 2,500 cm^{-1}. The question stem spectrum, however, shows a strong, sharp peak at 3,300, which is indicative of an amide. For this reason, answer choice C is correct. This question requires more knowledge of IR spectroscopy peaks than is necessary for the MCAT®.

83. **B is correct.** Although questions requiring memorization of spectroscopy peaks are not common on the MCAT®, they do sometimes occur. The two most commonly asked about are those that occur in IR spectroscopy at 1700 cm^{-1} for a carbonyl group and the broad dip at 3200-3600 cm^{-1} that represents an alcohol. This question asks about the peak that results from a carbonyl group, making the answer choice closest to 1700 cm^{-1} most likely to be correct. Choice B is thus more likely to be correct than choices A, C, or D.

84. **C is correct.** Note that this question is asking about C^{13} NMR spectroscopy. While less common, it is conceptually no different from proton NMR. In order to determine how many peaks would appear, it is necessary to identify how many unique carbons there are in each molecule. In methylcyclopentane, the methyl group carbon is unique, as is the carbon it is bonded to. The other four carbons, however, only constitute two pairs of unique atoms, since the molecule is perfectly symmetrical. This gives a total of four carbon peaks, meaning choice C is the only possible correct answer. Since a plane of symmetry can be drawn through 1,2-Dimethylbenzene that separates its eight carbons, the number of unique peaks will equal the number of unique carbons on one side of that plane. This number is also four. In other words, 1,2-Dimethylbenzene has four unique pairs of two carbons each.

85. **A is correct.** The peak at 3.6 ppm is the furthest downfield in this NMR readout, meaning the protons represented by this peak are the most deshielded in the molecule. The question stem does not indicate this is a 13C NMR, nor is NMR used to detect oxygen atoms, so choices B and C can be eliminated. The remaining answer choices involve protons attached to a β-carbon of a carbonyl or the carbon in a methoxy group. Both groups of protons are going to experience some deshielding due to electron withdrawal, but the methoxy protons should be more deshielded due to their closer proximity to an electron withdrawing oxygen. This means the 3.6 ppm peak likely represents the "D" hydrogens, making choice A correct and choice D incorrect.

86. **D is correct.** The parent peak, which occurs farthest to the right in a mass spectroscopy result, represents the mass of the molecular ion. In other words, it represents the mass of the molecule being studied. This makes choice C unlikely to be false. If the molecular mass of the molecule is 134 g/mol, the mass of its most abundant isotope cannot be 160 g/mol – choice D is false. Without more information it is impossible to say what the base peak of the molecule is, although 15 m/z is entirely possible. This means that although there is no way of knowing whether answer choice B is true nor false, it is plausible and not more likely to be false than true. Mass spectroscopy does not give the information necessary to determine whether the normal molecule carries a net charge, meaning there is also no way of determining choice A's veracity. For this reason, answer choice D is the only choice that must be false, and should be chosen.

87. **A is correct.** An IR spectroscopy peak at 3400 cm^{-1} should immediately trigger thoughts of a hydroxyl group. In this case, a hydroxyl group that was present in the reactants but not in the products. Hydroxyl groups are lost during elimination reactions, making choice A the correct answer. An addition reaction would add a new peak rather than removing an existing one, so choice B is incorrect. Hydration of an alkene is a type of addition reaction. Remember that any time one answer being correct would mean another must be correct, both choices can be eliminated. Reduction of an aldehyde would yield a new alcohol with a peak at 3400 cm^{-1} in the product, not the reactant, so choice D is also incorrect.

88. **B is correct.** UV absorbance occurs in molecules with conjugated systems, which are double bonds separated by single bonds. The longer the conjugated system, the higher the wavelength of UV light absorbed by the molecule. Whereas answer choices A, C, and D depict unconjugated molecules, choice B is fully conjugated, and thus the correct answer.

89. **D is correct.** This question requires no knowledge of PCR. It requires only the knowledge that a DNA polymerase replicates in the 5′ to 3′ direction, and that this replication occurs in the opposite direction (3′ to 5′) of the template strand. In other words, the DNA polymerase can only read from 3′ to 5′, so it must start at the 3′ end of the template DNA fragment. The complement of the 3′ end of the DNA fragment in the question stem is 5′-AGC-3′, making answer choice D correct. Choices A and C are not complementary to any portion of the depicted DNA strand, so both can be eliminated. Choice B would be reverse complementary to the template strand if it was written in reverse – but at the 5′ end of the template. A DNA polymerase could not work with this primer, making B incorrect as well.

90. **D is correct.** Restriction enzymes are proteins produced by bacteria that recognize and cut specific sequences of viral DNA, protecting the bacterium from the virus; Choice A is true and can be eliminated. Since these molecules or prokaryotic proteins, they are produced in the cytosol, making B true. It is important to remember that prokaryotes do not have membrane-bound organelles, including the endoplasmic reticulum. Restriction enzymes are typically targeted to palindromic sequences, which read the same forward and backward, so C is also true. While strands of DNA cut by the same restriction enzyme can be joined together, the same is not true of strands cut by different enzymes, which will form non-complementary ends due to their different target sequences. For this reason, answer choice D is false, and should be chosen.

91. **A is correct.** The illustration depicts a dideoxynucleotide (ddNTP), which is used during Sanger sequencing to terminate DNA replication. ddNTPs contain phosphate groups, as illustrated in the question stem, so answer choices C and D can be eliminated. What distinguishes a ddNTP from a regular nucleotide is its lack of a 3′ hydroxyl group. This makes it impossible to form a new phosphodiester bond and continue adding to the DNA strand, terminating replication; Choice B is incorrect and A is correct.

92. **B is correct.** The question stem indicates that cystic fibrosis is caused by a loss of function mutation in a specific transporter protein. In order to best study this phenomenon, a model should involve the complete loss of function of the protein or its mouse homologue. Since both RNA interference and substituting a weaker promoter will cause a partial loss of function, these methods would not be the best methods for making a model; Choices C and D can be eliminated. While choice A might initially sound appealing, it does not involve any practical loss of function. Expressing the human protein in mice might cause it to stop functioning normally, but the mouse homologue of the chloride transporter would not be affected, meaning the mice would be essentially wild type. A much more effective method for generating a model would be to generate a knockout for the homologous mouse gene. For this reason choice B is correct and choice A is incorrect.

93. **C is correct.** The polymerase chain reaction (PCR) relies on the power of exponential growth to multiply copies of a gene. Every time the reaction occurs, each copy of the gene is duplicated, meaning the total number of copies doubles. In a reaction starting with two copies of a particular gene, for example, one round of PCR should yield four copies (a gain of two), two rounds yields eight copies (a gain of four from round one and six overall), three rounds yields 16 copies, and four rounds yields 32 copies. Using a simple simulation like this can help to eliminate incorrect equations. Choice A gives the equation n^x. Substituting 2 for n and 4 for x (an initial value of two, after four rounds) gives a value of $2^4 = 16$. Since four rounds yields 32 copies, this equation cannot be correct. If n^{2x} was the correct equation, four rounds of PCR should yield $2^{2(4)} = 2^8 = 256$ copies. Since this is obviously incorrect, choice B can be eliminated. Choice D offers x^n, which would yield $4^2 = 16$ copies after four rounds of replication, rather than the correct number of 32. Only answer choice C, with the equation $n(2^x)$, would give the proper value of $2(2^4) = 32$ copies after four rounds of PCR.

94. **A is correct.** The lecture states that a gene that is up-regulated after some treatment will appear green on a gene chip, whereas a gene that is down-regulated will appear green. After eating, insulin levels generally rise (recall that insulin is necessary to help remove nutrients like glucose from the bloodstream for intracellular use and storage), likely corresponding with a rise in expression of the gene that codes for insulin. The spot on the chip specific to insulin mRNA, then, should appear green rather than red, making choice A correct and choice C incorrect. A yellow spot would indicate a gene that was neither up-regulated nor down-regulated, making choice B incorrect as well. There is no reason to suspect that no labeling would occur, so choice D can be disregarded.

95. **B is correct.** The most useful evidence for proving that an individual was at a crime scene is evidence that eliminates as many other suspects as possible, leaving only the individual in question. Evidence that the perpetrator has a rare blood disorder would be fairly useful, if not perfect, in this regard. Since the disorder is rare, it is likely that most other suspects can be eliminated based on this piece of evidence. RFLP or SNP analysis would be even more useful, since these techniques can be used to identify a single individual's genetic "fingerprint." For these reasons, answer choices A, C, and D can be eliminated. Blood type, on the other hand, would not be a very powerful piece of evidence. In a large population there will be many people with each blood type, making it a much less useful identification technique than the other three described. This makes choice B the best answer.

96. **D is correct.** One of the main disadvantages of standard knockout models is that they cannot be used to study genes that are essential for survival during development. Knocking out these genes is lethal to the embryonic mouse, making breeding (and continuation of the knockout line) impossible. For this reason, a *Hox* gene necessary for neurulation could only be studied using conditional knockouts or a similar method like RNA interference. This makes choice D the best answer. Although both the genes named in choices B and C could be studied using a conditional knockout, they are also accessible via traditional knockout technology, so conditional knockout technology would not be *most* helpful for their study. *LacZ* is a prokaryotic gene that is not expressed normally in mice, so choice A can also be eliminated.

Photo Credits

Covers

Front cover, DNA on abstract background: iLexx/iStockphoto.com

Lecture 1

Pg. 1, Phospholipid, collagen, amylose, ATP: Computational results obtained using Discovery Studio Visualizer 3.5 from Accelrys Software Inc.

Pg. 1, Cellular micrograph, TEM: © Steve Gschmeissner / Science Source

Pg. 2, Dolomedes fimbriatus on Black Water: © Alasdair James/ iStockphoto.com

Pg. 3, Overhead shot of food containing Omega 3: © Tooga/Getty Images

Pgs. 3-5, Fatty acids, triacylglycerols, phospholipids, glycolipids, sphingolipids, steriods, terpenes, waxes, phosphoglyceride: Computational results obtained using Discovery Studio Visualizer 3.5 from Accelrys Software Inc.

Pg. 4, Fat cells, TEM. © Steve Gschmeissner/Photo Researchers, Inc.

Pg. 5, Vitamin supplements: © Sarah Lee/iStockphoto.com

Pg. 6, Plant Cells (SEM): © Alice J. Belling, colorization by Meredith Carlson/Photo Researchers, Inc.

Pg. 6, Colored SEM of a liver cell (hepatocyte): © Professors Pietro M. Motta & Tomonori Naguro/Photo Researchers, Inc.

Pg. 7, The big graze: © Ken Banks/Flickr, adapted for use under the terms of the Creative Commons CC BY 2.0 license (http:// creativecommons.org/licenses/by/2.0/legalcode)

Pg. 8, The discoverers of the structure of DNA: © A. Barrington Brown/Science Source

Pg. 10, DNA molecule: © Sci-Comm Studios/Science Source

Pg. 12, Peanuts: © RedHelga/iStockphoto.com

Pg. 15, Picture symbolizing high-protein diet (meat, fish, vegetables): © Ulrich Kerth/Getty Images

Pg. 17,Human Bone, Microscopic View: © David Scharf/Getty Images

Pg. 17,Small child: © Jaroslaw Wojcik/iStockphoto.com

Pg. 18,Hexokinase: Computational results obtained using Discovery Studio Visualizer 3.5 from Accelrys Software Inc.

Pg. 22,Pancreas cell, SEM: © Steve Gschmeissner/Photo Researchers, Inc.

Lecture 2

Pg. 29, Conceptual computer illustration of the DNA double helix: © David Parker/Science Photo Library

Pg. 32, Human female mitotic chromosomes: Hans Rins/Cell Image Library

Pg. 34, Cell nucleus and chromosomes stained by Spectral karytyping (SKY): National Human Genome Research, NIH

Pg. 45, Col TEM of structural gene operon from E. coli: © Professor Oscar Mille/Photo Researchers, Inc.

Pg. 48, 46 human chromosomes with telomeres: Hesed Padilla-Nash and Thomas Ried, the National Cancer Institute, NIH

Pg. 54, Cancer cell: © Quest/Photo Researchers, Inc.

Pg. 55, Human egg cell and sperm cells: © Thierry Berrod, Mona Lisa Production/Science Source

Pg. 55, Sperm: © Juergen Berger/Science Source

Lecture 3

Pg. 67, Basketball © Amanda Mills/CDC Public Health Image Library

Pg. 83, Mitochondrion, SEM: © Dr. David Furness, Keele University/ Photo Researchers, Inc.

Pg. 86, Shopping Woman © Amanda Mills /CDC Public Health Image Library

Lecture 4

Pg. 89, Western Blot: Maggie Bartlett/National Human Genome Research, NIH

Pg. 91, Iceburg: © Paul Souders/The Image Bank/Gettyimages.com

Pg. 93, GCMS sample: © Tek Image/Photo Researchers, Inc.

Pg. 95, Southern Blotting: © James King-Holmes/Photo Researchers Inc.

Pg. 105, Mass Spectrometer: Pacific Northwest National Laboratory/ Office of Biological and Environmental Research Information System of the U.S. Department of Energy Office of Science

Pg. 111, Well-plates in PCR thermal cycler: Maggie Bartlett/National Human Genome Research, NIH

Pg. 112, Purified DNA: Mike Mitchell, National Cancer Institute Visuals Online

Pg. 112, A row of DNA sequencing machines on SteelSentry tables: © Steve Jurvetson, adapted for use under the terms of the Creative Commons CC BY 2.0 license (http://creativecommons.org/licenses/by/2.0/legalcode)

Pg. 112, Computer Screen with Sequence Trace: Office of Biological and Environmental Research of the U.S. Department of Energy Office of Science

Pg. 112, DNA sequencing readout from an automated sequencer: National Human Genome Research, NIH

Pg. 113, Microarrays: National Human Genome Research, NIH

Pg. 114, Genetically modified mosquito larva. © Sinclair Stammers/Science Photo Library

About the Author

Jonathan Orsay is uniquely qualified to write an MCAT® preparation book. He graduated on the Dean's list with a B.A. in History from Columbia University. While considering medical school, he sat for the real MCAT® three times from 1989 to 1996. He scored in the 90 percentiles on all sections before becoming an MCAT® instructor. He has lectured in MCAT® test preparation for thousands of hours and across the country. He has taught premeds from such prestigious Universities as Harvard and Columbia. He was the editor of one of the best selling MCAT® prep books in 1996 and again in 1997. He has written and published the following books and audio products in MCAT® preparation: "Examkrackers MCAT® Physics"; "Examkrackers MCAT® Chemistry"; "Examkrackers MCAT® Organic Chemistry"; "Examkrackers MCAT® Biology"; "Examkrackers MCAT® Verbal Reasoning & Math"; "Examkrackers 1001 questions in MCAT® Physics", "Examkrackers MCAT® Audio Osmosis with Jordan and Jon".

An Unedited Student Review of This Book

The following review of this book was written by Teri R—. from New York. Teri scored a 43 out of 45 possible points on the MCAT®. She is currently attending UCSF medical school, one of the most selective medical schools in the country.

"The Examkrackers MCAT® books are the best MCAT® prep materials I've seen-and I looked at many before deciding. The worst part about studying for the MCAT® is figuring out what you need to cover and getting the material organized. These books do all that for you so that you can spend your time learning. The books are well and carefully written, with great diagrams and really useful mnemonic tricks, so you don't waste time trying to figure out what the book is saying. They are concise enough that you can get through all of the subjects without cramming unnecessary details, and they really give you a strategy for the exam. The study questions in each section cover all the important concepts, and let you check your learning after each section. Alternating between reading and answering questions in MCAT® format really helps make the material stick, and means there are no surprises on the day of the exam-the exam format seems really familiar and this helps enormously with the anxiety. Basically, these books make it clear what you need to do to be completely prepared for the MCAT® and deliver it to you in a straightforward and easy-to-follow form. The mass of material you could study is overwhelming, so I decided to trust these books—I used nothing but the Examkrackers books in all subjects and got a 13-15 on Verbal, a 14 on Physical Sciences, and a 14 on Biological Sciences. Thanks to Jonathan Orsay and Examkrackers, I was admitted to all of my top-choice schools (Columbia, Cornell, Stanford, and UCSF). I will always be grateful. I could not recommend the Examkrackers books more strongly. Please contact me if you have any questions."

Sincerely,
Teri R—

BIOLOGICAL SCIENCES

DIRECTIONS. Most questions in the Biological Sciences test are organized into groups, each preceded by a descriptive passage. After studying the passage, select the one best answer to each question in the group. Some questions are not based on a descriptive passage and are also independent of each other. You must also select the one best answer to these questions. If you are not certain of an answer, eliminate the alternatives that you know to be incorrect and then select an answer from the remaining alternatives. A periodic table is provided for your use. You may consult it whenever you wish.

PERIODIC TABLE OF THE ELEMENTS

1 **H** 1.0																	2 **He** 4.0
3 **Li** 6.9	4 **Be** 9.0											5 **B** 10.8	6 **C** 12.0	7 **N** 14.0	8 **O** 16.0	9 **F** 19.0	10 **Ne** 20.2
11 **Na** 23.0	12 **Mg** 24.3											13 **Al** 27.0	14 **Si** 28.1	15 **P** 31.0	16 **S** 32.1	17 **Cl** 35.5	18 **Ar** 39.9
19 **K** 39.1	20 **Ca** 40.1	21 **Sc** 45.0	22 **Ti** 47.9	23 **V** 50.9	24 **Cr** 52.0	25 **Mn** 54.9	26 **Fe** 55.8	27 **Co** 58.9	28 **Ni** 58.7	29 **Cu** 63.5	30 **Zn** 65.4	31 **Ga** 69.7	32 **Ge** 72.6	33 **As** 74.9	34 **Se** 79.0	35 **Br** 79.9	36 **Kr** 83.8
37 **Rb** 85.5	38 **Sr** 87.6	39 **Y** 88.9	40 **Zr** 91.2	41 **Nb** 92.9	42 **Mo** 95.9	43 **Tc** (98)	44 **Ru** 101.1	45 **Rh** 102.9	46 **Pd** 106.4	47 **Ag** 107.9	48 **Cd** 112.4	49 **In** 114.8	50 **Sn** 118.7	51 **Sb** 121.8	52 **Te** 127.6	53 **I** 126.9	54 **Xe** 131.3
55 **Cs** 132.9	56 **Ba** 137.3	57 **La*** 138.9	72 **Hf** 178.5	73 **Ta** 180.9	74 **W** 183.9	75 **Re** 186.2	76 **Os** 190.2	77 **Ir** 192.2	78 **Pt** 195.1	79 **Au** 197.0	80 **Hg** 200.6	81 **Tl** 204.4	82 **Pb** 207.2	83 **Bi** 209.0	84 **Po** (209)	85 **At** (210)	86 **Rn** (222)
87 **Fr** (223)	88 **Ra** 226.0	89 **Ac**= 227.0	104 **Unq** (261)	105 **Unp** (262)	106 **Unh** (263)	107 **Uns** (262)	108 **Uno** (265)	109 **Une** (267)									

*	58 **Ce** 140.1	59 **Pr** 140.9	60 **Nd** 144.2	61 **Pm** (145)	62 **Sm** 150.4	63 **Eu** 152.0	64 **Gd** 157.3	65 **Tb** 158.9	66 **Dy** 162.5	67 **Ho** 164.9	68 **Er** 167.3	69 **Tm** 168.9	70 **Yb** 173.0	71 **Lu** 175.0
=	90 **Th** 232.0	91 **Pa** (231)	92 **U** 238.0	93 **Np** (237)	94 **Pu** (244)	95 **Am** (243)	96 **Cm** (247)	97 **Bk** (247)	98 **Cf** (251)	99 **Es** (252)	100 **Fm** (257)	101 **Md** (258)	102 **No** (259)	103 **Lr** (260)